THE CLASSICS
OF WESTERN
SPIRITUALITY

THE CLASSICS OF WESTERN SPIRITUALITY
A Library of the Great Spiritual Masters

Bishop Kallistos of Diokleia—Fellow of Pembroke College, Oxford, Spalding Lecturer in Eastern Orthodox Studies, Oxford University, England.

Jean Leclercq—Professor of Spirituality, Institute of Spirituality and of Religious Psychology, Gregorian University, Rome, Italy.

George A. Maloney—Spiritual Writer and Lecturer, Seal Beach, Calif.

John Meyendorff—Professor of Church History, Fordham University, Bronx, N.Y., and Professor of Patristics and Church History, St. Vladimir's Seminary, Tuckahoe, N.Y.

Seyyed Hossein Nasr—Professor of Islamic Studies, George Washington University, Washington, D.C.

Heiko A. Oberman—Professor for Medieval, Renaissance and Reformation History, University of Arizona, Tucson, Ariz.

Raimundo Panikkar—Professor, Department of Religious Studies, University of California at Santa Barbara, Calif.

Jaroslav Pelikan—Sterling Professor of History and Religious Studies, Yale University, New Haven, Conn.

Annemarie B. Schimmel—Professor of Indo-Muslim Culture, Harvard University, Cambridge, Mass.

Sandra M. Schneiders—Associate Professor of New Testament Studies and Spirituality, Jesuit School of Theology, Berkeley, Calif.

Huston Smith—Thomas J. Watson Professor of Religion Emeritus, Syracuse University, Syracuse N.Y.

John R. Sommerfeldt—Professor of History, University of Dallas, Irving, Tex.

David Steindl-Rast—Spiritual Author, Benedictine Grange, West Redding, Conn.

David Tracy—Greeley Professor of Roman Catholic Studies, Divinity School, University of Chicago, Chicago, Ill.

Rowan D. Williams—Lady Margaret Professor of Divinity and Dean of Christ Church, Oxford, England.

Birgitta of Sweden

LIFE AND SELECTED REVELATIONS

EDITED, WITH A PREFACE BY
MARGUERITE TJADER HARRIS

TRANSLATION AND NOTES BY
ALBERT RYLE KEZEL

INTRODUCTION BY
TORE NYBERG

PAULIST PRESS
NEW YORK • MAHWAH

Cover Art: A Benedictine nun of the Abbey of Regina Laudis in Bethlehem, Connecticut, MOTHER PLACID DEMPSEY, O.S.B., has brought her artistic skills to many media: painting, book-illustration graphics and also stage and architectural design where she recently collaborated in the building of a small outdoor theater. For her, all these various artistic gifts come together at a new range through the contemplative monastic life where they find expression in monastic hospitality, working creatively with the many people who come to the Abbey. "It is this," she says, "which has made illustrating the cover for St. Birgitta so meaningful to me. For it was St. Birgitta's contemplative union with God, her 'seeing' of him, and consequently of all things through him, that allowed her to look upon the world around her with a pure and penetrating eye, to see into the real nature of the situations of her time. Her *Revelations* express what she saw and challenge us to do as she did: become a medium of Christ's Light 'in a world of darkness.' "

Copyright © 1990 by the Order of St. Birgitta, Rome. Translation, Notes and Foreword copyright © 1990 by Albert Ryle Kezel.

Library of Congress Cataloging-in-Publication Data

Bridget, of Sweden, Saint, ca. 1303–1373.
    [Revelationes. English. Selections]
    Life and selected revelations/Birgitta of Sweden; edited with a
preface by Marguerite Tjader Harris: translation and notes by
Albert Ryle Kezel; introduction by Tore Nyberg.
       p. cm.—(The Classics of Western spirituality)
    Translation of: Revelationes, Books 5 and 7, and the Four prayers
from the Revelationes.
    "The life of Blessed Birgitta by Prior Peter and Master Peter": p.
[69]–98.
    Includes bibliographical references.
    ISBN 0-8091-0434-2—ISBN 0-8091-3139-0 (pbk.)
    1. Private revelations—Early works to 1800. 2. Visions—Early
works to 1800. 3. Bridget, of Sweden, Saint, ca. 1303–1373.
4. Christian saints—Sweden—Biography—Early works to 1800.
I. Harris, Marguerite Tjader, 1901–1986. II. Kezel, Albert Ryle.
III. Petrus Olai, of Alvastra, ca. 1307–ca. 1390. Vita b. Brigide.
English. 1990. IV. Title. V. Title: Birgitta of Sweden, life and
selected revelations. VI. Series.
BX4700.B62E5   1990
271'.97—dc20
[B]   89-48062
                                                      CIP

Published by Paulist Press
997 Macarthur Boulevard
Mahwah, New Jersey 07430

Printed and bound in the United States of America

CONTENTS

Author of the Preface

The late MARGUERITE TJADER HARRIS was born in New York City in 1901. She was the daughter of a Swedish father, inventor, evangelist, Richard Tjader and an American mother, founder of the International Union Mission, Margarate Thorne Tjader. Mrs. Harris attended Bryn Mawr College and received her B.A. in 1925 from Columbia University. In 1928 she met Theodore Dreiser and became his literary secretary from 1933–34, and later in 1944–45. From 1937 until 1945 she edited and published *DIRECTION* magazine, whose contributors included Dreiser, John Dos Passos, Paul Rand, Erskine Caldwell, and John Hyde Preston.

A world traveler and linguist, Mrs. Harris devoted time and energy to many causes for world peace, including the ecumenical movement. She became a Roman Catholic in 1957 and donated her family home in Connecticut to the Birgittine Sisters to establish a convent.

Her published literary works (listed under Marguerite Tjader) include: a novel, *Borealis* (1930), *Theodore Dreiser: A New Dimension* (1965) and *Mother Elizabeth* (1972).

Translator of this Volume

ALBERT RYLE KEZEL showed early interest in classical languages and received encouragement from his parents and from the Sisters of Mercy at St. John's School in Stamford, Connecticut. He followed the traditional Jesuit classical course at Fairfield College Preparatory School and has degrees in classical philology from Fairfield University (B.A.), Fordham (M.A.), and Yale (M.Phil.). In 1977 he returned to Fairfield Prep as a teacher of Greek, Latin, and Shakespeare. Since 1982 he has taught Greek and Latin at St. Basil College, the minor seminary of the Ukrainian Catholic Church in the United States. Since 1983, Mr. Kezel has worked with the Ukrainian Church's committee for liturgical translations on a new English version of the Greek liturgical books of the Byzantine Rite. In 1987 and 1988 he prepared two experimental versions of the committee's *Liturgy of St. John Chrysostom*, which were used at the public celebrations of the Millennium of Christianity in Kievan Rus'.

Author of the Introduction

DR. TORE S. NYBERG was born in Uppsala, Sweden, and studied history at Uppsala and Lund Universities. He received the licentiate degree in 1960 and the fil. dr. at Lund in 1965 on the topic of Birgittine monastic history in the Middle Ages. Since 1970, Dr. Nyberg has been employed at the University of Odense, Denmark. His special fields of teaching and research include: Birgittine history and the Christianization of Scandinavia, the establishment of the Christian Scandinavian kingdoms, Military Orders and the mission in the Baltic, fifteenth century religious and cultural history in Europe, and Buddhist kingdoms of Southeast Asia.

PREFACE

I. A HISTORY OF THE BIRGITTA TRADITION

Birgitta of Sweden was a major personality and one of the most multifaceted saints of the latter part of the Middle Ages. She was a cousin of the Swedish King Magnus, married at thirteen, and had eight children before her husband died. Then she transformed her life completely, to become "the bride of Christ," and developed her naturally mystical nature and intellect into that of an ascetic and an ambassador of Christ. She was both a contemplative and a woman of action. A controversial figure in her day, she founded a new order, sought to reform the dissolute court of Stockholm, admonished knights, priests and bishops, calling them to account for their deeds, and entreated three popes, Clement VI, Urban V, and Gregory XI, who had established themselves in Avignon, to bring the papacy back to Rome.

She faced the anger and scorn of many because of her courageous attitudes. Her strong, prolific writings demonstrated her concern for the entire political situation in the Europe of her day. She attempted to end the strife between the French and English kings, Philip VI and Edward III, who were then embarking on what is known as the Hundred Years' War.

She followed a destiny which led her across Europe from her land which she described as the "most northerly in the world and beyond that there is no country where men can live" (*Revelations of Saint Birgitta*, hereafter *Revelations*, Book III, Chapter 31 and in shortened form, Rev. III, Ch. 31, or, simply III, 31). For twenty years she lived in Rome, and died there, in the house on the Piazza Farnese where she had established a center of hospitality for pilgrims from the north. Here she served the sick and the poor, always working toward the goal of returning to Sweden to found her new order at Vadstena when the time was ripe. For in Sweden she had received her first revelations, instructing her exactly how this was to be done, and even how the walls of her convent and her church should be constructed. It was also in her prayer and divine revelations that she had been told to undertake pil-

1

grimages, to live at the Cistercian monastery of Alvastra, to travel to Rome, and, lastly, to the Holy Land. All of these actions were the carrying out of divine commands. Her revelations as she wrote or dictated them comprise a record of her experiences, exterior and interior. It is her life that is the key to the understanding of her revelations.

Birgitta was born in 1302 or 1303 at her father's estate of Finsta in the Province of Uppland, about fifty miles north of Stockholm. He was a lawman of noble birth, one who was versed in the laws of the day, and so had authority and respect. God-fearing and just, he had undertaken several long religious pilgrimages, as had his father before him. Birgitta's mother was also pious and careful to nurture her children in the Faith. At the age of seven, Birgitta had her first vision. She saw an altar opposite her bed, and a woman in a shining dress sitting above it who said: "Come, Birgitta" and handed her a crown. When Birgitta sprang from her bed to take it, the lady pressed it on her brow. She remembered the feeling of the ring around her head. Then all disappeared. But she never forgot it. It was a foretaste of her life to come.

Betrothed to a young nobleman by her father at the age of thirteen, she married, bore eight children, and lived a full life, including several years at the court of King Magnus, her cousin. But supernatural experiences had always been a part of her life and when her husband died, she underwent the profound conversion of her being into the bride of Christ. The revelations that had already marked her days then multiplied. She was divinely guided to act, to travel, to send messages, to denounce the evils of her day, and to work for the foundation of her "vineyard," as she called it, the new order that became one of the most influential of medieval times in the northern countries.

Her story is told in the *Vita*, written by her two confessors, and in her *Revelations* that reflect her life in Sweden, in Italy, and in the Holy Land. They show her contacts with many leaders of the church and of secular power and reveal her impact on the Europe of her day. She is as much a part of Swedish history as Joan of Arc is of that of France.

When Birgitta died in Rome, as related at the end of the *Vita*, her daughter Katherine accompanied her body back to Vadstena, on Lake Vettern, where land and a castle had been donated to her by King Magnus. Here, building had already begun. Her revelations had specified how her convent should be built. The walls of the early castle were to be lowered to avoid pride or *superbia*, as Birgitta called it. A central church was to rise much higher with wide nave and side aisles. Built of huge granite blocks, it stands today as one of the finest examples of

Gothic art in Sweden, called the Blue Church because of the bluish cast of its granite.

Katherine found the beginnings of a small community waiting for her and it was she who became the first abbess of the Order of the Most Holy Savior (*Ordo Sanctissimi Salvatoris*), as it was named by Birgitta. It attracted many vocations of both nuns and monks. Under Petrus of Alvastra, the first chaplain of the community, and then under Magnus Petri who followed him, the spiritual and cultural character of the Birgittine life was established.

According to her revelations, her order was to be a double community of some sixty nuns directed by thirteen priest-monks with twelve brothers whose convent would adjoin the sacristy of the church they were to serve. The nuns, in an entirely separate building on the rear side of the nave, had access only to a large choir in a gallery above; they received communion or went to confession through a grilled passageway behind the altar.

One of the most important early revelations was that of the Rule or *Regula,* which Birgitta received during her years at Alvastra. The Rule went through several revisions before it was accepted by Rome, but its mystical symbolism remained the same.

The Holy Virgin Mary was represented by the abbess; the sixty nuns and twelve brothers were the seventy-two disciples of the early Christian community. The thirteen priests were the apostles. There was a fine balance of duties and mutual trust. The abbess was to rule both communities. Priests were to be scholars and preach to the parishioners and pilgrims in the large central convent churches that Birgitta had planned, so that spiritual instruction could be given to her nuns and also be shared with the laity. The new order was well planted and its fruit was plentiful. Soon miracles began to occur around her relics and pilgrims streamed to Vadstena even before the Blue Church was completed.

The order continued to grow. In the next decades more than twenty-five abbeys grew up in Europe: in Germany, Denmark, Poland, Finland, Holland, Spain, and in England, the renowned convent of Syon Abbey.

The Vadstena Fathers arranged for the first printing of Birgitta's revelations in Lübeck, Germany, in 1492. Other editions followed: Antwerp, 1489; Nuremberg, 1500; Rome, 1556, and later, many others. Birger Bergh related in a text study that in a comparatively short time, Birgitta's revelations acquired great fame in Europe. In several foreign lands, interest in her work and personality was aroused in a much greater degree than in her own land. The revelations were translated from the Latin original into several popular languages, including an Old Swedish text.

To illustrate the wide influence of Birgitta's work, these are the circumstances of how her order reached Spain. Marina de Escobar, daughter of a wealthy family in Valladolid, then the capital of Spain, was drawn early on to the mystical life and, like Catherine of Siena, wished to remain in her own room, constantly praying. When her family saw her determination, they asked her why she did not join her friend, Teresa of Avila, who was then founding a convent of her Carmelite order in Valladolid. Marina told them that Christ with his Mother and Saint Birgitta had come to her and told her that she was to bring the Order of the Most Holy Savior to Spain. After great perseverance, Marina was finally given a small palace in Valladolid where she was able, with the help of an established group of nuns, to bring Birgitta's order to Spain. It flourished and still maintains five convents, in Valladolid, Vitoria, Paredes de Nava, Azcoitia, and Lasarte (San Sebastian). From Vitoria, convents were later founded in Mexico.

The parallel development of Birgittine priests and brothers produced many noted preachers and scholars. Outstanding among these was Richard Reynolds, who was martyred under Henry VIII. He was canonized by Pope Paul VI in 1970 together with other English recusant martyrs. Gervinus, who was general confessor of the order, defended Birgitta at the Council of Constance in 1495, after she had been attacked by the Councilor Gerson. Two centuries later, the distinguished Birgittine Father Christopher Langen worked to preserve the Dutch abbeys, and Father Simon Hörmann of Altomünster led a general chapter in Cologne, in 1675. The last monks of St. Birgitta were disbanded in the nineteenth century.

II. MODERN INTEREST IN BIRGITTA

Historical circumstances, the Reformation in particular, overshadowed Birgitta and her order in the north. Other saints and mystics of Europe supplanted her in popularity and many of her convents were destroyed. However, in the twentieth century she reappeared in a revival of interest in Sweden that was also evident in Germany, France, and England. Her order experienced a resurgence in 1911.

PREFACE

In 1901, the Swedish writer Werner von Heidenstam published *Holy Birgitta's Pilgrimage*, a romanticized story that was popular with readers of all ages. This book failed to take into account her mystical qualities. A little later a Lutheran bishop, Tor Andrae, described Birgitta but came no nearer to the truth about her spirituality. August Strindberg, the Swedish dramatist, wrote about Birgitta, but his study is considered little more than a caricature. Selma Lagerlöf wrote a more appreciative but sentimental story called *Birgitta's Last Days*.

Knut B. Westman, a well-known historian and clergyman, published a study of Birgitta in 1911. He was the first modern writer in Sweden who appreciated Birgitta's significance. Westman explained her spiritual importance as well as her place in history. He praised her vision of God's work through history and her consciousness of being called to a task in the great struggle between good and evil forces in the world. In this respect she followed the great tradition of heroes, prophets, and bearers of the revelations that have historical meaning. He even placed Birgitta in what he calls "the great complex of tradition which the church carries along" and which included the apostles and Christ himself. Of other books on Birgitta having literary quality and discernment, the work of Emilia Fogelklou stands as a permanent tribute. First published in 1919, it was long kept in print and has now been reissued in paperback. An accomplished writer and a Quaker, she had studied many spiritual books and approached Birgitta with a deep understanding of medieval life.

From the nineteen forties on, scholarly and spiritual interest grew around Birgitta, a true "renaissance," as it was called by Sven Stolpe, a prolific writer and lecturer on the subject. Among the many serious scholars who have made contributions to the knowledge of Birgitta and her writings are: Salomon Kraft, Tony Schmid, Carl Gustaf Undhagen, Sten Eklund, Sara Ekwall, Ingvar Andersson, Elias Wessén, Lennart Hollman, Tryggve Lundén, Birgit Klockars, Aron Andersson, Tore Nyberg, Birger Bergh, and others listed in the bibliography.

Prominent among modern books about Birgitta is the work of the Danish writer Johannes Jörgensen, who had formerly made studies of Saint Francis of Assisi and Saint Catherine of Siena. He had been collecting material for his story of Birgitta for many years. By the time he finished the book in 1943, he had encumbered himself with so many details that he produced a literary pageant almost too rich for the figure of Birgitta to emerge clearly from its many characters and historical references.

The sources of Birgitta's thought have been explored by Birgit Klockars, a Finnish scholar, in her books, *Birgitta and Her World* and *Birgitta and the Books* (meaning the books of her time). Appearing in 1966 and in 1973, they give an authentic background to her development. Dr. Klockars describes in detail the *Pentateuch Paraphrase*, a classic of the time, and quotes passages from it, comparing them with parallel passages from the *Revelations*. She also examines the Old Swedish *Legendariet* relating the lives of saints and martyrs. Both of these books were owned by Birgitta who spent many hours studying them as well as the Bible. Dr. Klockars describes the Rhineland mystics, the Dominican Meister Eckhart, John Tauler, and Henry Suso; the English mystics, Julian of Norwich, Richard Rolle, Walter Hilton; John Ruusbroec in Flanders; and Catherine of Siena—all of the same period as Birgitta. It is unlikely that Birgitta knew any of their works, except that of Suso, which was widely circulated in German, Latin, and Old Swedish, before his death in 1366. Klockars drew parallels between his *Book Concerning the Eternal Wisdom*, and some of the revelations. The figure of Christ as the Eternal Wisdom is used by Birgitta. She also says, as Suso teaches, that the way to Wisdom is through meditation on the Passion. Both give descriptions of the Passion through words put into Mary's mouth. In other incidents they compare God's anger to a stormy sky, or to a thunderstorm. In *Revelations*, Book VIII, Chapter 31, Birgitta states: "It is written that Christ says that all the elements suffered with me when I died; they drew back their right and abandoned their natural behavior." This can, of course, be traced to the gospel that speaks of the sun's being darkened and the earth quaking when Jesus died. The same phrase—"Nature suffered with its Creator"—is found where Suso speaks of Mary's pain when her Son died on the cross. Other parallels seem to indicate that Birgitta had read and been impressed by Suso's book.

Birgitta was certainly familiar with the church fathers, Saint Ambrose, Saint Augustine, Saint Jerome, and Saint Gregory. Saint Ambrose spoke to her when she visited his shrine in Milan (*Rev.* III, Ch. 6). She had a special devotion to Saint Francis. In Rome she had a vision in which he "invited her to his room." In Assisi, when she went to his church, he appeared to her again and said: "This is not the room I spoke of. My room is true obedience, which I always observed" (see *Rev.* VII, Ch. 3). There is also another revelation which Birgitta received in the Assisi church at a later time in which Christ himself praises Saint Francis (*Extravagantes* 90).

These and other revelations testify to the love that Birgitta had for Saint Francis, as her daughter Katherine relates in her biography. Some have stated that Birgitta was a tertiary of the Franciscan order, as she is often painted in a brown pilgrim's habit. Although there is no proof of this, the influence of Saint Francis over her was certainly great (see also *Extravagantes* 23).

A special study of Birgitta's canonization process was made by the Swedish scholar Isak Collijn, whose work was published in Uppsala from 1924 to 1931. This large volume of over 600 pages gives the text of the Process of Canonization in Latin. It is preceded by Collijn's introduction in Swedish. The process consists of two parts: the *Acta* and the first transcript of the *Vita* by Petrus of Alvastra and Petrus of Skänninge. This is introduced by a long statement of the ex-bishop Alfons, the *Attestaciones*, consisting of the *Interrogaciones* and other accounts of her miracles included in the revelations and called *Depositio Copiosissima* (some of these also appear in the *Vita*).

Collijn relates that Magnus Petri delivered these documents, together with Alfons' edition of the revelations, to Pope Boniface IX on August 1, 1391. He had had these books copied for the cardinals at his own expense. Special sponsors were Alfons, Petrus of Alvastra, Petrus of Skänninge, Katherine, and Magnus Petri of Eka. The process had started under Gregory XI, continued under Urban VI, and the final canonization took place under Boniface IX on October 7, 1391.

The modern wave of interest in Birgitta mounted as Swedes prepared to celebrate the 600th anniversary of Birgitta's death in 1973. A number of books were in preparation. Two volumes by Sven Stolpe, *Birgitta in Sweden* and *Birgitta in Rome*, were laudable, lively accounts. Andreas Lindblom, who had completed his restoration of Birgitta's original convent at Vadstena, published an account of his labors in *The Vadstena Convent's Destiny*. This was the massive, simplified structure which had been built on Birgitta's orders, using the foundations and the walls of the castle given to her by King Magnus. It is not to be confused with the great castle standing in Vadstena, further down the lake, that was built by Gustav Vasa two hundred years later. Across the grass courtyard from the convent rises the tall bulk and graceful spire of Birgitta's Blue Church.

It was in this church and convent and on the grass court in between that a three-day commemoration of Birgitta was held during the week of July 23rd, 1973. The gathering was brought about through the united efforts of historians, scholars, and churchmen, Lutheran and Roman

Catholic. Perhaps the most active agent was the Societas Sanctae Birgittae, a spiritual fellowship organized by the Lutheran archbishop Nathan Söderblom, and Countess von Rosen, a devotee of Birgitta. They felt that by reviving devotion to the saint, a spiritual renewal of the Lutheran church might follow, which has indeed been the case. For some thirty years, a band of men and women, wearing the gray cloaks and habits of the former Birgittines, had gathered at Vadstena on the anniversary of her death to honor Birgitta through speeches, music, and liturgies. It was this society that had first invited the Roman Catholic Sisters, then attempting to revive the medieval Order of Saint Birgitta in Rome, to attend such a celebration in 1925. It was a magnificent expression of the ecumenical spirit for which Archbishop Söderblom was noted. And in 1973, the same spirit was manifested in the great gathering at Vadstena. A series of lectures by churchmen and scholars offered free exchange of views and knowledge. Ecumenical services in the Blue Church were celebrated together in an atmosphere of fraternal love.

Later, on the canonization feast of Saint Birgitta on October 7th, ceremonies were held in Stockholm attended by the king, the Lutheran and Roman Catholic bishops, and many other churchmen and scholars. In Germany, an important exhibition presenting Birgitta was opened at the museum in Munich and a memorable church service was held in the historic convent of Birgitta at Altomünster, with Cardinal Döpfner presiding.

The climax of these celebrations came in Rome at the house on the Piazza Farnese where Birgitta had lived and died. Here Pope Paul VI addressed a large crowd of visitors, many from Vadstena and Stockholm. The pope's message was spread by press, radio, and television so that Birgitta's renaissance was made known in Italy, as it was in Germany and Sweden.

Another manifestation of Birgitta's return to the modern world of scholarship was the monumental work of Tryggve Lundén. He translated the *Revelations* into Modern Swedish with an introduction and much new information. It was published in four handsome volumes by the firm of Allhem in Malmö, 1957–1959. Its illustrations include almost all the known artworks made of Birgitta. A volume of extracts from this complete collection with an introduction by Sven Stolpe was sold in the jubilee year. Until the publication of Lundén's work, there existed in Modern Swedish only a small selection of revelations translated by R. Steffen, a renowned archivist on the island of Gotland.

Aron Andersson, director of Stockholm's historical museum, has written three books noted for their lucid style, fine illustrations, and printing. On the occasion of the jubilee year, he arranged a full-scale exhibition at the museum devoted to Birgitta and her time.

Birgitta was known to the art world, especially in Sweden and in Italy. After her canonization many churches throughout Scandinavia contained stone or wooden statues of Birgitta and also painted frescoes and altarpieces depicting scenes from the revelations. Her influence on the iconography of Scandinavia and of Europe was remarkable. Following her vision of the Nativity as given in Book VII, many painters showed the Christ child lying naked on the ground as his mother knelt beside him. The Virgin is often depicted with flowing hair, her hands folded in prayer or worship before the newborn child from which "radiates an ineffable light." Soon we find representations, murals, or paintings of variant or identical iconography by Gentile de Fabriano, Fra Angelico, Lorenzo Monaco, and later by such men as Filippino Lippi, Pesellino, and Lorenzo di Credi.

Birgitta's vision of the passion, also in Book VII, influenced painters in many lands. The German master Matthias Grünewald followed Birgitta in the painting of his colossal altarpiece of the crucifixion for a church in Isenheim. Michelangelo made a number of studies for a large scene of the passion for his friend Vittoria Colonna that has now been lost. His impressive drawings show a strong Christ figure stretched on a Y-shaped cross, such as Birgitta had described in an earlier vision given to her through the Virgin Mary (*Rev.* IV, Ch. 70).

The depiction of the *Pietà* was also changed after Birgitta's vision of the sorrowing mother who had taken the body of Jesus on her lap, not limp, but already stiffening in death. Detailed studies and comparisons have been made of Birgitta's influence on religious painting. Scenes from purgatory and hell were often influenced by Birgitta's revelations as illustrated by an altarpiece from Törnevalla Church in Östergötland, Birgitta's province.

III. BIRGITTA'S PERSONALITY

To a very intense degree, Birgitta lives on in her *Revelations*. Some writers reveal their lives more than others in the works they leave behind them. Birgitta is here, in her stories and visions, recreating the scenes around her, and, through her extraordinary sensitivity or intuition, receiving supernatural messages, divine mandates, and prophetic admonitions. So she shows herself to be as much at home in the spiritual world as at the unruly court of Sweden or in the tumultuous Italy of her time.

Here are plots, true incidents, homely illustrations from nature, or household realities. Then the scene may suddenly be raised to the level of conversations between heavenly persons which Birgitta "attends," because she is "allowed to see and hear spiritual things."

Often, Birgitta received messages for specific people who were playing important parts in the history of her time, sometimes predicting disaster for them if they did not listen to God's commands. This was the case when the Swedish King Magnus recklessly invaded the Baltic States, or when the warring French and English kings were engaging in what turned out to be the Hundred Years' War (Birgitta's *Revelations* characterized them as "wild beasts").

Perhaps the most remarkable of her prophecies was the one concerning Vatican City. Birgitta was distressed to see the many selfish or greedy prelates, sometimes corrupt or warring among themselves over properties and possessions. The pope himself had abandoned Rome for the luxurious papal palace at Avignon in the South of France. Birgitta had a vision and a message that one day God would create a State for the Church alone. She saw almost the exact boundaries of the present Vatican City which was set aside by Mussolini when he was seeking to obtain favor with the Church in 1921.

At the time of Birgitta's 600th Jubilee celebrated in both Rome and Vadstena, the Lutheran Bishop Sven Silén characterized Birgitta as having five spiritual qualities: humility, patience or waiting for God, devotion to the humanity of Christ, love for the Virgin Mary, and concern for the condition of the world. Her humility was shown after her husband died and Christ told her she was to become his bride. She undertook many penances, made frequent confessions, as she felt herself unworthy, but accepted the responsibility of doing his will. She was called upon to denounce many persons of high standing but always did so with a sense of her own sinful nature. However, many resented this and ridiculed Birgitta. Once when she was passing through a narrow street, a nobleman whom she had called to account threw his dirty wash basin water down on her head. She calmly went on, thanking God for this insult to increase her humility.

When Birgitta was told to embark on a pilgrimage to Rome after the death of her husband Ulf, she had already been given her key mission: to work for the return of the popes to Rome. The city had sadly deteriorated; many of its churches and great buildings had fallen into decay and there was grass growing in some of its streets and squares. Birgitta was offered a small palazzo on the Campo dei Fiori and tried to establish a center to welcome pilgrims from the north. But as she walked about the sprawling town, she was shocked by the conditions she encountered. Chapter 33 of Book IV is a very long description of the terrible state of Rome. Birgitta bewails shocking conditions among priests and deacons; many living in concubinage have abandoned their clerical dress, but still say masses and conduct funerals for the rich. Finally Birgitta cries out: "So don't be surprised, my Lord, that I call Rome unfortunate. The Catholic faith may soon go under. . . . Some of the priesthood still love God, but with the pope not being there, they feel fatherless. . . ."

Birgitta's contacts with the successive popes of her lifetime were typical of her anxiety over the state of Rome and the Church. The Lord had entrusted her with this overriding mission. She was to work all her life for the restoration of the papacy in Rome. At first she addressed Pope Innocent VI (1352–62). He failed to heed Birgitta because he was surrounded by evil people and would not leave Avignon.

Urban V came to Rome and Birgitta was able to present him with her *Supplica* for the foundation of her new order. When she heard that he was returning to France, she followed him to Monte Fiascone, his summer residence. Then she received a prophecy: if he left, he would have an attack, "his teeth will chatter and fall out. His sight will grow dim, all his limbs will shake and the glow of the Holy Spirit will die out in him" (*Rev.* IV, Ch. 137). Indeed, Urban went back to Avignon and died soon afterwards, in the fall of 1370.

Finally, to Gregory XI (1370–78) Birgitta made her last appeals: "A person that did not sleep but persevered in prayer was rapt in spirit. Then it seemed that all the strength in her body disappeared, but her heart was kindled and rejoiced with the glow of love; her soul felt elevated, her spirit was filled with divine strength, and all her consciousness was filled with spiritual understanding. She then received the following revelation. She heard a beautiful voice say: 'I am the one who bore God's Son, the true God Jesus Christ. I had formerly said some words to you concerning Urban, the pope. And now I wish to say something to you which should be sent to Pope Gregory.' Then follows an illustration of how a Mother tenderly picks up her son from the ground and caresses him. 'In the same way the Mother will love and help Gregory if he listens to her plea to come to Rome'" (*Rev.* IV, Ch. 139).

PREFACE

In chapter 141, Christ speaks to the bride as she prays for Gregory. He is like a lame man who cannot make up his mind to come to Rome, but the Son assures Birgitta that he will someday come, though she may not see it. The time is not hers to know. Finally, in chapter 143, Birgitta sent a last message to Gregory through Alfons, who was still in Avignon at her bequest. She writes "If Gregory asks for signs, give him three: . . . That God has spoken wonderful words through a woman. To what purpose if not for the salvation of souls and their bettering. . . . It is my will that he come now, this fall, and that he comes to stay. Nothing is dearer to me than this: that he come to Italy."

Birgitta died only a few weeks later. Almost with her last breath she continued to serve her Lord. So the meaning of her life comes through, beyond her accomplishments, in its essential quality: a life of courageous action perfectly coordinated with her mystical life of prayer, the two interwoven.

Its challenge is alive today and can offer a way of facing up to the troubled life of our times.

Introduction

SPIRITUAL BACKGROUND AND EARLY LIFE

Mystic union with God, redeeming words and deeds born out of a burning heart—all that we summarize under the heading "spirituality" —is not to be labelled male or female. It is both and at the same time either of them; seemingly a contradiction. In studying the mystics and the great men and women of spiritual life we find this contradiction dissolved into a kind of dynamic interaction between the level of the splendor of eternity, and the level of human relations in the sphere of creation. Many great spiritual men had the comfort of a female companion on their path. Catholic tradition shows that Francis of Sales had the countess Jeanne Françoise de Chantal, Francis of Assisi had St. Clare as an intimate associate, and the early story of Western monasticism offers the striking model for both of them and for many others: St. Benedict with his sister St. Scholastica.

The relationship of two such personalities was always one of deep interior affection and feeling of oneness, and yet at the same time restrained, demanding distance to a degree which sometimes seems incomprehensible to outsiders. Still more striking is this in the lives of women chosen to spiritual preeminence. Hildegard of Bingen, Elisabeth of Schönau, the two Mechtilds of the thirteenth century, Catherine of Siena, and many others had their confessors: men of high human and educational standards, dedicated to serving God, humbly impressed by God's work in a woman assigned to their spiritual direction and care, a woman in whom they often recognized higher gifts of grace than the ones to which they could pretend in their own lives. Such men saw that if theirs was the gift of discursive thinking and literary form, they would have to use these gifts to channel an overwhelming spiritual eruption, or the boundless richness of images and messages brought forth in a woman committed, under their care, to a higher vocation.[1]

Such, in short, was the situation of the three priests, theologians, and spiritual directors who play such an eminent role in the life and development of Birgitta of Sweden. First, there is the remarkable and learned theologian, Canon Matthias of Linköping, the first Swede known to have translated and ingeniously commented upon the Bible in the Old Swedish language and whose commentary on the Apocalypse of St. John has been copied in a number of manuscripts from all parts of Europe. Then there are the two Peters: the Cistercian prior Peter Olavsson from Alvastra, who practically gave up his monastic seclusion to be able to assist Birgitta during her many years abroad; and Magister Peter Olavsson from Skänninge, a gifted spiritual director, theologian, and musician. The two Peters are the authors of the *Life of St. Birgitta* which forms the first section of this volume.

A *Life*, a *Vita*, had been a fixed literary pattern for centuries,[2] and the two confessors in composing their work had to follow the reading habits of the 1370's and of the papal court, since such texts were meant to be used in the investigations leading up to a canonization. Ancestry, childhood, and early evidence of God's special calling would have to come first, followed by examples of heroic faith and action in the person's mature life. Attention is always paid to supernatural events in this kind of literature. The two confessors were not short of material in any respect. Their account became a sober document marked by humble confidence in God's prophetic call through Birgitta. Many things which the modern reader might have wished to know are lacking, e.g., her Christian life with her husband on the estate of Ulvåsa, her social attitude toward servants and beggars during that half of her life. Now, we only know of these aspects from witnesses during the canonization process.[3]

There are two main versions of the *Vita*.[4] The fullest account, well worked out stylistically as well as in regard to signs of Birgitta's holiness and divine election, is the one rendered in English here below. There has been, however, an important scholarly discussion on this version of the *Vita*, its origin and function. We find the text in its fully elaborated form among the acts of the process of canonization, and there its purpose is perfectly clear: to underline all characteristics of Birgitta which were most properly fitting to a saint of the Church, according to the standards of the late fourteenth century. As such, the *Vita* is a final evidence of attachment, affection, and awe among those who were able to follow her posthumous fame until the solemn declaration of her sanctity by Pope Boniface IX in 1391, only eighteen years after her death.

Although the canonization process was brought to its fulfillment by a pope who represented only a part of European Christendom—the Roman obedience in the Great Schism, as opposed to the Avignonese obedience to which, among others, France, Spain, and Scotland adhered—its juridical form was nevertheless lawful and traditional. Its validity was not questioned once the Great Schism was brought to an end at the Council of Constance by the election of Pope Martin V (1417). The so-called "Canonization of St. Birgitta at the Council of Constance," which took place on 2 February 1415, was nothing but a vain effort undertaken by the leader of the short-lived Pisan obedience, Baldassare Cossa, the antipope John XXIII, to vindicate, in the last minute, his authenticity as the only true bishop of Rome by invoking the prophetic voice of Birgitta. Yet this restating of the canonization may have worked as a preparation for the final solution of the Great Schism among his own adherents.[5] In all these events the *Vita Processus,* as it is called, was the authorized document making evident Birgitta's sanctity and divine election.[6]

There is, however, a shorter version of Birgitta's *Vita,* preserved in the MS C 15 of the University Library of Uppsala,[7] one of the numerous manuscripts from the medieval library of Vadstena Abbey happily saved and handed down to our days. As always in the case of two versions, the question was raised: is the *Vita Processus* the original version and the *Vita C 15* a shortened form of it, or is the *Vita C 15* the true original text which was later embellished and enriched upon? And if the second alternative is true, then were elements added to the *Vita Processus* which were not altogether authentic?[8]

The Swedish scholar Sara Ekwall, who studied this question carefully, brought forth in 1965 her conclusion: the *Vita C 15* must be the original one. Several characteristics led her to this view. The text shows a structure with chapters of basically equal length having each its own heading, whereas in the *Vita Processus* some chapters are unreasonably long (e.g., that on Birgitta's stay in Alvastra, which contains a number of anecdotes on persons who experienced Birgitta's help and the strength of her prayer during this period: Gerekin, Bishop Hemming, a nun called Catherine, Master Matthias, and the Dominican master Algot). Another long passage without heading is devoted to some of Birgitta's mystical experiences of early years. This, says Sara Ekwall, cannot have been omitted in a shorter version produced out of a fuller one; but it may well have been added to a shorter version to make it more rich and attractive.

What is rendered in the addition should not be suspected of being untrue; it simply stems from another source, or it may have been added at some later point by the original authors, who thereby changed the original cast of the text. In same manner, the chapter on how the devil tempted Birgitta (below, p. 87) brings forward short events which carry the mark of having been added later, says Sara Ekwall. Basically, the same may be true for the final portion of the *Vita* dealing with Birgitta's life in Rome and Italy. The passage on Naples and Jerusalem carries so strongly the character of a conclusion that the original *Vita* may have ended here (below, p. 95).[9]

There are also a number of significant differences between the two versions pointed out by Sara Ekwall. In several passages the fuller version has a more correct Latin but also uses more literary and devotional formulas than the shorter one. In the shorter version Birgitta is often called "God's bride," but in the longer version the expression "Christ's bride" is much more common. The shorter version does not enter upon Birgitta's noble ancestry in the way the longer version does, where she is more often called "Lady Birgitta" (*domina Brigida* by the Italian form of the name). A number of persons are anonymous in the shorter version, while in the longer one their name and social status are given. The word *divinitus*, "divinely" revealed, which is common in the long version, is not used at all in the shorter one.

As decisive evidence, Sara Ekwall quotes a testimony of Prior Peter Olavsson and Master Peter Olavsson given in the canonization process. They recount how they wrote the *Vita* of St. Birgitta in Rome shortly after her death, but that they knew much more which they were not able to write down then because of their approaching departure from Rome in the fall of 1373 with Birgitta's earthly remains destined for Sweden.[10]

These arguments amount to a strong support of the view that the two confessors, shortly after Birgitta's death, wrote a concentrated *Vita* of her life without yet having an explicit purpose of convincing the judges of a canonization process about Birgitta's sanctity in canonical forms. Someone later worked the text over thoroughly and extended it with the canonization process in sight. But if this was not done by the two confessors, who created the final version, the *Vita Processus* translated here below? Sara Ekwall is not in doubt. After stylistic and other comparisons with texts whose origin and author are secure, she reaches the conclusion that no one but Alphonsus Pecha, bishop of Jaen, is the author and redactor of the final, full version of the *Vita*.[11]

The question of who put the last finishing touch to the *Life of St. Birgitta*, then, enables us to arrive at a better understanding of the world of Birgitta as a spiritual writer. Four men guided her development successively: Master Matthias, Prior Peter Olavsson, Master Peter

Olavsson, and Bishop Alphonsus Pecha. From their *Vita* and other sources, we can follow Birgitta's life in its main lines.

Born in the winter of 1302–03—probably around St. Sylvester, says Birgit Klockars, the able biographer of her childhood, youth, and married life in Sweden—Birgitta was surrounded by spiritual impulses preparing the way for her first confrontation with divine election: her first revelations in the period 1344–49.[12] She was guided by Master Matthias in interpreting them. Birgitta's religious experiences in childhood are faithfully recorded in the *Vita*. Nils Hermansson or Nicolaus Hermanni, a cleric born around 1326, prepared the way. He was perhaps the teacher of young Karl, Birgitta's eldest son, although probably of the same age as he. Later he was teacher to Birgitta's next son Birger. He became canon and bishop of Linköping and was one of Birgitta's faithful supporters in establishing Vadstena Abbey. He was a model for a cleric and a priest in Birgitta's eyes, serving God in daily prayer, pastoral care, and spiritual friendship. He died in 1391 and was venerated as a saint throughout the rest of the Middle Ages.[13]

Master Matthias's influence upon Birgitta has been studied by scholars like Bengt Strömberg, Hjalmar Sundén, and Anders Piltz.[14] Sundén, applying Jungian psychology to Birgitta's relationship to Master Matthias, based himself upon the image of Matthias as a theologian and a spiritual writer that Strömberg had created in 1944. Piltz has deepened our understanding of Matthias's theology considerably since then. "There is something anachronistic about him: he was a dedicated anti-dialectician some hundred or two hundred years behind his times. He would have been better off with John of Salisbury or Saint Bernard or Roger Bacon, and he echoes, as it were, their warnings against the perils of biblical studies detached from the biblical texts," says Piltz. He then quotes Matthias as saying: "A great corruption has prevailed in the Church for a long time, since theology is taught in a philosophical way and the philosophers are venerated instead of theologians."[15] This gives us an indication of how Matthias strove for a biblically centered theology and pastoral teaching.

Strömberg has demonstrated how Matthias found the model for his theological work among the Dominicans and the Franciscans, the preachers of those centuries. In his great theological treatise which starts *Homo conditus in omnibus bonis habundabat* (Created man overflowed in everything which is good) biblical quotations recur in every paragraph, whereas long philosophical deliberations are entirely lacking. Man's beauty according to God's creation is placed at the very beginning, man's corruption through sin and seduction constitutes the background for the full story of redemption, restitution, fullness of grace, and vision of God.

Faith, hope, charity are the healers of the sickness of the soul, which is sin. Suffering and Christ's God-willed passion reopen the path to the Father; the sacraments are the signs that communicate to us what Christ has won. Vices have their remedies in the virtues, the burden of which we impose upon ourselves. Christ in the gospel texts is our example and the saints guide our path in daily life through example and intercession.

Whereas *Homo conditus* probably was written for the use of parish priests, a more advanced and confidential teaching was presented in the same author's *Alphabetum distinctionum,* a selection of biblical passages in alphabetical order. Its commentaries often elaborate upon evils of the Church and of the clergy; the tone is not very different from what we often find in Birgitta's writings.[16]

It is not impossible that Master Matthias arranged Book I of Birgitta's *Revelations,* the first 60 spiritual texts which she apparently already received in Sweden. The famous introduction of Master Matthias to the *Revelations* called, after its first words, *Stupor et mirabilia* (Amazing and marvelous things are being heard on our earth) was meant to introduce the start of this new revelation of God's message through a woman. Birgitta was still living as a God-devoted widow in Sweden, planning the foundation of a monastery, writing letters to Pope Clement VI (1342–52) to have him act as a peace negotiator in the war between England and France.[17] There was not yet any prospect of her passage from Sweden to stay abroad for the rest of her life.

This changed with the Crusade which King Magnus Eriksson of Sweden and Norway launched against the city of Novgorod in 1347–48, and with the clash of opinions on how to carry out the Crusade—where apparently Matthias also entertained views of his own.[18] The situation was decisively altered when the great pestilence, the Black Death, started its ravaging tour across Europe. It is generally assumed that Master Matthias died in the great pestilence around 1350. He was buried in the Church of the Dominicans in Stockholm, but his body was later transferred to Vadstena, where he was venerated as a saint.[19]

Master Matthias, in his preface, presents the text of Birgitta's first recorded revelation, the text of which is given here in full:[20]

INTRODUCTION

The devil sinned in three ways: by pride, because I had created him good; by desire, to be not only similar to me, but superior to me; and by lust to enjoy so much my divinity that he willingly would have killed me, had he been able to, so that he might reign in my place. Because of this he fell from heaven, filled the earth with these three sins and so violated all mankind. Therefore I took on humanity and came into the world, to annihilate his pride by my humility, to destroy his desire by my poverty and simplicity. And I submitted to the most immense penance of the cross in order to annihilate his abominable lust and to open heaven, closed through his sins, to man by the blood of my heart and by my death—yet so far as he inserts his will to work for it, according to his ability. But now the men of Sweden, especially those who call themselves courtiers or knights, sin in the same manner as the devil did before them. They take pride in their well-shaped bodies, which I gave them. They surround themselves with fortunes which I did not give them. They overflow with their abominable lust to such a degree that they had rather killed me, were it possible for them, than abstained from their lusts or endured my frightful justice, which threatens them for their sins. Therefore their bodies, which they take pride in, shall be slain by sword, lance, and axe. These precious limbs, which they boast of, wild animals and birds shall devour them. Let strangers make spoil of all that they have drawn together against my will, and let them be wanting (Cf. Ps. 108:11). Because of their abominable lusts they offend my Father so that he does not hold them worthy of being admitted to see his face. And since they had rather killed me, if they could, they will be given over into the hands of the devil to be slain by him by eternal death. But I would have let this judgment pass over Sweden long before, if the prayers of my friends, who live in the midst of them, had not resisted; they moved me to mercy. Therefore, the time shall come when I shall draw these friends of mine to me, so that they shall not see the evil which I will make befall this country. Verily, some of my friends will live then, and they will see in the fullness of their merits. But now, since kings and princes and prelates do not want to recognize me in my good deed, and come to me, I will gather the poor, the wicked, the minors and the wretched, and with them I will fill up the place of the others, so that my army will not be weakened because of their absence.

The collaboration of the two, Master Matthias and Birgitta, grew into a procedure for cautious self-control. In his testimony at the canonization process Prior Peter Olavsson stated:

In case she was experiencing an illusion in these [revelations], she herself submitted all her visions and her way of experiencing them to the examination of Master Matthias, her aforementioned confessor, and of other masters in theology, and of men highly skilled in the knowledge and way of the spirit. She bowed totally to their decision, which was that . . . these ways of experiencing visions and of having visions were a gift of the Holy Spirit, taking into account the person seeing them, and the matter of the visions, and the ways they were seen.[21]

The first book of the *Revelations* contains themes and passages of great weight and impressiveness. In contrast to Books IV and VI, there is no mixture here of long and short, extravagant and straight, more and less important texts. Nothing seems to have been added or deleted—the number sixty indicates an original arrangement, just as the thirty revelations of Book II probably reproduce the very first plan for the arrangement of these texts. All the sixty chapters of Book I have been carefully worked out, each around its principal theme. They are often already in dialogue form, as later on in Birgitta's life, but here speeches or messages in direct form spoken by Christ or our Lady predominate. Sometimes there are additional teachings or explanations by angels (ch. 10), John the Baptist (ch. 31), St. Peter (ch. 41). Numerous quotations and allusions to the Old Testament make their mark upon Book I. The basic Jewish-Christian experience laid down in Exodus recurs often: Yahweh's witness to himself in the blazing of the bush is echoed in chapter 47; the staff of Moses in chapters 53 and 60; the plagues of Egypt in chapters 44 and 56; the Exodus from Egypt in chapters 26, 41, 49, and 60; the pillar of cloud in chapter 26; the march through the Red Sea in chapters 15, 45, 48–49, 53, and 60. The giving of the Law on Mount Sinai is referred to in six revelations: 10, 26, 45, 47–48, 53; the Golden

Calf in three: 48, 53, 60. A similar amassing of references to the Exodus themes is not to be found in any other single book of the *Revelations*.[22]

One example from chapter 53 of Book I shows us how Birgitta interprets three great deeds performed by the staff of Moses. First, the staff is transformed into a serpent, to the fright of the enemies of Israel. Secondly, it divided the Red Sea in two halves to allow the people to walk safely in the middle to reach the other shore.

> Lastly, the rock gave out water by means of that staff. The rock is the hard parts of the people, for if they are struck with the fear of God and love, remorse and tears of repentance flow out. No one is so unworthy, no one is so evil that his tears do not flow from his eyes and all his limbs are quickened toward virtue if he turns to me interiorly, considers my suffering, realizes my power and thinks of the goodness which lets earth and trees bear fruit.

Here the stories from Exodus 4:2ff; 7:8ff; 14:16ff; 17:5ff have been drawn together and condensed into one single application containing three stages of God's action toward mankind. Very often this is the way Birgitta's meditation of Holy Scripture is echoed in her revelations.

THE MONK ON THE LADDER

During her Swedish years as a widow, Birgitta's relationship to God and to his intermediary, Master Matthias, underwent a deep change. Recent scholarly work on this process seems to be unanimous in one respect: something like a "crisis" must have taken place.[23] There is no unanimity, though, concerning this crisis, or the deeper cause behind it. K. B. Westman (1911) and others understood it as the result of Birgitta's confrontation with God's calling to her after the death of Ulf, her husband—a "vocational" crisis, as it were, leading her under the guidance of Matthias straight to its logical historical scope. Sundén (1973) adhered to the idea that the crisis was due to the deterioration in Birgitta's relationship with the king because of the importance this relationship had for the future of the planned monastery for which the king had donated Vadstena royal castle. As Birgitta Fritz has shown recently (1985), however, this interpretation is open to doubt for chronological reasons. The more subtle problems of religious psychology have not yet been tackled in this regard.[24] But there seems to be one important agreement between scholars today: that Book V of the *Revelations* is a vestige of this crisis and thus constitutes a primary document of what really was at stake during this period of transition in Birgitta's life. Before entering upon other sections of the main bulk of the *Revelations* and the story of their redaction, then, we will have to halt for a moment and have a closer look at Book V, which makes up an important portion of the texts printed below.

Book V has been analyzed several times by scholars, primarily from the point of view of the texts and their authenticity,[25] and secondarily from the vantage point of C. G. Jung's school of psychoanalysis.[26] Some basic stages of research into this work, however, seem to have been forgotten. First of all, the sequence of questions which make up the basic pattern of this treatise conceived by Birgitta in the summer of 1349 has not yet been lucidly explained. The treatise consists of sixteen challenging interrogations directed to "the judge" by the "monk on the ladder, full of guile and devilish malice," who seemed, "in his most restless and unquiet bearing, to be more devil than humble monk." Each interrogation has five or seven questions and the corresponding answers of the judge. Thirteen longer or shorter messages and visions in the form of revelations have been irregularly inserted between the interrogations. One part of the scholarly discussion has been devoted to the problem of whether these revelations were put there by Birgitta herself or distributed in such manner by the redactors. Before entering upon this topic, let us follow the sequence of questions. This sequence is identical in the Latin text and the Old Swedish translation of the Latin text, whereas the insertion of revelations does not follow the same pattern in the two versions.

The first four interrogations, each consisting of five questions, belong so closely together that the Old Swedish text made one introductory chapter of the first three of them. A monk is seen standing on a ladder in front of Jesus Christ as judge; the judge is surrounded by all the heavenly host. The first questions are all modelled upon the questioner's individual needs: why, judge, did you give us senses and limbs, property, law, diversion, food, will, sex, vitality, if we may not use these things as we want? Why ought I feel pain when enjoying created things? Why should I suffer when the world is full of happiness and I myself, of noble birth, am meritorious, rich, and honorable and therefore deserve my reward? God's answers to these egotistic questions

22

remain extremely short, never exceeding six lines in the critical Latin edition of the text. The common characteristics seem to make out of interrogations 1 to 4 (= chapters 1–2 in the Old Swedish text) a first separate entity of Book V.

With interrogation 5, the answers of the judge become fuller and more extensive. Even the pattern of questioning changes. Instead of questions like "Why did you give" and "Why should I," the monk now asks: "Why did you create . . . ?" "Why does N. N. suffer . . . ?" "Why did you make . . . ?" "Why did you not make . . . ?" This goes on from interrogations 5 to 8, with the exception of interrogation 7, which has six questions instead of five; they center again around the monk himself in his relationship to the created world. The answers of the judge show a similar shift: instead of the iterated "I have" in the answers to interrogations 1 to 4, we find at the opening of the first answer in interrogation 5 the decisive: "I created." This aspect is stressed again when it comes to the worship of idols in interrogation 8. The monk's questions insist upon created goods and their place in God's plan: How can you, judge, advocate being the originator of sickness, fear of death, bad judges, wild animals, and the well-being of evil men, all that which is a threat to happiness in this world? Why do you accept that many peoples adore idols, why don't you appear convincingly in your glory to all the world, why don't you show quite openly how detestable the demons are, so that all men avoid and detest them?

It has escaped scholars so far that there is a switch in the sequence after interrogation 8. Until now, Birgitta or her redactors have practically no comment in the form of a message, a revelation, in addition to the answers of the judge. After no. 8, commenting or concomitant revelations are added to each single set of answers.

Then there is the switch of subject. By interrogation 9 the monk leaves the order of creation and moves into the order of salvation. He signifies it by addressing for the first time the judge as son of Mary. Why are the gifts of creation so unevenly distributed between angels, men, animals, and unspirited matter? Interrogation 10 enters deeper into the mystery of incarnation by accusing the judge, now precisely as Christ, for having submitted himself to these insulting human conditions without really being obliged to do so according to the plan of salvation. Christ ought to have followed another plan, as implicitly stated in interrogation 9. Number 11 elaborates on the same subject in that the monk is accusing Christ of having become subject to time instead of having revealed his glory and majesty in one second.

INTRODUCTION

The set of interrogations proceeds according to a distorted salvation history. The basic plan of God's incarnation having been attacked by the monk, he now pursues his attack in detail: why did you not prove openly that Mary was a virgin, that you were God born to mankind? Why did you flee to Egypt letting the innocent children die for you—and how could you allow yourself to be so insulted during your passion? After this fulminating accusation in interrogation 12, there is an end to the sequence of subjects belonging to the order of salvation.

The last four interrogations (13 to 16) seemingly return to themes touched upon earlier. In fact, however, the uneven distribution of grace, which is the object of the monk's attacks in number 13, does not concern gifts of the creational order, but clearly belongs to the order of grace, connected to the working of the Holy Spirit. Why do you call men so differently with your grace, the monk asks? Some are called in their youth, some in old days; some receive a good understanding and some are as stupid as an ass. Some are always tempted, some are continually being consoled; the evil man gets a better life than the good man. The answers of the judge are now getting very discursive. This is also true for the answers of interrogation 14, where the monk turns to the injustice of children carrying their fathers' sins, of giving birth in pain, of fear for the unforeseen and of the good end of evil men, whereas the good sometimes are stricken unprepared by sudden death.

Central issues of faith are broken into pieces in the questions of the last two interrogations. Why do you not always listen to the prayers of the faithful? Why does the evil man not have your permission to go on being evil? Why do evil things happen to the good ones, and why does the devil stay for years with some and not with others? And finally: How can you find joy in separating the good from the evil on the day of judgment, the date of which you do not even know, although you are coequal with the Father? And why, at all, did you postpone your incarnation so long, if it really was so necessary? How can the gospels be so full of contradictions if the Holy Spirit spoke through the evangelists? And why did your word not yet reach out to all the world?

Interrogations 1 to 4 bring forward a set of questions concerning individual doubts of a single person only. For the other interrogations we arrive at this scheme:

4 interrogations (5, 6, 7, 8) move within the order of creation;
4 interrogations (9, 10, 11, 12) move within the order of salvation;

4 interrogations (13, 14, 15, 16) move within the order of sanctification.

Birgitta's treatment of human doubts is, then, fundamentally trinitarian
in its set-up. Book V demonstrates her situation in the summer of the
great European pestilence, the Black Death, when she was faced with
the decision to leave Sweden or not for the sake of faith. We meet her
here thoroughly imbued and animated by the revelation of the Triune
God, Father, Son, and Holy Spirit. Book V is a sequence of doubts,
growing out of the monk's personal discomfort, accelerating from his
doubts about the reasonable purpose of creation, via his doubts about
God's plan of salvation, to a challenging reproach to God for a number
of allegedly false principles of spiritual life laid down in the Christian
teaching of man's sanctification, of life in the unction of the Holy
Spirit.

Understood according to this structure, Book V is evidently a challenge to any theologian acting as a confessor to the interpreter of such
doubts, Lady Birgitta. The plotting out of revelations among interrogations 8 to 16 may well have seemed ephemeral to Birgitta herself, if hers
was such a clear spiritual insight into trinitarian theology. In the first
long revelation summing up interrogations 1 to 8 (or 5 to 8) the imagery
of the doctor healing the sick is displayed. The distribution and subjects
of subsequent messages can be seen in a table:

INTERROGATION NO.	IMAGERY OF ADDED REVELATION	REVELATION NO.
9	Christ on the merits of his Mother	4
10	Christ on the love of poverty	5
11	Christ on submitting oneself to spiritual hardships and endur-ance	6
12	Christ on frequent confession of sins	7
9 to 12	Summary: Christ on the damna-tion of the voluptuous	8
13	Christ on the dwellings of the Holy Spirit	9

There is every reason to stress the importance of revelation 13 of Book V, as Hjalmar Sundén has done.[27] This message of the Father—only rarely does the Father and not Christ speak—appears as the solution to all sixteen sets of doubts laid down in strategical and trinitarian order in the sequence of interrogation. It is no wonder that Sundén found in this arrangement a confirmation of his Jungian interpretation of Book V as a testimony of the process of individuation which Birgitta allegedly went through prior to her departure for Italy. The monk is, according to Sundén, the *animus* of Birgitta; the doubts are but her own doubts projected upon the figure of the monk, who then takes over all the negative elements, whereas Master Matthias, who might have given rise to many of these problems, is free from being accused in the last run.

Seen in the perspective of the literary form, the sixteen interrogations without regard to the series of revelations added to them are powerful enough to be evaluated even outside the key of Jungian psychology. If God's action is seen as a sequence, it does not necessarily mean that it is being understood as a sequence in time, either in Joachimite terms as ages of world history,[28] or in Jungian terms as stages in the history of a soul.[29] It could also refer to the different ways God turns his face to mankind: sometimes in his power over creation, sometimes in his message through human word and action, sometimes in the transformative, continuous stream of divine inner working. The symbolic arrangement of four times four interrogations evokes a pattern of limitless extension and expansion of God's power in all the four quarters of the world. For that reason, one might even imagine the set-up of Book V according to the geometrical pattern of the triangular pyramid, where one side is always at the bottom and the appearance from any side is a tripartite one, although it has four sides and four edges.

On the other hand, this does not ridicule a Jungian interpretation of the same text. One might rather see it as an explanation of how Sundén could arrive at his conclusions. For if God acts with man according to his different attitudes in a series of approaches, some points in time will inevitably become more important, more decisive than others to a person, since the human person is bound by the conditions of time and space. To the one person, God's action in the order of creation will be decisive, to the other, his action in the order of salvation. Most decisive to all, however, must be God's action in the order of sanctification, to which the gospel words on the unforgivable sins against the Holy Spirit have always been linked. The ultimative character of the order of sanctification certainly does not rest upon an arbitrary divine decision, but is based upon the internal order of things in themselves—for how can there be access to God if no attention is paid to the basic call of the Spirit to complete conversion and attachment to God through contrition, repentance, remission of sins, and the works of the Holy Spirit?

Sundén, therefore, is certainly right in focusing upon the process of Birgitta's identification and purification of self by and through the concepts about God's action which she brought forth in Book V. Only Sundén's assignment of Birgitta's crisis to a certain historical moment and a very specific situation in Birgitta's life may have been too much influenced by the doctrines inherent in Jung's psychology. Much of the process may have been far behind Birgitta in the summer of 1349. Her task was then to summarize all in the face of the imminent judgment of God—maybe also as a testament to her life in Sweden, to leave behind a document of the essence of her mystical relationship to God, as she had experienced it so far.

SALVATION HISTORY

Birgitta's exodus from a Sweden overflowing with pride and concupiscence took place in late 1349. The prospects were good and bad at the same time. Master Matthias had supported her prophetic task and King Magnus Eriksson had been won over to the idea of transforming the castle of Vadstena ("Watz stena," the stone house on the water [of lake Vättern]) into a monastery (1346) and of proceeding in the form of a crusade against Novgorod east of Swedish Finland (1348). But then there was the expected "Egyptian Plague," the Black Death. The ravaging sickness, for which there was no known remedy, reached Norway's western coast by ship from England early in 1349, and rumors already spread fear and terror in advance. After having depopulated large stretches of Norway's cultivated valleys, it reached Sweden only in early 1350.[30] No doubt Birgitta fled as God's judgment approached. Birgitta must have felt like crossing the Red Sea with the chosen people of God, traversing Europe in the middle of death, protected as it were by the pillar of cloud through the desert. Her arrival in Rome, probably toward the opening of the Holy Year 1350, meant the end of Master Matthias's guidance in her life and the opening up of a new chapter, characterized by her two confessors by name of Peter Olavsson. From then on, they were her spiritual directors until she met the Spanish bishop Alphonsus Pecha, the "guardian angel" of her last years and of her spiritual heritage to future generations.

Prior Peter Olavsson, a Cistercian monk of Alvastra, joined Birgitta in Rome, but soon left again for Sweden. Because of his frequent travels, we cannot exactly follow his role in Birgitta's spiritual life during these first years abroad. Instead, Master Peter Olavsson from Skänninge must have been her most intimate guide during the early 1350's when she stayed in a flat at San Lorenzo in Damaso in Rome. He was a key person in the long process—over at least a year—when an angel regularly appeared to Birgitta, dictating to her a dogmatic treatise on salvation history known as "The Sermon of the Angel."[31] This treatise is best understood as a unit in itself, as one single revelation, yet received and written down during a long period of time. Its particular function in Birgitta's world is closely bound up with her hopes for the establishment of a monastic community. The *Sermo Angelicus*, divided into twenty-one long lessons, became the daily readings in the weekly Office of Our Lady of the nuns in the Order of the Holy Savior.[32]

The three times seven lessons assigned to seven days' matins (the night prayer office of monks, nuns, and other religious) treat seven stages in salvation history. Antiphons, responsories, prayers, and other liturgical items were written to match the main subject of each of the seven days and were repeated in identical manner every week through the year. The ordinary year of the Church from Advent to Christmas, Easter, Pentecost, and Last Judgment was present through the priestly office prayed by Prior Peter, Master Peter, and other priests and members of Birgitta's household. So it was a considerable advance for the spirituality of a female community when, instead of a simple Marian office prayed in the same way every day, the so-called *Officium parvum Beatae Mariae Virginis*, the nuns of the Order of the Holy Savior could pray and sing a "Great Marian Office" proper to their own order. Here the priest who must have been Birgitta's spiritual advisor during this period enters into the picture: it seems indisputable that Master Peter Olavsson actually wrote the liturgical texts of the Great Marian Office and even composed or adapted Gregorian chant to the texts, to fit the twenty-one lessons "dictated" to Birgitta by the angel.[33]

The Sunday texts were devoted to God's work of creating the world according to the most beautiful "model" for it, which was the Mother of God, the Virgin existing in God's consciousness and premeditation before all ages. The office proceeds on Monday to the angels, their beauty and fall; on Tuesday to Adam's fall, to the patriarchs and to the premeditated protection of the people of God through the Virgin, the Mother of God to come. Wednesday deals with the birth of the Virgin, her childhood and youth while chosen and elected with preeminence among all women. Thursday is devoted to the incarnation of the Word Divine, and Friday to the suffering and death of Christ in his manhood.

On Saturday, contrary to what one might expect, the meditation does not stay with Christ in his tomb, in expectation of the day of resurrection. Characteristically, it concentrates upon the theme of the Virgin's faith in Christ, in spite of all odds—her confidence during the first great Sabbath, when Christ went down to the nether world, that he would rise again, and, finally, her bodily assumption into God's presence. Nowhere is Birgitta's Mariology brought to a fuller expression.[34] And yet there is nothing entirely new compared to the revelations from her Swedish period collected in Book I. A good number of them start with the introductory: "I am the Queen of Heaven" or "I am Mary," if speaking to Birgitta, or referring to Birgitta as seeing her in a vision, or to the Mother as speaking to the Son. But whereas Mary in Book I is speaking and acting, the Sermon of the Angel is at face value a treatise on her role in salvation history—and therefore Mariology, not Marian piety. It is the doctrine of what she means in God's plan, not the story of her intervention in the present-day life of the Church. But on the other hand, being Mariology, and inasmuch as salvation history is present and working in any epoch of world history and in any stage of an individual's life, the Sermon of the Angel also tells of the daily, eternal story of Motherhood and Virginity interceding in any salvific events that surround us.

Master Peter's engagement in the shaping of the Marian Office for the nuns is revealing. It raises the question if, by chance, there was something in his religious outlook which helped bring Birgitta into a state of mind where this perspective on salvation history was close at hand. We cannot know this, since there are no distinct literary works known to be exclusively written by Master Peter. But considering the importance of confessors, the Sermon of the Angel may be taken as the fullest expression of Birgitta's first meeting with Rome, the city of martyrs, on the one hand, and the guidance of Master Peter on the other. In this situation the strict theological training of Master Matthias ceased to press its mark upon Birgitta, and the Italian milieu, perhaps also imbued with fresh experiences of Franciscan piety, made its impression upon her. As Toni Schmid has pointed out (1940), Birgitta's understanding of the Immaculate Conception of Mary is close to that of the Franciscans of the fourteenth century, more distant from that of the Dominican school, whereas for the assumption she deviates somewhat from the Franciscan view, absolutely stating against skeptics, however, the Virgin's bodily assumption (VI, 60).[35]

Psychologically and spiritually the Sermon of the Angel marks the end of crisis, Birgitta's arrival into the promised land in an even deeper sense. What used to be a perverted, chaotic world, an "inverse salvation history" presented by the monk on the ladder in his challenging God, has now turned into a cosmos, in which the essence of womanhood and motherhood has become the center toward which all doctrines and dogmas of faith are being oriented. In this case, as for the *Book of Questions*, the literary result of the process no doubt lags far behind the real event that made it possible. The moment Book V was conceived and written down, Birgitta must have overcome the crisis described in it and may already have arrived at a new cosmos, which was then activated and made productive in a literary sense by the apparition of the angel. God's answers to the monk's attacks may have paved the way for this new history of salvation.

MONASTIC FAMILY

Two great revelations of Birgitta have been mentioned so far: Book V from the summer of 1349 and the Sermon of the Angel from 1352–53. These two texts give witness to Birgitta's transition from a life of a noble lady in Sweden to that of a noble guest and pilgrim in the holy city. She exchanged a life at home for that of a foreigner—a transition we encounter most dramatically in the Irish monks of the early Middle Ages taking lifelong exile as the most harsh form of penance, which it also certainly is in all ages of mankind. But the third great revelation of Birgitta, that of her vision of the Rule of the Holy Savior, has not yet been treated here, although it probably came first in time. There is a general assumption that Birgitta had this vision in Vadstena on one of the occasions when she stayed with King Magnus Eriksson and Queen Blanca in the royal palace, which was later to become the first monastery of the Order of the Holy Savior.[36]

The problem of the text is that we do not possess any original version to bring us back to the very moment of her vision.[37] What we have is an echo of the primary mystical experience she had, worked out to fit the exigencies of canon law, but framed by revelations retelling the circumstances surrounding her vision. If we remove the surrounding revelations, the division into chapters, the chapter headings, and a number of particular directives clearly intended at adjusting the text to the genre of a monastic rule, we become aware of three stages of mystical experience gradually broadening Birgitta's understanding of the task God wanted to entrust to her.

The first field of the vision is the young virgin chosen by Christ the Lord to lead a life of the elect in the sisterly community under the guidance of her mother abbess. In a solemn rite of transition she is taken out of the secular world, and removes her secular clothes, to be invested by Christ, here in the person of the bishop, in the gown of the chosen ones, and crowned with Christ's five marks of passion.

In the second field of the vision we meet the sisterly community of the elect in need of the complementary element of male assistance to represent the fullness of divine redemption. In a grand general view, the recruitment of this sister- and brotherhood of the elect is being sketched: how dowries and gifts are to be accumulated until a certain level of self-support has been attained, and how, thereafter, any surplus is to be distributed to the poor and needy.

The third field of the vision reveals the community's purpose: first, perpetual service of God in the love of a burning heart, where everything has to be directed towards this goal, on the human as well as on the material scale; second, ascetic practice, confession of sins, the preparation of the altars for the daily sacrifice of the mass, and the disciplinary supervision exerted by the bishop. In the final passage death is evoked: the daily rehearsal of the rite of *memento mori* is prescribed to prove that death is conquered by this perpetual, neverending praise of God, which lets individual death become nothing more than birth into a new life, making room for a new member to enter into the community of the elect.[38]

The Rule of the Holy Savior does not have its like in the history of monastic rules. Few other rules ever approved were composed of so few basic elements, and paid so little attention to all the practical needs of a monastic community. This perhaps explains the thorny path of this visionary text from its first version probably produced by the Swedish confessors in the 1340s, through its first presentation to the pope probably around 1367, its first summary approval by Pope Urban V in 1370, and the final approval of a revised version by Pope Urban VI in 1378, although formally only as constitutions to be added to the rule of St. Augustine.[39] But at that time Birgitta had already left the scene, and sons and daughters of her monastic family had to be content with this image of an original visionary impetus. And yet they found access to the fresh water in the vessel in which it was contained.

The Rule of the Holy Savior has been for hundreds of followers to the call the first acquaintance they ever had with Birgitta's visionary world. It is a text derived from the walk of her soul with Christ, her Lord and bridegroom, a walk in which he, with delicate care, introduces her to one secret after the other in stages of well-measured time. In like manner, new recruits to the Order of the Holy Savior met Christ taking their hands to introduce them with subtlety into the three stages of the community life of the elect: the personal decision and election; the human fullness of divine praise and its continuation through the generations; and the perfect sacrifice of the chosen people in spite of material limitations and individual death.

THE SEVEN BOOKS

There are, as we have seen, three great revelation texts in Birgitta's writings. Their relative sequence in time is: Monastic Rule, *Book of Questions*, Sermon of the Angel. But probably only the lastmentioned revelation got its final shape comparatively soon after it had been given. The *Book of Questions* was enriched by inserted revelations, the Rule was probably worked over again and again, so that the text, as we know it, is more recent than those of the other two great visions.

The bulk of Birgitta's writings consists of about six hundred longer or shorter texts stylized as sayings of God the Father, Christ, his

Mother, or another saint.[40] Birgitta herself as the bride is often found speaking in the text, sometimes even opening it up by a question or by the retelling of something which happened to her. So many messages, spread out over a period of maybe thirty mature years, had to be arranged according to some external criteria. Scholars have discussed which one of Birgitta's confessors is to be credited for the arrangement of most of the texts in eight "books": one of the two Peters, or Bishop Alphonsus. The conclusion of Salomon Kraft (1929) was that the sequence is partly chronological, but on the basis of a scheme laid down by Bishop Alphonsus.[41] We can discern characteristic traces of the division in eight books. The first book, already treated above, contains sixty distinct revelations, all from Birgitta's time in Sweden. The second, third, and seventh books each contain thirty texts or a little more—30, 34, and 31, respectively. This is hardly accidental. The number of items joined into a unit was taken as a form to mirror a basic order inherent in matter. It seems to me very probable that an ideal number of 60, 30, 30, and 30 texts collected into four units may have been projected at a very early stage of the arrangement. This corresponds to the four different origin situations of the four groups:

Book I: 60 great revelations from Sweden
Book II: 30 other revelations from Sweden
Book III: 30(?) revelations from Italy
Book VII: 30(?) revelations from the Holy Land

An examination of Book III shows that among the 34 texts of the authorized version some are extremely short exhortations, of a type which can be found more often in Books IV and VI and among the *Extravagantes*, but is clearly exceptional here: chapters 9, 25, 32. Also chapters 22, 23, and 34 are comparatively short. It is easy to assume that four of these six texts have been added to an original number of 30 chapters. In Book VII, on the other hand, long and short texts have the same value inasfar as they each refer to a particular phase of Birgitta's journey to the Holy Land. Possibly chapter 9 is a later addition, a short promise to Birgitta increasing the total number from a planned 30 to 31 chapters; but this, of course, is a guess.

In any case, four books are arranged to give an approximate number of 150 revelations. To play a little with the numbers, one might also put it in another way: three opening books render a total of approximately 120 chapters. This is interesting, since Book IV at some stage seems to have consisted of 130 chapters, at the end of which the authorized version says: "This is the end of Book IV according to Alphonsus." What follows is an addition of special revelations addressed to popes and high prelates, raising the total number to 144 chapters. Of the first 130 chapters there are many rather short ones: 26–32; 35; 41–43; 56–57; 66; 73; 84; 91; 116–23. One might easily imagine ten of these texts to have been squeezed in among an original number of 120 chapters, which would bring a rather neat balance between Books I–III on the one hand, and Book IV on the other, as two units with 120 texts each.

One might even consider the 109 chapters of Book VI as a result of an increase from 90; adding Book VII to Book VI, then, would render a third great unit of roughly 120 chapters.

Whatever the plan might have been, it could not, however, not even with adjustments, comprise the total number of Birgitta's revelations. Some texts apparently unknown or discarded in the first run appeared again and again, as, e.g., when Prior Peter returned to Sweden in 1380.[42] It was, then, hopeless to try to force all the texts into the framework of the seven books which can be proved to have existed first. A Book VIII, containing political messages, was added; and yet there were still 116 revelations floating around that finally—after re-sultless efforts to arrange them in different series—were brought together and called the *Extravagantes*—texts outside the main collection (also inadequately called Book IX).

The story of the confessors trying to bring order into the mass of divine messages left behind by Birgitta is itself witness to the incredible span of inspiration in her mystical and literary heritage. Some texts are visions written down, with or without a summary, a goal indicating the inner tendency of the vision. Many texts are doctrinal, ascetic, or didactic treatises, in which an original visionary nucleus is surrounded by constructions such as applications to the moral life, often in a scholastic set-up. This fits perfectly well into the pattern worked out by Peter Dinzelbacher (1981),[43] who is able to identify a similar mixture of visionary and didactic elements in much female mystical writing of the fourteenth and fifteenth centuries.

No effort has been made yet among scholars to treat Books I, II, and III as a unit of some sort, the parts of which remain characteristically distinct. Is it merely accidental that *Book II* starts with the threefold temptation by the devil at Birgitta's calling? And that Book III initiates a sequence of personal messages to bishops and priests, some spoken by saints of Italian shrines—St. Ambrose (Milan), chapters 5–7; John the Baptist (St. John Lateran), chapter 11; St. Agnes (Rome), chapters 12 and 30; St. Dominic, chapters 17–18; St. Benedict, chapters 20–22— some directly addressing the moral corruption of the eternal city of Birgitta's years (chapter 27ff.)? The common link between Books I, II, and III seems to be the transition in Birgitta's calling from the Swedish to the Italian scene, demonstrated in magisterial and solemn visionary texts, as if the redactor(s) wanted to collect in these first books the clearest, most outspoken, most predicative messages that Birgitta had received. One might easily imagine that in between she might have received many of the short glances of the divine will which we encounter so often in the many short texts of Books IV and VI, and among the *Extravagantes*. The proportion between great visions and short, didactically formulated insights in God's mysteries might have been about the same as that transmitted in Book VII, for the reasons stated above. This, then, makes Book VII, which is rendered in full in this translation, much more interesting.

First, however, what makes Book IV differ most from Books I, II, and III is probably the subject matter and the addressees of the revelations.[44] There is an opening sequence of revelations addressed to kings; there are visions of Rome, of the judgment; several times St. Agnes is speaking, once, John the Evangelist. The sequence in chapters 26–32 of several short messages by the Blessed Mother may indicate the end of a first section, for then, in chapter 33, a series of grand visions starts again: on Rome, on penitence, on the corruption of religious orders, on priests, on the government of the Church on earth: pope, bishops, priests. Chapters 64–66 constitute short, perhaps concluding messages of the Blessed Mother. New items are treated next: from chapter 67 onward great messages on obedience, temptation, and the passion of Christ are introduced, followed by the important messages on Christian knighthood and on "God's friends." *Amici Dei*, rendered "die Gottesfreunde" in German, was a special notion in Birgitta's time: a term used by groups of believers to designate themselves as Christians withdrawing from the world, cultivating an intimate, unpretentious friendship with God without immersing in worldly interests and desires, but also without formally joining a religious order.[45] Again, some very short texts are inserted here, e.g., chapters 83–85, 93–98. Somewhere around chapter 100 we meet still another type of text: the famous political messages to the kings of England and France; Birgitta's conversation with St. Denis, the patron saint of France; Christ's teaching on repen-

tance, penitence, pride, humility, and good intention; and, in conclusion, a tremendous judgment vision on a bishop, as well as a mysterious
vision of seven animals with strong symbolism (chapters 125–26). The
unity of Book IV is indicated by the curious fact that the vision in
chapter 2 is explained in chapter 129—the second last chapter in Book
IV "according to Alphonsus."

Thus, Book IV is certainly more than a hodgepodge of everything
which does not fit elsewhere. One might easily consider Books I, II, and
III as a result of a first selection of solemn, magisterial revelations, those
dealing with the most universal subjects of Christian faith. In Book IV,
then, the redactor(s) may have undertaken a second selection, collecting
texts directed to more specific categories of Christians and treating
more specific matters of faith and morals. This very general attempt to
explain the genesis of Books I, II, and III, in relation to Book IV is, of
course, no more than a working hypothesis for further study; nevertheless, it may be worthwhile to try to see the texts in the light of such a
hypothesis.

There is enough evidence to show that Books I, II, III, and IV were
kept together as such at a very early stage of redactionary work and then
generally followed by Book V, which by force of its extraordinary
character may have been placed there as a kind of first conclusion to the
preceding books. Westman and Kraft made the puzzling discovery that
in the second earliest extant manuscript dated 1388, Book V is followed
by Book VII, and only then comes what we afterward know as Book
VI.[46] This seems to indicate that Book VI is indeed the arrangement of
a number of remaining texts which probably did not reach the level of
"great visions" and also were not, like Book VII, kept together by a
common origin like the pilgrimage to Jerusalem. If the order of Books
VI and VII can be reversed, it would be worthwhile to find out if Book
VI also contains subgroups corresponding to units of some 30 revelations. Is this the case?

There are in fact some striking cuts in the sequence of the originally
109 (at present 122) texts of Book VI. How is it to be explained, for
example, that chapter 34 starts out with a message of the value of the
revelations in general and turns it into a message on the conflict between England and France—and that chapter 63 deals with the letter
Birgitta was to send to Pope Clement concerning the same conflict?
Between chapters 34 and 63 we find a number of texts testifying to the
credibility of God's message: a knight at his judgment (ch. 39), sins of
kings (ch. 41), purgatory (ch. 52), and the sequence of Marian texts on

her Immaculate Conception, assumption, flight to Egypt, the birth and ascension of Christ, etc. (ch. 55–62). It seems reasonable to see chapters 34 and 63 as a kind of brackets, marking the beginning and end of the second section of Book VI. Chapter 65 is the opening of the third section: the very extensive revelation on Mary and Martha as symbols of the two vocations, the contemplative and the active. All the remaining texts, chapters 66–109, can be understood as illustrating both vocations: the contemplative way of priests and religious, the active way of men and women serving God in the world. Book VI, chapters 1–33, then, appears to concentrate on moral values, expanding upon impatience (ch. 6), pride (ch. 5, 15), luxury (ch. 19), temptation (ch. 6 and 17), repentance (ch. 20, 24), and conversion (ch. 26). Chapter 33, on the mutual love of bride and bridegroom—an old imagery with many symbolic implications—would be justly understood as the final summing up of such a first section of Book VI. Taking into account later additions to Book VI, we may assume an original plan of a third unit of 120 texts (90 for Book VI and 30 for Book VII) to balance Books I, II, and III on the one hand, and Book IV on the other.[47]

This allows us finally to turn to Book VII, in its entirety contained in the following translation.[48] There are 31 chapters, all dealing with the preparations and stages of Birgitta's pilgrimage to the Holy Land in 1372. This book was long regarded as the last of the whole collection, until Book VIII was added. Thematically Book VII starts with a prophecy from "after the year of the jubilee," that Birgitta was to go to Jerusalem and Bethlehem (ch. 1), a vision of the sorrows of Mary which Birgitta had in the church of Santa Maria Maggiore on 2 February (ch. 2, possibly in 1351, the first Lenten season Birgitta spent in Rome), and finally that very intimate experience she had of St. Francis on one of his feast days in the church dedicated to him in Trastevere (ch. 3). To share our Lady's sorrows and St. Francis's food and drink meant to enter on the narrow path to follow Christ on his earthly way from birth and childhood to manhood and death on the cross. This was prepared through Birgitta's visit to St. Thomas's relics in Ortona (ch. 4), her message to young Elziario of Ariano in Naples (ch. 5), and, finally, Christ's calling to her on 25 May 1371, to prepare herself for the pilgrimage to the Holy Sepulchre (ch. 6).

This is the signal for another series of six texts, chapters 7 to 12, dealing with subtle matters of conscience and spiritual distinctions, and basically located in Naples. A new series of six revelations starts with Birgitta's long-lasting doubts concerning the spiritual destiny of her own son Karl, who had a liaison with the queen of Naples (ch. 13). Expressedly, it is stated that her anxiety over the destiny of Karl followed her to the Holy Land. In such manner the scene is dramatically turned to Jerusalem, where Christ appears and talks to Birgitta on the grace of pilgrims (ch. 14), showing her the entire story of his passion and death (ch. 15) and the meaning of it (ch. 16). After this a short chapter on Birgitta's lodging (ch. 17) leads to the matter of Cyprus: first a letter she wrote to the king of Cyprus giving advice (ch. 18), then her confrontation with the actual situation there—apparently new to her— including the Greek Church and its representatives on Cyprus (ch. 19). Perhaps the letter in chapter 18 was added later, for there follows another sequence of six texts: the long chapter 20 dealing with the Franciscan Rule and the true followers of St. Francis, the four visionary texts from Bethlehem (ch. 21–24), and, finally, the speech of our Lady on humility (ch. 25). Then we reach the last section: Birgitta's last visits, which gave her the vision of the assumption of our Lady (ch. 26), the return to Italy by way of Naples (ch. 27 and 28), her letter to a bishop of Ancona (ch. 29), one of the great visions of the Judge (ch. 30), and, finally, Birgitta's last revelation five days before her death (ch. 31).

Regardless of the length of time which Birgitta spent in these different places, the redactor, doubtless Bishop Alphonsus, handed down to us in Book VII a wonderful piece of literary art, built up and held together by means of carefully selected texts and revelations. Much has been written on the profound devotion expressed in Birgitta's words when she describes Christ's and our Lady's appearances to her in the Holy Land.[49] But it ought not to be forgotten what a high degree of spiritual attachment has been laid down in the redactionary work found in this collection, so that each one of the great visions from the Holy Land stands out in its own force to convey the message of the divine meeting a chosen woman and revealing to her the secrets of heaven. No geographical or chronological affinity is comparable to this unity, stemming from the maturity of someone beholding God's mysteries after a long life of loving and suffering in God's presence.

Scholars agree that the first seven books of *Revelations* constitute the main corpus of God's message through Birgitta. But not everybody will consult such a huge collection of texts. The need for a digest was urgent already in the fourteenth century. Alphonsus himself took the first steps to comply with such wishes. He had three groups of addressees in mind:

1) kings and other civil authorities
2) pontiffs and bishops
3) the monastic family of the Order of the Holy Savior.

For each of these groups he produced a compilation in which texts already placed in one of the Seven Books were mixed with other texts of Birgitta which Alphonsus had either not known at the time he created the seven books, or which he had ruled out during the process.[50] The first compilation he called "The Book of the Heavenly Emperor to the Kings"; this has since that time been called "Book VIII" of the *Revelations*, although about half of the texts—there were originally 58 chapters, later 3 more were added—were already part of other books.[51]

The second collection, addressed to popes and bishops, *Ad pontifices*, has in fact not survived; it is found only in one manuscript. Its content is spread around at the end of Book IV and as sequences among the *Extravagantes*.[52]

The third collection, meant for the religious of the order, has been widely spread and studied under the name of *Celeste viridarium*, "The Heavenly Pasture," or, in the classical and renaissance sense of the word, "The Heavenly Garden." Book VIII has been adopted into the main collection probably partly because Alphonsus wrote his magnificent preface to it: "The Letter of the Hermit to the Kings," where he defends Birgitta against attacks which were bound to come, although at the time he wrote, in 1379, they were not yet as fierce as they became later on.[53]

Finally there are the extraordinary *Four Prayers* also translated and included in the present selection of texts.[54] The knowledge we have of these prayers and their origin is limited. They are extensive meditations in the form of prayers of praise to God for his blessings to mankind through the life on earth of our Lady and of Christ (first and second prayers), and through the beauty of Christ in his manhood (third prayer), and of our Lady (fourth prayer). This type of prayer and meditation was widespread in the Middle Ages: Christ's head, face, lips, eyes, ears, tongue, shoulders, intestines, breast, arms, hands, legs, and feet are the objects of meditation for the part they play in the salvific action of God. Of all these devotions we have kept in our epoch only one: that to the Sacred Heart, which is also part of the third of Birgitta's four prayers. The same is true for the meditations on the limbs of our Lady in the fourth prayer.

INTRODUCTION

THE DOCTRINE

The doctrine of St. Birgitta is certainly, as can be derived from what has been said so far, most aptly understood as the result of a dialectical process partly between Birgitta and her confessors and spiritual advisors, partly between her own experiences and her mental and affective life.

The basic stages of spiritual development are all present in her life: purification from sin through contrition and acceptance of God's majesty, mercy, and care; illumination through steady progress in the virtues and through an ever greater understanding of and affection for God's salvific action towards his people by innumerable means; union of the soul with God as a bride is embraced by the bridegroom.[55] This spiritual development is decisively Christian in that Birgitta accepts God's grace in and through the Messenger, the Messiah, the Anointed One, Jesus Christ. With Christ the heavenly host is always present in dynamic activity and yet all-enduring peace and communion with God —Christ's Mother Mary, all the angels and saints. On the periphery the fallen angels, angry at not being allowed to participate in God's essence, are trying to disturb as much as possible the path of the human soul toward its goal.

Let us examine for a moment the teaching in Birgitta's revelations on the first steps of the path to heaven: contrition and repentance for sins, the return of the erring child to the caring love of its parents. "Come and rise quickly through penance and contrition, then I will forgive the sins and give you patience and strength to be able to withstand the plots of the devil" (VI, 30). It is Christ's program for the bride to proceed from the first to the second stage of spiritual life. There is "true" contrition if the person has a perfect intention of making good what was formerly destroyed, as in the parable of the goldsmith (II, 14), or, in a more subtle distinction, if the person has the firm intention of doing no more evil and of persevering in good deeds (VI, 24). If, as the words given to a Swedish lady in Rome show, contrition is not as deep as the lust in doing evil was great, God's special love is necessary to fill out the gap (VI, 102). As when two lovers meet in stages such as sending letters, talking together, and embracing, penance and contrition are like the second stage, the mutual talk between bride and bridegroom by which they become one heart and one soul, to proceed to the union of the naked human soul with God, which is pure love and heavenly desire (IV, 75).

40

INTRODUCTION

Praying to God with contrition entitles one to be called God's friend precisely because of this contrition; and if contrition is firm, not only sin but also the penance for sin will be forgiven (III, 26). The symbols of a golden key, a silver vase, and a crown adorned with precious stones, all offered to God by an angel, denote the three stages of spiritual life. Here, the golden key is "pure" contrition for sins, by which the heart of God is being opened to let the sinner in (IV, 107). Two ways lead to the heart of God: the first is humility's true contrition leading man into spiritual discourse with God; the second way is meditation on Christ's passion, so that the hardness of man's heart is weakened and he runs with joy to the heart of God (IV, 101). All sorrow and tears of contrition are recalled in the scene when Birgitta suffers for her son Karl in Naples (VII, 13). Once contrition is likened to golden shoes which enable you to walk (III, 24), once to an undershirt which is closest to the body and therefore comes first when you dress (I, 7).

Contrition is like the point of a sword in the warrior's hand, since it kills the devil (IV, 89). Here, contrition hits and strikes; but on other occasions it also purges and Birgitta can place it in the intestines because this is where the cleaning process of the body takes place (IV, 115). Even the devil knows perfectly well the disastrous effects of contrition on his affairs. In a speech concerning a bad monk he characterizes it as a whirlwind which, if it leads to confession of sins and is strongly upheld, is the most secure path to peace with God—"and just from such heights," the devil declares, "I succeeded in pushing him down by his own desire to sin" (IV, 102).

Birgitta often returns to the theme of contrition immediately before death and its effect upon the eternal destiny of the soul, as, for example, when "for charity's sake" a contrition characterized as "divine" was given to a person shortly before his death; this contrition separated him from hell (IV, 9). Once the "Word" from the "Pulpit" told Birgitta that many who are guilty of numerous crimes receive the gift of full contrition before death, and that such contrition might even be so perfect that not only sins were forgiven, but also the punishment that ought to have been suffered after death (VIII, 48). But there is another side, as is clear from another passage: someone confessed his sins, but there was very little contrition in his confession, and so he was not saved—he did not deserve the kingdom of heaven. As the conclusion states: "If my friends want to be reconciled with my grace and friendship, they must needs make penitence and have contrition of all their heart for having offended me, their Creator and Redemptor." The next step after contrition is confession of sins, the third is communion with the faithful, the Church (IV, 7, cf. below, VII, 27).

A person who had lived all his life without confession and communion in despair of salvation (such was possible even in the Middle Ages!) confessed his sins several times shortly before his death, so that the devil, with whom he had entered into a covenant and to whom he had given an oath of fidelity, fled. This was precisely because of his contrition. This contrition was given to him as a gift of God because the man had always felt some type of compassion with the Mother of God when he thought and heard of her, without, however, really loving her in his heart. But this was enough for a *compendium salutis suae*, as the text runs—an expression which might mean the "property" or the "area" of his salvation, but which could also mean "compendium of salvation" in the modern sense (VI, 97). The same expression is used for the bishop of Växjö, to whom contrition and confession are a *compendium* for life in this world (III, 12).

It is interesting to note that God's answers to the monk on the ladder in Book V do not enter upon contrition. It is as if God—being here the accused one—does not want to open his heart to the conversion of the monk, but rather marks the distance between what the monk propounds and what is in reality the true context of things. Contrition is a gift of God and a concept to denote a very intimate relationship between the soul and its Creator, as the likeness of the lovers tells us. The monk on the ladder has nothing that can serve as a vessel or a vehicle for the gift of contrition. Not the slightest compendium of salvation is present in him, only doubts and reasoning.

One explanation for this might be hinted at by another symbolic interpretation of the key. The only key to open and to close is the desire for God alone, so that man does not want anything but God, and him only because of his love. Only husband and wife, only God and the soul, can dispose of the key to their partner's intimate chamber, so that their common desire for each other is the only key to open it (II, 27). That contrition for sins can range among the meanings carried by the key indicates that it also has this character of intimate confidence which is peculiar to the act of opening and closing the door with the key.

The full doctrine of the spiritual life is again propounded in one of the revelations placed after Birgitta's journey to Jerusalem. The first stage is penance and contrition of heart because of the offense one has committed against the Creator and Redemptor. Confession of sins, humble and iterated, marks the beginning of the second stage which consists in making reparation for sins according to the advice of the confessor, so that God can approach and the devil withdraws from the person. The third stage, then, consists not only in the participation in the sacrament of the altar—our meaning of "communion"—but also in the "receiving of my body with a firm intention never to fall back into previous sins but to endure in good until the end" (VII, 27). "My Body" here obviously means the full communion and unity with the Church, Christ's mystical body.

Penance, characteristic of the second stage of spiritual life, may sometimes be only an empty gesture, as we saw in some examples above—penance without real and worthy contrition for sins. But generally Birgitta's teaching is that penance is a proof of the socialization of the person in that he or she starts to confess their sins regularly and to take the advice and submit to the guidance of their confessor. "While I abhorred penance I felt heavy as if in chains, but since I started to go to confession I feel so relieved and peaceful in my soul, that I don't care for honors nor if I suffer losses in my property," runs a personal comment added to a revelation (VI, 20). The grace of penance keeps a person in God's hands, even though he or she justly ought to have been handed over to the devil because of crimes (*Extravagantes* 89). Penance can wash clean what has become dirty (II, 26, and IV, 39), but this is true also for confession (VI, 16). The evil smell of a sinner, registered by Birgitta, can only be healed by penance, to evade God's wrath (*Extravagantes* 81). There will be no more account for those sins for which penance has been done; sins for which there was no penance done will have to be cleansed in other ways or remedied here and now (I, 36). In open words the Mother of God stated to Birgitta before she left for Jerusalem that God will never deny his grace to a sinner with a true contrition, a will to satisfy for sin, honest penance, and humble prayer with burning love to receive God's mercy (VII, 7).

But remedy for sins committed also implies hard efforts and training in acts of self-denial. To this and many other forms of mastering one's own will, feelings, thoughts, and abilities, Birgitta often uses the word *labor*, work, in more or less the modern sense of the word. "My friends should work diligently that justice be observed and upheld, that care be taken of society, that God's honor grow and that rebels and criminals be punished," says Christ to one of the kings (VIII, 18). This "work" is certainly understood as part of what in religious terms is called penance: "God's friends . . . ought to work in order that the evildoer improves and the good reaches perfection" (IV, 21). To preach and show others the way can be a "work" (I, 40), and by this same word ("before I started my work") Christ can refer to the beginning of his active three years of pronouncing the message (II, 15). We often have also the other meaning which the Latin word *laborare* can take: to suffer, to endure hardships. Mary says about Jesus: "He worked with his hands" (VI, 58), and a mother's prayers and tears for her son can be called her "work" or "suffering" for him (VII, 13). There is intellectual work, as can be seen from a speech between two masters (II, 22), and the five senses can be said to have each their work to do (VI, 66). God's friends ought to work in order to save souls (VI, 47), and someone will have to work with the ground to earn his living (*Extravagantes* 83). Even the devil works, not against man's bodily existence, but against virtues, patience, and moderation in man (VI, 43), or to make him deaf and mute (IV, 107). But there is difference between work and work: some work only for material reasons and they receive no "crown," no eternal glory for that; but if this work is God's precept to them, then they serve him in their work (IV, 74). To attain true love we need humility, mercy, and the "work" or "suffering" of love, *labor caritatis* (III, 12, and IV, 126).

We get very close to Birgitta personally in her little dialogue with the Mother of God upon Birgitta's question: "Should I never work in order to earn my living?" The Blessed Mother gives her a question in reply: "What are you doing just now and every day?" Birgitta answers—in fact, the text reads, very exceptionally: "And I answered"—"I learn grammar and pray and write." Then the Blessed Mother said: "Don't give up such a work for physical work!" (IV, 46).

We reach another dimension, that of "good works" or "good deeds," when Christ speaks to Birgitta about Jacob who worked long to win Rachel as his wife. Love made his work easier, and this is true, then, for the spiritual life: "Many work in a manly way with prayers and good deeds in order to reach heaven, but when they think they have attained the peace of being with God, they get involved in temptations, their troubles increase, and just as they envisage themselves perfect, they discover that they are totally imperfect" (V, revelation 6).

It is in the nature of things that the third stage of spiritual life, called "the peace of contemplation," here rendered as "the peace of being with God," cannot be described in ordinary words, since it is a wordless union beyond letters and sentences—see the imagery of the lovers quoted above (IV, 75). If "communion" stands for this third stage, it is clear to us that this word cannot denote solely the act of receiving the Blessed Sacrament, the Body of Christ under the shape of the unleavened bread, and the Blood of Christ under the shape of wine mixed with a drop of water. Not even the "confession" of the second stage can be understood in Birgitta's writings as just the holy sacrament of penance. It means a more specific readiness to admit to all the fellowship that we are sinners, and that therefore we are called to appear in God's presence to be at his disposal in his salvific action towards all mankind. In like manner, the "communion" of the third stage must mean a permanent union with God's friends in whom God appears visibly to us and to our human eyes and understanding.

Taking this as basic to what Birgitta meant by "communion," we may have a closer look at some of her visions and messages belonging to this dimension.

Once in Italy on the first Sunday after Easter, Birgitta was inspired by 1 John 5, read on that day at mass. "There are three who give witness on earth: Spirit, Water, and Blood; and three who give witness in heaven: Father, Son, and Holy Spirit." The three are then linked to faith, baptism, and adoption in God, and Birgitta, as daughter of the Godhead, is told to receive the Body and Blood of Christ's manhood from the hands of the priest thereby to signify her readiness to do "our" will (says the Triune God) and in order that Christ testifies to her being his and belonging to him. In Christ, then, the Father and the Holy Spirit also testify to the same effect, that she belongs to all the three Persons by force of her true faith and her love (III, 23). No doubt "faith" here stands for the beginning, the first stage of spiritual life; "baptism" for the second stage, corresponding to contrition and confession in the texts quoted earlier. To be the daughter of God, adopted as it were, to be "his" without any further addition, then, must refer to the unitive stage of spiritual life; and precisely here Birgitta is told to receive the Body and Blood of Christ in the sacrament of the altar. Not the divinity of Christ, but the humanity of Christ is the way to union with God according to Birgitta's teaching here, for then the Godhead—Son, Father, Holy Spirit—testify to where their daughter belongs.

In like manner, the feast of Pentecost once revealed to Birgitta some of the most evanescent of God's expressions of love. During early morning mass, Birgitta saw a fire descend and surround the altar. In the fire she saw the priest with the Host in his hand, and in the Host she saw a lamb, and in the lamb "an inflaming face, like that of a man." The vision was interpreted to her by a voice telling her about the fire of Pentecost inflaming the hearts of the disciples. But the voice continued its message: "Through the word the bread becomes the Living Lamb, which is my Body, and the Face is in the Lamb, and the Lamb in the Face, for the Father is in the Son and the Son in the Father, and the Holy Spirit is in both." "And then," the text adds, "in the hand of the priest the bride saw, at the elevation of the eucharist, a young man of extraordinary beauty, who said: I bless you who believe; to those who don't believe I am a judge" (VI, 86). From what she saw first: an inflaming face like that of a man, Birgitta is carried on finally to stand face to face with Christ in the shape of a young man of extraordinary beauty. The transition is made possible by the fire from heaven and the final stage is closeness; but the intermediate stage is the short passing through doctrine and clarification of the Triune God before entering into the final union and communion, signalled by the elevation of the Host.

The last week of Birgitta's life sets forth an immemorial record of her union with the bridegroom. For a long time in June-July 1373 (the text does not say how long) Birgitta had felt the emptiness and desolation of her heavenly spouse not being with her—that feeling of night which other mystics have written more about. Sunday, the 17th of July, the fourth Sunday after Pentecost, she attended mass in her house. It may have been the Sunday named after its entrance verse: *Dominus illuminatio mea*—"The Lord is my Light and my Savior," and the gospel may then, as later, have been Luke 5:1–11, on the faith of St. Peter towards Jesus at the great fishing in the Lake Genesareth. Monday or Tuesday, Christ finally spoke to Birgitta, giving her relief with the words: "I was to you just like a spouse generally is, when he hides from his bride in order that she has greater desire for him. . . . So now after this probation proceed and be prepared, for now the time has come when that shall be fulfilled what I promised you, that . . . you shall be counted not only my bride, but also a nun and the mother in Vadstena" (VII, 31). On Friday, July 22, fell the feast of St. Mary Magdalene, and on Saturday, July 23, Birgitta died in her room which still exists at the Piazza Farnese in Rome.

The third stage of spiritual life, to her, was the indissoluble union with God, in which no element of mystical love was lacking.

Notes

1. Recent publications with further references: *Temi e problemi nella mistica femminile trecentesca* (Todi, 1983), and Peter Dinzelbacher and Dieter R. Bauer, eds., *Frauenmystik im Mittelalter* (Ostfildern bei Stuttgart, 1985).

INTRODUCTION

2. Michael Goodich, *Vita perfecta: The Ideal of Sainthood in the Thirteenth Century* (Stuttgart, 1982, = Monographien zur Geschichte des Mittelalters, 25), pp. 48–68.

3. Isak Collijn, ed., *Acta et processus canonizacionis beate Birgitte* (Uppsala, 1924–31, = Samlingar utgivna av Svenska Fornskriftsällskapet, Ser. 2: Latinska skrifter, I).

4. Sara Ekwall, *Vår äldsta Birgittavita och dennas viktigaste varianter* [summary: La plus ancienne vie de sainte Brigitte et ses deux variations les plus importantes] (Lund, 1965, = Kungl. Vitterhets Historie och Antikvitets Akademiens Handlingar, Historiska Serien, 12).

5. Karl Kup, "Ulrich von Richenthal's Chronicle of the Council of Constance," *Bulletin of The New York Public Library* (April, 1936). Eric Colledge, "Epistola solitarii ad reges: Alphonce of Pecha as Organizer of Birgittine and Urbanist Propaganda," *Medieval Studies* 18 (1956): 19–49, here pp. 44–45.

6. Claes Annerstedt, ed., *Vita Sanctae Birgittae*, in *Scriptores Rerum Suecicarum medii aevi*, III, 2 (Upsaliae, 1876), pp. 188–206, and I. Collijn, ed. (*supra*, note 3), pp. 73–101. Another version of this text was published by I. Collijn, *ibid*, pp. 612–41, and by the same editor as facsimile in *Corpus Codicum Suecicorum Medii Aevi*, VII (Copenhagen, 1946).

7. John E. Kruse, "Vita metrica s. Birgitte," *Acta Universitatis Lundensis* (Lund, 1891–92): 10–28.

8. Ekwall, *op. cit.*, pp. 16–17.

9. *Ibid*, pp. 62–63.

10. *Ibid*, p. 70, from *Acta et processus*. (note 3), p. 73: et quod plura alia sciunt de vita dicte domine Brigide, sed propter eorum repentinum recessum ad partes Swecie ea scribere et testificari protunc non poterant.

11. Ekwall, *passim*. Colledge (note 5) does not yet consider Alphonsus redactor of the *Vita*.

12. Birgit Klockars, *Birgittas svenska värld* [The Swedish World of Birgitta] (Stockholm, 1976), pp. 32–33.

13. *Ibid*, pp. 136, 152. Tryggve Lundén, ed., *Processus canonizacionis beati Nicolai Lincopensis* (Stockholm, 1963). *Idem, Nikolaus Hermansson, biskop av Linköping* (Lund, 1971), with summary in German, pp. 62–70, and edition of liturgical texts composed by Nikolaus, pp. 77–138.

14. Bengt Strömberg, *Magister Mathias och fransk mendikantpredikan* [summary: Magister Mathias et la prédication des religieux men-

diants français] (Lund, 1944). Hjalmar Sundén, "Den heliga Birgitta och hennes biktfar magister Mathias," *Kyrkohistorisk årsskrift* 73 (1973): 15–39. Anders Piltz, *Prolegomena till en textkritisk edition av magister Mathias' Homo conditus* (Uppsala, 1974, = Acta Universitatis Upsaliensis, Studia Latina Upsaliensia 7).

15. The quote is from Anders Piltz, "Magister Mathias of Sweden in his theological context. A preliminary survey," lecture given in Stockholm 1984, unprinted. Cf. *idem,* ed., *Magistri Mathiae canonici Lincopensis opus sub nomine Homo Conditus vulgatum* (Angered 1984, = Samlingar utgivna av Svenska Fornskriftsällskapet, Ser. 2: Latinska Skrifter, IX:1).

16. *Idem,* "Mathias Ouidi," *Svenskt Biografiskt Lexikon,* 2nd ed. (Stockholm 1918–   ), 25: 248–51.

17. Carl-Gustaf Undhagen, ed., *Sancta Birgitta Revelaciones Lib. I* (Uppsala, 1978, = Samlingar utgivna av Svenska Fornskriftsällskapet, Ser. 2: Latinska Skrifter, VII:1), pp. 229–40. Birgitta Fritz, "Den heliga Birgitta och hennes klosterplaner," *Festskrift til Thelma Jexlev* (Odense, 1985): 9–17.

18. Anders Piltz, "Mathias Ouidi" (as in note 16). The crusade: J.L.I. Fennell, *The Emergence of Moscow 1304–1359* (London, 1968), pp. 265–67. *Idem,* "The Campaign of King Magnus Eriksson against Novgorod in 1348," *Jahrbücher für Geschichte Osteuropas,* 14 (1966): 1–9. John Lind, "The Russian Sources of King Magnus Eriksson's Campaign against Novgorod 1348–1351 Reconsidered," *Mediaeval Scandinavia* 12 (1986): pp. 248–72.

19. Anders Piltz, "Mathias Ouidi" (as in note 16).

20. Undhagen (note 17), pp. 237–38.

21. Collijn, *Acta et processus,* p. 485, quoted from Birger Bergh, "A Saint in the Making: St. Bridget's Life in Sweden (1303–1349)," in Francis Cairns, ed., *Papers of the Liverpool Latin Seminar* 3 (1981): 371–84, here p. 378.

22. As can be gathered from the excellent indices in Birgit Klockars, *Birgitta och böckerna. En undersökning av den Heliga Birgittas källor* (Lund, 1966, = Kungl. Vitterhets Historie och Antikvitets Akademiens Handlingar: Historiska Serien, 11). The observation of the Exodus theme has been made also by Roger Ellis, "A Note on the Spirituality of St. Bridget of Sweden," *Spiritualität heute und gestern,* ed. James Hogg (Salzburg, 1982, = Analecta Cartusiana, 35): 157–66, here p. 166.

23. Birger Bergh (note 21) with further references.

INTRODUCTION

24. Knut B. Westman, *Birgitta-studier* (Uppsala, 1911), pp. 107–16. Hjalmar Sundén, *Den heliga Birgitta. Ormungens moder som blev Kristi brud* (Uddevalla, 1973), pp. 66–89. Birgitta Fritz (note 17).

25. Birger Bergh, ed., *Sancta Birgitta Revelaciones Lib. V: Liber Questionum* (Uppsala, 1971, = Samlingar utgivna av Svenska Fornskriftsällskapet, Ser. 2: Latinska Skrifter, VII:5). Sundén (note 24). Bergh (note 21).

26. Sundén (note 24). Bergh (note 21) and Fritz (note 17) do not basically challenge Sundén's position.

27. Sundén (note 24), pp. 85–89.

28. Recently, e.g., Robert E. Lerner, "Antichrists and Antichrist in Joachim of Fiore," *Speculum* 60 (1985): 553–70, with further references.

29. As in Sundén above.

30. Yngvar Ustvedt, *Svartedauen* [The Black Death] (Oslo, 1985), pp. 82–92.

31. A. Jefferies Collins, ed., *The Bridgettine Breviary of Syon Abbey* (Worcester, 1969, = Henry Bradshaw Society Vol. XCVI), pp. xvii–xxx. Tryggve Lundén, ed., *Den heliga Birgitta och den helige Petrus av Skänninge, Officium parvum beate Marie Virginis*, I–II (Lund, 1976, = Acta Universitatis Upsaliensis, Studia Historico-Ecclesiastica Upsaliensia, 27–28), pp. xi–xxxi (summary: The Lady-offices of Saint Bridget and Venerable Peter of Skänninge, pp. cv–cxii). Sten Eklund, ed., *Sancta Birgitta Opera Minora II: Sermo Angelicvs* (Uppsala, 1972, = Samlingar utgivna av Svenska Fornskriftsällskapet, Ser. 2: Latinska Skrifter, VIII:2).

32. Lundén, *op. cit.*, and Dom Ernest Graf, *Revelations & Prayers of St. Bridget of Sweden* (London, 1928).

33. Collins and Lundén, *op. cit.*

34. Gabriele M. Roschini, *La Madonna nelle "Rivelazioni di S. Brigida" nel sesto centenario della sua morte (23 luglio 1373)* (Roma, 1973), pp. 69–86.

35. Toni Schmid, *Birgitta och hennes uppenbarelser* [Birgitta and her Revelations] (Lund, 1940), pp. 94–98, 108–10.

36. Sten Eklund, ed., *Sancta Birgitta Opera Minora I: Regvla Salvatoris* (Lund, 1975, = Samlingar utgivna av Svenska Fornskriftsällskapet, Ser. 2: Latinska Skrifter, VIII:1), pp. 21–23. Cf. Fritz (note 17).

37. Eklund (note 36) uses a special letter for this unknown early version. Discussion of fragments in Old Swedish: Jostein Gussgard, *To*

fragmenter på svensk af den Hellige Birgittas skrifter (Uppsala, 1961, = Samlingar utgivna av Svenska Fornskriftsällskapet, 230).

38. Tore Nyberg, "Analyse der Klosterregel der Hl. Birgitta," *Festschrift Altomünster 1973*, ed. Toni Grad (Aichach, 1973), pp. 20–34.

39. Eklund (note 36) and review of Eklund by Tore Nyberg in *Theologische Revue*, 77 (1981):221–24.

40. Tore Nyberg, "Birgitta von Schweden—die aktive Gottesschau," *Frauenmystik im Mittelalter* (note 1), pp. 275–89, here p. 281.

41. Salomon Kraft, *Textstudier till Birgittas revelationer* (Uppsala, 1929, also in: *Kyrkohistorisk årsskrift* 29 (1929): 1–196), pp. 52–69.

42. Known through his witness in the canonization process, the so-called *Depositio copiosissima*, cf. Lennart Hollman, ed., *Sancta Birgitta Reuelaciones Extrauagantes* (Uppsala, 1956, = Samlingar utgivna av Svenska Fornskriftsällskapet, Ser. 2: Latinska Skrifter, V), pp. 85, 90–91.

43. *Vision und Visionsliteratur im Mittelalter* (Stuttgart, 1981, = Monographien zur Geschichte des Mittelalters, 23).

44. The critical edition of Book IV is being prepared by Hans Aili, Stockholm.

45. Francis Rapp, "Gottesfreunde," *Theologische Realenzyklopedie* (Berlin, 1975–), 14:98–100.

46. Westman (note 24), p. 264. Kraft (note 41), p. 68–69. Undhagen (note 17), p. 174–77. The ms. is W. 318 of Historisches Archiv der Stadt Köln.

47. The critical edition of Book VI is being prepared by Birger Bergh, Lund.

48. Birger Bergh, ed., *Sancta Birgitta Revelaciones Lib. VII* (Uppsala, 1967, = Samlingar utgivna av Svenska Fornskriftsällskapet, Ser. 2: Latinska Skrifter, VII:7).

49. Karl Kup, "Bene veneris . . . filius meus. An Early Example of St. Birgitta's Influence on the Iconography of the Nativity," *Bulletin of the New York Public Library* 61 (1957): 583–89. Lottlisa Behling, "Symbole der Revelationes der Hl. Birgitta in Beziehung zum Isenheimer Altar des Matthias Grünewald, insbesondere für die Darstellung der knienden Maria im Goldtempel," *Festschrift Altomünster 1973* (note 38), pp. 138–62.

50. Colledge (note 5), p. 33–34.

51. Kraft (note 41), p. 71–72.

52. Colledge (note 5), p. 33, correcting Westman. The MS is Harley 612 of the British Library, London.
53. Colledge (note 5), pp. 40–42, with further references.
54. See pp. 221–35.
55. Adolphe Tanquerey, *The Spiritual Life*, 2nd ed. (Tournai, 1930).

TRANSLATOR'S FOREWORD

Marguerite Tjader Harris was a woman of many interests and remarkable personality. At the end of World War II, she became a Catholic through the influence of a dying cousin who had been released from the German concentration camps. In 1958, her former family home, "Vikingsborg," in Darien, Connecticut, was transformed into the first Birgittine convent established in the United States. There Marguerite Tjader Harris assembled a small working collection of Birgittine literature and artifacts.

As time passed, her interest increasingly focused on the text of Saint Birgitta's *Heavenly Book of Revelations.* Despite their fame as a historical memory, inaccessibility of printed editions and rarity of translation have left the saint's writings relatively unknown and unread.

For anyone who encounters the *Heavenly Book,* the first and lasting impression is of its great bulk. As we read in paragraph 27 of the *Life of Blessed Birgitta,* the saint became aware of the true importance of her experiences in 1345 or 1346 (see note 32); and, with the aid of her confessors, she compiled a record of her daily prayer that ended only with her death in Rome on July 23, 1373.

The extent and diversity of the material left to us is astonishing; and one can only regret that the final arrangement of the texts is more topical than clearly chronological. This volume of material has predictably attracted few translators, and no one has as yet attempted a complete translation into Modern English. Nor has there been a full Modern English translation of any of the individual books of revelations until now. Several versions, however, were attempted in the Middle English period; and seven fifteenth-century manuscripts are extant, only two being reasonably complete, while the others are anthologies (Cumming xi–xxii). In 1491, Caxton printed a Birgittine anthology; and since then others have occasionally appeared in English (Emery 300).

These anthologies have chiefly emphasized Birgitta's few revelations about the life of Christ and thus have contributed to the seriously inaccurate impression of her as a fourteenth-century Catherine Emmerich. The small devotional anthologies have also given inappropriate prominence to a short series of prayers honoring Christ's passion and called in English the *Fifteen O's*. Birgittine authorship of these prayers is highly doubtful, and they have never been included in any of the critical Latin editions of her works. The *Fifteen O's* are, in themselves, pious and unobjectionable; but their history is tainted by a scandalously superstitious set of instructions and absurd promises. On June 30, 1671, the Congregation of the Index prohibited their further circulation "unless the prologue is deleted" (Vernet 1956)—a stipulation that has not always been obeyed. In any case, the *Fifteen O's* have enjoyed centuries of use in English Catholic piety, and they too have had a marked effect on the saint's reputation while her authentic works went unread (cf. Kirby).

It was this almost unknown book that increasingly engaged the attention of Marguerite Tjader Harris. In 1975, she began a purely personal study of Birgitta's writings, using the four volumes of the Modern Swedish translation, the work of Professor Tryggve Lundén. As she read, Marguerite Tjader Harris kept notes on each revelation; and soon it was apparent that she had laid the foundations for a more ambitious project. Not long after, Paulist Press began to publicize its forthcoming series, *The Classics of Western Spirituality;* and Marguerite Tjader Harris suggested to then editor-in-chief, Richard Payne, the inclusion of a volume on Birgitta of Sweden.

Inclusion in *The Classics of Western Spirituality* raised the question of the original Latin texts, which are now appearing in critical editions under the direction of Professor Birger Bergh at the University of Lund in Sweden. It is the Latin text which must be regarded as the saint's intended original. Therefore it was clear that Marguerite Tjader Harris's version from the Modern Swedish translation would have to be compared to the original Latin in the new critical editions; and it was at this point that I first became seriously involved with this project, whose course I had been following from a distance for several years.

From April to July of 1979, Marguerite Tjader Harris and I worked our way through her translation of the Modern Swedish version, diligently comparing it to the newly edited Latin texts. For motivation and encouragement in this reorientation of the project, we were highly indebted to the helpful and bracing comments of an insightful reader, the Rev. Canon T.C. Teape-Fugard of Killala, County Mayo, Ireland. In this, my first real participation in the project, I ventured to suggest only those changes that were absolutely required by the original Latin.

At the same time, I began to record those places where the meaning of the text was still unclear.

From June 23 to July 15, 1979, Professor Tore Nyberg of Odense University visited the Vikingsborg convent; and during that time, he examined the translation and discussed it with us. In 1980, it was decided that the translation needed further work; and my brother, Dr. John Ryle Kezel, and I were asked by Dr. Ewert Cousins of Fordham to read the Tjader Harris translation one more time against the Latin text, making any corrections that were required. In the end, this task fell to me alone although my brother, with his facility in reading not only the classical languages but also Anglo-Saxon and the related forms of the old Scandinavian languages, has in fact made many contributions to this book. Finally, however, it proved necessary to undertake a completely new translation.

In January of 1985—with the written consent of Marguerite Tjader Harris—I formally undertook the responsibility of making a fresh translation of the Latin text and a new set of notes. Professor Nyberg assumed the task of writing the introduction.

During the summer of 1985, I completely retranslated the *Book of Questions*. I also translated the *Four Prayers*, which had not previously been a part of the Tjader version. The pressures of teaching and my continuing participation in Byzantine liturgical translations forced me to postpone the completion of the new Birgitta translation until the summer vacation of 1986. Unfortunately, on April 7, 1986, Marguerite Tjader Harris died at the age of 84, before the translation and notes were completed with the help of suggestions from Professors Bergh, Eklund, and Nyberg.

Thus the present volume is the result of a long and complicated history. But the final product is an exact and accurate representation of the Latin original. The succession of revisions has ended in a radically new translation; but certain good things have been appropriately retained from the earliest version: some fine turns of speech and various clever resolutions of Birgitta's long and tangled sentences.

The present translation, however, is a new version in nearly every way; and I alone bear the responsibility for its final form.

Having outlined the history of the present volume, I would now like to describe the principles and certain details of the present translation.

The process of translation focuses on three aspects of a text. First there is the *meaning*. In some ways, this is the easiest part of the task;

for every reasonably articulate language can somehow manage to say most of the things that another language has said. It is here that I would include the translator's obligation to convey the tone of the meaning in the original—reverence, hostility, playfulness, etc. The last quality mentioned should not be overlooked when evaluating such curiosities as the shepherds' startling request in *Revelations* 7.23.2 or the salutation to our Lady's nostrils in *Four Prayers* 92. In the thirty-ninth chapter of the *Book of Margery Kempe*, we read that in 1414, there were still people in Rome who remembered Birgitta for her homely kindness and her laughing face. Certainly not everything in her *Heavenly Book* is grim.

The translator's second and more difficult concern is the *imagery*—i.e., all that dimension of the original word that conveys sense-information. This is an area requiring much thought and great sensitivity to the exact significance of the word being translated. In the end, it is sometimes found that the translation language has no words that can convey the original meaning in the original image; and the latter must be sacrificed.

Under the heading of imagery, I would include the handling of the "tropes" or non-literal meanings of a word—i.e., synecdoche, metonymy, metaphor, conceit, and allegory. All of the Birgittine corpus is marked by a skillful and interesting use of images and tropes, and great care has been taken to convey them properly in the present translation.

The third concern of the translator lies in the area of *structure,* whether of the grammatical forms and syntactical relationships or of the word order. Such elements make an important—but easily overlooked —contribution to the effect of the original and should not be lightly discarded from the translation.

It is under this heading that I would include the "schemes"—i.e., all those rhetorical devices that create visible or audible patterns of letters, syllables, words, phrases, or clauses. This, of course, is the most difficult area for the translator to convey; and because meaning and imagery are usually more important, it is often this area of structure that will suffer most in translation.

An example of departure from original structure in the present translation is the decision to render both *tu* and *vos* as "you." Another is the frequent and necessary recasting of Birgitta's very long and often very unperiodic sentences, in which the grammar sometimes approaches a state of chaos that detracts from the interest of the thought and the beauty of the words. However, the present translation intentionally avoids all unnecessary rewriting or "improvement" of the original—in which passages of unusual beauty may be followed by pedestrian paragraphs of point-by-point cataloguing. Both types of writing have their place; and both have been rendered in this translation as honestly as possible.

Since this is the first Modern English rendering of most of this material, it seemed particularly important to give the English-speaking reader a very accurate impression of the Latin. If, as a result, this translation has a slight flavor of Bible English, that flavor is deliberate and entirely appropriate. Birgitta's own excellent medieval Latin style is everywhere suffused with the flavor of the Vulgate.

Perhaps a word should be said about the choice of texts for this translation. The first three selections were chosen by Marguerite Tjader Harris, and their arrangement has remained the one firm constant in the course of this enterprise. The fourth selection—*Four Prayers*—was suggested by me as a more manageable alternative to Marguerite Tjader Harris's original idea of an abridgement of the *Extravagantes*.

The first selection—*The Life of Blessed Birgitta by Prior Peter and Master Peter*—is an eyewitness account prepared by her confessors for the process of her canonization. From it and from other materials, later writers compiled the lives that appear in the collected editions of her works and in the liturgical offices for her feast. This early and important life by the confessors was critically edited by Isak Collijn on pages 73 to 101 of his monumental *Acta et processus canonizacionis beate Birgitte* (Uppsala: 1924–1931). That text has been translated here. It should be noted that the present English translation exactly follows the layout and paragraphing of the latest critical texts available. In the case of the *Life of Blessed Birgitta,* I have introduced a system of numbering for Collijn's paragraphs in order to facilitate references.

The second selection—the fifth of the seven original books of the *Heavenly Book of Revelations*—is the famous *Book of Questions*. This book is the most organized and unified section of the Birgittine corpus; for it is the record of one single day on which the saint experienced one long and unforgettable vision interwoven with a "subplot" of thirteen revelations—all climaxing in the statement and solution of a great prophetic riddle. For this translation I have used the critical edition of Birger Bergh (Uppsala, 1971). It should be noted that like the *Shepherd of Hermas* and the *Summa Theologiae*, Birgitta's *Book of Questions* requires a cumbersome system of citation because of its division into 16 "interrogations" and 13 "revelations." The manuscript tradition is divided on the question of format: either interweaving interrogations with revelations or arranging them in two separate groups. Professor Bergh regards the interwoven arrangement as the original; and his opinion has been followed in the present volume. He has done much to make citation easier by introducing a new numbering of *sections* within each interrogation or revelation. Thus, in the present translation, *Rev.* 5, Int. 7.12 means *Heavenly Book of Revelations*, Book 5, Interrogation 7, section 12.

The third selection is the seventh, and originally the last, of the books of Birgitta's collected revelations. This Seventh Book also has a strong feeling of unity because it is a chronological record of the visions that first predicted and then accompanied the pilgrimage of the saint to the Holy Land in 1372. The last chapter—a variant of the last chapter of the *Life*—recounts the scene of Saint Birgitta's death in Rome on July 23, 1373. I have used the critical edition of Professor Bergh (Uppsala, 1967). Here too he has introduced a new numbering of sections within the traditional chapters. In this book, the thirty-one chapters follow each other without interruption; and there are no difficulties of citation.

The fourth selection—*Four Prayers*—is provided here in its traditional place as an appendix to the books of revelations. These *Four Prayers* give a brief but striking introduction to the fervent spirit of prayer that lay at the center of Birgitta's daily life. Tradition identifies these four prayers with that "most beautiful prayer" that was divinely given to her at a date earlier than 1345, as we read in the fifteenth paragraph of the *Life*. In translating the *Four Prayers*, I have had to use the second edition of the critical text of Bishop Gonzales Durante (Rome: 1628).

The present translation, however, was read by Professor Eklund during the winter of 1986–87. He compared it to the text of his own forthcoming critical edition and generously indicated to me those few places in which slight changes would bring my translation into line with the readings of his edition. He also confirmed my suspicion that several odd readings in Durante are, in fact, misprints. All of these departures from Durante have been documented in the notes.

Professor Eklund also proposed that I adopt the new section numbering that will appear in his edition; and he personally inserted the new numbers into a copy of my translation for that purpose. Moreover, he provided me with the Latin text of the prologue that he intends to print so that I might use it for this translation in place of the later prologue of Durante.

Thus, the present translation can now be regarded as the equivalent of the forthcoming critical edition. Scholars are rarely so open-handed with their unpublished material, and I am extremely grateful to Professor Eklund for his kindness in contributing to the critical accuracy of the present translation.

Concerning the notes, I should first observe that those to the *Life* and to the *Four Prayers* are entirely my own work—although they do incorporate some suggestions from Professor Nyberg (in the *Life*) and Professor Eklund (in the *Prayers*). I believe that these notes are the first real commentary ever published on these two texts. The notes to Books Five and Seven have had published predecessors in the comments of Torquemada, of Durante, and of Professor Bergh. My notes include virtually all of the biblical citations and other sources given in the editions of Professor Bergh. However, I have supplemented them in a number of areas, and I have added summaries of the relevant "articles" from Cardinal Torquemada's defense of Saint Birgitta.

The notes as a whole have been written with concern, not so much for the professional scholar, as for the ordinary reader interested in such studies. They have therefore been designed to be read in sequence with the text; and, as the reader progresses, the more difficult matters of Birgittine scholarship are slowly introduced. Thus the scholar should be warned from the start that topics, omitted in the earlier notes, were omitted there deliberately.

One important scholarly question excluded from the notes merits being called "The Birgittine Question" because it bears a striking resemblance to the more famous "Homeric Question." As in the case of Homer, the "Question" is a very serious one: can Birgitta really be regarded as the author of the writings attributed to her? The problems involved in answering this question are very real, and they involve the further question of just what sort of revelations these texts are claiming to be. Such difficulties cannot simply be ignored; and, while I have not emphasized them in the notes, I cannot avoid a brief outline of the Birgittine Question here.

The Latin texts that we have contain plain statements of six important facts about the writing of the *Heavenly Book of Revelations:*

1) Birgitta's original verbalization of her mystical experiences was in Old Swedish. Occasionally, she herself wrote out a text in Old Swedish. At other times she dictated in Old Swedish to her confessor who translated her words into Latin on the spot.

2) The Latin translation was either written out by the confessor him self or was taken down in Latin by a *scriptor* (writer) (*Life* 37).

3) When this rough draft in Latin was complete, it was examined by Birgitta herself in consultation with her confessors. Inevitably, at this point, the text was polished and, apparently, augmented with biblical and patristic allusions that supported and clarified Birgitta's original insight. We are repeatedly assured that Birgitta took an active role in reading and approving the Latin text, and the examiners for her canonization were particularly careful to question each witness for confirmation of Birgitta's knowledge of Latin (cf. note 96).

4) It would seem—though here the documentary evidence is poor—that once the saint was satisfied with the Latin text little more attention was given to whatever first drafts there may have been in Old Swedish. There now exist three sheets of revelations written in Old Swedish by Birgitta's own hand (cf. Haugen 233–34; Högman). It is not known how many similar sheets may have perished; and there is no evidence that, at any time, there ever existed a complete set of such sheets covering the whole corpus of the *Revelations*. In fact, the evidence suggests that many chapters may have never had an Old Swedish "first draft" apart from the moment of the saint's dictation for her Latin translator. Certainly, one gets the impression that the extant Old Swedish sheets survived more as relics of the saint than as a control on the accuracy of the Latin version.

5) The Latin versions—and whatever Old Swedish sheets there may have been—were kept fairly secret during Birgitta's lifetime, and—apart from those revelations sent to private recipients—they were not generally available. But with the arrival of Alphonsus of Jaen (ca. 1370), Birgitta formulated a plan for the eventual publication of her work; and we are told (*Life* 78) that on her deathbed she instructed her confessors to give everything to Alphonsus for final editing, with special emphasis on polishing the Latin style and guaranteeing the theological orthodoxy of her expressions. Much of Alphonsus' work was actually done after the saint's death and resulted in the ("addition"-less) seven-book form of the *Revelations* submitted for the canonization process.

6) However, there still remained unpublished material that had been kept back because of its sensitive nature or simply because it had been left behind in Sweden when the saint departed on the Holy

Year pilgrimage of 1350. This material was eventually published by Birgitta's confessor, Prior Peter. Where he found items that directly related to existing chapters in the seven books of Alphonsus, Peter inserted them there as "additions" or "declarations." Whatever else was left he collected under the title *Extravagantes* or "stray" revelations. The actual process of adding Peter's "additions" and *Extravagantes* to the manuscripts was a slow one. The Birgittine monks of Vadstena felt that a complete and final arrangement of the text was achieved only with the first printed edition in 1492. Thus it took more than a century for the saint's whole work to be made public (cf. note 522).

Apparently in the decades immediately after the saint's death, someone undertook the task of "retranslating" her Latin book into Old Swedish. The actual survival of several manuscripts of this Old Swedish version raises questions. Were there more Old Swedish holographs of the saint than we now know of? Have any of those (hypothetical) sheets been simply transcribed into the extant Old Swedish version? Can any of the Old Swedish version be shown to be more truly the saint's original than the official Latin version is?

In general, most editors have rejected the idea of any superiority of the Old Swedish over the Latin, of which they feel that the Old Swedish is simply a translation. While not rejecting the theoretical possibility that the Old Swedish could contain passages derived from holograph sheets, most scholars have found little evidence in the Old Swedish text that would support an identification of these "authentic" passages.

However, certain recent developments have led Professor Eklund to issue a strong challenge to those who too easily neglect the possible importance of the Old Swedish version. The cause of Eklund's new position is the recent discovery, in Oslo, of a small fragment of a hitherto unknown *Latin* version of part of the *Four Prayers*. Never before has there been known evidence of any Latin version except the official one. While the Oslo version is clearly related to the version traditionally printed, it is strikingly simpler and stylistically rougher than the traditional version. Moreover, where the Oslo fragment is simpler through the omission of laudatory adjectives and epithets that do occur in the traditional Latin version, the very same adjectives and epithets are absent from the Old Swedish version too. One is led to suspect that, whatever their own interrelationship may be, the Oslo

fragment and the Old Swedish version—at least of the *Four Prayers*—
are apparently giving us readings from an earlier draft of the prayers
than that in the printed editions.

As Professor Eklund admits, this is only one small clue to the question of Birgitta's early drafts; and much work remains to be done. But
now, at last, we have a documented example of how the Latin version
was polished into its final shape. However, there still remains the question of whether the extant Old Swedish was translated from the Latin
text represented in the Oslo fragment or is itself the actual Old Swedish
original of Birgitta herself.

This Oslo fragment sheds light on only one small section of the
Birgittine corpus. For almost every other section, we have little warrant
yet for looking to anything but the traditional Latin text, which—as we
are repeatedly told—the saint clearly intended to be the final statement
of her message.

Inevitably a thought arises in the modern mind—so concerned with
originality and authenticity—as it considers the remarkably complicated history of the text, the number of hands that worked on it, and the
long lapse of time between Birgitta's "vocation vision" of 1345 (cf. *Life*
26) and the first authoritatively complete edition of her *Revelations* in
1492. Are we really reading Birgitta at all? Can we really believe that
these priests and scholars scrupulously transmitted her exact words?
Can we really listen to the claim that these words were in some way
revealed by God? Is it not possible that this wealthy and pious woman
was somehow being used by a group of reform-minded priests who thus
gained greater attention for their message? These are very serious and
reasonable questions, and they have been raised and refuted a number of
times over the centuries (cf. Pourrat 2:95–98).

Are we really reading Birgitta? For the best answer, we should look to
the internal evidence of the text itself. My own impression—after
working so long and so closely with the text—is of a single, distinc-
tively recognizable human personality at the bottom of all this writing: a
person who prayed and read and thought and asked questions with a
vigorous concern for the things of God. In the notes I have often
pointed out exegetical or theological questions that would most naturally arise in an attentive mind as it prayed the yearly cycle of the Roman
liturgy. In my opinion, the rhythm and flow of the Birgittine writings
springs not from the calculated design of a committee, but from an
individual life vigorously lived. I see no reason to doubt that we are
reading the experiences of the woman Birgitta.

Nor do I see any reason to doubt the traditional account of the role of the priest-translators. We are several times plainly told that they polished Birgitta's words and brought them into line with correct theological terminology. We are told that they discussed the Latin translation with Birgitta, which means that she was willing to listen to their ideas about her words and perhaps accepted from them suggestions of biblical and patristic allusions in support of her insights. We are also told that the priests went on working with her texts after her death—an editorial phenomenon that has countless parallels in the posthumous publications of many other writers. Is it possible that, here and there, the priest-editors may have added things that would never have occurred to Birgitta?

The Oslo fragment has shed a new light of reassurance on the traditional text. For the first time, we can begin to see the actual process of revision that the Latin text underwent at the hands of Birgitta's priests. And what we see is what the traditional text has always described: polishing of Latinity and refinement of theological terminology. In the change from the Oslo version to the traditional version, some words were replaced with better Latin synonyms; the *clausulae* were rewritten in the accentual *cursus;* and many traditional epithets of honor were added to the invocations of Jesus and Mary. Nevertheless, the two texts are essentially the same; the later text has simply been polished, not significantly changed. In fact, the very nature of these differences between the two texts is the best evidence that the Oslo fragment represents the earlier draft. If the Oslo version were an abridgment of the traditional text, the abbreviator might plausibly drop the epithets; but he would hardly redo the *clausulae* without the *cursus* (cf. Eklund, "Re-assessment" 13–14).

From the priests' point of view, the polished text represented the sort of thing that Birgitta had wanted to publish. However, by their polishing, they did move the text one step further away from the actual words that came from Birgitta's lips—a fact that is inevitably disturbing to the modern mind. But there seems to be no reason to reject the traditional account, which insists that the traditional Latin version accurately represents what the saint wished to have published. After all, an author's intended final version of a work has a certain authority that cannot really be compromised by the chance survival of scattered fragments of the text's early drafts. And when the survival of such early drafts is more hypothetical than really demonstrated, the authority of the final version carries great weight.

We are still confronted with the problem of "revelation." With such a history of composition; with so much polishing, so much improving and augmenting, in what sense does this text claim to be a revelation from God? The question is most pressing for those who cannot conceive of revelation except as a literal dictation, word by word, from God. Catholic tradition has always had reservations about such an extremely literal concept of revelation. Birgitta herself witnessed to this reserve, and her words about the inspired authors of the gospels should be carefully pondered (*Rev.* 5, Int. 16.15–31).

A more technical exposition of the Catholic position is given by the confessors themselves (*Life* 27) in their summary of St. Augustine's teaching on the three types of vision: corporeal, imaginary (also called "spiritual"), and intellectual. It is the last of these types—in which sense-data play no part—that tradition considers the highest and most important. In intellectual vision, the divine communication is somehow directly impressed upon the recipient, who must then struggle to put this "revelation" or "vision" into human words and images. In the two lower types of vision, the seer receives the mystical insight accompanied by an external (corporeal) or internal (imaginary) perception of the words or images already formulated.

God, in himself, is always above and beyond all words and images. For the person who has experienced intellectual vision—and the confessors testify (*Life* 27) that Birgitta had—words and images become important *after* the visionary experience. Verbalization allows the memory to retain the insight and enables the intellect to ponder it; and with the words come images. These words and images are even more pressingly needed if the visionary is to communicate the received insight to others.

But the struggle to balance and match insight and verbalization can be painful and prolonged. We can see this struggle in the case of Birgitta, where we have some limited control over several drafts of certain texts and a traditional account of a process of rewriting as a major factor in the recording of all the revelations. Far from being a process of degeneration from a "pure" text first spoken by the saint, it seems more likely that we are witnessing her struggle to communicate more clearly the things that she had found in prayer.

To the extent that she guided the process of rewriting and participated in it, we have no reason to criticize her desire to see the texts rewritten and even augmented in a way that would better convey her insights. And the confessors do warn us by the words "intellectual" and, more frequently, "spiritual" to remember that they did not indiscriminately view the mystical insight of a given revelation and its accompanying words or images as equally sacrosanct in every detail.

A word should be said about the special role of Alphonsus in the theological refinement of the text. First of all, we must lay aside any preconceived notion of a necessary conflict between mystical experience and official theology. As a sincere member of the Catholic Church, Birgitta would have instinctively rejected any "revelation" that plainly contradicted the faith that she had received. As a Catholic, she fully expected to find in her mystical prayer a deep penetration of the tradition of the Church rather than a corrective or a supplement for it. Therefore she was understandably eager to have her words examined and even refined by a skilled theologian like Alphonsus in order that they might be a more perfect reflection of God's *public* revelation in the Scriptures and in the traditional teaching of the Church.

After consideration of the preceding discussion and before forming a final opinion about the Birgittine Question, the reader should carefully reflect on the following text (*Extravagantes* 49.1–8; Hollmann 165–66), which presents crucial testimony concerning the composition of Birgitta's revelations. Two rubrics for this text survive, the longer of which gives certain details of interest:

> *Lady Birgitta had this revelation from God in the kingdom of Cyprus, in the city of Famagusta, when she was going to Jerusalem. In it Christ instructed her to give over all the books of heavenly revelations to Alphonsus the hermit, the sometime bishop, to the end that he might write, elucidate, and divulge them.*
>
> *2. That same bishop did not inscribe this revelation in the books of revelations in order to avoid arrogance and for the sake of humility; but, after his death, it was found in his breviary.*

The text itself follows, together with the shorter rubric that was printed in the first edition in 1492:

> *Christ, in giving these revelations, likens himself to a carpenter; and afterward he sent them to Lord Alphonsus, a bishop and at that time a hermit, to be elucidated, telling how the Holy Spirit sometimes leaves the elect to themselves. Chapter 49.*

The Son of God spoke to the bride, saying: "I am like a carpenter who, cutting wood from the forest, carries it off into his house and of it fashions a beautiful image and adorns it with colors and lineaments. 2. And his friends, seeing the image and that it could be adorned with colors still more beautiful, themselves applied their colors too, painting upon it. 3. Thus I, God, have cut from the forest of my Godhead my words that I have put into your heart. My friends, in fact, have redacted [*redegerunt*] them into books, in accord with the grace given to them, and have colored and adorned them. 4. Now, therefore, that they [i.e., the words] may be serviceable [*conueniant*] to more tongues, give over all the books of the revelations of these same words of mine to my bishop, the hermit, who is to write them together and to elucidate the obscure things and to hold to the Catholic sense of my Spirit. 5. Because my Spirit sometimes leaves my elect to themselves in order that they, in the manner of a pair of scales, may judge and examine my words in their heart, and, after much thought, may expound them more clearly and elicit the better things. 6. For just as your heart is not always capable and warm for uttering and writing those things that you sense, but now you turn and turn them again in your soul, now you write and rewrite them, until you come to the proper sense of my words, thus with the Evangelists and Doctors my Spirit ascended and descended because now they put some things that had to be emended, now some things that had to be retracted, now they were judged and reprehended by others. 7. And nevertheless others afterward came, who more subtly examined and more lucidly explained their words. But nevertheless it was from my Spirit, through infusion, that all my Evangelists had the words that they spoke and wrote. 8. Likewise say to the same hermit that he is to do and to fill the office of an evangelist."

The notes that I have written are chiefly intended to help the reader to appreciate Birgitta's sources, her style, and her ideas. In connection with the notes, the reader should be warned that the modern Birgittine editions are printed in medieval Latin spelling and, moreover, that the earlier system of medieval spelling used by Collijn is not identical in all details with the spellings used by Bergh. Ordinarily these spellings will be easily understood by those more used to classical spelling; but some words can look very curious indeed. For example, *vue* would be the medieval spelling of *uvae*, "grapes." For quotations from the *Four Prayers* and from the other parts of the *Heavenly Book* that have no modern edition, I have used the classical spelling as given in Durante's edition of 1628. This juxtaposition of different methods of spelling may seem confusing at first but is clearly preferable to any attempted regularization according to a system selected by me.

In the translation and the notes, the spelling of biblical names and titles follows the usage of the *New American Bible*, with one exception: the last book of the New Testament is always referred to as the Apocalypse in order to avoid confusion with the *Heavenly Book of Revelations*, whose parts are cited as *Rev. 1, Rev. 2*, etc. The reader must always keep in mind the fact that all biblical citations refer primarily to the text of the Latin Vulgate, specifically to *Biblia sacra iuxta vulgatam versionem*, ed. Robert Weber, O.S.B., et al. (Stuttgart: Deutsche Bibelgesellschaft, 1983). In the Psalms and in some other books (e.g., Tobit), the chapter and verse numbers will not always match those of the modern versions made from the Hebrew or Aramaic. They will, however, be easily found in the English versions of the Vulgate: namely, the Douay-Rheims, Challoner, or Knox versions. All biblical translations—unless otherwise noted—are from the Challoner version or have been done by me.

Throughout the course of this project, the English spelling of proper names has provided a recurrent topic for controversy. Marguerite Tjader Harris's original intention was to give the translation a Swedish flavor by having all names in the Modern Swedish forms found in the Lundén translation. But now that the translation has been redone directly from the Latin, I have, after careful consideration, adopted a simple rule for rendering the names: if the Latin text gives the standard Latin form of a name (e.g., *Carolus*), I have given the standard English equivalent (i.e., Charles); but, if the Latin gives a Latinized Swedish form that has no English equivalent (e.g., *Botuydus*), I have used the standard Modern Swedish name (i.e., Botvid).

The one exception to this rule is the use of the Swedish name "Birgitta"—pronounced "burr-GHEE-tuh," with a hard *g* as in "geese." Marguerite Tjader Harris absolutely rejected the use of the traditional "Bridget," "Brigid," or "Bride" in order to avoid the all too common confusion of Saint Birgitta of Sweden with Saint Brigid of Ireland. She had strong feelings on this point, and I have respected her wishes by using "Birgitta" in the present volume.

TRANSLATOR'S FOREWORD

The bibliography is chiefly intended to serve as a record of those works of Birgittine relevance that were consulted for the preparation of the present work, whether or not they are explicitly cited in the notes. Those who wish to go beyond the works listed here should consult the very full bibliographies in the various volumes of the modern editions of the Latin text, especially for such technical items as grammars or dictionaries. I have not reproduced their complete listing of these technical volumes here although I have included several titles that are not cited in the critical editions or that have appeared only recently.

In conclusion, I must express my gratitude to John Farina, Bernard McGinn and Georgia Christo of Paulist Press, and to four learned and generous professors—Birger Bergh (Lund), Ewert Cousins (Fordham), Sten Eklund (Uppsala), and Tore Nyberg (Odense)—for their unfailing encouragement of this project.

My special thanks go to my mother Mary and her sister Ann Ryle, to my brother John, and to my cousin Joseph Ryle for patient interest, assistance, and advice of a sort that made possible the achievement of this long and difficult labor.

Finally, I recommend to the readers' prayers the souls of Marguerite Tjader Harris and of my father Albert Patrick Cassidy Kezel, M.D. Without them, neither this book nor the studies that prepared for it would ever have been begun. *Requiescant in pace.*

The Life of Blessed Birgitta by Prior Peter and Master Peter[1]

1. One should know that this most humble handmaid of God never presumed to call herself or to have herself called the bride of Christ, or his channel,[2] because of vainglory or transitory honor or any temporal advantage, but at the instruction of Christ and of blessed Mary, his most worthy Mother, who both called her so. And it was not from presumption, but out of humble obedience to them, that she thus called herself in her writings.

2. *Of what parents Christ's bride, Lady Birgitta, was born.*

As we read about blessed John the Baptist and about Saint Nicholas, the merits of parents many times cooperate to produce in their children an even greater grace, which perseveres to the end. So Lady Birgitta of holy memory, the princess of Närke[3] in the kingdom of Sweden, the bride of Christ, came forth from just and devout parents, who were noble according to the flesh because they were of the noble race of the kings of the Goths,[4] but more noble according to God. For her father was a devout and just man and was called Lord Birger of Upper Sweden. Every Friday, he humbly confessed his sins; and he used to say this: "On Fridays, I want to prepare myself so well for God that on the other days I may be ready to bear whatever God may give."

3. He also visited, with great labor, the places of the saints—namely, of James and of others[5]—imitating the footsteps of his predecessors. For his father had been a Jerusalem pilgrim and so had his grandfather and his great-grandfather and his great-great-grandfather. And it is unheard of that men so magnificent and of such great wealth and glory from the ends of the world—namely, from the kingdom of Sweden—should undertake such a laborious journey—namely, to see the places of Saint James and of Jerusalem, where Jesus Christ became incarnate and suffered.[6]

4. Wherefore Christ later, among other words of the revelations, spoke to his aforesaid bride: "I tell you," he said, "but not for your praise, that your generation has come forth from a lineage of holy kings. And they themselves earned, by their merits, that my divine grace be made manifest with you." And similarly the mother of this same bride of Christ—her name was Lady Ingeborg[7]—was very noble and very de-

vout. Her father, named Lord Benedict, a man sprung of kingly seed, founded and endowed many churches and monasteries. The wife of this Benedict hid her devotion of mind and walked ways in accord with her noble rank and the customs of the nobility. One time when she and her household were passing through a certain monastery of nuns,[8] she was looked down upon by a certain nun. And indeed this nun began, with force, to disparage this same grandmother of the said Lady Birgitta and to murmur with the other nuns. And when, on the following night, the said nun had fallen asleep, a person of wonderful beauty appeared to her and said with angry countenance: "Why have you disparaged my handmaid by saying that she is haughty, which is not true? For from her offspring I shall cause a daughter to come forth, with whom I shall do my great deeds in the world; and I shall pour such great grace into her that all the nations will be astonished."

5. However, when the time came that this bride of Christ, Lady Birgitta, was still in her mother's womb, it happened that her mother suffered shipwreck in an inlet of the sea. And when many of either sex had already drowned, a duke of the kingdom, Lord Eric,[9] the king of Sweden's brother, who was there at the time, saw her in peril, and, by every means in his power, brought her alive to the shore. Then that very night, a person in shining garments stood by that same mother of Lady Birgitta and said: "You have been saved for the sake of the good that you have in your womb. Therefore nourish it with the love of God because it is God who has given it to you."

6. *How the birth of Christ's bride appeared to a priest.*

And so, with the coming of the time at which the girl Birgitta was born,[10] a certain parish priest of a nearby church—a man of proven life and advanced age—while awake and praying, saw in the night a shining cloud, and, in the cloud, a virgin sitting with a book in her hand. To the wondering priest the same virgin said: "To Birger has been born a daughter whose wonderful voice will be heard throughout the world."

7. *How she was as if tongueless[11] for three years.*

And so, as the girl Birgitta advanced in age,[12] she was as if tongueless for three years and did not have the use of speech. Her parents were in much doubt about this, believing that she was mute; but at the end of the third year, she so fully obtained the use of speech that she did not speak in the babbling manner of infants, but, contrary to what is natural at such an age, she sounded the words perfectly.

8. *How Birgitta's mother dies.*

In the meantime her mother, a woman virtuous in all things, was growing infirm. Several days in advance, she foreknew and foretold her own passing; and when she was just about to go forth from her body and saw her husband and the others sorrowing, she said: "Why do you sorrow? It is enough to have lived this long. We must rejoice because I am now called to a mightier Lord." And having called her children, she blessed them all and fell asleep in the Lord.

9. *How, while still a girl, she saw wonderful things.*

And so, when the girl Birgitta, the bride of Christ, had now attained the seventh year of her age, she once saw, while wide awake,[13] an altar just opposite her bed and a certain lady in shining garments sitting above the altar. The lady had a precious crown in her hand and said to her: "O Birgitta, come!" And hearing this, she arose from bed, running to the altar. The lady said to her: "Do you want to have this crown?" She nodded, and the said lady put the crown on her head so that Birgitta then felt, as it were, the circle of the crown touching her head. But when she returned to bed, the vision disappeared; and yet she could never forget it.

10. *How she saw Christ crucified.*

Round about her tenth year, on a certain occasion she heard a sermon preached in church about the passion of our Lord Jesus Christ. The following night she saw, in a dream, Christ as if he had been crucified in that same hour, and he said to her: "In such a way was I wounded." And she thought that this had happened at that hour and answered in her sleep: "O Lord, who has done this to you?" Jesus Christ answered: "Those who scorn me and neglect my love: they have done this to me." Then she came to herself; and from that day, she felt such affection for the passion of Christ that she could rarely recall the memory of it without tears.

11. *How an unknown girl was seen sitting beside her.*

Moreover, on a day in her twelfth year, she was intent upon some handiwork involving silk and gold in the company of other girls of her own age; and she felt much anxiety of soul because she could not do her work as she wished. Then her maternal aunt[14]—a very devout and praiseworthy lady into whose keeping Birgitta had come after her mother's death—walked into the house and saw an unknown maiden sitting beside Birgitta and doing that same piece of work with her. And since, at her entrance, that unknown girl had disappeared, the aunt then asked Birgitta who the girl was that had been working with her. Birgitta answered that she had seen no one. Her aunt, however, inspected the work and found that it was so finely done that anyone looking at it would be given to understand that it was not the work of a girl of such a tender age but was something divine. Therefore this lady herself used to hold it in regard[15] among her relics as something from God.

12. *How the aunt found Birgitta praying at night.*

One night, the aforesaid aunt secretly entered the bedroom of the maidens and found Birgitta kneeling naked before her bed and praying with tears. The aunt, suspicious of maidenly levity, ordered someone to bring a switch. But when she had begun to extend the switch to strike Birgitta, at once it broke into tiny pieces so that the said aunt, seeing this, wondered greatly and said: "What have you done, Birgitta? Have the women taught you some fallacious prayers?"[16] The maiden answered with tears: "No, my lady; but I arose from bed to praise him whose custom is ever to help me." And her aunt said: "Who is he?" To which the maiden said: "The Crucified One whom I saw." And because of this, from that day her aunt began to love and venerate her more fervently.

13. *How she saw the devil.*

Not long after, when Birgitta was wide awake and playing with girls, she saw the devil, as it were, having a hundred hands and feet and most deformed in every way. Thoroughly terrified, she ran to her bed, where the devil appeared to her again and said to her: "I can do nothing unless the Crucified were to permit." Since the women had seen and were asking what it was that had befallen her and why she was so thoroughly terrified, she answered: "A certain heartache seized upon me." And those women asked nothing more of her. But after some years, her aunt came and heard from her the whole truth and instructed her to cover her visions in silence and to be of good hope and to love God intimately and to beware of all levity.

14. *How she came to marriage and how she lived in her marriage.*

In the meantime, Lady Birgitta was betrothed to a rich young man, a noble and prudent knight who was called Lord Ulf of Ulvåsa, prince of Närke.[17] Between them they had so very honorable a marriage[18] that both spouses lived in virginity for one year, devoutly asking God that if they ought to come together he, the Creator of all, would from them create an offspring that would be at his service. She truly loved God and was most highly wary of herself so that no one might speak badly of her and that she might not give occasion for anyone to disparage her. Therefore she fled levities and places or persons for which she could be branded; and she had in her company honest handmaids and well-mannered companions. Indeed, together with the members of her household, she was intent upon work for divine worship or for the welfare of her neighbors.

15. *How she prayed and how a prayer was poured into her.*

In truth, the bride of Christ was so very fervent in prayer and tears[19] that when her husband was away, she passed almost whole nights in vigil and did not spare her body many genuflexions and cruel disciplining.[20] In fact, some time passed during which she constantly kept asking God in her prayers that some suitable manner of praying might be poured into her. One day, in a wonderful manner, she was elevated in mind; and then there was poured into her a most beautiful prayer[21] concerning the passion of Christ and concerning the life and the praise of the most Blessed Virgin Mary. She kept this prayer in her memory so that afterward she might read it every day. And so one time when blessed Mary appeared to her afterward, she said: "I merited that prayer for you; therefore when you read it, you will be visited with the consolation[22] of my Son."

16. *About confession.*

She continuously frequented confession; and for her confessor, she had a very expert and devout master of theology, called Master Matthias, who wrote an excellent gloss on the whole Bible and composed many volumes of books.[23] And it was he who composed the prologue for the books of the *Heavenly Revelations* of the aforesaid Lady Birgitta; and it was him that she obeyed in all her difficulties. Wherefore, this same confessor used to say familiarly to his friends: "In Lady Birgitta, it is a sign of some future grace that she so laments light matters as others lament things very serious and that she leaves nothing in her words or behavior unexamined."

17. *About fasting.*

When she could, she multiplied her great fasts and other acts of abstinence; and she very often abstained from delicacies in a hidden way so that it would not be noticed by her husband or by others.

18. *About reading.*

Indeed, when she was not occupied with manual labor, she was continually rereading the lives of the saints and the Bible, which she had caused to be written out for herself in her own language;[24] and when she could hear the sermons of upright men, she did not spare herself the labor of going to hear those same sermons.

19. *About almsdeeds.*

Right up to her death, she did very large almsdeeds.[25] In Sweden, she had a house set aside for the poor; and she served them in person when she could. She washed their feet and clothed them and visited them when they were infirm and handled their wounds and bodies with tender compassion and the greatest of maternal charity.

20. *How blessed Mary helped her in childbirth.*[26]

Now at one time Lady Birgitta was imperiled during childbirth, and her life was despaired of. That night, the women who were present to watch over her were awake; and as they looked, a person dressed in white silk was seen to enter and stand before the bed and handle each one of Lady Birgitta's members as she lay there—to the fear of all the women who were present. When, however, that person had gone out, Lady Birgitta gave birth so easily that it was a thing of wonder and not to be doubted that the Blessed Virgin, who gave birth without pain, was that person who mitigated the labors, the pains, and the peril of her handmaid, just as that same Virgin afterwards told her in a vision when she spoke this revelation:

21. *A revelation.*

"When you," she said, "had difficulty in childbirth, I, Mary, entered unto you. For that reason, you are an ingrate if you do not love me. Labor, therefore, that your children may also be my children."

22. *How she virtuously educated and nurtured her children.*

The bride of Christ, therefore, with great concern and diligence, virtuously educated and nurtured her sons and daughters, handing them over to teachers by whom they were instructed in discipline and good behavior.[27] She wept daily over her children's sins, fearing that they would offend their God. And so one time when Saint John the Baptist appeared to her, he said: "Because you wept over the fact that your son offended me by not fasting on my vigil,[28] and because you would prefer him to serve me rather than be a king,[29] I shall therefore help him and shall arm him with my arms." Mention is made of this more clearly at the end of the fourth book of the *Heavenly Revelations* given to the aforesaid lady.

23. *How she gained her husband for God and they both went to Saint James.*

When, however, Lady Birgitta had for a long time been making progress in the virtues, she also gained her husband for God. For even though he was a vigorous man and an important member of the king of Sweden's council, he occupied himself—at his wife's advice and admonishment—in learning to read the Hours[30] of the most Blessed Virgin Mary and the books containing the laws and legal judgments; and he studied to fulfill what belongs to justice and the law. And so, both of them—namely, this husband and wife—being fervent in their love for God and that they might more freely disengage themselves from the vanities of the world, went forth from their fatherland and from their kindred after Abraham's example, and, with great labors and expenses, proceeded into Spain to Saint James in Compostella. After they had made their pilgrimage to many places of the saints and while they were on the way back, her husband took sick in the city that is called Arras, near Flanders. As the sickness grew worse, the bride of Christ, being in a state of great anxiety of soul, merited to be consoled by Saint Denis,[31] who appeared and spoke to her at prayer: "I," he said, "am Denis, who came from Rome to these parts of France to proclaim God's word in my life. And so, because you love me with special devotion, I therefore proclaim to you that through you, God wills to be made known to the world and that you have been handed over to my guardianship and protection. Wherefore I shall help you always; and I give to you this sign: your husband will not die now of this sickness." And many other times, this same blessed Denis visited her in revelations and consoled her.

24. *A vision of future things.*

After some days, there in that same city of Arras, she again saw certain wonderful things in prophetic vision: namely, how she was going to travel to Rome and to the holy city of Jerusalem, and how she was going to depart from this world, and how a very handsome youth led her then in spirit through all the said places. All these things were thus fulfilled after much time.

25. *How, with her husband convalescing, she returned to her fatherland.*

However, after his long illness, her husband was convalescing; and they both returned to their fatherland. Between them, they maintained a mutual continence and decided to enter a monastery. And after all their affairs and goods had been set in order to this end, her husband—still having the same purpose—died in the year of our Lord, 1344.[32]

26. *How she was sent to a teacher and how, after her husband's death, she was visited by the Spirit.*

After some days, when the bride of Christ was worried about the change in her status and its bearing on her service of God, and while she was praying about this in her chapel, then she was caught up in spirit; and while she was in ecstasy, she saw a bright cloud; and from the cloud, she heard a voice saying to her: "Woman, hear me." And thoroughly terrified, fearing that it was an illusion, she fled to her chamber; and at once she confessed and then received the Body of Christ. When at last, after several days, she was at prayer in the same chapel, again that bright cloud appeared to her; and from the cloud, she heard again a voice uttering words like those before, namely: "Woman, hear me." And then that lady, again thoroughly terrified, fled to her chamber; and having confessed, she communicated as before, fearing that the voice was an illusion. Finally, after several days, when she was praying again in the same place, she was indeed caught up in spirit and again saw the bright cloud, and, in it, the likeness of a human being, who said this: "Woman, hear me; I am your God, who wish to speak with you." Terrified, therefore, and thinking it was an illusion, she heard again: "Fear not," he said; "for I am the Creator of all, and not a deceiver. For I do not speak to you for your sake alone, but for the sake of the salvation of others. Hear the things that I speak; and go to Master Matthias, your confessor, who has experience in discerning the two types of spirit.[33] Say to him on my behalf what I now say to you: you shall be my bride and my channel,[34] and you shall hear and see spiritual things, and my Spirit shall remain with you even to your death." After this, he added: "For three reasons, Lucifer fell," etc.,[35] as is more fully contained in the revelations of the *Heavenly Book*.

27. And this is the first revelation in the prologue, etc.[36] Therefore in the year of our Lord 1345,[37] the first divine revelations were made to Lady Birgitta not in sleep but while she was awake and at prayer, with her body remaining alive in its vigor, but while she was caught up from her bodily senses in ecstasy and in visions, either spiritual or imaginary, with the coming of a vision or a supernatural and divine illumination of her intellect, for she saw and heard spiritual things and felt them in spirit. Indeed, in the manner mentioned, she saw and heard corporeal images and similitudes; in fact, in her heart she felt something, as it were, alive, which moved more actively and more fervently in response to greater inflammations and infusions, but less when the infusions were less. Many times, indeed, the movement in her heart was so vehement that motion could be seen and felt even on the outside.[38]

28. *How, even before her husband's passing, she saw certain things.*

In the fourth year before her husband's passing, a saint of our land of Sweden, Botvid by name,[39] appeared to her, as it were, in an ecstasy of mind, and said: "I have, with other saints, merited for you God's grace —namely, to hear and to see and to feel spiritual things—and the Spirit of God will inflame your soul."

29. In the third year before her husband's passing, the most Blessed

Virgin Mary appeared to her and said: "I am the Queen of those in misery. I want to show you what my Son was like in his humanity and what he was like when he suffered on the cross. And this will be a sign to you,[40] that you will come to the places in Jerusalem where I lived in the body and there, with your spiritual eyes, you will see my Son." After twenty-eight years, all of this was thus accomplished, as it is more clearly recorded in the book of revelations that she had in Jerusalem and in Bethlehem.[41]

30. *How, at the beginning of the revelations, she was instructed to stay in a certain monastery.*

And so at the beginning of the revelations, she was at once instructed to obey that same Matthias, a master of theology, and to stay in a monastery of Cistercian monks, namely, Saint Mary's in Alvastra, which is in Sweden, in the diocese of Linköping. The Spirit said to her in a vision: "If it should please the mighty Lord to do a work that is singular, general works must not therefore be despised but must be loved all the more and with greater fervor. So I, the God of all, who am above all rules, permit you to reside at the present time near the monastery—not to abolish the Rule, nor to introduce a new custom, but rather to display my wonderful work in a holy place. For David, in a time of need, ate the hallowed loaves—an act that is nevertheless forbidden to some in a normal time."[42] There was a lay brother with the name Gerekin in this same monastery of the Cistercian order at Alvastra. For forty years he never went outside the monastery; but day and night, he was absorbed in prayers; and he had this grace: that, during prayer, he almost continually saw the nine choirs of angels; and at the elevation of the Body of Christ, he merited frequently to see Christ in the appearance of a child. When Lady Birgitta had come to the monastery and was residing there, this brother wondered in his heart and said: "Why does that lady settle here in a monastery of monks, introducing a new custom against our Rule?" Then this same brother was caught up in an ecstasy of mind and clearly heard a voice saying to him: "Do not wonder. This woman is a friend of God; and she has come in order that at the foot of this mountain she may gather flowers from which all people, even overseas and beyond the world's ends, shall receive medicine."

31. Again, on a second occasion, this same brother saw her raised from the earth, and, as it were, lightning going forth from her mouth. And then he heard in spirit: "This is the woman who, coming from the ends of the earth, shall give countless nations wisdom to drink. And this

will be a sign to you:[43] that she, from the mouth of God, is going to tell you the end of your life. And you will exult at her words and at her coming; and your desire will be fulfilled more quickly lest you see the evils that God is going to bring down upon this house."

32. Lord Hemming, bishop of Åbo,[44] performed her divine embassy[45] in France and England and saw that the kings were less than willing to receive the words of God—namely, those revelations touching the kings and the war between the kingdoms of France and England. These revelations are contained in the fourth book of the *Heavenly Revelations*, nearly at the end of the chapter "Disturbed in heart," etc.[46] As he slept, Lady Birgitta appeared to him and said: "Why are you disturbed? You will return to your fatherland successfully, and you will bear the fruit of souls. But know that the plague upon those to whom you were sent shall not yet end, for their hearts are hardened against God, and they shall be troubled yet a while until they are humbled."

33. There was a nun named Katharine in the monastery of Mount Saint Mary,[47] in the kingdom of Sweden. She received this grace: blessed Mary appeared to her, and, among other words, said: "I shall show to you that I am the Mother of God, and I shall present you to my Son." When this lady had seen Lady Birgitta and they were talking together familiarly, she replied: "O you happy lady! For I am not speaking so that either you or I would be boasting, because I have heard for very certain a voice that said this: 'Know that Birgitta shall yet be called happy because, if she is scorned on earth, she will be honored in heaven and those to be born will proclaim her name.' Therefore stand firm because without doubt it will thus be accomplished, even as I have heard."

34. When Master Matthias, her confessor—of whom mention was made above—was stricken with a certain temptation, it was said to Lady Birgitta in spirit: "He will be knowledgeable from 'In the beginning,' i.e., from the beginning of the Bible and of the book of Genesis, which thus commences: 'In the beginning, God created heaven and earth,' right through to 'Alpha and O,' i.e., right through to the Apocalypse, where 'Alpha and O' is thus written.[48] And he will be liberated from his temptations, and I shall give to him the fervor of my Spirit." And at once he felt himself liberated and given rest from his temptation. Also, on the same day that this Master Matthias died in his fatherland, Lady Birgitta, who was staying in Rome, heard in spirit: "Happy are you, Master Matthias, because of the crown that was fashioned for you in Sweden. Come now to wisdom that will never end!"

35. When, in old age, Brother Algot of the Order of Preachers, a master of theology and a most familiar friend of Lady Birgitta, for three years experienced blindness and suffered violently from calculi, he asked the said Lady Birgitta to offer prayer to God for him. When, in compliance with his request, she asked for him to be healed, this answer came to her in spirit: "He is a gleaming star. It is not expedient that his soul be blackened by his body's health. Now he has competed and he has reached the finish. Nothing remains save that he be crowned.[49] This will be a sign to him:[50] now, from this hour, the pains of his flesh will be alleviated; now all of his soul will be inflamed with my charity." And not many days afterward, he expired.

36. The aforementioned Lady Birgitta also had, from God, these special graces of great virtue and wonder: the first is that when she was saying anything that would be an offense to God, at once she felt in her mouth a very great bitterness, as it were, of sulphur. And by this she knew at once that she had offended God; and, bringing that word back into her memory, at once and without delay she confessed it to her confessor with great sorrow and tears. Also, when anyone spoke to her any sly or vicious words that would offend God, at once she felt in her nostrils a horrible stench of sulphur, which she could hardly tolerate. And this was a sign that God had then been offended by the words of that person—a thing that we proved almost an infinite number of times.[51]

37. Moreover, when any person asked her about some doubt in his conscience and sought from her advice and a special remedy that would be very good, she then used to answer him: "Pray to God about this. And we too shall think, and we shall do what we can for you—although I am an unworthy sinner." In fact, after three days or so and sometimes on the very same day, she would answer that same person—if the person were spiritual and honest—having first lifted her hands toward heaven and saying this: "I am a sinner unworthy to say such things; nevertheless, know that Jesus Christ appeared to me at prayer and told me what reply I might make to the fact that you asked such and such, etc." And then she gave him the words that she had had from Christ or from the Blessed Virgin Mary as the response to this matter. Or else when she was well, she wrote down with her own hand and in her mother tongue the words divinely given to her; and she had them most faithfully translated into the Latin tongue by us, her confessors. And afterward, she listened to the translation together with her own writing that she herself had written, so that there might be not one word more

81

added there or missing but only what she herself had divinely heard and seen in the vision. If, in fact, she was ill, she called her confessor and her writer—a secretary specially assigned to this—and then, with great devotion and fear of God and sometimes with tears, she reported to him those words in her own vernacular and with a certain attentive elevation of mind, as if she were reading them in a book. And then the confessor said these words in the Latin tongue for the writer, and he wrote them down right there in her presence. And afterward, when the words had been written out, she wanted to listen to them; and she listened very diligently and attentively. And so she gave or sent this writing to those who were making the inquiry. This has often—yes, very often—been proven in experience by the lady queen and the archbishop of Naples; also by the queen and the king and the princes and many others from the kingdom of Cyprus and from the kingdom of Sicily; and by men, and by women too, from Italy, from Sweden, and even from Spain.[52]

38. Moreover, it also happened very often that to the same Lady Birgitta were revealed the most secret thoughts and doubts of those who came to her and even of certain other persons who were absent—things that they themselves had never at all made public by word or by writing or by sign. Witnesses to this are: Lord Nicholas of Nola, rector of the Patrimony; Lord Gomez de Albornoz, rector of the duchy of Spoleto; the lord count of Fondi;[53] and many others, both religious and secular, to whom she told or wrote the innermost things of their hearts.

39. One also had to wonder at another grace that the aforesaid lady had from her bridegroom, Jesus Christ. For very often it happened that with devotion and charity, various persons asked her to pray to God for certain souls of some of their departed. And if it seemed to her that they were in purgatory—a place where they would need intercessory prayers—they asked her to tell this to them, the living questioners, and to make known to them by what alms and sacrifices or by what intercessory prayers of the living the dead could be freed from those pains. Indeed, she received in writing the names of the departed; and with utmost charity and compassion, she prayed to God for them. And then, in prayer, she obtained answers from God as to whether those souls were in purgatory—and even about the manner of that purgatory and of those pains where they were—or whether they were in hell or in heaven.[54] She was also given to know, clearly and distinctly, the manners of intercessory prayer and of almsgiving through which those souls could be freed. Good proof of this was experienced by some of the

aforesaid living persons who were named above and who devoutly asked her about such things, and, concerning this, had divine answers from her in writing. Indeed when she herself, or any of us in her house, was anxious or doubtful about anything, at once and without great delay, through the revelations divinely given to her, she humbly brought back from Christ, her glorious bridegroom, or from our Lady, the Virgin Mary, a most precious answer explaining that business.

40. What more is there? For the testimony to so many virtues, to such great holiness and excellence, to such flowing and abundant grace divinely shining in her is all disclosed in the books of the *Heavenly Revelations*, which were divinely given to her, and in the *Book of Questions*, which was also given to her divinely, through an infusion from the Holy Spirit, in a wonderful manner and, as it were, in a single hour, while she was riding her horse and journeying to her villa in Vadstena, as is more fully recorded at the beginning of that same *Book of Questions*.[55] Testimony is also provided by visual experiences, for very often these things were seen by us ourselves and by many others in various parts of the world. For we have often seen that things that she had prophetically foretold many years ahead of time, afterwards actually came about in our experience. This is something that many others also saw and experienced. From them it may be clearly gathered (and it can be tested by the sayings of the saints) that she had from God the true spirit of prophecy and that intellectual vision had been divinely given to her.[56] The miracles too that since her death are happening through her merits and intercession bear now, and will in future bear, the clear witness of truth to the great graces that divinely sparkled[57] in her. Indeed, after this lady had been called into the Spirit of God, she prophesied not only about the future—as did the prophets—but also about the present and the past;[58] and she also clarified many things concerning certain doubtful matters in Sacred Scripture.[59]

41. Moreover, like the apostles, she relinquished all that she owned; and, at God's instruction, she sent letters to the major personages of the whole of Christendom: namely, to the supreme pontiffs; to the emperors; to the kings and queens of France and of England, of Sicily and of Cyprus; to princes and princesses; to various prelates; to seculars and to religious; to kingdoms, and to lands and to cities. She also visited many lands personally, showing God's will to great and small alike for the good of their souls, redeemed by Christ's blood.

42. Like the holy evangelists, she wrote also about the birth of Christ

and about his glorious life, and, in a similar way, about his death and about his resurrection and about his eternal glory, as is shown clearly enough in her revelations.[60]

43. In truth, she was not without experience of martyrdom; for she mortified her body by living in toil and abstinence, by exposing herself to dangers on land and on sea, and by patiently enduring, for the sake of Christ's name, the reproaches and affronts of many, whether she was in grave physical infirmity or in health. From her innermost heart, she continually returned thanks to her bridegroom, Jesus Christ, for all adversities; and she prayed suppliantly to God for those who offended her.

44. *How a certain lady who had died appeared to her and foretold to her the future.*

Now, during the first month that Lady Birgitta came to the said monastery of Cistercian monks—namely, Saint Mary's of Alvastra—a certain lady, already dead and very well known to her, appeared to her at prayer and said: "To you shall be given understanding of spiritual things; in all things, therefore, humble yourself. And that you may know this with greater certainty, behold, I give to you a threefold sign. The first is that I have been gravely purged for the stubbornness of my conscience. The second: that my husband, who is not my husband, now seeks something carnal—namely, carnal intercourse with another woman in opposition to God—and it will be, for him and his posterity, a cause of tribulation. The third is that you will cross the sea; and you will die in a glorious place, in Rome."

45. Moreover, the lady appeared to her a second time and said: "I want to inform you of my situation; for it thus pleases God that as we have loved each other while both living in the flesh, so we should now love each other in spirit. I—to speak using a similitude—have been put, as it were, in thick glass and can hear,[61] but not yet reach, the things that I wish for. Thus, I can understand and desire and hope for those everlasting joys; but I have not yet attained to the full until the glass, by God's will, becomes more thin and sheer. And this has been because two things weighed me down in the world: namely, a facility of anger; and the fact that I was not content with the things that I had, but wanted always to have more. Therefore induce those who were my friends to have chalices made for me, in which the sacrifice of my Lord Jesus Christ may be offered; and second, to have remembrance of me made during the year[62] by those who are the friends of God. For by such

means I shall, without a doubt, be more quickly freed from this punishment."

46. *What sort of things happened during life to that aforesaid lady who was the sister of Lady Birgitta's husband and who thus appeared to her.*

That said lady who after death appeared to Lady Birgitta was very famous for her fasts and prayers. And one time, when she was seriously ill, the devil appeared to her in a most hideous form, intending as if to snatch her as she lay there. In fact, violently terrified, she called out: "For eternity," she said, "I shall be damned!" As she many times repeated these words, her confessor spoke to her: "Why," he said, "do you speak these words, my Lady, when you have always loved God with all your heart?" She, however, could make no answer save as before: "I shall be damned for eternity!" Finally, she fell silent in the hands of those who held her; in a wonderful way, her face began to change and to take on colors and to be, in color, now white and now a rosy red. While those present were wondering, she said in a loud voice: "Blessed are you, my God, who have created and have freed me. I confess you and I bless you."[63] But when she had regained her breath and was returning to herself, she called her confessor and other virtuous men and said to them: "I saw the devil in a most vile form. Taking fright at his appearance, I believed that I would be damned. And while I was in this terrible anxiety, I saw Christ, as it were, standing on the cross.[64] As the devil fled away, Christ said: 'When a year has rolled by, you will see the same vision, but not the devil. And this will be a sign to you,[65] when you see it, that at once your life will be at an end.'" And so it happened; for when the year had rolled by, on that very same date she saw Christ; and then her soul was loosed from the flesh after long purgation.

47. *How this lady appeared a third time to Christ's bride, Lady Birgitta.*

This said lady also appeared a third time after her death to that same Lady Birgitta and said: "What I longed for, I now have. My former torments have been consigned to oblivion, and my love is now perfect. But as for you: be obedient! For you are going to come into the society of the great."[66]

48. *How, after the death of her husband, Lady Birgitta distributed her goods.*

With her husband dead, at once Lady Birgitta distributed all her goods among her children and the poor. She changed her way of living and dressing; and she would have done even greater things but for the obstacle of the fact that she had been instructed in a revelation to make a pilgrimage to Rome. And when she was scorned by the nobles for the sudden change and the cheapness of her clothing, she answered: "It is neither for you that I start, nor for you that I stop. For I have determined in my heart to tolerate injurious words. Pray, therefore, for me that I may be able to persevere."

49. *How she was divinely instructed to go to the king of Sweden.*

And so, when she had been instructed in spirit to go to the king of Sweden, and when she pleaded the excuse that she did not know what to say to him, this answer was made to her by God: "When you arrive," he said, "open your mouth; and I will fill it."[67] Therefore, when she arrived, divine words were at once poured into her—not only words that pertained to the king, but also many that were about the future.

50. *How she was sent to a bishop and he acknowledged her coming.*[68]

This same Lady Birgitta also came to a certain bishop of proven life and devotion and said to him some words divinely revealed to her. When he heard those words, he, in his own conscience, discovered—right down to the last point—what she herself had understood in spirit: namely, things that, except for God and himself, no human at all had ever known. For the said lord bishop had certain less rational desires, and, in some things, a zeal at variance with knowledge; and he practiced fasts that went beyond nature. Therefore, he more willingly accepted her charitable admonitions, corrected everything by the standard of charity, and spoke to her: "Last night," he said, "I definitely saw you entering toward me and removing from my heart very great burdens. Therefore, not only do I believe your words, but I also see in my soul that God is doing wonderful things with you."

51. *How she prohibited the king from imposing unjust imposts and tributes.*

When the king of Sweden was hard pressed to pay a certain sum of money and was arranging to put the burden on the community of the realm contrary to the statutes and his oaths, Lady Birgitta replied to him: "My Lord, do not do this; for you will not be immune from the wrath of God. But take instead my two sons; and pawn them as hostages until you can pay; and do not offend your God." Then, on that very day, there came to her the following vision in which Christ spoke to Lady Birgitta and said this: "Just as a kingdom has sometimes been saved because of the charity of one human being,[69] so some kingdoms have been lost because of one person's new inventions and burdensome taxes. I give you an example of this in the case of the following kingdom. For its king himself trusted in money—exacted by fraud or feigned justice from his people and from travelers—more than he trusted in me. Therefore, he lost his life and left his kingdom in trouble. Others who succeeded him turned his crooked inventions into custom, and, as it were, into law. But if a king trusts in me, his God, and the community of the realm is petitioned for assistance with charity, then I am able to save and to restore to peace more quickly because of that charity. Therefore, if the king desires to prosper, let him keep his promise to me and keep truth with the community of his realm; and let him especially beware of introducing new inventions or tributes or technicalities.[70] In his difficulties, let him follow the advice of those who fear God, and not the advice of the covetous; for it is better to suffer some adversity in this world than to sin knowingly against me and against his own soul."

52. *How the devil wanted to deceive her.*

One day, when Lady Birgitta was going, at the Spirit's instruction, to visit a certain man obsessed by the devil, the horse on which she was accustomed to ride, and which had previously been very gentle, suddenly so reared up from the ground that the horseshoes on its hooves could all be seen. As a result of this rearing, that same lady suffered pain in her back for a long time, whereby she was given to understand that the devil begrudged this sinner's conversion. In fact that man being visited—a man noble, by the world's standards, and great—was vexed by the devil; and especially in her presence, he was disturbed, as it were, more gravely than usual. Then that same man spoke many horrible things against God and said to her: "Oh, how unlike are your spirit in you and my spirit in me! But when it pleases the Spirit who is in you, I shall be perfectly healed; for he himself, because of my disbelief and my hidden demerits, has given me over into the hands of a cruel exactor." She answered him: "I promise you that you shall be quickly healed, but I ask why you speak such great abominations against God." And he said: "I do not rule myself." When he had said this word, he began to speak, as it were, more bitterly against God and to blaspheme him, saying: "Him who created heaven and earth, I worship; about your new God Christ, be silent!"[71] Then the bride of Christ said: "Be silent, wretched devil, in your speech against God; for even if you are this creature's punisher, nevertheless you shall not be his eternal owner." And at once that man, as if drowsing, fell silent; but after several days, he was cured.

53. Still another miracle took place. In a revelation, it had been divinely told to the aforementioned Lady Birgitta that on God's behalf she should instruct a certain Brother Peter—the prior of the Cistercian order's monastery of Saint Mary of Alvastra in Sweden—to write the books of the revelations that had been divinely given to that same Lady Birgitta in spiritual vision. This same prior was a very simple man; and he would for no reason set his hand to writing; for he reckoned himself, because of his ignorance, less than suitable for so great a work. Then he was driven by Christ with the fear of death—and almost died—until he consented. And when his consent was given, he was suddenly cured without any lapse or interval of time.[72]

54. So too a demoniac in East Gothland.[73] In the presence of two trustworthy witnesses, at words from the mouth of the aforesaid religious—words whose form this lady heard from Christ and which the brother said to the demon according to Christ's instruction—then indeed the demoniac was cleansed.

55. Moreover, another demoniac in Sweden was cleansed in the same manner by the same religious, in the presence of trustworthy witnesses, at the instruction of the aforesaid Lady Birgitta.

56. Moreover, through the intervention of the Blessed Virgin Mary, who with Christ appeared to the said Lady Birgitta, a certain public prostitute was converted through the prayer of that same Lady Birgitta.

57. Moreover, many magnates in the kingdom of Sweden were converted when at one and the same time and place—with the exception of those ungrateful to Christ—they experienced a movement of their hearts for the better: a movement caused by him at the words of the same Lady Birgitta and which they confessed had been sent by him.

58. *How Lady Birgitta was judged by a certain bishop in his heart, and what things came to her.*

One time, at a banquet, when the bride of Christ was sitting at table with a certain devout bishop and, in God's honor, was making use of the delicacies that had been served, she was judged by the bishop interiorly in his mind; for he said in his heart: "Why does this lady of such great spirit not abstain from delicate foods?" Then, toward vespers, she herself, knowing nothing of such thoughts, heard these things in spirit: "Say to the bishop, 'I am he who filled the shepherd with my Spirit. Was this because of the shepherd's fasting?[74] I am he who made married men prophets. What had they done to merit this? I commanded a prophet to take an adulteress as his wife. Did he not obey?[75] I am he who spoke as well to Job in his delights as when he sat upon the dunghill. Therefore, because I am wonderful, I do all things that please me without dependence on preceding merits.' " And so, hearing this, the bishop recognized himself and now humbled asked the same Lady Birgitta to pray for him. And then, on the third day, the most Blessed Virgin Mary appeared to that same bride of Christ and said to her: "Say to that same bishop that because he is accustomed to begin all his sermons with praise of me[76] and because his judgment was made with charity rather than envy, his charity thus merits consolation. Tell him, therefore, that I want to be a mother to him and that I want to present his soul to God. And now I shall expound to you how he is the seventh animal of the animals shown to you and how he will carry my words into the presence of kings and pontiffs." This revelation of the seven animals is more fully recorded in the book of the revelations.[77]

59. *How Lady Birgitta returned from the king of Sweden and how her son died.*

And so, when Lady Birgitta returned from the king of Sweden to the monastery of Alvastra, she found that a son of hers—who, when she left, had long been infirm—was now *in extremis*.[78] And she wept much over his long infirmity and reckoned that it was happening because of the sins of his parents. Then the devil appeared to her and said: "Why, woman, with all this water of tears, are you weakening your sight and laboring in vain? Could water ascend to heaven?"[79] In the same hour, Christ appeared to his bride in his human form and said: "This boy's infirmity has not been caused by constellations of stars—as the foolish say—nor by his sins. He has become infirm because of his physical condition and so that his crown will be greater. Therefore, if he has hitherto been called by his own name, Benedict, Ulf's son, from now on he shall be called the son of tears[80] and prayers; and I shall put an end to his distress. In fact, on the fifth day afterward, there was heard a most sweet singing, as it were, of birds between the boy's bed and the wall;[81] and, behold, then the boy's soul went forth; and the Holy Spirit said to that same Lady Birgitta: "Behold what tears accomplish! Now the son of waters has passed over to his rest. Therefore the devil hates the tears of good people, which proceed from divine charity."

60. *About a brother who lay in his infirmity for three years and more.*

In the said monastery of Alvastra, a certain lay brother of holy life was infirm for three years and more. At Christ's command, his bride visited the brother and said to him: "Repent with greater attention[82] because there is something hidden in your heart. As long as you keep it hidden, you will not be able to die." When he answered that he had nothing that had not been disclosed in penance, she said: "Ask with what intention you entered the monastery and with what intention you have lived up to now." Then he dissolved in tears and said: "Blessed be God who has sent you to me. Now that you have spoken, I want to tell the truth; for I do have something hidden that I never dared to betray because, as often as I repented, my tongue was always, as it were, tied and indeed excessive shame invaded me so that I did not open the matter. Therefore, as often as I made my confession, I invented for myself a new conclusion to my words, saying at the end: 'I declare to God and to all God's saints that I am culpable of all the crimes that I have told to you, Father, and of all those that I have not told.' I believed that through this conclusion, all was forgiven. But now, if it should please God, I would gladly tell the whole world." And when a confessor had been called, he fully explained everything with tears; and he did not survive long afterward.

61. *About a temptation to gluttony with which Lady Birgitta was tempted.*

Now at one time, Lady Birgitta was so gravely tempted with gluttony[83] that for hunger, she could scarcely think of anything else. Finally, in spirit, she saw an Ethiopian[84] holding in his hand, as it were, a morsel of bread and a certain very handsome youth holding a gilded vessel. And the youth said: "Why do you solicit that woman who has been given over into my custody?"[85] The Ethiopian responded: "Because she glories in an abstinence that she has not had; for she does not cease to fill her belly until it is full of delicate dung. I therefore hold forth my morsel that grosser things may, for her, become sweet." The youth responded: "You know quite well that she does not have an immaterial nature as we do but, rather, a sack made of earth.[86] Since earth is slippery and restless, she needs continual re-creation." The Ethiopian said: "Your Christ[87] fasted, eating nothing; and the prophets ate bread and drank water in moderation. Therefore they merited lofty things. And how will that woman merit when she always feels a satiety?" The youth responded: "Is Christ not yours too as well as ours?" To which the other said: "By no means at all! For I will never humble myself to him but will rather act in opposition to him because I shall not return to his glory!" The youth responded: "Our Christ taught us to fast, not so that the body would be weakened beyond measure, but so that it would be humbled and not grow insolent in opposition to its soul. Our Christ does not ask for things impossible to nature but for moderation; he does not ask the quality or the quantity of what one eats but, rather, the quality of the eater's intention and charity." To which the Ethiopian said: "It is just that what that woman did not experience in youth, she should feel in old age." In rebuttal, the youth said: "The praiseworthy thing is abstinence from sin. There is no obstacle to heaven in purple dye or in delicate flesh when these things are possessed together with the love of God. Sometimes the customs of one's upbringing must be maintained well, with thanksgiving, lest the flesh be too seriously weakened." After this, at that same hour, the Virgin Mary appeared to her—wearing a crown—and said to the Ethiopian: "Be silent, you negotiator; look askance, because she has been assigned to me!"[88] And the Ethiopian spoke: "If I cannot do anything else," he said, "I will cast a bramble of the Christ's-thorn plant onto the hem of her garments." To which the Virgin said: "I will help her. And as often as you cast it on, it shall be cast back into your face; and her crown will be doubled." Not long after this vision, the whole temptation to gluttony[89] was taken away.

62. *How she was tempted at prayer.*

During her prayers, the bride of Christ was sometimes tempted even with unclean thoughts. Blessed Mary appeared to her and said: "The devil is like an envious spy, seeking to accuse and impede the good. Therefore try and pray[90] as long as you are being tempted because your desire and good effort will count for you as prayer; and if you cannot cast out of your mind the sordid matters that come to it, those efforts will count for you as merit provided that you not consent and as these things are against your will."

63. *How the prayer of the bride of God was of profit to someone.*

A certain religious was tempted for twelve years concerning the Sacrament of the Body of Christ and concerning the name of blessed Mary, whom he could never name without sordid thought and blasphemy. And so for a long time he omitted even the Angelic Salutation.[91] With tears, he asked Lady Birgitta, the bride of Christ, to pray for him; and, obtaining her prayers, he was so freed that, afterward, he rarely pronounced the name of blessed Mary without great joy; and the Body of Christ became so sweet[92] to him that he could not rest on a day when he did not celebrate Mass. For a long time, this same man had a desire to visit the holy places in Jerusalem; but, out of obedience and because of his profession, he was not permitted to do so. When he was *in extremis,* he was enraptured and saw all those places in spirit just as did those who have seen them in body; and when he had shown the arrangement of those places to those who had previously visited them, he passed away, exulting in the Lord.

64. *How the bride of Christ was instructed to go to Rome and to testify to the grace of God.*

However, after the passage of almost two years in the Cistercian order's aforesaid monastery of Saint Mary of Alvastra, Christ instructed her to go to Rome, even as it is recorded in the following revelation.

65. *A revelation concerning the same thing.*

Our Lord Jesus Christ once spoke to this same Birgitta and said: "Go to Rome, where the streets are paved with gold and reddened with the blood of saints and where there is a compendium—i.e., a shorter way—to heaven because of the indulgences that the holy pontiffs have merited by their prayers. Moreover, you shall stay there in Rome until you see the supreme pontiff and the emperor there at the same time in Rome, and to them you shall announce my words."

66. *What she did on the way to Rome.*

After she had gone forth from her fatherland, she was divinely instructed in a vision to give up her customary reading and learn grammar.[93] This was when she was given blessed Agnes[94] for her solace and Master Peter,[95] her confessor, for a teacher to instruct her and that she might obey him. Moreover, the said lady, in a brief time, made so much progress in grammatical knowledge that she knew in part how to read, to understand, and to utter Latin speech.[96]

67. *How she was divinely instructed to go to Naples and visit there the places of saints.*

After she had stayed a long time in Rome, Christ spoke to her thus and said: "Permission is given you to visit the holy places in Sicily[97] because in that place are the bodies of many who loved me with all their heart. Outstanding among them is Thomas, my apostle. When you arrive there, I am going to show you certain secrets." And since she hesitated somewhat lest her money for expenses chance to fail on the way, the Lord answered: "One who possesses a meadow does not spare the meadow in preference to his laboring horse. So I, the Lord, provide for my friends when their own providence fails; and I stir up the souls of others to do good to them." Look in the *Book of Heavenly Revelations* for a certain vision that was given to Lady Birgitta by Christ in the city of Ortona and which speaks about the praise of blessed Thomas and about that kingdom.[98]

68. *How in Rome she was divinely instructed to go to Jerusalem although the instruction did not determine the time.*

Christ once spoke to her and said: "I am like an eagle that foresees those flying in the air who want to harm its young and forestalls them by its own flight lest they do the harm; so I foresee the times and the ways and the ways' difficulties and the dispositions of souls. And so I say to you:[99] sometimes, 'Stand and wait'; now, 'Go and hurry.' Therefore, because it is already the time, go now to the places previously shown to you: where there was a vessel, clean and not clean; and where there was a lamb, shorn and not shorn; where a lion roared and did not roar; where a serpent moved and did not move; where an eagle flew to a place from which it has never withdrawn." See in the *Book of Questions,* in the last and the next-to-last chapters, where these things are recorded and divinely clarified.[100] And when she complained of bodily infirmity and of decrepit age, then an answer came to her from Christ: "Who is the Establisher of nature? Is it not I? Therefore I will increase your strength. I will provide for the way. I will guide you and lead you back[101] to this place in Rome."

69. On a certain occasion—fifteen years before the incident that we last mentioned above—when Lady Birgitta was praying in Rome, the Virgin Mary appeared to her and said: "Because of the exceeding love that you have for me, I tell you that you will go to Jerusalem when it pleases my Son; and then you will go also to Bethlehem; and I then will show to you how I gave birth to my Son, Jesus Christ."[102] This promise the Virgin Mary fulfilled sixteen years later, when Lady Birgitta was in these said places—as is more amply recorded in the books of revelations, in a certain revelation made to her in Bethlehem that speaks of the Virgin Mary's childbearing.[103]

70. *How she was divinely commanded, while she was in Jerusalem, to return again to Rome.*

On a certain occasion, while Lady Birgitta was praying in Jerusalem, Christ appeared to her and said: "All the places that other pilgrims visit, you too will visit. For there are still other places where I was in the body and which should be visited; but it is sufficient for you to seek out the nearer ones because of your infirmity and because it is not yet the time of that mercy of which mention has been made; for there are very few who reflect upon the charity of my passion and of my patience. But when you have come back from the Jordan, prepare yourselves[104] for your journey; for there are still some things to be sent to the supreme princes of the earth." Look for the many and beautiful revelations that are contained in the *Heavenly Book* and which were made to that same Lady Birgitta in Jerusalem and in Bethlehem.[105]

71. *About a special sign of the Spirit.*

One should also know that from the first time that the bride of God was visited by the Spirit of God she had this sign: that, when she was approached by human beings full of diabolic spirit or who were averse to goodness, she felt so great a stench in her nostrils and so bitter a taste in her mouth that she could hardly bear it.[106] Wherefore, when a certain man—who had undergone a change away from goodness and had returned to his earlier sins—had sat down with the bride of God and was speaking with her, he said to her: "What is this about a spirit that you are said to have? Is it from you or from someone else or from a demon?" To this she—who scarcely had the strength to bear his stench—responded: "You have a fetid indweller, and fetid things proceed from your mouth. Repent, therefore, lest there come upon you the vengeance of God!" The man went away angry; and, when he had gone to sleep, he heard voices without number saying: "Let us drag the pig to the places for pigs because he has spurned the warnings of salvation." Returning to himself, he perfectly corrected his life; and his odor was perceived by the said lady to have changed into sweetness.

72. A similar thing, as it were, happened to the same Lady Birgitta in Famagusta, in the kingdom of Cyprus, with a certain religious to whom she was speaking;[107] and with many other people, this similarly happened to her.

73. *Item concerning the same thing.*

The bride of God had also this special trait: that, in the twenty-eight years from the time she began to have the Spirit of God, she never went or made any change to other cities nor ever tarried in any place except in accord with the infusion and instruction of the Holy Spirit.

74. *About the city of Milan.*

When she was in Milan, she stayed there a long time; and there, amidst other words, the Blessed Virgin Mary responded to the words of a certain great master of theology, as is recorded in the *Book of Heavenly Revelations.*[108]

75. *About Rome.*

In truth, the said Lady Birgitta stayed in Rome a rather long time, not only because of the indulgences but also because of the promises to be fulfilled. There, in manifold ways, she experienced visitations both concerning the state of the City and concerning the reparation of all states.[109] There too, she was informed with certainty about many things in the future, as is shown in the revelations made to her, which are more amply recorded in her books.

76. There also in Rome the promise was fulfilled that had been made to her in a revelation in Sweden many years before: namely, that she would go to Rome and would stay there until she saw there the pope and the emperor.

77. Moreover, when the lord pope, Urban V, wanted to return from Italy to Avignon, the Virgin Mary appeared to the said Lady Birgitta and said to her some words in a vision, saying that this same lord pope should not return from Rome, nor from Italy, to Avignon; otherwise, the outcome would be to his loss in a brief time—as is more amply recorded in that revelation which the same Lady Birgitta, with her own hand, presented to that same lord pope in Montefiascone. And present there, on that occasion, was our lord pope, Gregory XI, who was then called Cardinal Beaufort.[110]

78. Moreover there, on that occasion in Montefiascone, the Virgin Mary instructed her to tell, on her own behalf, a certain hermit-priest Alphonsus, a friend and acquaintance of hers, to write down and copy the books of the revelations that had been divinely given to her and which indeed until then had been kept secret. At the death of this same lady, Christ confirmed this by instructing the same Lady Birgitta to tell her confessors to hand over to the said hermit all the secret revelations and all others that they had not yet handed over in order that this same hermit might have them written out and that he might publish them to the nations for the honor and glory of God.[111]

79. Moreover, in Naples and in Jerusalem too, she stayed for a long time; and there she saw some visions concerning the state and the tribulation of kingdoms and concerning the nativity and the passion of Jesus Christ and concerning the calling of the nations. Wherefore, in Jerusalem, Christ spoke to her: "My words," he said, "must for a long time be heard and proclaimed; works and signs will come afterward. Therefore, know that there are many not yet born who are going to receive my words sweetly. Wherefore, as it says in my gospel: 'Blessed are they who hear the words of God';[112] so I say now: 'Blessed are they who now hear my words and will perform them in deed.' Nevertheless, know that after your passing more will receive my words and will follow them with sweetness, for they are not like a flower that will fall but like a fruit that lasts for eternity."

80. One should know also that although during her husband's life

Lady Birgitta had done some penance in a hidden way, nevertheless after his death she was not content with this penance. Indeed, for thirty years she used no linen garments except the veils for her head.

81. Also, before her bed, she had them put on the pavement a coverlet and a little cushion for under her head; and thus she used to sleep there, having over her a single garment or a mantle. When questioned as to how she could rest there in the very intense cold that prevails in those parts of Sweden, she spoke in answer: "I feel," she said, "within myself so great a warmth from divine grace that the cold that is without does not much urge me toward a softer bed."

82. Day and night, however, she was accustomed to perform so many genuflections, bows, and prostrations[113] that it was a wonder that so tender a person could endure such great labors.

83. It was her custom too, on Fridays, to pour on her bare flesh flaming drops from a burning candle so that they left wounds remaining; and if at any time before the next Friday these wounds healed somewhat by themselves, she then at once put her nails in and plowed them so[114] that her body would not be without the suffering of wounds; and this she did for the sake of the memory of the passion of Christ. She also had knotty bands of cord with which she girded herself right against her flesh and which she never removed, day or night, whether she was ill or well.

84. When, however, she came to these parts of Rome and of Italy, she visited the holy places with devotion and great frequency; and with sufficiently great toil to herself, she observed the practice of not speaking voluntarily[115] with anyone on the way unless she happened to have been asked a question—in which case she replied with very few words to the one speaking to her. And whenever she uttered any unconsidered word, then at once, on the cord that hung upon her breast for saying the paternoster,[116] she diligently noted that word by which she had offended God, in order that she might not neglect to confess it and make satisfaction for it by means of penance.

85. Similarly too, when she visited shrines, she held her eyes in check so as not to look voluntarily[117] at the faces of human beings. When, however, it happened that she had suddenly looked into someone's face, at once, on that same chaplet that hung at her neck, she kept a token,[118] until, through penance, satisfaction for it had been made.

86. From her infancy, she was accustomed to confess every Friday. But nevertheless, she was not content with this; no, she also confessed more than once on every day of the year concerning light words and

thoughts. For in her there was fear of God together with great love of him.

87. On Fridays, indeed, because of Christ's passion and the bitterness of the drink of gall proffered to him before his death, she was accustomed to hold in her mouth a certain very bitter herb, which is called *genciana*.[119] She also did this on other days when she had uttered some unconsidered or incautious word.

88. In making her confession, she was very humble and very prompt in fulfilling whatever things were enjoined upon her.

89. Moreover, she so loved true humility that in no place did she wish to be without an instructor whom she humbly obeyed in all things.

90. Moreover, she so loved poverty that everything that she had in her possession she put into the hands of another; and when she wished to have something, she asked her confessor the master for it in the name of Jesus Christ as humbly as if she had never possessed it.

91. She attended to the welfare of the persons living with her even more than she did to her own. For sometimes she was actually concealing her own ruined shoes even while asking for new ones to be given to others;[120] and she acted similarly concerning other necessary things.

92. Indeed, she very patiently endured everything that came; and the Blessed Virgin once spoke to her thus in a vision: "You," she said, "should be like a mirror, clear and clean, and like a sharp thorn—a mirror through honest and godly behavior and through good example, but a thorn through denunciation of sinners.[121] In fact, Lady Birgitta well demonstrated the latter point; for, wherever she was, she did this to the best of her ability. She showed it well in Famagusta while, in the presence of the king and the queen and the princes and the other magnates of the kingdom of Cyprus, she seriously and boldly narrated a revelation made to her in Jerusalem concerning the kingdom of Cyprus —despite the fact that at that time she was physically weak and infirm. This revelation too is contained in the books of the *Heavenly Revelations*.[122]

93. Moreover, in Naples too she did not keep silent about a revelation made to her concerning the people of that same city but related it in the presence of the archbishop and three masters of theology and other doctors of canon and civil law and the other lords and prudent men, both clerical and lay. She intrepidly reproved the sins of the city and showed how they might amend their lives—just as Jesus Christ had instructed her in a revelation and as it is more clearly and more amply recorded in the books of revelations.[123]

94. Furthermore, while she was in Jerusalem, she began to weaken; and this infirmity of hers lasted for a whole year. And both at sea and on land, she most patiently endured fatigue and pain; and it was of this infirmity that she died in Rome.

95. It happened, finally, in Rome—five days before the day of her passing—that our Lord Jesus Christ appeared to her in front of the altar that stood in her chamber. He showed himself with a joyful face and said to her: "I had done to you what a bridegroom usually does, concealing himself from his bride so that he may be more ardently desired. Thus I have not visited you with consolations during this time; for it was the time of your testing. Therefore, now that you have been tested, go forward and prepare yourself; for now is the time when—as I had promised you—before my altar, you shall be clothed and consecrated as a nun. And henceforth you shall be counted not only as my bride, but also as a nun and a mother in Vadstena."[124] This is a certain villa that is called by this name; and there stands that monastery of nuns and brothers whose construction was revealed to her by God and where the said lady was to be buried. Finally Christ said to her: "Nevertheless, know that you will lay down[125] your body in Rome until it come to the place prepared for it. For it pleases me to spare you from your labors and to accept your will in place of the completed action."[126]

96. After these and many other things had been said, she made mention of and arrangements for some persons living with her and whom, before death, she said she had seen standing in God's presence.[127]

97. After those things had been heard, the Lord added these words: "On the morning of the fifth day, after receiving the sacraments, call together one by one all those whom I named above; and to them tell the things to be done. And thus, amidst these words and their hands, you will come to your monastery—i.e., into my joy; and your body will be placed in Vadstena."[128] Then, as the fifth day approached,[129] at the moment of dawn, Christ appeared to her again and consoled her. But when Mass had been said and after she had received the sacraments, in the hands of the aforesaid persons[130] she sent forth her spirit.[131]

The Fifth Book of Revelations
or
Book of Questions [132]

Here begins the prologue to the fifth book of heavenly revelations which is called the Book of Questions.[133]

Here begins the fifth book of Christ's heavenly revelations to blessed Birgitta of the kingdom of Sweden. It is deservedly entitled the *Book of Questions* because it proceeds by means of questions to which Christ the Lord gives wonderful solutions. 2. It was revealed to that same lady in a wonderful way, as she and her confessors often testified in their own words.[134] 3. For it once happened that on a certain day,[135] she was riding a horse[136] and traveling to her castle at Vadstena[137] in the company of many members of her household who were riding along with her. Then, as she was thus riding along the road, she began to raise her mind to God in prayer. 4. And at once she was caught up in spirit and went, as it were, outside herself, alienated from the senses of her body and suspended in an ecstasy of mental contemplation. 5. She saw then, in spirit, a ladder[138] which was fixed in the earth and whose top touched the sky. And at its top, in the sky, she saw the Lord Jesus Christ seated on a wonderful throne like a judge judging. 6. At his feet stood the Virgin Mary; and round about the throne, there was an infinite army of angels and a teeming multitude of saints. 7. And, in the middle of that same ladder, the aforesaid Lady Birgitta saw a certain religious, known to her and at that time still alive in the body[139]—a man of great erudition in the science of theology but full of guile and diabolic malice. 8. Because of his extremely impatient and restless gestures, this man looked more like a devil than a humble religious. 9. And then the said lady saw the thoughts and all the internal affections of the heart of that religious and how he manifested them with inordinate and restless gestures, by means of questions, to Christ the Judge seated on the throne—as follows below. 10. And then the Lady Birgitta herself saw and heard in spirit how Christ the Judge, with most meek and dignified gestures, replied briefly to each question with great wisdom and how, at times, our Lady, the Virgin Mary, spoke some words to the same Lady Birgitta—as this book will show in greater detail[140] below.

11. Moreover, after the lady had in her mind, in a single instant, the whole of this book by means of one and the same revelation and while she was now approaching the aforementioned castle, the members of her household grasped the bridle of her horse and began to shake her and, as it were, to awaken her from that rapture. 12. And when she had returned to herself, she was exceedingly grieved by the fact that she was now deprived of such divine sweetness.

13. This *Book of Questions* then remained fixed in her heart and her memory as effectively as if it had all been carved on a marble tablet. 14. But she herself immediately wrote it out in her own language;[141] and her confessor translated it into the literary tongue,[142] just as he had been accustomed to translate the other books of revelations.

FIRST INTERROGATION

I saw a throne in the sky, and on it sat the Lord Jesus Christ as Judge.[143] Before his feet sat the Virgin Mary; and around the throne, there was an army of angels and an infinite multitude of saints. 2. A religious,[144] very learned in theology, stood on a high rung[145] of a ladder which was fixed in the earth and whose summit touched the sky. His gestures were very impatient and restless, as if he were full of guile and malice. He questioned the Judge, saying:

3. *First question.* "O Judge, I ask you: You have given me a mouth. May I not say the things that please me?"

4. *Second question.* "You have given me eyes. May I not see with them those things that delight me?"

5. *Third question.* "You have given me ears. Why am I not to hear with them those things that please me?"

6. *Fourth question.* "You have given me hands. Why am I not to do with them what agrees with me?"

7. *Fifth question.* "You have given me feet. Why shall I not walk with them as I desire?"

8. *Christ's response to the first question.* The Judge, who sat on the throne and whose gestures were meek and very dignified, replied: "Friend, I gave you a mouth that you might speak rationally about things that are useful for your body and soul and about things that belong to my honor."

9. *Response to the second question.* "Second, I gave you eyes that you might see evils to be fled and healthful things to be kept."

10. *Response to the third question.* "Third, I gave you ears that you might hear those things that belong to truth and honesty."

11. *Response to the fourth question.* "Fourth, I gave you hands that with them you might do those things that are necessary for the body and not harmful to the soul."

12. *Response to the fifth question.* "Fifth, I gave you feet that you might draw back from love of the world and go to your soul's rest and love and to me, your Creator and Redeemer."

SECOND INTERROGATION

First question. Again the same religious appeared on his rung as before and said: "O Christ, Judge, you voluntarily bore most bitter pain. Why may I, for that reason, not treat myself honorably and take pride in this world?"

2. *Second question.* "Item.[146] You have given me temporal goods. Why then may I not possess those things that I crave?"

3. *Third question.* "Item. Why have you given me limbs for my body if I am not to move them and exercise them as I will?"

4. *Fourth question.* "Item. Why have you given law and justice if not for doing vengeance?"

5. *Fifth question.* "Item. You have permitted us to have rest and quiet. Why have you arranged for us to feel weariness and tribulation?"

6. *Response to the first question.* The Judge replied: "Friend, man's pride is long tolerated out of my patience in order that my humility may be exalted and my virtue may be manifested. 7. And because pride was not created by me but was invented by the devil, it therefore must be fled because it leads to hell. But humility must be practiced because it leads to heaven. And I, God, have taught it by my word and my example."[147]

8. *Response to the second question.* "Item. I have given and entrusted temporal goods to man that man might have the use of them in a rational way and that he might exchange these created things for that which is uncreated—namely, for me, the Lord and Creator—by praising and honoring me for my good things and by not living in accord with the desire of the flesh."

9. *Response to the third question.* "Item. The body's limbs are given to man so that they may represent for the soul a similitude[148] of the virtues and be for the soul, as it were, its instruments for duty and virtue."[149]

10. *Response to the fourth question.* "Item. Justice and law have been instituted by me that they may be accomplished with supreme charity and compassion and that divine unity and concord may be strengthened among humans."

11. *Response to the fifth question.* "Item. I enabled man to have bodily rest and quiet in order to strengthen the weakness of the flesh and to make the soul gain power and strength. 12. But because the flesh is sometimes imprudently insolent, one must cheerfully tolerate tribulations and all those things by which the flesh may be corrected."

THIRD INTERROGATION

First question. Again the same religious appeared on his rung as before and said: "O Judge, I ask you: Why did you give us bodily senses if we are not to move and live according to the feelings of the flesh?"

2. *Second question.* "Item. Why have you given us things to nourish and sustain the flesh—namely, foods and other delights—if we are not to live to our own satisfaction according to our carnal appetites?"

3. *Third question.* "Item. Why have you given us free will if not to follow our own choice?"

4. *Fourth question.* "Item. Why have you given men and women sexual organs and the seed for intercourse if it may not be spilt according to the appetites of the flesh?"[150]

5. *Fifth question.* "Item. Why have you given a heart and a will if not to like that which tastes sweeter and love that which is more delightful to enjoy?"

6. *Response to the first question.* The Judge replied: "Friend, I gave man sense and intelligence that he might consider and imitate the ways of life, and flee the ways of death."

7. *Response to the second question.* "Item. I gave foods and the necessities of the flesh for the body's moderate sustenance and so that it might more vigorously execute the virtues of the soul and not be weakened by excessive consumption."

8. *Response to the third question.* "Item. I gave man free will for this reason: that he himself might abandon his own will because of me, his God, and that thereby, man might gain greater merit."

9. *Response to the fourth question.* "Item. I gave the seed for intercourse for this reason: that it might germinate in the proper way and in the proper place and that it might bear fruit for a just and rational cause."

10. *Response to the fifth question.* "Item. I gave man a heart so that he might enclose in it me, his God, who am everywhere and incomprehensible, and so that his delight might be in thinking of me."

The first revelation in the Book of Questions—*made to Lady Birgitta by the Virgin Mary—in which Mary informs her about five virtues which she ought to have inside herself and five others outside.*[151]

The Mother speaks: "Daughter, you must have five inward things and five outward. First outwardly: a mouth clean of all detraction, ears closed to idle talk, modest eyes, hands busy with good works, and withdrawal from the world's way of life. 2. Item. Inwardly, you must have five things: namely, fervent love for God, a wise longing for him, the distribution of your temporal goods with a just and right intention and in a rational way, humble flight from the world, and a long-suffering and patient expectation of my promises."

FOURTH INTERROGATION

First question. Again the same religious appeared on his rung as before and said: "O Judge, why should I search for God's wisdom when I have the wisdom of the world?"
2. *Second question.* "Why should I mourn and weep when the world's joy and glory are mine in abundance?"[152]
3. *Third question.* "Item. Tell me why or how I ought to rejoice in the afflictions of the flesh."
4. *Fourth question.* "Item. Why should I fear when I have the force of my own strength?"
5. *Fifth question.* "Item. Why am I to obey others if my will is in my own control?"
6. *Response to the first question.* The Judge replied: "Friend, everyone who is wise toward the world is blind toward me, his God. And therefore, to acquire my divine wisdom, it is necessary that one seek after it with diligence and humility."
7. *Response to the second question.* "Item. Everyone who has the world's honors and its joy is driven by various cares and is involved in bitter things that lead to hell. 8. Therefore, in order not to deviate from the way of heaven, it is necessary to be devoutly cautious, to weep,[153] and to pray."

9. *Response to the third question.* "Item. It is very useful to rejoice amidst the affliction and infirmity of the flesh because my mercy draws near to one who has afflictions of the flesh; and through that mercy, such a person more easily approaches eternal life."

10. *Response to the fourth question.* "Item. Everyone who is strong gets his strength from me, and I am stronger than he. Therefore, one must everywhere fear that strength will be taken away."

11. *Response to the fifth question.* "Item. Whoever has free will in his own hands ought to fear and truly understand that nothing so easily leads to eternal punishment as one's own will without a leader. 12. Therefore, one who relinquishes his own will to me, his God, and obeys me will have heaven without punishment."

FIFTH INTERROGATION

First question. Again, the same religious appeared as before and said: "O Judge, why have you created worms which can harm and cannot profit?"

2. *Second question.* "Item. Why have you created ferocious beasts that also harm human beings?"

3. *Third question.* "Item. Why do you send infirmities and pains into bodies?"

4. *Fourth question.* "Item. Why do you suffer the iniquity of unjust judges who afflict their subjects and scourge them as if they were bought slaves?"[154]

5. *Fifth question.* "Item. Why is man's body troubled even in the moment of death?"

6. *Response to the first question.* The Judge replied: "Friend, I, God and Judge, created heaven and earth and all that is in them—but nothing without a reason and nothing without a similarity[155] to spiritual things. 7. For, just as the souls of the saints resemble the holy angels who have life and happiness, so the souls of the unjust resemble the demons who have everlasting death. 8. Therefore, because you have asked why I created worms, I answer you that I created them to show the manifold power of my wisdom and goodness. 9. For even though they can harm, nevertheless they do not harm except by my permission and because sin requires it in order that man, who scorns submission to his own superior, may groan over his ability to be troubled by this lowest of things and thus may know that he is nothing without me, whom even irrational things serve and at whose beckoning all things stand.[156]

10. *Response to the second question.* "Item. As to why I created ferocious beasts, I answer: All that I created was not only good, but even very good,[157] and was created either for man's benefit and testing or for the good of the other creatures and so that man, being so much happier than all others, might serve me, his God, all the more humbly. 11. Moreover, beasts do harm in temporal things for two reasons: first, for the recognition and reproof of wickedness so that the wicked may understand from their scourges that they must obey me, their superior. 12. Second, beasts also harm the good in order to advance their virtue and to purge them. And because man, by sinning, has raised himself up against me, his God, therefore all things which had been subject to man have been raised up against him."

13. *Response to the third question.* "Item. As to why infirmity comes to the body, I answer: This happens as a major warning and also because of the vices of incontinency and excess, in order that man may learn spiritual moderation and patience by bridling his flesh."

14. *Response to the fourth question.* "Item. Why is there toleration for unjust judges? This happens for the purging of others and because of my own patience. Just as gold is purged in the fire, even so, through the malice of the wicked, souls are purged and educated and drawn back from things that must not be done. 15. Therefore, I patiently tolerate the wicked so that the ears of the devil's grain may be separated from the wheat of the good and so that out of my hidden and divine justice their desire may be fulfilled."

16. *Response to the fifth question.* "Item. Why does the body suffer punishment in death? It is just that man be punished in ways similar to the ways of his sinning. And because he sins through inordinate pleasure, it is right that he be stricken with a measure of bitterness and pain. 17. Therefore, for some, death begins here—a death that will endure without end in hell. For others, death ends in purgatory; and then begins everlasting joy."

The second revelation in the Book of Questions, *in which the Virgin Mary speaks to blessed Birgitta and says that one who desires to taste divine sweetness must first endure bitterness.*

The Mother speaks: "Which of the saints had the sweetness of the Spirit without first experiencing bitterness? Therefore, one who craves sweetness must not flee away from things that are bitter."

SIXTH INTERROGATION

First question. Again there appeared on the rung the same man as before, and he said: "O Judge, I ask you why one infant comes forth alive from its mother's womb and obtains baptism while another, after receiving a soul, dies within its mother's viscera?"

2. *Second question.* "Item. Why, for the just, do many things have an untoward outcome while, for the unjust, all things are as they wish?"

3. *Third question.* "Item. Why do plagues and famines come—and the inconveniences that afflict the body?"

4. *Fourth question.* "Item. Why does death come so unexpectedly that it can very rarely be foreseen?"

5. *Fifth question.* "Item. Why do you suffer men to go to war with deliberate wrath and envy and in a spirit of vengeance?"

6. *Response to the first question.* The Judge replied: "Friend, you question[158] not out of charity but only because I permit it. And that is why I answer you in a way that resembles words.[159] 7. You ask why one infant dies within its mother's viscera and another comes forth alive. 8. The reason is this. All the strength of a child's body is taken from the seed of its father and mother; but if it is conceived without due strength because of some infirmity of the father or the mother, it quickly dies. 9. As a result of the parents' neglect or lack of care—and also as a result of my divine justice—many things happen so that what was joined together quickly separates. 10. Nevertheless, although the soul had no longer time to vivify the body, it will not therefore meet with a harsh punishment but rather with a mercy known to me. 11. When the sun streams into a house, its rays alone are seen. Only those who gaze at the sky see the sun as it is in its beauty. So it is with the souls of such children. Because they lack baptism, they do not see my face. Nevertheless, they do draw nearer to mercy than to punishment—although not in the same way as my elect."[160]

12. *Response to the second question.* "Item. As to why untoward things[161] befall the just, I answer: My justice is that every just man should obtain what he seeks. But no man is just who does not desire to suffer untoward things for the sake of obedience and the perfection of justice and who does not do good to his neighbor out of divine charity. 13. My friends consider what I, their God and Redeemer, have done for them and what I have promised to them; and also they attentively see the wickedness in the world. Therefore, as a precaution, they more gladly seek—for my honor, for their own salvation, and for the avoidance of

sin—the untoward things of the world rather than its prosperity. 14. And therefore I permit tribulations to befall them. If some of them suffer with too little patience, I do not permit this to happen without a reason; and I stand by them in their trouble. 15. When a son, in his boyhood, is rebuked by a charitable mother, he does not know enough to thank her because he cannot weigh the cause for which he is being reproved; but when he has reached the age of discretion, he thanks his mother because through her instruction he has been drawn away from wrongdoing and has become accustomed to discipline and good behavior. I treat my elect in a similar way. 16. Because they entrust their will to me and love me above all things, they have tribulations for a time. And although, at present, they may not fully understand my benefactions, nevertheless I am doing what is best for them in the future. 17. But because the impious do not care about justice and are not afraid to inflict injuries and because they seek the transitory things of the world and love earthly delights, therefore, out of my justice, they prosper for a time, free from scourges, lest they sin the more if they be touched by untoward things. 18. However, not all the wicked are given what they desire—in order that they may know that it lies within my power to give gifts to whomever I will. For I grant good things even to the ungrateful and although they do not deserve them."

19. *Response to the third question.* "Item. As to why plagues and famines come, I answer: It is written in the law[162] that one who commits a theft must give back more than he took. 20. Because the ungrateful accept my gifts and abuse them and do not pay me the honor that is my due from them, I therefore exact of their bodies more trouble in the present in order to spare their souls in the future. 21. Sometimes, too, I spare the body and punish man in and through that which he loves so that he, who would not acknowledge me when he was happy, may recognize and understand me when he is troubled."

22. *Response to the fourth question.* "Item. As to why death comes suddenly, I answer: If man knew the time of his death, he would serve me out of fear and faint with sorrow. 23. Therefore, in order that man might serve me out of charity and that he might always be solicitous about himself and secure about me, the hour of his exit is uncertain— and deservedly so. 24. For, when man deserted that which was certain and true, it was necessary and right that he be afflicted with uncertainty."

25. *Response to the fifth question.* "Item. As to why I permit men to proceed to war while filled with wrath, I answer: Everyone who has the

full intention of harming his neighbor is like the devil and is the devil's member and his instrument. 26. I would be doing an injury to the devil if I deprived him of his servant without justice. 27. Therefore, even as I use an instrument of my own for whatever pleases me, so it is justice that in one who would rather be the devil's member than mine the devil operates and does his own deeds either for the purgation of others or for the completion of his malice—but only as I permit and as sin demands."[163]

SEVENTH INTERROGATION

First question. Again, the same religious appeared on his rung as before, and said: "O Judge, I ask you. Why are ugliness and beauty spoken of in the world?"

2. *Second question.* "Item. Why must I hate the world's beauty when I myself am beautiful and of noble descent?"

3. *Third question.* "Item. Why may I not extol myself above others although I am rich?"

4. *Fourth question.* "Item. Why may I not prefer myself to others although I am more honorable than they?"

5. *Fifth question.* "Item. Why may I not seek my own praise although I am good and praiseworthy?"

6. *Sixth question.* "Item. Why am I not to demand remuneration if I do convenient things[164] for others?"

7. *Response to the first question.* The Judge replied: "Friend, the ugliness and the beauty of this world are like bitterness and sweetness. The ugliness of the world—which is its contempt and its adversity—is a profitable sort of bitterness that heals the just. 8. The world's beauty is its prosperity; and this is a flattering sort of sweetness, but false and seductive. 9. Therefore he who flees the beauty of the world and spits out its sweetness will not come to the ugliness of hell or taste its bitterness, but will ascend to my joy. 10. Therefore, in order to escape the ugliness of hell and to acquire the sweetness of heaven, it is necessary to go after the world's ugliness rather than its beauty.[165] 11. For even though all things were well created by me and are all very good,[166] nevertheless one must beware especially of those things which can furnish an occasion for the loss[167] of the souls of those who use my gifts irrationally."

12. *Response to the second question.* "Item. As to why you must not

glory in your descent, I answer that what you received from your father was worthless, putrid, and dirty;[168] and that in your mother's womb you were as if dead and totally unclean. 13. It was not in your power to be born of noble or ignoble parents, but it was my pity and my goodness that brought you into this light. 14. Therefore, you who call yourself noble, humble yourself under me, your God, who arranged for you to be born of nobles. Conform yourself to your neighbor; for he is of the same matter as you—although by my providence you have come from what is, in the eyes of the world, a lofty lineage and he from a lowly one. 15. O you noble! Fear even more than he who is not noble, for the nobler and richer you are, the stricter will your accounting be and the greater your judgment because you have received more."[169]

16. *Response to the third question.* "Item. As to why you must not take pride in riches, I answer: The world's riches are yours only for your necessary nourishment and clothing. 17. The world was made in order that man—having sustenance for his body—might return, by means of labor and humility, to me, his God, whom he disobediently despised and for whom, in his pride, he had no care. 18. Moreover, if you say that temporal goods are yours, I tell you for very certain that you, as it were, violently usurp for yourself all those things that you have beyond your necessities. For all temporal goods ought to be common and, out of charity, equal for those in need.[170] 19. But you superfluously usurp for yourself things that should be given to others out of compassion. And yet, it is reasonable that many people have much more than others; they own it rationally and they distribute it with discretion. 20. Therefore, lest you be reproved more gravely at the judgment because you have received greater things than others, you are advised not to put yourself above others by boasting and by hoarding.[171] 21. For delightful as it is in this world to have more temporal things than others and to enjoy an abundance, at the judgment it will be a fearsome and exceedingly grave matter if one has managed even licit things unreasonably."

22. *Response to the fourth and fifth questions.*[172] "Item. As to why one must not seek personal praise, I answer: No one is good of himself except me, God alone;[173] and everyone who is good has received that goodness from me. 23. If then you, who are nothing, seek your own praise and not the praise of me, to whom belongs every perfect gift,[174] false is your praise and you do an injustice to me, your Creator. 24. Since all the goods that you have are from me, you should give to me all praise. And since I, your God, bestow upon you all temporal things— strength and health, conscience and discretion to think of what is more

beneficial to yourself, and time and life—it is I who should be honored for all these things that have been given to you, if you manage them well and reasonably. 25. But if you manage them badly, the fault and the ingratitude are yours alone."

26. *Response to the sixth question.* "Item. As to why one must not seek a temporal reward for good deeds in the present, I answer you: 27. If anyone does good to others with the intention of caring not for a recompense from man but only for such as I, God, choose to give him, such a person shall have much in return for little, the eternal in place of the temporal.[175] 28. But he who seeks something earthly in exchange for something temporal will have what he desires but will lose what is everlasting. Therefore, in order to obtain the eternal in exchange for what is transitory, it is better to seek recompense not from man but from me."[176]

EIGHTH INTERROGATION

First question. Again the same religious appeared on his rung as before and said: "O Judge, I ask you: Why do you permit it that gods are placed in temples and honored as yourself when your kingdom is nobler than any other?"

2. *Second question.* "Item. Why do you not cause your glory to be seen by humans in this life so that they may more fervently desire it?"

3. *Third question.* "Item. Since your saints and angels are more noble and more holy than all other creatures, why are they not seen by humans in this life?"

4. *Fourth question.* "Item. Since the pains of hell are incomparably horrible, why do you not cause them to be seen by humans in this life so that they may be fled?"

5. *Fifth question.* "Item. Since the demons are so incomparably deformed and horrible, why do they not appear to humans in a visible way? For then no one would follow them or consent to them."

6. *Response to the first question.* The Judge answered: "Friend, I am God, the Creator of all. I do not act less justly to the wicked than to the good; for I am justice itself. 7. My justice decrees that entrance into heaven must be obtained through steadfast faith and rational hope and fervent charity. 8. That which is more fervently loved by the heart is more frequently thought of and more diligently adored. 9. Such is the case with the gods that are placed in temples although they are neither

gods nor creators; for there is only one sole Creator—namely, I, God, the Father and the Son and the Holy Spirit. Nevertheless, the people and the owners of the temples love these gods more than they love me—their purpose being prosperity in this world and not life with me. 10. Therefore, if I were to annihilate those things which humans love more than they love me and if I were to permit myself to be adored against their will, I would indeed do them an injustice by taking away their free will and desire.[177] 11. And so, because they do not have faith in me, and since they have in their hearts something more delightful than I, it is therefore reasonable for me to permit them to fashion externally what they love and long for in their minds. 12. They love created things more than me, the Creator, whom they can know in a provable way from signs and deeds if only they would use their reason. Therefore, since they are blinded, cursed are their created works and cursed are their idols. 13. They will be put to shame and judged for their foolishness because they are unwilling to understand how sweet am I, their God, who with fervent love created man and redeemed him."[178]

14. *Response to the second question.* "Item. As to the reason why my glory is not seen, I answer: My glory cannot be spoken, and it cannot be compared to any other sweetness or goodness. 15. Therefore, if my glory were to be seen as it is, then man's perishable body would weaken and fail as did the senses of those who saw my glory on the mountain.[179] And also because of the soul's joy, the body would faint from its labor and would be incapable of physical activities. 16. Therefore, because there is no entrance into heaven without the labor of charity, and so that faith may have its reward and the body may be capable of work, my glory is hidden for a time in order that, through desire and faith, it may be seen all the more fully and happily forever."

17. *Response to the third question.* "Item. As to why the saints are not seen as they now exist, I answer: If my saints were seen openly and visibly spoke, they would be honored as I myself; and then too, faith would have no merit. 18. Nor would the frailty of flesh be strong enough to see them. Moreover, my justice does not will that such brightness be seen by such frailty. 19. Therefore, my saints are not heard or seen, as they now exist, in order that all honor may be shown to me and that man may know that no one is to be loved above me. 20. However, if my saints do sometimes appear, they do so, not in that form of glory in which they truly exist, but in that form in which—by hiding the fullness of their virtue—they can be seen without disturbing a corporeal intelligence."[180]

21. *Response to the fourth question.* "Item. As to why the pains of hell are not seen, I answer: If hell's pains were visibly seen as they now exist, man would be totally frozen with fear and would seek heaven out of fear and not out of love. 22. Since no one ought to seek heavenly joy out of fear of punishment but rather out of divine charity, these pains are therefore now hidden. 23. Indeed, before the separation of soul and body, those who are good and holy cannot taste that ineffable joy as it is; nor can the wicked taste their punishments. But when the soul has been separated from the body, then they will feel and experience what they were unwilling to probe with their understanding when it was still possible."

24. *Response to the fifth question.* "Item. As to why the demons do not appear visibly, I answer: If their horrible deformity were seen as it now exists, a soul seeing this would go out of its mind at the very sight; the whole body would begin to quiver like a trembling man's; drained by fear, the heart would die; and the feet would not be strong enough to support the other limbs. 25. Therefore, in order that the soul may remain stable in its sense, that the heart may be vigilant in its love for me, and that the body may be capable of laboring in my service, the demons' deformity is hidden—and so that the demons' evil endeavor may be restrained."

The third revelation, in which Christ speaks to his bride, blessed Birgitta, and gives her—in a similitude—instruction concerning a true physician who is a healer, a false physician who is a murderer, and a man who makes a guess. He says that if a man takes responsibility for sinners[181] and gives them help or opportunity for sinning and if they then die in sin, God will exact an account of the death[182] of those souls at his hand. But if he takes responsibility for them in order that they may cease from sinning and that they may be instructed by him in the virtues and if, through his teaching, they do amend, then he and they shall have a great reward from God.

The Son of God speaks: "When there is a sick man in the house, if a professional physician[183] goes in to see him, the physician quickly considers, from outward signs, what sickness the man has. 2. Therefore, if a physician who knows the sick man's illness gives him a remedy which results in death, he is denounced as a murderer and is not a true physician. 3. If someone knows how to cure and practices medicine for the sake of worldly repayment, he will receive no recompense from me. But if someone practices medicine for love of me and for my honor, then I am obligated to give him recompense.[184] 4. If someone who is not a master of medicine believes, according to his own guesswork, that this or that is good for the sick man and gives him something with a kind intention, then he must not be declared a murderer if the sick man dies—but rather, a presumptuous fool. 5. If, however, the sick man recovers as a result of the fool's medicine, then the fool must have the reward, not of a master, but of a guesser; for he gave the medicine, not out of knowledge, but only according to his own guesswork.

6. "Behold, I will tell you what these things mean. Those people known to you are spiritually sick and are inclined to pride and cupidity through following their own will. 7. Therefore, if their friend—whom I compare to a physician—grants them help and advice which causes them to transgress[185] through pride and ambition and to die spiritually, then I will indeed exact an account of their death at his hand. 8. For, although they die of their own iniquity, nevertheless—because he has been the minister and the cause of their death—he shall not be immune from punishment. 9. If, however, led by natural love, he coddles them and raises them up in the world for his own comfort and for worldly honor, he is not to hope for recompense from me. 10. But if, like a good physician, he thinks of them wisely and says to himself: 'These people are sick and need medicine. Therefore, although to them my remedy may seem bitter, nevertheless—because it is healthful—I will give it to them in order that they may not die a hard death. 11. Therefore, while restraining them, I shall give them food lest they faint from hunger; and I shall give them clothes that they may walk honestly in accord with their station; I shall keep them under my regimen that they may not become insolent; I shall also provide for their other needs in order that they may not be lifted up by pride or grow dissolute through presumption or have occasion to do harm to others.' 12. Such a physician as this will have a large recompense from me, for such admonishment is pleasing to me. 13. However, if their friend—thinking to himself—says this: 'I will give them the necessities, but I do not know whether this is expedient for them or not. Nevertheless, I do not believe that I am displeasing God or hindering their health;' and if they then die—or rather, transgress—because of his gift, their friend will not be declared a murderer. 14. Moreover, although the friend will not have a full recompense, nevertheless—to the extent that he loves their souls—his good will and kindly affection will relieve the sick and will cause them to grow toward that health that they would have more difficultly obtained without the cooperation of his charity. 15. However, one piece

of advice is necessary here. For according to a popular proverb,[186] a harmful kind of animal cannot do injury if it is enclosed; and being enclosed and receiving the necessities, it becomes just as strong and fat as the animal that lives at large and on its own. 16. Now, since these people are the kind whose heart and blood seek lofty things and whose will thirsts more the more it drinks, therefore their friend is not to give them any occasion to transgress; for they desire to inflame their appetites but lack the strength to extinguish them."[187]

THE NINTH INTERROGATION

First question. When these things had been said, the same religious appeared on his rung as before and said: "O Judge, I ask you: Why do you seem so unfair in your gifts and graces that you preferred your mother Mary to every other creature and exalted her above the angels?"

2. *Second question.* "Item. Why did you give the angels a spirit without flesh and the gift of being in heavenly joy, whereas to man you gave an earthen vessel[188] and a spirit—and birth with wailing, life with labor, and death with sorrow?"

3. *Third question.* "Item. Why did you give man a rational intellect and senses, whereas to animals you did not give reason?"

4. *Fourth question.* "Item. Why did you give life to animals, but not to the other created things that lack senses?"

5. *Fifth question.* "Item. Why is there not such light at night as there is in the day?"

6. *Response to the first question.* The Judge replied: "Friend, in my Godhead all that is going to exist or happen is foreseen and foreknown from the beginning as if it had already occurred. 7. The fall of man was foreknown, and out of God's justice it was permitted; but it was not caused by God and did not have to happen because of God's foreknowledge. Foreknown too from eternity was man's liberation, which was to happen out of God's mercy. 8. You now ask why I preferred my mother Mary to all others and loved her more than any other creature. It was because the special mark of virtues was found in her.[189] 9. When a fire is kindled and many logs surround it, the log most apt and efficient for combustion will be the quickest to catch the flame and burn. So it was with Mary. 10. For when the fire of divine love—which in itself is changeless and eternal—began to kindle and appear and when the

Godhead willed to become incarnate, no creature was more apt and efficient for receiving this fire of love than the Virgin Mary; for no creature burned with such charity as she. 11. And although her charity was revealed and shown at the end of time, it was nevertheless foreseen before the beginning of the world. 12. And so, from eternity, it was predetermined in the Godhead that as no one was found comparable to her in charity, so too no one would be her equal in grace and blessing."

13. *Response to the second question.* "Item. As to why I gave the angel a spirit without flesh, I answer: In the beginning and before time and the ages, I created spirits in order that of their own free choice they might live according to my will and thus rejoice in my goodness and glory. 14. But some of them took pride in their goodness and did evil to themselves by using their free will in an inordinate way. And because there was nothing evil in nature and creation except the inordinacy of their individual wills, they therefore fell. 15. But other spirits chose to take their stand in humility under me, their God; and therefore they merited eternal stability. 16. For it is right and just[190] that I, God, who am an uncreated spirit and the Creator and Lord of all, should also have in my service spirits more subtle and swift than other creatures. 17. And because it was not fitting for me to have any diminishment in my hosts, I therefore created, in place of those who fell, another creature—namely, man—who, through his free choice and his good will, might merit the same dignity that the angels deserted.[191] 18. And so, if man had a soul and no flesh, he would not be able to merit so sublime a good nor even be able to labor. The body was joined to the soul for the attainment of eternal honor. 19. Therefore, man's tribulations increase in order that he may experience his free will and his infirmities, to the end that he may not be proud. 20. And so that he may desire the glory for which he was created and that he may undo the disobedience that he voluntarily committed, he has therefore been given, out of divine justice, a tearful entrance and a tearful exit[192] and a life full of toils."

21. *Response to the third question.* "Item. As to why animals do not have a rational intellect as man does, I answer you: 22. Everything that has been created is for man's use or for his needs and sustenance or for his instruction and reproof or for his consolation and humiliation. 23. But if brutes had intelligence as man does, they would certainly be a trouble to him, causing harm rather than profit.[193] 24. Therefore, in order that all things may be subject to man[194]—for whom all things were made—and that all things might fear him, while he himself is to

fear no one but me, his God, animals have not been given a rational intellect."

25. *Response to the fourth question.* "Item. As to why insensate things have no life, I answer: Everything that lives is going to die, and every living thing moves unless it is impeded by some obstacle. 26. If, therefore, insensate things had life, they would move against man rather than for him. 27. And so, in order that everything might be for man's solace, higher beings—namely, the angels, with whom man shares reason and immortality of the soul—have been given to man for his protection; 28. and lower beings, whether they are sensate or not, have been given to him for his use and sustenance and instruction and training."

29. *Response to the fifth question.* "Item. As to why it is not always daylight, I will answer you by means of an example. Under every vehicle, i.e., a cart, there are wheels so that the burden placed upon it may be more easily moved; and the back wheels follow those in front.[195] 30. A similarity exists in spiritual matters. For the world is a great burden, burdening man with worries and troubles. And no wonder; for when man disdained the place of rest, it was right that he experienced a place of work. 31. Therefore, in order that the burden of this world may be more easily borne by man, mercifully there comes a change and alternation of times—namely: day and night, summer and winter[196]— for the sake of man's exercise and his rest. 32. When contrary things come together—namely, the strong and the weak—it is reasonable to condescend to the weak so that it can exist beside the strong; otherwise the weak would be annihilated. 33. So it also is with man. Even though, in the strength of his immortal soul, man could continue forever in contemplation and labor, nevertheless the strength of his weak body would fail.[197] 34. For this reason, light has been made so that man, who has a common bond with higher and lower beings, may be able to subsist by laboring in the day and remembering the sweetness of the everlasting light that he lost. 35. Night has been made that he may rest his body with the will of coming to that place where there is neither night nor labor, but rather everlasting day and eternal glory."[198]

The fourth revelation in the Book of Questions, *wherein Christ most beautifully praises all the limbs of his Virgin Mother Mary—moralizing the said limbs in a spiritual way by comparing them to virtues—and he pronounces this same Virgin most worthy of her queenly crown.*[199]

The Son speaks: "I am a crowned king in my Godhead, without beginning and without end. A crown[200] has neither beginning nor end, thus signifying my power which had no beginning and shall have no end. 2. But I had still another crown in my keeping; and this crown is I myself, God. 3. This crown was prepared for the one who had the greatest love for me; and you, my sweetest Mother, won it and drew it to yourself with your justice and your charity.[201] 4. For the angels and the other saints bear witness to the fact that in you there was a love for me more ardent than any other and a chastity more pure; and this pleased me more than all else. 5. Truly, your head was like gleaming gold[202] and your hair like the rays of the sun. For your most pure virginity—which in you is, as it were, the head of all your virtues—and your freedom from all illicit impulses[203] pleased me and shone in my sight with all humility. 6. Therefore, you are deservedly called a crowned queen over all that is created: "queen" because of your purity and "crowned" because of your excellent dignity. 7. Your brow was of an incomparable whiteness—signifying the modesty of your conscience, in which resides the fullness of human knowledge and in which the sweetness of divine wisdom shines upon all. 8. Your eyes were so lucid in my Father's sight that in them he gazed upon himself; for, in your spiritual vision and in your soul's intellect, the Father saw all your will—that you wanted nothing but him and desired nothing which did not please him. 9. Your ears were most pure and were open like the fairest windows when Gabriel made my will known to you and when I, God, became flesh in you. 10. Your cheeks were of the finest color—namely, white and ruddy[204]—for the fame of your praiseworthy deeds and the beauty of your character[205] daily burning within you pleased me. 11. At the beauty of your character, God my Father truly rejoiced; and he never turned his eyes away from you. And, out of your love, all have obtained love. 12. Your mouth was like a lamp—burning within and shining without—because the words and affections of your soul burned inwardly with divine understanding and shone outwardly in the praiseworthy control of your bodily motions and in the lovely harmony of your virtues. 13. Truly, dearest Mother, the word of your mouth[206] drew, in a way, my Godhead into you; and the fervor of your godly sweetness never separated me from you; for your words are sweeter than the honey and the comb.[207] 14. Your neck is nobly erect and beautifully elevated because the righteousness of your soul is entirely directed upward to me and moves in accord with my will, and has never inclined to any wickedness of pride. 15. For just as the neck curves with the head, so your every intention and operation bows to my will. 16. Your breast was so full of all the sweetness of the virtues that there is no good in me that would not be in you; for you drew all good into yourself through the sweetness of your character when it pleased my divinity to enter into you and my humanity to dwell with you and drink the milk of your breasts. 17. Your arms were beautiful through your true obedience and your tolerance of labors. Your bodily hands touched my humanity, and I rested in your arms with my divinity. 18. Your womb was as perfectly clean as ivory and shone like a place built of exquisite stones;[208] for your constancy of conscience and of faith never cooled and could not be spoiled by tribulation. 19. Of this womb—i.e., of your faith[209]—the walls were like the brightest gold; and on them was inscribed the fortitude of your virtues and your prudence and justice and temperance and your perfect perseverance; for all these virtues of yours were perfected by divine charity. 20. Your feet were clean and washed and drenched, as it were, with fragrant herbs; for your soul's hope and affections were directed to me, your God, and were fragrant with good example for others to imitate.[210] 21. To me, this place of your womb—the spiritual as well as the corporeal—was so desirable and your soul was so pleasing that I did not disdain[211] to come down to you from high heaven and tarry within you. No! This deed was my sweetest delight. 22. Therefore, dearest Mother, that crown which I had in my keeping —that crown which is I myself, God, who was to take flesh—was not to be placed on anyone but you because you are truly a mother and a virgin."

TENTH INTERROGATION

First question. Again the same religious appeared on his rung as before and said: "O Judge, I ask you: Since you are most mighty, most beautiful, and most virtuous, why did you cloak your divinity—which shines incomparably brighter than the sun—in such sackcloth[212]—namely, your humanity?"

2. *Second question.* "Item. How does your Godhead enclose all in itself and yet not be enclosed by anything? How does it contain all and yet not be contained by anything?"

3. *Third question.* "Item. Why did you will to lie so long a time in the

Virgin's womb? Why did you not come forth as soon as you had been conceived?"

4. *Fourth question.* "Item. Since you can do all things and are everywhere present, why did you not immediately appear in the stature that you had when you reached your thirtieth year?"

5. *Fifth question.* "Item. Since you were not born of Abraham's seed through a father,[213] why did you will to be circumcised?"

6. *Sixth question.* "Item. Since you were conceived and born without sin, why did you will to be baptized?"

7. *Response to the first question.* The Judge answered him: "Friend, I answer you with an example. There is a certain kind of grape whose wine is so strong that it comes forth from the grape without the touch of man.[214] 8. When the attentive owner sees the time of ripeness, he places a vessel down below. The wine is not waiting for the vessel, but the vessel for the wine. 9. But if several vessels are placed below, the wine pours into the vessel that is nearest. 10. This grape is my Godhead, which is so full of the wine of divine charity that all the choirs of angels are replenished with it, and of it, all existing things partake. But through disobedience, man made himself unworthy of that grape. 11. Therefore, when at the time foreseen from eternity God my Father willed to display his charity, he sent his wine—i.e., me, his Son—into the vessel that stood nearest, expecting the advent of the wine, namely, into the womb of the Virgin, who had a love for me more fervent than that of any other creature. 12. This Virgin so loved and desired me that there was no hour in which she did not seek me out of longing to become my handmaid.[215] 13. Therefore she received the choice wine; and this wine had three traits: first, strength, because I came forth without the touch of man; second, a most beautiful color because I, fair in beauty,[216] came down from high heaven[217] to fight; third, a most excellent sweetness, inebriating[218] with its supreme blessing. 14. And so that wine—which is I myself—entered a virginal womb so that I, the invisible God, might be made visible and so that lost man might be liberated. 15. I could quite well, indeed, have taken on another form; but it would not have been justice in God if form were not given for form and nature for nature, and if the manner of satisfaction did not accord with the manner of fault. 16. Moreover, which of the wise could have believed or guessed that I, God almighty, would will so to humble myself that I would take on the sackcloth of humanity, except for the fact of my incomprehensible love, because of which I willed to live[219] visibly with man? 17. Because I saw that the Virgin burned with so fervent a love, my divine

severity was conquered and my love was shown in order that man might be reconciled to me. 18. Why do you marvel? I, God—who am love itself[220] and who hate none of the things that I have made[221]—arranged to give man not only my best gifts but also myself, as his price and his prize,[222] so that all the proud and all the devils might be cast into confusion."

19. *Response to the second question.* "Item. As to how my Godhead encloses all things in itself, I answer: I, God, am spirit.[223] I speak and it is done.[224] I instruct and all things obey me. 20. Truly, I am he who gives existence and life to all.[225] Before I made the sky and the mountains and the earth, in myself I AM.[226] I am above all and beyond all. I am within all; and all are in me; and, without me, there is nothing. 21. And because my spirit breathes where it will;[227] because it can do all things when it will; because it knows all things and is more swift and agile than all the spirits; because it has all strength and sees all things—present, past, and future—therefore my spirit, i.e., my Godhead, is deservedly incomprehensible even while it comprehends all."[228]

22. *Response to the third question.* "Item. As to why I lay so long a time in the Virgin's womb, I answer: I am the establisher[229] of all nature; and for each nature I have arranged a due manner, time, and order of birth. 23. Thus, if I, the establisher, had gone forth from the womb as soon as I was conceived, I would have acted against my arrangement of nature; and my assumption of humanity would have been fantastical and untrue. 24. I willed to be as long a time in the womb as other children so that even I myself might comply with the arrangement of nature that I had made and ordained so well."

25. *Response to the fourth question.* "Item. As to why, at the time of my nativity, I was not immediately as large as I was in my thirtieth year, I answer: 26. If I had done this, all would have wondered and feared, following me out of fear—and because they saw miracles—rather than out of love. 27. How then would the prophets' words have been fulfilled? They had foretold that as a child I would be placed in a manger among animals[230] and be adored by kings[231] and be offered in the temple[232] and be persecuted by enemies.[233] 28. Therefore, to show that my humanity was real and that the prophets' words were fulfilled in me, my limbs grew through the intervals of time[234]—but in fullness of wisdom I was as great at the beginning of my birth as at the end."

29. *Response to the fifth question.* "Item. To your questioning why I was circumcised, I answer: Although I was not of Abraham's lineage through a father,[235] nevertheless I was of that lineage through my

Mother, although without sin.[236] 30. Because I instituted the law in my divinity, I willed also to suffer the law in my humanity that my enemies might not slander me by saying that I had given precepts that I myself would not fulfill."

31. *Response to the sixth question.* "Item. As to why I willed to be baptized, I answer: Everyone who wills to establish or begin a new way must himself—as the establisher and beginner of that way—walk on it ahead of others. 32. Now, to the ancient People,[237] there was given a carnal way, namely, circumcision, as a sign of obedience and future purgation. In faithful persons who kept the law, it wrought some effect of the future grace and promise before there came that promised truth —namely, I, the Son of God. 33. Because the law was only, as it were, a shadow, it had been determined in eternity that with the coming of truth the ancient way would retire, lacking its effect. 34. Therefore, that the truth might appear, the shadow yield, and an easier way to heaven be shown, I, God and man, born without sin, willed to be baptized out of humility and as an example to others and so that I might open heaven to those who believe. 35. As a sign of this, when I had been baptized, the heavens were opened; the Father's voice was heard; the Holy Spirit appeared in the form of a dove;[238] and I, God's Son, was shown in a true human being[239] in order that all the faithful might know and believe that the Father opens heaven for the faithful who have been baptized. 36. The Holy Spirit is with the baptizer, and the virtuous power of my humanity is in the element,[240] although in the Father and in Me and in the Holy Spirit there is only one operation and one will.[241] 37. And so, with the coming of truth—i.e., when I, who am truth,[242] came into the world—then, at once, the shadow vanished; the shell of the law was broken and the kernel appeared;[243] circumcision gave way and in me baptism was confirmed[244]—by means of which, heaven is opened for the young and the old; and the children of wrath[245] become children of grace and of life everlasting."

The fifth revelation in the Book of Questions, *in which Christ speaks to his bride, blessed Birgitta, instructing her not to be worried about the care of earthly riches and informing her of the patience to be had in times of tribulation together with the virtues of perfect self-denial[246] and humility.*

The Son of God speaks to the bride and says: "Be diligently attentive[247] to yourself!" She answers: "Why?" The Lord says to her: "Because the world is sending to you four servants who wish to deceive you. 2. The first is the worry of riches. When he comes, answer him:[248] 'Riches are transitory; and the greater their abundance, the greater the accounting of them that one must give. Therefore, I do not care about them because they do not follow their owner, but leave him.' 3. The second servant is the loss of riches and the deprivation of things that had been bestowed.[249] Answer him thus: 'He who gave the riches has himself taken them away.[250] He knows what is expedient for me. May his will be done!' 4. The third servant is the tribulation of this world. Speak to him thus: 'Blessed be you, my God, who permit me to be troubled. 5. For through tribulations I know that I belong to you because you permit tribulation in the present that you may spare in the future. Therefore, distribute[251] to me patience and strength to endure.' 6. The fourth servant is scorn and insults. Answer them thus: 'God alone is good, and[252] to him all honor is due. 7. But I, who have done all wicked and worthless deeds, whence or why should I have honor? I am worthy, rather, of every insult because the whole of my life has blasphemed God. 8. Why does honor mean more to me than insult? For it only excites pride and diminishes humility: and God is forgotten.[253] Therefore, to God be all honor and praise.' 9. For the sake of these reasons, stand fast against the servants of the world; and love me, your God, with all your heart."

ELEVENTH INTERROGATION

First question. Again the same religious appeared on his rung as before and said: "O Judge, I ask you: Since you are both God and man, why did you not show your divinity as well as your humanity? Then all would have believed in you."

2. *Second question.* "Item. Why did you not cause all your words to be heard in a single moment? Then it would not have been necessary for them to be preached through the intervals of time."

3. *Third question.* "Item. Why did you not do all your works in one hour?"

4. *Fourth question.* "Item. Why did your body grow through the intervals of time and not in one moment?"

5. *Fifth question.* "Item. At the approach of death, why did you not show yourself in the might of your divinity; and why did you not show your severity on your enemies when you said, 'All is consummated'?"[254]

6. *Response to the first question.* The Judge answered: "O Friend, it is

you that I answer—and yet, not you. On the one hand, I answer you in order that the malice of your thought may be noted by others. On the other hand, it is not you that I answer, for these things are shown, not for your own improvement, but as a benefit and as a warning for others in the present and in the future. 7. For you do not intend to alter your obstinacy; and therefore you will not pass over from your death into my life because in your own life you hate true life. 8. Nevertheless, others who have heard about your life—I should say: your 'death'—will pass over and will fly to my life[255] because, as it is written, for the saints, all things work together for good;[256] and God permits nothing without a cause. 9. Therefore, when spiritual things are discussed between us, I answer you, not as those who speak in human fashion, but in order that what you think and crave may be expressed in similitudes for others.[257]

10. "You ask, therefore, why I did not openly show my divinity as well as my humanity. The reason is that the divinity is spiritual and the humanity is corporeal. 11. Nevertheless, the divinity and the humanity are, and were, inseparable from the first moment that they were joined.[258] The Godhead is uncreated, and all things that exist were created in it and through it, and all perfection and beauty is found in it. 12. If, therefore, such great beauty and perfection were to be shown visibly to eyes of clay, who would endure the sight? Who could look at even the material sun in its clarity? 13. Who would not be terrified by the sight of lightning and the sound of thunder? How much greater the fear if the Lord of lightnings and Creator of all were seen in his glory! 14. Thus it was for a two-fold cause that my Godhead was not shown openly. First, because of the weakness of the human body, which is earthen in its substance. 15. If any human's body were to see the Godhead, it would melt like wax before a fire;[259] and the soul would rejoice with such great exultation that the body would be annihilated like a cinder. 16. Second, because of the divine goodness and its immutable stability. For if I showed to corporeal eyes my Godhead, which is incomparably more splendid than fire or the sun, I would be acting contrary to myself; for I said: 'No human shall see me and live.'[260] 17. Not even the prophets saw me as I am in the nature of my Godhead; for even those who heard the voice of my Godhead and saw the smoking mountain were terrified and said: 'Let Moses speak to us, and we shall hear him.'[261] 18. Therefore, in order that man might better understand me, I, God the merciful, showed myself to him in a form like himself that could be seen and touched—namely, in my humanity, in which the Godhead exists but, as it were, veiled—in order that man might not be

terrified by a form unlike himself. 19. For, insofar as I am God, I am not corporeal and not corporeally portrayed;[262] therefore, it was in my humanity that I could be heard and seen more tolerably by man."[263]

20. *Response to the second question.* "Item. As to why I did not speak all my words in one hour, I answer you: 21. Just as, materially, it goes against the body for it to take in one hour as much food as might content it for many years, so it is against the divine arrangement that my words, which are the food of the soul, would all have been spoken in one hour. 22. But just as bodily food is taken in little by little, to be chewed and, when chewed, to be carried to the interior, so my words were not to be spoken in one hour, but rather through the intervals of time, in accord with the intelligence of those who were making progress, in order that the hungry might have something by which to be satisfied and that when satisfied, they might be excited to higher things."[264]

23. *Response to the third question.* "Item. As to why I did not do all my works in one moment, I answer: Of those who saw me in the flesh, there were some who believed and some who did not believe. 24. For those who believed, it was necessary that they be instructed in words, through the intervals of time, and be occasionally aroused by examples and strengthened by works. 25. As for those who did not believe, it was just that they showed their malicious disposition and were tolerated as long as my divine justice might permit. 26. If I had done all my works in a single moment, all would have followed me out of fear rather than out of love. And how, then, would the mystery of man's redemption have been fulfilled? 27. Therefore, just as at the beginning of the world's creation, everything was brought to pass at distinct hours and in distinct ways—although everything that was to be made existed then, at one and the same time, without change, in my divine foreknowledge—so also, in my humanity, all things were to be done rationally and distinctly, for the salvation and instruction of all."

28. *Response to the fourth question.* "Item. As to why my body grew for a number of years and not in one moment, I answer: The Holy Spirit, who is eternally in the Father and in me, the Son, showed to the prophets what I would do and suffer when I came in the flesh. 29. Therefore it pleased the Godhead that I should take on such a body, in which I could labor from morn to evening and from year to year, even to the end of death. 30. Therefore, lest the prophets' words seemed empty, I, the Son of God, took on a body like Adam except for sin[265]—a body in which I would be like those whom I was going to redeem—in order that through my charity, man, who had turned away, might be led

back; that man, who had died, might be revived; that man, who had been sold, might be redeemed."

31. *Response to the fifth question.* "Item. As to why I did not show the power of my Godhead and the truth of my divinity to all when, on the cross, I said: 'It is consummated,'[266] I answer: All that was written about me had to be fulfilled. 32. Therefore, I fulfilled all those things even to the last point.[267] But, because many things had been foretold about my resurrection and ascension,[268] it was therefore necessary that these words too should have their effect. 33. If the power of my Godhead had been shown at my death, who would have dared to take me down from the cross and bury me? In the end, it would have been a very small matter for me to come down from the cross[269] and scatter my crucifiers; but how, then, would prophecy have been fulfilled; and where, then, would the virtue of my patience be? 34. And if I had come down from the cross, would then all have really believed? Would they not have said that I had used the evil art? For if they were indignant because I raised the dead and healed the sick, they would have said even worse things if I had come down from the cross. 35. Therefore, that captives might be loosed, I—the free—was captured; and that the guilty might be saved, I—the guiltless—stood fast upon the cross. And through my steadfastness, I steadied all that was unstable and strengthened the weak."[270]

The sixth revelation in the Book of Questions *in which Christ speaks to his bride, blessed Birgitta, and teaches her—saying that in the spiritual life, labor and vigorous perseverance and humble acquiescence in an elder's advice and manly[271] resistance to temptations will gain, for her, repose of mind and eternal glory. He proposes as an example Jacob, who worked as a servant to win Rachel. He says that for some the strongest temptations come at the beginning of their conversion to the spiritual life; for others, in the middle of the spiritual life or at its end. Therefore one must fear and, with humility, persevere in virtues and in labor to the very end.*

The Son speaks: "It is written that Jacob worked as a servant for Rachel's sake and that the days seemed few to him because of his great love; for the greatness of his love lightened his labors.[272] 2. But when Jacob believed that he had attained his desire, he was outwitted;[273] nevertheless, he did not yet cease from his labor because love does not debate about difficulty until it reaches what it desires. 3. So it is in spiritual matters. To obtain the things of heaven, many labor manfully in prayers and pious works; but when they think that they have attained the repose of contemplation, they become involved in temptations. Their tribulations increase; and just when they are considering themselves almost perfect, they find that they are totally imperfect. 4. And no wonder; for it is temptations that probe and purge and perfect man. And so for some, temptations increase in the beginning of their conversion to the spiritual life; and such persons are more perfectly strengthened in the end. 5. Others are more gravely tempted in the middle of their lives and at the end. These must look to themselves carefully, never having any presumption about themselves, but laboring all the more bravely. As Laban said: 6. 'It is the custom to take the elder sister first.'[274] It was as if he were to say: 'First practice labor, and afterward you will have the repose you desire.' 7. Therefore, daughter, you are not to marvel if even in old age temptations increase. For as long as life is permitted, temptation too is possible. The devil never sleeps,[275] because temptation is an opportunity for perfection so that man may not presume. 8. Behold, I show you the example of two persons. One was tempted at the beginning of his conversion, and he persisted and progressed and attained what he sought. 9. The other experienced in his old age grave temptations that he had little known in his youth. He became so involved in them that he almost forgot all prior ones. 10. But because he stood by his resolve and did not cease to labor—even though he had become cold and tepid[276]—therefore he came to his desires and to repose of mind. He recognized in his own case that the judgments of God are hidden and just and that if it had not been for those temptations, he would have had difficulty in reaching eternal salvation."

TWELFTH INTERROGATION

First question. Again the religious appeared, standing on his rung as before and saying: "O Judge, I ask you: Why did you prefer to be born of a virgin rather than of another woman not a virgin?"

2. *Second question.* "Item. Why did you not show with a visible sign that she was both a mother and a pure virgin?"

3. *Third question.* "Item. Why did you so hide your nativity, which was known to but a very few?"

4. *Fourth question.* "Item. Why did you flee before Herod into Egypt, and why did you permit innocent boys to be killed?"

5. *Fifth question.* "Item. Why do you allow yourself to be blasphemed and falsehood to prevail over truth?"

6. *Response to the first question.* The Judge replied: "O friend, I preferred to be born of a virgin rather than of a woman not a virgin because for me, God the most pure, all purest things are fitting. 7. As long as man's nature[277] remained in the order of its creation, it had no deformity; but when my command was violated, there arose at once a certain ability to blush for shame—as happens to persons who sin against their temporal lord and who blush even at the limbs with which they sinned. 8. With the arrival of shame for the violation, inordinate impulses soon increased, and most of all in that organ which was set in place for the sake of fruitfulness.[278] 9. But so that this impulse might not be fruitless, by the goodness of God it was converted into something good; and through the institution of a divine command, the work of carnal intercourse was granted as the means by which nature could bear fruit.[279] 10. However, it is more glorious to extend oneself beyond a command by doing whatever additional good one can out of love; 11. and this is virginity. For it is more virtuous and more magnificent to be in the fire of tribulation and not burn, than to be without fire and yet wish to be crowned. 12. Now, since virginity is a most beautiful path to heaven—while marriage is, as it were, a road[280]—it befitted me, God the most pure, to rest in the purest virgin. 13. Just as the first man was made from the earth when it was, in a way, a virgin—for it had not yet been polluted with blood—and because Adam and Eve sinned while their nature was still healthy, so too I, God, willed to be received by the purest receptacle so that through my goodness all things might be reformed."[281]

14. *Response to the second question.* "Item. As to why I did not show by open signs that my Mother was both mother and virgin, I answer: I made all the mysteries of my incarnation known to the prophets so that it might be all the more firmly believed, the longer it had been predicted. 15. That my Mother truly was a virgin both before and after childbirth was sufficiently attested to by Joseph, who was the guardian and the witness of her virginity. 16. Even if her chastity had been shown by a more evident miracle, the distrustful, in their malice, would still not have ceased from blasphemy. They distrust that a virgin conceived through the power of the Godhead because they do not attend to the fact that it is easier for me, God, to do this than it is for the sun to penetrate glass.[282] 17. It was an act of my divine justice that the mystery of God's incarnation was hidden from the devil and from mankind, to

be revealed in the time of grace. Now, however, I say that my Mother truly is a mother and a virgin. 18. Just as, in the molding of Adam and Eve, there was the wonderful power of the Godhead and, in their cohabitation, a delightful honesty,[283] even so, in my Godhead's approach to the Virgin, there was a wonderful goodness—for my incomprehensible divinity descended into that closed vessel without doing it violence. 19. And that place was a delightful habitation for me; for I, God—who was everywhere in my divinity—was, in my humanity, enclosed.[284] Here, too, there was wonderful power; for I, God, who am bodiless, went forth with a body from her womb, while preserving her virginity. 20. Because man made difficulties about believing and because my Mother is a lover of total humility, it therefore pleased me to hide her beauty and her perfection for a time in order that my Mother too might have some merit with which she might be more perfectly crowned and in order that I, God, might be more fully glorified at that time in which I would fulfill my promises of reward for the good and retribution for the wicked."

21. *Response to the third question.* "Item. As to why I did not show my nativity to mankind, I answer: Although the devil lost the dignity of his previous rank, he did not lose his knowledge, which he possesses for the testing of the good and for his own confusion. 22. Therefore, in order that my human nature might grow and might reach the predetermined time, the mystery of my pity[285] had to be concealed from the devil because I willed to come in secrecy to make war on the devil and because I chose to be despised in order to subdue the arrogance of mankind. 23. The very teachers of the law, who read about me in their books, despised me because I came in humility; and because they were proud, they would not hear the true justice that comes from faith in my redemption. Therefore they shall be confounded when the son of perdition[286] comes in his pride. 24. But if I had come with great power and honor, how then would the proud have been humbled? Or will the proud now enter heaven? Not at all! 25. And so I came humbly in order that man might learn humility; and I hid myself from the proud because they wished to understand neither my divine justice nor themselves."

26. *Response to the fourth question.* "Item. As to why I fled into Egypt,[287] I answer: Before the violation of the commandment, there was a single way to heaven, broad and bright: broad in its abundance of virtues and bright with divine wisdom and with the obedience of a good will. 27. And when that will had changed, two ways began.[288] One led to heaven; the other led away. Obedience led to heaven; disobedience led

astray. 28. Therefore, because it was in the power of man's free will to choose good or evil—namely, to obey or not to obey—he sinned because he willed otherwise than I, God, wanted him to will. 29. In order that man might be saved, it was just and right[289] that someone came able to redeem him—someone who would possess perfect obedience and innocence and, in whose regard, those who so wished could show love and those who so wished could show malice. 30. But in order to redeem mankind, it was not an angel that ought to be sent; for I, God, do not grant my glory to another.[290] Nor was there any human found who could placate me on his own behalf, much less for others. Therefore, I, God, who alone am just, came to justify all. 31. The fact that I fled into Egypt showed the weakness of my humanity and fulfilled a prophecy.[291] And I also gave an example to coming generations: that sometimes persecution must be eluded for the greater glory of God in the future. 32. Because I was not found by my pursuers, my divine plan prevailed over that of men; for it is not easy to fight against God. 33. The fact that the infants were slain[292] was a sign of my future passion and a mystery of election and divine charity.[293] 34. Although these speechless infants did not bear witness to me with their voices or their mouths, they did so through their death, as befitted my own speechless infancy;[294] for it had been foreseen that God's praise would be accomplished[295] even in the blood of the Innocents. 35. For, although the malice of the unjust afflicted them unjustly, nevertheless it was my divine permission, always kind and just, that exposed them, not without justice, in order to show the malice of mankind and the incomprehensible counsel and pity of my Godhead. 36. Therefore, where unjust malice boiled up against the children, there merit and grace justly abounded; and where confession of the tongue and age were lacking, there the blood that had been shed accumulated a most perfect goodness."[296]

37. *Response to the fifth question.* "Item. As to why I allow myself to be blasphemed, I answer: It is written that when King David eluded his son's persecution, a certain man cursed him on the way; 38. and when his servants wanted to kill that man, David prohibited them for a double reason: first, because he had hope of returning; second, because he considered his own weakness and sin, the foolishness of the curser, and God's patience and goodness towards himself.[297] 39. Figuratively, I am David. Man truly persecutes me with his evil deeds—as the servant persecuted his lord—casting me out of my kingdom, i.e., out of his soul, which I created and which is my kingdom. 40. Then he rebukes me for being unjust in judgment and even blasphemes me because I am patient.

Indeed, because I am meek, I suffer their[298] foolishness; and because I am a judge, I await their conversion even to the very last moment. 41. Finally, because man believes falsehood rather than truth—loving the world more than me, his God—it is therefore no wonder if the wicked man is tolerated in his wickedness; for he wills neither to seek the truth nor to recover from his evil."

The seventh revelation in the Book of Questions, *in which Christ speaks to his bride, blessed Birgitta, and praises frequent confession in order that man may not lose the divine grace that he has.*

The Son of God speaks: "When there is a fire in the house, it is necessary to have a venthole through which the smoke can go out so that the inhabitant may enjoy the warmth. 2. Thus, for everyone who desires to keep my Spirit and my divine grace, frequent confession is useful so that through it, the smoke of sin may escape. 3. For although my divine Spirit is in itself unchangeable, nevertheless it quickly withdraws from the heart that is not guarded by humble confession."

The eighth revelation in the Book of Questions, *in which Christ speaks to the bride and says of those who find their pleasure in carnal and earthly delights—neglecting heavenly desires and charity and the memory of his passion and of eternal judgment—that their prayer is like the sound of stones colliding and that they will be abominably cast forth from God's sight as if they were an abortion or the soiled napkin of a menstruous woman.*[299]

"That man sang: 'Deliver me, O Lord, from the unjust man.'[300] This voice is in my ears like the sound of two stones struck together. Indeed, his heart calls to me as if with three voices. 2. The first says: 'I want to have my will in my own hands; I want to sleep and to arise and to talk of pleasant things. I shall give nature what it craves. 3. I long for money in my purse and the softness of garments on my back. When I have these and other things, I count them a greater happiness than all of the soul's other spiritual gifts and virtues.' 4. His second voice is this: 'Death is not too hard, and judgment is not as severe as it is written. We are threatened with harsh things as a precaution, but they are mitigated out of mercy. 5. Therefore, if I can have my will in the present, let my soul pass over as best it can in the future.'[301] 6. The third voice is this: 'God would not have redeemed man if he did not wish to give man heavenly things; nor would he have suffered if he did not wish to lead us back to our Father's home. Why, indeed, did he suffer? Who ever compelled him to suffer? 7. Obviously, I have no intelligence of heavenly things except by hearsay; and whether one should trust the Scriptures is something that I do not know.[302] If I could only have my will, I would take it in place of the heavenly kingdom.' 8. Behold, such is that man's will. Therefore, in my ears his voice is like the sound of stones.

9. "But, O friend, I answer your first voice: 'Your way does not tend toward heaven, and the passion of my charity is not to your taste. Therefore hell has opened for you; and because you love things base and earthly, you will therefore go to the regions below.' 10. To your second voice, I answer: 'Son, death will be hard for you, judgment unendurable, and flight impossible, unless you amend yourself.' 11. To your third voice, I say: 'Brother, all my works were done out of charity in order that you might be like me and, though turned away, might come to me again. But now my works are dead in you, my words are burdensome, and my way is neglected. 12. And so what awaits you is punishment and the company of the demons because you turn your back to me, you trample underfoot the signs of my humility, and you give no attention to the state in which I stood before you—and for you—on the cross.[303] 13. In a threefold state, I stood there for your sake: first, as a man whose eye was penetrated by a knife; second, as a man whose heart was perforated by a sword; third, as a man whose every limb trembled with the pain of pressing tribulation. 14. Indeed, my passion was to me more bitter than a puncture in the eye;[304] yet I suffered it out of charity. 15. My Mother's sorrow moved my heart more than my own; yet I bore it.[305] For a long time, all my inner and outer parts trembled out of pressing pain and suffering; and yet I did not dismiss it or draw back. 16. Thus I stood before you, but all this you forget and neglect and despise. Therefore you shall be cast forth as an abortion; and, like the napkin of a menstruous woman, you will be cast out.' "[306]

THIRTEENTH INTERROGATION

First question. Again the same religious appeared on his rung as before and said: "O Judge, I ask you: Why is your grace so quickly withdrawn from some while others are long tolerated in their wickedness?"

2. *Second question.* "Item. Why is grace granted to some in their youth while others, in old age, are deprived of it?"

3. *Third question.* "Item. Why are some troubled beyond measure while others are, as it were, secure from tribulation?"

4. *Fourth question.* "Item. Why are some given intelligence and an incomparable genius for learning while others are like asses without intellect?"

5. *Fifth question.* "Item. Why are some excessively hardened while others rejoice in wonderful consolation?"

6. *Sixth question.* "Item. Why is greater prosperity given in this world to the wicked rather than to the good?"

7. *Seventh question.* "Item. Why is one called in the beginning and another toward the end?"

8. *Response to the first question.* The Judge replied: "Friend, all my works are in my foreknowledge from the beginning; and all things that have been made were created for the solace of man. 9. But because man prefers his own will to my will, therefore, out of justice, the goods gratuitously given to him are taken from him in order that man may know that with God all things are rational and just. 10. And because many are ungrateful for my grace and become more undevout the more their gifts are multiplied, the gifts are therefore quickly taken from them in order that my divine plan may be more swiftly manifested and lest man abuse my grace to his own greater doom. 11. Item. As to why some are long tolerated in their wickedness, the reason is that amidst their evils, many have some tolerable trait.[307] 12. For either they are of profit to some, or they are a caution to others. When Saul was denounced by Samuel, Saul's sin[308] seemed slight in the sight of men while David's sin seemed greater.[309] 13. However, under the pressure of testing, Saul disobediently abandoned me, his God, and consulted the pythoness.[310] But David, in temptation, became more faithful, patiently enduring the things that bore down upon him and considering that they befell him for his sins. 14. The fact that I patiently endured Saul demonstrates Saul's ingratitude and my divine patience. The fact that David was chosen shows my foreknowledge and David's future humility and his contrition."

15. *Response to the second question.* "Item. As to why grace is taken away from some in their old age, I answer: All are given grace in order that the Giver of grace may be loved by all. 16. But because many, toward their end, are ungrateful for my divine grace—as Solomon was[311]—it is therefore just that what was not carefully kept before the end should, in the end, be withdrawn. 17. For my gift and my divine grace are taken away sometimes because of the recipient's negligence in

134

attending[312] to what he has received and to what he should give in return, sometimes as a caution for others so that everyone in the state of grace may always fear and feel dread at the fall of others. 18. For even the wise have fallen through negligence; and even some, who seemed to be my friends, have been supplanted because of their ingratitude."

19. *Response to the third question.* "Item. As to why some have greater tribulation, I answer: I am the Creator of all. Therefore no tribulation comes without my permission, as it is written: 20. I am God 'creating evil'[313]—i.e., permitting tribulation—because no trouble befalls even the gentiles without me or without a rational cause. 21. For my prophets foretold many things concerning the adversities of the gentiles in order that they, being negligent and abusive of reason, might be taught by scourges and in order that I, God—permitting all—might be known and glorified by every nation. 22. If therefore I, God, do not spare the pagans from scourges, far less will I spare these who have more copiously tasted of the sweetness of my divine grace. 23. The fact that some have less tribulation, and others more, occurs so that mankind may turn away from sin and may, after troubles in the present, obtain consolation in the future. 24. For all who are judged and who judge themselves in this age will not come to future judgment.[314] As it is written: They will pass 'from death into life.'[315] 25. The fact that some are protected[316] from the scourge occurs lest, having been scourged, they murmur and thus incur a heavier judgment, for there are many who do not deserve to be scourged in the present. 26. There are even some in this life who are not weighed down by any bodily or spiritual annoyance and who live as carelessly as if God did not exist or as if God spares them because of their works of justice. 27. But they should be greatly afraid and should grieve lest I, God, who spare them in the present, come unforeseen and damn them more harshly because they have no compunction.[317] 28. There are some who have health in the flesh but are troubled in soul because of their contempt for God. Others enjoy neither bodily health nor inner consolation of soul, and yet they persevere in serving and honoring me according to their ability. Indeed, some—from their mother's womb and right up to the end—are afflicted by infirmities. 29. But I, their God, so moderate the tribulations of all these people that nothing happens without a cause and a recompense, for of those who slept before their temptations the eyes of many are opened in tribulation."

30. *Response to the fourth question.* "Item. As to why some have greater intelligence, I answer: The abundance of one's wisdom does not

profit the soul toward eternal salvation unless the soul also shines with a good life. On the contrary, it is more useful to have less knowledge and a better life. 31. Therefore, each person has been given a measure of rationality by means of which he can obtain heaven if he lives piously. However, rationality varies in many according to their natural and spiritual dispositions. 32. For just as, by means of divine fervor and the virtues, man makes progress toward perfection of the virtues, so too, through bad will and bad disposition of nature and wrong upbringing, man descends into vanities.[318] 33. Many times nature suffers a defect when one strives against nature and one sins. Therefore, it is not without cause that in some, rationality is great but useless, as in those who have knowledge but not life. 34. In others, there is less knowledge but better practice. In some, of course, rationality and life are in agreement; but in others, on the contrary, there is neither rationality nor life. 35. This variety comes from my well-ordered and divine permission— sometimes, for the benefit of humans or for their humiliation and instruction; sometimes, because of ingratitude or temptation; sometimes, because of a defect of nature or latent sins; 36. sometimes, in order to avoid the occasion of a greater sin; and sometimes, because a nature is not suited to receive anything greater. Let everyone who has the grace of intelligence therefore fear that, because of it, he will be judged more heavily if he is negligent. 37. Let him who has no intelligence or talent rejoice and do as much as he can with the little that he has; for he has been freed from many occasions of sin. 38. In youth, Peter the apostle was forgetful and John was no trained expert;[319] but they grasped true wisdom in their old age because they sought wisdom's beginning.[320] 39. When young, Solomon was docile and Aristotle was subtle;[321] but they did not grasp the beginning of wisdom because they neither glorified the Giver of knowledge as they ought, nor imitated the things that they knew and taught, nor learned for themselves, but for others. 40. Balaam, too, had knowledge but did not follow it; and therefore the she-ass rebuked his folly.[322] Daniel when young, judged his elders.[323] 41. Erudition, without a good life, does not please me; therefore, it is necessary that those who abuse rationality be corrected. For I, the God and Lord of all, give knowledge to mankind; and I correct both the wise and the foolish."

42. *Response to the fifth question.* "Item. As to why some are hardened, I answer: The fact that Pharaoh was hardened was his own fault, and not mine, because he would not conform himself to my divine will.[324] 43. For obduracy is nothing other than the withdrawal of my

divine grace; and grace is withdrawn because man has not given to me, God, that free thing he has, namely, his own will, as you will be able to understand through an example. 44. There was a man who possessed two fields, of which the one remained uncultivated and the other, at certain times, bore fruit. 45. His friend said to him: 'Since you are wise and wealthy, I wonder why you do not cultivate your fields more diligently or hand them over to others for cultivation.' 46. He answered: 'One of these fields—no matter how much diligence I display—produces nothing but very bad herbs—which noxious beasts seize upon, and then the beasts befoul the place. 47. If I apply an enrichment,[325] the field grows so insolent and wanton that even if it produces a modicum of grain, even more weeds[326] spring up, which I disdain to gather because I desire no grain unless it is pure. 48. Therefore, the better plan is to leave such a field uncultivated; for then the beasts do not occupy the place and the beasts do not hide in the grass. And if some bitter herbs do sprout, they are useful for the sheep, for after tasting them, the sheep learn not to be fastidious about things that are sweet. 49. The other field is laid out according to the temperature of the seasons. A part of it is stony and needs enrichment; another part is moist and needs warmth; another part is dry and needs moisture. For that reason, I will to regulate my work according to the field's condition.' 50. I, God, am like that man. The first field is the free movement of the will given to man. He moves it more against me than for me. 51. And if man does some things that please me, in many more things he provokes me, for man's will and mine are not in agreement. 52. So too Pharaoh acted, for, although through sure signs he recognized my power, nonetheless he strengthened his resolution of standing fast in his wickedness against me.[327] 53. Therefore, he experienced my justice, for it is just that he who does not make good use of trifles should not pride himself on things that are very great. 54. The second field is the obedience of a good mind and the rejection of one's own will. If such a mind is dry in devotion, it must wait for the rain of my divine grace. 55. If it is stony through impatience or obduracy, it must, with composure, endure purgation and rebuke. If it is moist through carnal wantonness, let it embrace[328] abstinence and be like an animal prepared for its owner's will; for in such a mind I, God, take much glory. 56. Therefore, the fact that some become hardened is caused by man's will being contrary to mine. For even though I will that all be saved,[329] nevertheless this is not accomplished unless man has personally cooperated by making his entire will conform to my will.[330] 57. The fact that not all are given equal grace and progress is an act of my hidden judgment, for I know and I regulate for each person what is expedient and necessary for him; and I restrain man's attempts lest he fall too deeply. 58. For many have the talent of grace and would be able to work; but they refuse.[331] Others abstain from sin out of fear of punishment or because they do not have the means to sin or because sin does not amuse them. Therefore, to some, greater gifts are not given because I, who alone know the minds of human beings know how to distribute my gifts."

59. *Response to the sixth question.* "Item. As to why the wicked sometimes have greater prosperity in the world than the good, I answer: This is an indication of my great patience and charity and a testing for the just. 60. For if I gave temporal goods only to my friends, the wicked would despair and the good would grow proud. Therefore, temporal goods are given to all so that I, the Creator and giver of all, may be loved by all and so that, when the good grow proud, they may be instructed in justice by means of the wicked. 61. Indeed, let all understand that temporal things are not to be loved or preferred to me, God, but are to be had for sustenance alone; and let them be all the more fervent in my service, the less the stability that they find in temporal things."

62. *Response to the seventh question.* "Item. As to why one is called at the beginning and another at the end, I answer: I am like a mother who sees in her children the hope of life and gives stronger things to some and lighter things to others. With those for whom there is no hope she also sympathizes, and she does for them as much as she can. 63. But if the children become worse from the mother's remedy, what need is there then to labor? 64. This is the way I deal with man. One, whose will is foreseen as more fervent and whose humility and stability are foreseen as more constant, received grace in the beginning; and it will follow him to the end. 65. Another, who, amidst all his wickedness, still attempts and strives[332] to become better, deserves to be called toward the end. But he who is ungrateful does not deserve admission to his mother's breasts."[333]

The ninth revelation in the Book of Questions, *in which Christ speaks to his bride, blessed Birgitta, and shows her that she has already been rescued and delivered from the house of the world and of vices and that she has now been brought to dwell in the mansion of the Holy Spirit. And therefore he warns her to conform herself to that same Spirit by always persevering in purity, humility, and devotion.*

The Son speaks to the bride: "You are she who was nurtured in a house of poverty[334] and then came into the society of the great.[335] In a house of poverty, there are three things, namely, stained walls, harmful smoke, and pervasive soot. 2. But you have been led into a house where there is beauty without stain, warmth without smoke, and sweetness that fills without cloying. 3. The house of poverty is the world. Its walls are pride, oblivion of God,[336] abundance of sin, and disregard of the future. These walls stain because they annihilate good works and hide God's face from mankind. 4. The smoke is love of the world. It harms the eyes because it darkens the soul's understanding and causes the soul to worry about superfluous things. The soot is pleasure; for even if it delights for a time, it never satisfies or replenishes with eternal goodness. 5. From these things, therefore, you were drawn away; and you were led into the mansion of the Holy Spirit.[337] He is in me, and I am in him, and he encloses you in himself.[338] 6. He, indeed, is most pure and most beautiful and most steadfast; for he sustains all things. Therefore, conform yourself to the Inhabitant of the house by remaining pure, humble, and devout."

FOURTEENTH INTERROGATION

First question. Again the same religious appeared on his rung as before and said: "O Judge, I ask you: Why do animals suffer inconveniences when they will not have eternal life and do not have the use of reason?"

2. *Second question.* "Item. Why are all things born with pain when there is no sin in the birth of anything?"

3. *Third question.* "Item. Why does an infant carry the sin of its father when it does not know how to sin?"

4. *Fourth question.* "Item. Why does the unforeseen so frequently occur?"

5. *Fifth question.* "Item. Why does a wicked man die a good death like the just; and the just sometimes a bad death like the unjust?"

6. *Response to the first question.* The Judge replied: "Friend, although this inquisition of yours[339] does not come from love, nevertheless I do answer you so that others may love.[340] You inquire why animals suffer infirmities. 7. It is because in them—as in everything else—all things are disordered. For I am the establisher of all natures, and I gave to each

nature its own temperament and order by which each thing might move and live. 8. But after man—because of whom all things were made—opposed his lover, i.e., me, his God, all other things began to take on his disorder; and all that should have revered him began to oppose and resist him. 9. Therefore, it is out of this vice of disorder that so very many annoyances and adversities befall both man and the animals. 10. However, animals also sometimes suffer because of the intemperance of their own nature—sometimes for the mitigation of their wildness and the purging of nature itself; sometimes because of mankind's sins so that, when the things that man loves are plagued or withdrawn, man himself may attentively consider what great punishment he deserves, for he has the use of a greater thing, reason.[341] 11. Indeed, if mankind's sins did not demand it, the animals that are in man's hands would not be so singularly afflicted. But not even they suffer without great justice. 12. For either it will be to them for a swifter end of life, or for less labor of misery and consumption of strong nature, or because of the change of seasons or out of the carelessness of man when labor is forthcoming.[342] 13. Let man therefore fear me, his God, more than everything else and be all the more gentle toward my creatures and animals, on whom he must have mercy for the sake of me, their Creator. 14. For this reason, I, God, gave man the precept concerning the Sabbath,[343] for I care about every one of my creatures."

15. *Response to the second question.* "Item. As to why all things are born with suffering, I answer: When man scorned the most beautiful delight, he immediately incurred a toilsome life. 16. And because disorder began in man and through man, it is my justice that the other creatures too—which exist for man's sake—should have some bitterness for the tempering of their delight and the fostering of their nourishment.[344] 17. Therefore, man is born with pain and makes progress with labor so that he may be eager to hasten to his true rest. He dies naked and poor so that he may bridle his inordinate impulses and so that he may fear future examination. 18. And thus, even animals give birth with pain so that bitterness may temper their excesses and so that they may be partners with man in labor and pain. Therefore, man, who is so much nobler than the animals, should all that more fervently love me, the Lord God, his Creator."

19. *Response to the third question.* "Item. As to why the child carries the sins of the father, I answer: Could anything that comes from something unclean be clean itself? 20. Therefore, when the first man lost the beauty of innocence because of his disobedience, he was cast out of the

paradise of joy and became involved in unclean things. No one was found able, of himself, to recover this innocence. 21. Therefore I, the merciful God, came in the flesh and instituted baptism, by means of which a child is liberated from wrong uncleanness and from sin. Because of this, the son will not carry the sin of the father;[345] but each one will die in his own sin. 22. However, it happens many times that children imitate the sins of their parents; and therefore the parents' sins are sometimes punished in the children. This is not because the sins of the parents will not be punished in the parents themselves, although the punishment of these sins may be deferred for a time. But each one will die in, and be punished for, his own sin. 23. Sometimes, too, the sins of the fathers—as it is written—are visited even upon the fourth generation;[346] for when the children do not endeavor to mitigate my wrath in their own behalf or on behalf of their parents, it is my divine justice that they be punished together with the parents whom they followed against me."

24. *Response to the fourth question.* "Item. As to why the unforeseen so frequently comes about, I answer: It is written that man shall be punished through those things through which he sins.[347] And who shall be able to understand the plan of God?[348] 25. Many seek me, not in accordance with knowledge, but for the sake of the world. Some fear more than is right; others presume too much; others are proud in their designs. Therefore, I, God, who work the salvation of all,[349] cause sometimes the occurrence of that which man most fears: 26. sometimes, the removal of a thing that is loved more than is right; sometimes, the delay of a thing that is too anxiously anticipated and desired, in order that, above all things, man may always fear, love, and acknowledge me, his God."

27. *Response to the fifth question.* "Item. As to why a wicked man dies a good death like the just, I answer: The wicked sometimes have certain good traits and do certain works of justice for which they are to be repaid in the present.[350] 28. Similarly, too, the just sometimes do certain bad things for which they are to be scourged in the present, or they should be expected to be.[351] 29. Therefore, because at present all things are uncertain and all things are reserved for the future and because there is one entrance for all, therefore there must also be one exit for all,[352] for it is not the exit but the life that makes a man blessed.[353] 30. However, the fact that the wicked meet with an exit like that of the just is a result of my divine providence, for they themselves desired that exit.[354] 31. The devil, foreseeing the exits of his friends, sometimes

foretells to them their time of death to cause in them presumption and vainglory and the deception—as it is found in those books entitled Apocrypha[355]—that after death they will be praised as if they were just. 32. On the other hand, the just sometimes meet with a lamentable exit for their own greater merit so that they who, in their lifetime, always were careful about the virtues, may, through a contemptible death fly[356] free to heaven—insofar as not even offscourings[357] would be found in need of cleansing. As it is written, a lion killed a disobedient prophet and did not eat of the cadaver but guarded it.[358] 33. In that the lion killed the body, what else is hinted at if not my divine permission that the prophet's disobedience be punished? 34. That the lion did not eat of the cadaver was a showing of the prophet's good works so that purged in the present, he might be found to be just in the future. 35. Therefore, let each one fear to examine my judgments; for even as I am incomprehensible in virtue and power, so am I terrible in my plans and my judgments. Indeed, some who wished to comprehend me in their wisdom have failed in their hope."[359]

The tenth revelation in the Book of Questions, *in which Christ speaks to the bride and warns her not to be disturbed if his divine words, given to her in revelations, are found to be sometimes obscure, sometimes dubious, and sometimes uncertain; for this happens from certain causes designated here and out of the hidden justice of God. He advises, however, that the events and promises of his words must always be awaited with patience and fear and humble perseverance lest the promised grace be revoked for ingratitude. He says also that many things, said in a corporeal way, will not be accomplished in the body but in the spirit.*

The Son speaks to the bride: "Be not disturbed if I speak one word obscurely and another more expressly; or if I now say that someone is my servant or son and friend and, another time, the contrary is found. 2. For my words can be interpreted in diverse ways: just as I said to you of one man that his hand would become his death, and of another, that he would approach my table no more.[360] 3. These things are said either because I am going to tell you why I have spoken thus or because you, in fact, will see the final truth—just as it is now clear in the case of those two. 4. Sometimes, too, I say things obscurely in order that you may both fear and rejoice—fearing that they may come to pass in another way because of my divine patience, which knows the changes of hearts, and rejoicing too because my will is always fulfilled. 5. So too, in the Old Law, I said many things that were to be understood more spiritually than corporeally—as concerning the temple and David and Jerusalem —in order that carnal mankind might learn to desire spiritual things. 6. For to test faith's constancy and the solicitude of my friends, I said and promised many things which, according to the diverse effects of my Spirit, could be understood in different ways by the good and the wicked, and so that in their different states they each might have opportunities in which they could be trained and tested and taught by me. 7. That some things have been said obscurely happens out of my justice so that my plan may be hidden, and so that each one may patiently await my grace lest, perchance—if my plan were always made known[361] with a definite date—all might grow tepid while waiting. 8. And I have promised many things that have been withdrawn because of man's ingratitude; and many things have been said corporeally which shall be accomplished in a spiritual way, as concerning Jerusalem and Zion.[362] For the Jews are, as it is written, the blind and deaf People of the Lord."[363]

FIFTEENTH INTERROGATION

First question. Again the same religious appeared, standing on his rung as before, and said: "O Judge, I ask you: Why have many things been created that seem to be of no usefulness?"

2. *Second question.* "Item. Why are souls—remaining in the body or going forth from the body—not commonly seen?"

3. *Third question.* "Item. Why are your praying friends not always heard?"

4. *Fourth question.* "Item. Why are many who want to do evil not given permission?"

5. *Fifth question.* "Item. Why do evils come upon some who do not deserve them?"

6. *Sixth question.* "Item. Why do those who have the Spirit of God sin?"

7. *Seventh question.* "Item. Why does the devil adhere to some, being always present to them, but never to others?"

8. *Response to the first question.* The Judge replied: "Friend, just as my works are many, so too they are wonderful and incomprehensible. And, many though they are, none are without cause. 9. Man, indeed, is like a boy nurtured in a prison, in darkness. If one were to tell him that

light and stars exist, he would not believe because he has never seen.[364] 10. Similarly, ever since man deserted the true light, he delights only in darkness in accord with the popular saying: To a man accustomed to evil, evil seems sweet.[365] 11. And so, although man's intellect is darkened, nevertheless there is no shadow or change in me. I do arrange, and have arranged, all things so temperately and honestly and wisely that nothing has been made without a cause or a use, 12. not the highest mountain, nor the desert, nor the lakes; not the beasts, nor even the venomous reptiles. I provide for the usefulness of all creatures as well as of mankind. 13. I am like a man who has certain places for strolling; other places for keeping utensils; other places for animals, tame and wild; other places for fortifications or for the mysteries of his council;[366] other places because of the congruent position of the land; other places for mankind's reproof. 14. Thus I, God, have arranged all things in a rational manner: some things for man's use and delight, some to be refuges for animals and birds, some for the training and bridling of human cupidity, 15. some for the harmony of the elements, some for the admiration of my works, some for the punishment of sin and for the harmony of things higher and lower, some for a cause known and reserved to me alone. 16. For behold: the bee—so brief and small—knows how to extract much from many sources for the confecting of honey.[367] So too the other creatures, both minute and large, surpass man in the shrewd distinguishing of herbs and in the consideration of their usefulness; and there are many things profitable for them which are harmful to man. 17. What wonder then if man's sense is weak in discerning and understanding my marvels, since he is already surpassed by the tiniest creatures? 18. Behold: what is more ugly than a frog or a serpent; what is more contemptible than a burr or a nettle or similar things? And yet they are very good for those who know how to discern my works. 19. And so, whatever exists is of use for something; and each thing that moves knows how its own nature will be able to subsist and gain strength. 20. Therefore, because all my works are wonderful and all praise me, let man, who is so much more beautiful and preferred than the others, know that he is all that more obligated than the others to honor me. 21. Moreover, if the impact of the waters were not confined by some boundary of mountains, where would mankind dwell in safety? And if the beasts had no refuge, how would they escape the insatiable greed of man? And if man had everything as he wished, would he then require the things of heaven? 22. But if the beasts neither toiled nor feared, they would grow dissolute and infirm. Therefore, very many of my works are in concealment in order that I, the wonderful and incomprehensible God, may be known and honored by mankind out of admiration for my wisdom in the creation of my so many creatures."

23. *Response to the second question.* "Item. As to why souls are not seen by man, I answer: the soul is of a far better nature than the body because it is from the power of my Godhead and is immortal, having a partnership with the angels, and more outstanding than all the planets and nobler than the whole world. 24. Therefore, because the soul is of a most noble and fiery nature—giving the body life and warmth—and because it is spiritual, it can in no way be seen by corporeal beings except through corporeal similitudes."[368]

25. *Response to the third question.* "Item. As to why my friends, petitioning me in their prayers, are not always heard by me, I answer: I am like a mother who sees her son making a request contrary to his welfare and puts off listening to his petition while stemming his tears with some indignation. 26. Indeed, such indignation is not anger but great mercy. Thus I, God, do not always hear my friends because I see—better than they themselves would see—the things that are more useful for their welfare. 27. Did not Paul[369] and others pray with energy and yet were not heard? But why? 28. Because amidst their abundant virtues, my friends themselves have certain weaknesses and things to be purged; and therefore they are not heard in order that they may be all that more humble and fervent toward me, the more lovingly they are defended by me and preserved unscathed in temptations to sin. 29. It is therefore a token of great love that the prayers of my friends are not always heard—for the sake of their greater merit and for the proving of their constancy. 30. For just as the devil tries, if possible, to spoil the life of the just through some sin or through a contemptible death in order that the constancy of the faithful may thus grow tepid, so too I permit, not without cause, the testing of the just in order that their stability may be known to others and that they themselves may be more sublimely crowned. 31. And just as the devil does not blush to tempt his own because he sees that they are quite prompt in sinning, so for a time I do not spare my elect because I see that they are prepared for all good."

32. *Response to the fourth question.* "Item. As to why some who wish to do evil are not given permission, I answer: If a father has two sons, the one obedient and the other disobedient, that father resists the disobedient one as much as he can, lest the son transgress with malice.[370] 33. But the father tests the obedient son and urges him on to greater

things so that by his activity even the disobedient son may also be incited toward better things. 34. So too I, many times, do not permit the wicked to sin, because in the midst of their evils they do some good things by which they profit either themselves or others. 35. Therefore, justice demands that they not be handed over to the devil at once and that they not always have success in fulfilling their will."[371]

36. *Response to the fifth question.* "Item. As to why evils come upon some who do not deserve them, I answer: Only I, God, know how good each person is and what each one deserves.[372] Because many things appear beautiful when they are not, even gold is proved in the fire.[373] 37. Therefore, the just man is sometimes troubled as an example to others and for a crown for himself. So too Job was tested.[374] He was good before his scourges; but during and after them, he became more known to mankind. 38. And yet, who would want to examine why I scourged him? Who could know it but I myself, who anticipated him with my blessings[375] and preserved him from sinning and upheld him in temptations? 39. And just as, without merits of his own, I anticipated him with my grace, so too I tested him with justice and mercy; for no one will be justified in my sight except through my grace."

40. *Response to the sixth question.* "Item. As to why those who have my Spirit sin, I answer: The Spirit of my Godhead is not bound but blows where it will[376] and draws back when it will. It does not dwell in a vessel which is subject to sins[377] but in one which has charity. 41. For I, God, am charity;[378] and where I am, there is freedom.[379] Therefore he who accepts my Spirit has the ability to sin if he wishes, because every human being has free will.[380] 42. And so, when man moves his will against me, then my Spirit, which is in him, withdraws from him;[381] or man himself is rebuked in order that he may correct his will. 43. Thus, Balaam willed to curse my people; but I did not permit him. For although he was a wicked and covetous prophet, nevertheless he sometimes spoke good things, not of himself, but from my Spirit.[382] 44. Many times, the gift of my Spirit is given to the good and to the wicked. Otherwise, those great and eloquent speakers would not have disputed about such lofty things if they had not had my Spirit; nor would they have raved so foolishly against me if their thoughts had not been contrary to me and if they had not inclined toward pride, wanting to know more than they ought."

45. *Response to the seventh question.* "Item. As to why the devil is more present to some and adheres to them, I answer: The devil is, as it were, the lictor[383] and the examiner of the just. Therefore, with my

permission, he vexes the souls of certain people; he overshadows the consciences of others; and of some he vexes even the bodies. 46. He vexes the souls of those who sin against reason and give themselves over to every impurity and infidelity. He disturbs the consciences and bodies of those who are purged and vexed, in the present, for some sins. 47. Indeed, such vexation also comes upon infants of either sex—whether pagan or Christian—either because of the parents' lack of care or a defect of nature, or for the terror and humiliation of others, or because of some sins. But my justice mercifully arranged that these infants, who are spared the occasions of sin, either are not too gravely punished or are more sublimely crowned.[384] 48. Similarly, many such things also happen to brutes either for the punishment of others, or for a quicker end to life, or because of the intemperance of their own nature.[385] 49. Therefore, that the devil adheres to some and is nearer to them is the result of my permission, either for greater humiliation and caution; or for a greater crown and a greater solicitude in seeking me; or because of sins to be purged in the present; or because, through the demands of their guilt,[386] the punishment of some begins in the present and will endure without end."

The eleventh revelation in the Book of Questions, *in which Christ speaks to his bride, blessed Birgitta, and tells her why and when he began to administer and infuse into her the words of divine revelations in spiritual vision. And he tells her that the aforementioned words of the revelations, which are contained in these books, have principally these four virtues: they spiritually satisfy one who thirsts for true charity, they warm the cold, they gladden the disturbed, and they heal weak souls.*

The Son of God speaks: "By means of natural things, a healthful[387] drink can be made—namely, of cold iron and hard stone,[388] of a dry tree and a bitter herb. 2. But how? Certainly, if steel[389] were to fall upon a sulphurous mountain[390] with force, then fire would go forth from the steel to ignite the mountain. 3. Out of its warmth, an olive tree[391] planted nearby—outwardly dry but inwardly full of unction[392]—would begin to flow so greatly that the bitter herb, planted at the olive's foot, would be sweetened by the downflow of oil; and thence a healthful drink could be made. 4. This is what I have done for you in a spiritual way. For your heart was as cold toward my love as steel; and yet, in it there moved a modest spark of love for me, namely, when you thought me worthy of love and honor above all others. 5. But that heart of yours then fell upon the sulphurous mountain when the glory and delight of the world turned against you and when your husband, whom you carnally loved beyond all others,[393] was taken from you by death. 6. In truth, mundane pleasure and delight are well compared to a sulphurous mountain;[394] for they are accompanied by swollenness of the soul, the stench of concupiscence, and the burning of punishment. 7. And when at your husband's death your soul was gravely shaken with disturbance, then the spark of my love—which lay, as it were, hidden and enclosed —began to go forth, for, after considering the vanity of the world, you abandoned your whole will to me and desired me above all things. 8. And so, because of that spark of love, you relished the dry olive tree, i.e., the words of the gospels and the conversation[395] of my Doctors, and abstinence so pleased you that all the things that previously seemed bitter began to be sweet for you. 9. And when the oil began to flow and the words of my revelations came down upon you in spirit,[396] then one stood upon the mountain[397] and cried, saying: 'By this drink, thirst is quenched; the cold are warmed; the disturbed are gladdened; and the infirm convalesce.' 10. It is I myself, God, who cry. My words—which you hear from me frequently in spiritual vision[398]—like the good drink, satisfy those who thirst for true charity; second, they warm those who are cold; third, they gladden those who are disturbed; and fourth, they heal those who are weak in soul."

SIXTEENTH INTERROGATION

First question. Again the same religious appeared, standing on his rung as before and saying: "O Judge, I ask you: Why, according to the word of the Gospel,[399] will the goats be placed at your left and the sheep at your right? Surely, you do not delight in such things?"

2. *Second question.* "Item. Since you are God's Son, coequal to the Father, why is it written that neither you nor the angels know the hour of judgment?"[400]

3. *Third question.* "Item. Since your Holy Spirit spoke in the evangelists, why is there such great discrepancy in the gospels?"

4. *Fourth question.* "Item. Since, in your incarnation, there is so great a salvation for the whole human race, why did you delay so long a time to take on flesh?"

5. *Fifth question.* "Item. Since man's soul is better than the whole

148

world, why do you not send your friends and preachers everywhere and at all times?"[401]

6. *Response to the first question.* The Judge answered: "Friend, you do not ask in order to know but so that your malice may be known.[402] Now then, in the Godhead there is nothing carnal, or carnally portrayed, because my Godhead is spirit.[403] And with me, the good and the wicked cannot dwell together at one time any more than light can dwell together with darkness. 7. Neither is there in my Godhead a right or a left—portrayed, as it were, corporeally—nor will they be happier for being at my right rather than at my left. These things have been said as a similitude.[404] 8. For, by 'right,' the loftiness of my divine glory is understood; by 'left,' the lack and loss of all good. 9. Neither sheep nor goats exist in that wonderful glory of mine, where there is nothing corporeal or stained or changeable. However, the behavior of mankind is many times described in similitudes and in the figures of animals. Just as the sheep signifies innocence, the goat signifies wantonness, i.e., incontinent mankind, and must be placed at the left where there is a lack of all good. 10. Therefore, know that I, God, sometimes use human words and similitudes in order that the little one may have something to suck and that the perfect may become more perfect[405] and for the fulfillment of the Scripture, which says that the Son of the Virgin has been set in place for contradiction so that out of many hearts thoughts may be revealed."[406]

11. *Response to the second question.* "Item. As to why I, the Son of God, said that I was ignorant of the hour of judgment,[407] I answer: It is written that Jesus advanced in age and wisdom.[408] Everything that waxes and wanes has mutability; but the Godhead is immutable. 12. Therefore, the fact that I, God's Son, coeternal with the Father, advanced was the result of my human nature. What I did not know was what my humanity did not know. In my Godhead, I knew and know all things. 13. For the Father does nothing other than the things that I, the Son, do.[409] Or does the Father know things unknown to me, the Son, and to the Holy Spirit? Not at all. 14. But only the Father—with whom I, the Son, and the Holy Spirit are one substance, one Godhead, and one will[410]—knows that hour of judgment—not the angels and not any creature."[411]

15. *Response to the third question.* "Item. If the Holy Spirit spoke in the evangelists, why is there such great discrepancy[412] among them? I answer: It is written that the Holy Spirit is manifold in his operations; for to his elect he distributes his gifts in many ways.[413] 16. Indeed, the

Holy Spirit is like a man who has a pair of scales in his hand,[414] and, in many ways, balances and adjusts its extremities until the very movement of the scales[415] arrives at stability. 17. Such a pair of scales is handled in different ways by those accustomed to it and by those not accustomed, in different ways by the strong and by the weak. So too the Holy Spirit—in the manner of the scales—now ascends in human hearts and now again descends. 18. He ascends when he elevates the mind through subtlety of understanding and through devotion of soul and through the inflaming of spiritual desire. He descends when he permits the mind to be involved with difficulties, to be worried by superfluous matters, and to be perturbed by tribulations. 19. And as the scales have no fixity without the moderation of their loads and the application of the hand that controls them, so too, in the operation of the Holy Spirit, moderation is necessary, and a good life and simplicity of intention and discretion of works and virtues. 20. Therefore, when I, God's Son, visible in the flesh, preached different things in different places, I had different imitators and hearers; 21. for some followed me out of love, others to find opportunity[416] and because of curiosity. And some of those who followed me were subtle by nature; others were simpler. 22. Therefore, I spoke simple things by which the simple were instructed; and I also spoke higher things at which the wise wondered. 23. Sometimes, too, I spoke in parables and obscurely—about which some received an opportunity of speaking.[417] Sometimes I repeated things previously said, and sometimes I expanded or condensed them. 24. Therefore, it is no wonder if those who arranged the narrative of the gospels[418] have set down things that are different, but nevertheless true, because some of them set down word for word and others set down the sense of the words, but not the words themselves. 25. Some wrote things that they had heard but had not seen. Others wrote earlier things later. Some wrote more about my divinity. And each one of them wrote just as the Holy Spirit enabled him to speak.[419] 26. However, I want you to know that acceptance is to be given only to those evangelists whom my Church accepts.[420] Many who had zeal tried to write, but not in accordance with my own knowledge. 27. For behold, I said that which was read today: 'Destroy this temple and I shall rebuild it.'[421] 28. Those who testified that they had heard these things were truthful according to the word that they had heard, but they were false witnesses[422] because they did not attend to the sense of my words. For I spoke that word that it might be understood in reference to my body.[423] 29. Similarly, when I said: 'If you do not eat my flesh, you shall not have life,' many went away[424] because they did not pay attention to the conclusion that I spoke: 30. 'My words are life and spirit,'[425] i.e., they have spiritual meaning and power.[426] It is no wonder that they erred, for they did not follow me out of love. 31. And so the Holy Spirit, in the manner of the scales, ascends in the hearts of mankind, now speaking corporeally and now spiritually. He descends when man's heart is hardened against God or becomes involved in heresies or worldly things and is darkened."

32. Then, at that same moment, the Judge said to the inquisitive religious, who was sitting[427] on a rung of the ladder: "You, O friend, have so often asked me subtle questions. Now, for the sake of my bride who is present nearby,[428] I ask you: 33. Why does your soul—which has discretion and understanding of good and evil—love decadent things more than the things of heaven and not live in accord with those things that it understands?" 34. That religious mentioned above answered: "Because I act against reason, and I make the senses of the flesh prevail over reason." Christ said: "Your conscience, then, shall be your judge." 35. Finally, Christ said to the bride: "Behold, daughter, how greatly there prevails in man not only the devil's malice but also a depraved conscience! This comes about from the fact that man does not wrestle against his temptation as he ought. 36. But this was not the behavior of that Master known to you.[429] In his case, the Spirit descended[430] by testing him with temptations to such an extent that it was as if all the heresies stood before him and said, as it were, with one mouth: 'We are truth.' 37. However, he did not trust his senses and did not think thoughts that were beyond him. Therefore he was liberated and was made knowledgeable from 'In the beginning' right through to 'Alpha and O,' just as it was promised to him."[431]

38. *Response to the fourth question.* "Item. As to why I delayed my incarnation for so long a time, I answer: My incarnation was truly necessary; for through it the curse was undone and all things were pacified in heaven and on earth. 39. Nevertheless, it was necessary that man first be taught through the natural law and, then, through the written law. 40. For through the natural law, the quantity and quality of man's love appeared. Through the written law, man understood his weakness and misery and then began to require medicine. 41. It was therefore just that the physician came then, when the infirmity was aggravated, so that where disease abounded, medicine might even more abound.[432] 42. Nevertheless, both under the natural law and under the written law, there were many who were just; and many had the Holy Spirit and foretold many things and instructed others in all that was

honest and waited for me, the Savior. These met with[433] my mercy and not with eternal punishment."

43. *Response to the fifth question.* "Item. As to why, since the soul of man is better than the world, preachers are not sent everywhere and at all times,[434] I answer: Truly, the soul is more worthy and more noble than the whole world and more stable than all things. 44. It is more worthy because it is spiritual and equal to the angels and created for eternal joy. It is more noble because it was made, in the image of my Godhead, both immortal and eternal. 45. Therefore, because man is more worthy and more noble than all creatures, man ought to live more nobly than all; for he, in preference to others, has been enriched with reason. 46. But if man abuses reason and my divine gifts, what wonder is it if, at the time of justice, I punish that which was passed over in the time of mercy? 47. Therefore, preachers are not sent everywhere and at all times because I, God, foresee the hardness of many hearts and spare the labors of my elect lest they be troubled for an empty purpose. 48. And because many who sin intentionally and with sure knowledge, deliberately resolve to persevere in their sins rather than be converted, they are not worthy to hear the messengers of salvation. 49. But, O friend, now I will end, with you, my response to your thoughts; and you shall end your life. Now you shall experience the profit that you have had from your wordy eloquence and the favor of man. Oh how happy you would be if you had paid attention to your profession and your vow!"

50. Item. The Spirit said to the bride:[435] "Daughter, he who was seen to have asked such things at such length lives still in the body; but he is not going to remain alive one day.[436] 51. The thoughts and affections of his heart have been shown to you through similitudes, not for his greater reproach but for the salvation of the souls of others.[437] But behold: together now with his thoughts and his affections, his hope and his life will end."[438]

The twelfth revelation in the Book of Questions, *in which Christ speaks to his bride, blessed Birgitta, and says to her that she must not be disturbed by the fact that he does not do justice at once in the case of a man who is a great sinner. For he defers the sentence of his justice in order that his justice—which is to be done in this man's case—may be made manifest to others. He also says that his divine words which are contained in this book of* Heavenly Revelations *must first grow and bear fruit even to full maturity and, afterwards, produce the effect of their virtue in the world. Indeed, these words are like oil in a lamp, i.e., in a virtuous soul, which they enrich with their unction[439] and which, with the Holy Spirit coming upon it, they make to burn and shine with wonderful splendor. He adds that the said words of the revelations will first rise up and bear fruit in a place other than the kingdom of Sweden, where they began to be revealed by God to that same bride.*

The Son of God speaks: "Why are you disturbed because I put up with that man[440] so patiently? Do you not know that it is a grave thing to burn eternally? Therefore, even to the last point, I suffer him in order that in him my justice may be manifested to others. 2. And so, wherever dye-plants[441] have been sown, if they are cut before their time, they do not have the strength to color a thing as well as if they were cut in due time. 3. Thus, my words—which are to be manifested with justice and mercy and ought to grow and bear fruit even to the fullness of maturity —then indeed will be more fit for the thing to which they will be applied and will fittingly color my virtue.[442] 4. However, why are you disturbed because that man distrusts my words unless more evident signs be shown? Was it you that bore him, or do you know his interior as I do? 5. Indeed, this man is, as it were, a burning and radiant lamp. When fat[443] is put into it, the wick[444] soon draws near, firmly adhering to it. Thus he is a lamp of virtues, a lamp fit to receive my divine grace. 6. As soon as my words will be poured into him, they will liquify completely and will descend to the interior of his heart. And what wonder is it if the fat liquifies when fire burns in the lamp—a fire that liquifies the fat and makes the lamp burn?[445] 7. Truly, that fire is my Spirit, which exists and speaks in you; and the very same Spirit also exists and speaks in him, although in a more hidden and, for him, more useful way. 8. This fire kindles the lamp of his heart to labor in my honor. It also kindles his soul to receive the tallow[446] of my grace and of my words, by which the soul is sweetly sustained[447] and more fully fattened, when it comes to works. 9. Therefore, do not fear; but persist steadfastly in faith! If these words came from your own spirit or from the spirit of this world, then deservedly you would have to dread. 10. But, because they are from my Spirit, which the holy prophets also had, you must, therefore, not fear but rejoice, unless, perhaps, you are more afraid of the empty name of the world than of the postponement[448] of my divine words.

11. "Listen further to what I say: This kingdom is entangled in a great and long-unpunished sin.[449] Therefore my words cannot yet rise

up and bear fruit here; as I shall now make clear to you, speaking by means of a similitude. 12. If a nut had been planted in the earth and something heavy had been placed over it so that it could not rise up, the nut, being naturally sound and fresh, but hindered in its ascent by the pressing weight above it, searches about in the earth for a place to rise where there is less weight.[450] 13. There it fixes roots so deep and stable that it not only produces most beautiful fruit but also grows a strong trunk that annihilates all that impedes its ascent and extends itself over that heavy object. 14. Thus, this nut signifies my words, which due to sin would not now be able to have their rise conveniently in this kingdom and will first rise up and make progress in another place[451] until the hardness of this kingdom's earth decreases and mercy can be disclosed."[452]

The thirteenth revelation in the Book of Questions, *in which God the Father speaks to blessed Birgitta and subtly informs her about the virtue of those five sacred places which are in Jerusalem and Bethlehem, and about the grace received by pilgrims who, with devout humility and true charity, visit those places. He says that in the said places there was a vessel that was closed and not closed, a lion born that was seen and not seen, a lamb that was shorn and not shorn, a serpent placed that lay and did not lay, and an eagle that flew and did not fly. He expounds all these things figuratively, and there follows an exposition and clarification of the figurative words aforesaid.*

God the Father[453] speaks: "There was a certain lord whose servant said to him: 'Behold, your fallow land has been cultivated; and the roots have been pulled out. When is the wheat to be sown?' 2. The lord said to him: 'Even though the roots seem to have been pulled out, nevertheless the hardened old trunks and stumps are still left. In spring, the rains and the winds are going to loosen them. Therefore, patiently await the time for sowing.' 3. To this, the servant replied: 'What am I to do between the seasons of spring and harvest?' The lord said to him:[454] 'I know five places.[455] Everyone who goes to them shall have fivefold fruit if only he comes pure and empty of pride and warm with charity. 4. In the first place, there was a vessel, closed and not closed; a vessel, small and not small; a vessel, luminous and not luminous; a vessel, empty and not empty; a vessel, clean and not clean. 5. In the second place, there was born a lion that was seen and not seen, that was heard and not heard, that was touched and not touched, that was recognized and was not known,[456] that was held and not held. 6. In the third place, there was a lamb, shorn and not shorn; a lamb, wounded and not wounded; a lamb, calling and not calling; a lamb, suffering and not suffering; a lamb, dying and not dying. 7. In the fourth place, there was put a serpent that lay and did not lay, moved and did not move, heard and did not hear, saw and did not see, felt and did not feel. 8. In the fifth place, there was an eagle that flew and did not fly, and that came to a place from which it has never withdrawn, that rested and did not rest, that was renewed and not renewed, that rejoiced and did not rejoice, that was honored and not honored.' "

9. *The exposition and clarification of the things said figuratively above.* The Father speaks: "That vessel[457] of which I spoke to you was Mary, Joachim's daughter,[458] the mother of Christ's human nature.[459] 10. She was indeed a vessel closed and not closed: closed to the devil but not to God. For just as a torrent—wishing to enter a vessel opposed to it and not being able—seeks other ways in and out, so the devil, like a torrent[460] of vices, wished to approach Mary's heart by means of all his inventions; 11. but he never was able to incline her soul toward even the slightest sin because it had been closed against his temptations. For the torrent[461] of my Spirit had flowed into her heart and filled her with special grace. 12. Second, Mary, the mother of my Son,[462] was a vessel small and not small: small and modest in the contempt of her lowliness;[463] great and not small in love for my Godhead. 13. Third, Mary was a vessel empty and not empty: empty of all hedonism and sin;[464] not empty but full of heavenly sweetness and all goodness. 14. Fourth, Mary was a vessel luminous and not luminous: luminous because every beautiful soul is created by me; but Mary's soul so grew toward the full perfection of light that my Son fixed himself in her soul, at whose beauty heaven and earth rejoiced.[465] 15. But this vessel was not luminous in the sight of mankind because she scorned the world's honors and wealth. 16. Fifth, Mary was a vessel clean and not clean: truly clean because she was all beautiful[466] and because there was not found in her even enough uncleanness in which to fix the point of a needle; 17. not clean because she came forth from Adam's root and was born of sinners, although herself conceived without sin in order that, of her, my Son might be born without sin.[467] 18. Therefore, whoever comes to that place,[468] namely, where Mary was born and reared, will not only be cleansed but will also be a vessel to my honor.[469]

19. "The second place is Bethlehem, where my Son was born like a lion.[470] He was seen and held in his humanity; but in his Godhead, he was invisible and unknown.

20. "The third place is Calvary, where my Son, like an innocent lamb,[471] was wounded and died in his humanity; but in his Godhead, he was impassible and immortal.

21. "The fourth place was the garden of my Son's sepulchre, in which his humanity was placed,[472] and it lay like a contemptible serpent;[473] but in his Godhead, he was everywhere.

22. "The fifth place was Mount Olivet,[474] from which my Son, like an eagle, flew[475] up to heaven in his humanity; but in his Godhead, he was always there. He was renewed[476] and he rested in his humanity; but in his Godhead, he was always at rest and always the same.

23. "Therefore, one who comes to these places pure and with a good and perfect will, will be able[477] to see and taste how sweet and pleasant I, God, am.[478] And when you come to these places, I shall show you more."[479]

The Seventh Book of Revelations[480]

Here begins the prologue to the last book.[481]

This book of the *Heavenly Revelations* is the last. The revelations in this book were received by Lady Birgitta in Rome and also when she went on pilgrimage for the first time to Naples and to Sant' Angelo on Monte Gargano.[482] 2. After her return and while she was in Rome, she received others that are contained here. And in that same place, it was divinely told to her by Christ in a vision that she was to go overseas[483] on a pilgrimage to the holy city of Jerusalem.[484] 3. Moreover, on that overseas voyage, she had very many revelations—in Naples as well as in Jerusalem and in Bethlehem—just as it had been divinely promised to her beforehand and as it is contained above in the *Book of Questions* in the last revelation given to her in the kingdom of Sweden.[485] 4. After she returned to Rome from Jerusalem, she had still others that are contained here. And then the said lady died in the City.[486] To her, before her death, Christ foretold in a vision the time and the date on which she was to die. All of these things are contained here below in greater detail.[487]

A revelation which Lady Birgitta had[488] *in Rome after the year of jubilee*[489] *and in which the Virgin Mary foretells to her that she will go to Jerusalem and Bethlehem when it pleases God; and Mary promises her that she will then show her the manner in which she gave birth to her blessed Son. Chapter 1.*

When Lady Birgitta, the bride of Christ, was in Rome and was once absorbed in prayer,[490] she began to think about the Virgin Birth[491] and about the very great goodness of God who willed to choose such a very pure mother for himself. 2. And her heart then became so greatly inflamed with love for the Virgin that she said within herself: "O my Lady, Queen of Heaven, my heart so rejoices over the fact that the most high God forechose[492] you as his mother and deigned to confer upon you so great a dignity 3. that I would rather choose for myself eternal excruciation in hell than that you should lack one smallest point of this surpassing glory or of your heavenly dignity." 4. And so, inebriated with the sweetness of love, she was above herself, alienated from her senses and suspended in an ecstasy of mental contemplation.[493] The Virgin appeared then to her and said to her, 5. "Be attentive,[494] O daughter: I am the Queen of Heaven. Because you love me with a love so immense, I therefore announce to you that you will go on a pilgrimage to the holy city of Jerusalem at the time when it pleases my Son. 6. From there you will go to Bethlehem; and there I shall show you, at the very spot, the whole manner in which I gave birth to that same Son of mine, Jesus Christ;[495] for so it has pleased him."[496]

In Rome Lady Birgitta had this revelation which speaks about the glorious sword of sorrow that pierced the soul of the Blessed Virgin Mary and which the just man Simeon foretold to her in the temple. Chapter 2.

While Lady Birgitta, the bride of Christ, was in Rome, in the church called Saint Mary Major,[497] on the feast of the Purification of the Blessed Virgin Mary,[498] she was caught up into a spiritual vision,[499] and saw that in heaven, as it were,[500] all things were being prepared for a great feast. 2. And then she saw, as it were, a temple of wondrous beauty; and there too was that venerable and just old man, Simeon, ready to receive the Child Jesus in his arms with supreme longing and gladness. 3. She also saw the Blessed Virgin most honorably enter, carrying her young Son to offer him in the temple according to the law of the Lord.[501] And then she saw a countless multitude of angels and of the various ranks of the saintly men of God and of his saintly virgins and ladies, all going before the Blessed Virgin-Mother of God and surrounding her with all joy and devotion. 4. Before her an angel carried a long, very broad, and bloody sword which signified those very great sorrows which Mary suffered at the death of her most loving Son and which were prefigured by that sword which the just man Simeon prophesied would pierce her soul.[502] 5. And while all the heavenly court exulted, this was said to the bride: "See with what great honor and glory the Queen of Heaven is, on this feast, recompensed[503] for the sword of sorrows which she endured at the passion of her beloved Son." And then this vision disappeared.

A revelation which blessed Francis showed to Lady Birgitta wherein he invited her to his chamber to eat and to drink and explained to her spiritually that his chamber was obedience and that his food was to convert souls to God and that his drink was to see his converts loving God with all their strength and fervently absorbed in prayer and in the other virtues. Chapter 3.

On the feast of Saint Francis,[504] in his church in Trastevere in Rome,[505] Saint Francis appeared to the same bride of Christ and said to her, "Come into my chamber to eat and to drink with me." When she heard this, she at once prepared for a journey in order to visit him in Assisi. 2. After she had stayed there five days, she decided to return to Rome and entered the church to recommend herself and her loved ones[506] to Saint Francis. 3. He then appeared to her and said: "Welcome!"[507] For I invited you into my chamber to eat and to drink with me. Know now that this building[508] is not the chamber that I mentioned to you. No, my chamber is true obedience, to which I always so held that I never endured to be without an instructor.[509] 4. For I continually had with me a priest whose every instruction I humbly obeyed, and this was my chamber.[510] Therefore do likewise, for this is pleasing to God. 5. My food,[511] however, whereby I was refreshed with delight, was the fact that I most willingly drew my neighbors away from the vanities of worldly life to serve God with the whole of their hearts; and I then swallowed that joy as if it were the sweetest morsels. 6. My drink, however, was that joy I had while I saw some whom I had converted loving God, devoting themselves with all their strength to prayer and contemplation, teaching others to live good lives, and imitating true poverty.[512] 7. Behold, daughter: that drink so gladdened my soul that, for me, all things in the world lost their taste. Enter, therefore, into this chamber of mine; and eat this, my food; and drink this drink with me. Drink it so that you may be refreshed with God eternally."[513]

Lady Birgitta had this revelation in the city of Ortona, in the kingdom of Naples. Christ speaks to her and assures her that there are relics of the body of Saint Thomas the Apostle on the altar there and that he takes a most sweet delight in these relics and in those of his other saints, counting such relics as his precious treasure on earth and promising great merit and reward to those who honor them with due devotion. Chapter 4.

To a person who was wide awake and at prayer,[514] it seemed as if her heart were on fire with divine charity and entirely full of spiritual joy so that her body itself seemed to fail in its strength. She then heard a voice that said to her: 2. "I am the Creator and Redeemer of all. Know therefore that such a joy, as you now feel in your soul, is a treasure of mine. For it is written that 'the Spirit breathes where he will, and you hear his voice, but you know not whence he comes or whither he goes.'[515] 3. This treasure I bestow on my friends in many ways and by many means[516] and through many gifts. However, I wish to tell you about another treasure, which is not yet in heaven but is with you on earth. 4. This treasure is the relics and bodies of my friends. For, in truth, whether they are fresh or moldering, whether they have turned into dust and ashes or not, the bodies of my saints are most certainly my treasure. 5. But, you may ask, since Scripture says, 'Where your treasure is, there your heart is,'[517] how then is my heart with that treasure, namely, with the relics of the saints? 6. I answer you: my heart's supreme delight is to bestow—according to their will, their faith, and the toils of their journey—everlasting rewards on all those who visit the places[518] and honor the relics of my saints, namely, of those who have been glorified by miracles and canonized by the supreme pontiffs. Thus my heart is with my treasure. 7. Therefore, I want you to know for certain that in this place is my most choice treasure, namely, the relics of my apostle Thomas, which are not found elsewhere in such quantity as they are on this altar, where they are unspoiled and undivided. 8. For when that city[519] where my apostle's body was first buried was destroyed, then with my permission this treasure was translated by certain of my friends to this city and was placed on this altar. 9. But now it lies here as if concealed, for before the apostle's body came here, the princes of this land were of the disposition described in the Scriptures: 10. 'They have mouths and will not speak. They have eyes and will not see. They have ears and will not hear. They have hands and will not touch. They have feet and will not walk,' etc.[520] 11. How could such people then, with such an attitude toward me, their God, be able to pay due honor to such a treasure? 12. Therefore, anyone who loves me and my friends above all, and who would rather die than offend me in the least, and who also has the will and the authority to honor me and to instruct others, such a one, whoever it be, will exalt and honor my treasure, namely, the relics of this my apostle whom I chose and forechose.[521] 13. Therefore, it should be said and preached for very certain that, just as the bodies of the apostles Peter and Paul are in Rome, the relics of Saint Thomas, my apostle, are in Ortona."

14. The bride, however, answered and said: "O Lord, did not the princes of this kingdom have churches built; and did they not practice

great almsgiving?" 15. The Lord said to her: "They have done many things and have offered me much money to appease me. Yet the alms of many of them were to me less pleasing and acceptable because of the marriages that they had contracted contrary to the statutes of the holy fathers. 16. And even though those marriages that the supreme pontiffs permitted were ratified and to be upheld, nevertheless the will of those people was corrupt and was striving against the statutes of the Church. Therefore, at my divine judgment, this must be examined and judged."

Addition[522]

17. When the lady had gone to Ortona, it happened that she and her companions had to spend a whole night under God's open sky, in the cold and in a heavy rain. Then toward dawn, Christ said to her: 18. "For three reasons, tribulation comes to human beings: either for greater humility—as when King David was troubled;[523] or for greater fear and caution—as when Sarah, Abraham's wife, was taken away by the king;[524] or for a human being's greater consolation and honor. 19. And so it has happened to you. For I gave those who met you the impulse to proceed no farther that day. But you would not believe them, and so you suffered as you have. Therefore go now into the city, and my servant Thomas will give you what you desire."

20. *Item concerning the same thing.* Christ appeared in Ortona and said: "I told you earlier[525] that Saint Thomas, my apostle, was my treasure. This is certainly true. 21. For Thomas himself is truly a light of the world.[526] But human beings love darkness more than light."[527] Then Saint Thomas also appeared and said: "I will give to you a treasure that you have long since desired." 22. And in the same moment, a tiny splinter of a bone of blessed Thomas came forth from the very case of Saint Thomas's relics without anyone's touch. The lady received it with joy and reverently saved it.[528]

Lady Birgitta had this revelation in Naples at the request of Lord El-zear,[529] son of the countess of Ariano and, at that time, a young scholar of good disposition. He had then asked Lady Birgitta to pray to God for him. While she was at prayer, the Virgin Mary appeared to her and gave to her this revelation, by means of which she informs him about the measures to be maintained in his life and very beautifully says that reason must be the doorkeeper and guardian of the soul, to expel all temptations and resist them manfully[530] *lest they enter one's inner house. Chapter 5.*[531]

To almighty God, from whom all good things proceed, be praise and honor, especially for these things that he has done for you in the time of your youth! Of his grace one must ask that the love you have for him may increase in you daily even until death.

2. A mighty and magnificent king constructed a house, in which he placed his beloved daughter,[532] assigning her to the custody of a man and saying this: 3. "My daughter has mortal enemies and therefore you must guard her with all care. There are four things that you must beware with diligent premeditation and constant concern: 4. first, that no one undermine the foundation of the house; second, that no one climb over the top of the outer walls;[533] third, that no one breach the walls of the house;[534] fourth, that no enemy enter through the gates."

5. My Lord, this parable[535] that I write for you out of divine charity —God, the searcher of all hearts,[536] being my witness—must be understood spiritually. Therefore, by the house I mean your body, which the King of heaven formed out of the earth. 6. By the king's daughter I mean your soul, created by the power of the Most High and placed in your heart. By the guardian I mean human reason, which will guard your soul according to the will of the eternal King. By the foundation I mean a good, firm, and stable will. For on it must be built all good works, by which the soul is best defended. 7. Therefore, since your will is such that you wish to live for nothing else but to follow God's will, showing him by word and deed all the honor you can, and also serving him with your body and your goods and all your strength, as long as you live, in order that you may be able to commend your soul, preserved from all impurity of the flesh, to its Creator, 8. then, oh how vigilantly must you guard this foundation, i.e., your will, by means of the guardian, i.e., your reason, so that no one may be able to undermine it with his siege-engines[537] to the soul's harm. 9. By those who strive to undermine this type of foundation I mean those who speak to you thus and say: "My Lord, be a layman and take to yourself a charming, noble, and wealthy wife so that you may rejoice in your offspring and heirs and not be weighed down by the tribulation of the flesh." 10. And others perhaps reply in this manner: "If you want to become a cleric, then also learn the liberal arts, to the end that you may be called 'master' while procuring for yourself, by prayers or gifts, as much as you can of the goods and revenues of the Church. 11. Then you will have worldly

honor for your knowledge; and by your worldly friends and your many servants, you will be glorified[538] for the abundance of your riches." 12. Behold: if perhaps anyone should offer you such persuasion, immediately make the guardian, i.e., reason, answer him and say that you would be willing to endure all the tribulation of the flesh rather than lose your chastity. 13. Answer also that you want to acquire knowledge and the arts for the honor of God and the defense of the Catholic faith, for the strengthening of good people and for the correction of the erring and of all who need your advice and teaching; and say that you do not wish to desire anything in this life beyond sustenance for your body and for the household truly necessary to you and not overly enlarged for the sake of vainglory.[539] 14. Say also that, if perchance divine providence were to confer on you some added dignity, you desire to order all things wisely for the benefit of your neighbor and for the honor of God. 15. And so indeed the guardian, i.e., reason, will be able to expel those who are exerting themselves to undermine the foundation, i.e., your good will.

16. Reason must also constantly and diligently beware lest anyone climb over the top of the walls. By this top of the walls I mean charity, which is more sublime than all the virtues. 17. Know therefore most certainly that the devil desires nothing more than to leap over that wall. And so he incessantly tries as much as he can that mundane charity and carnal love may surpass divine charity. 18. Wherefore, my Lord, as often as worldly love attempts to advance itself in your heart in preference to divine charity, immediately send the guardian, i.e., reason, out to meet it with the commandments of God and saying that you would rather endure death in soul and body than live to such an end that you would, by word or deed, provoke a God so kind, 19. and, indeed, that you would not in any way spare your own life, your goods or possessions, or the favorable opinions of your relatives and friends provided that you might be able to please God alone in every respect and honor him in all things, 20. and that you choose to submit voluntarily to all tribulations rather than cause any harm, scandal, or trouble to any of your neighbors—whether higher or lower than yourself—and that, in accord with the precept of the Lord, you wish instead to love all your neighbors thoroughly and in a brotherly way. 21. And if you do this, my Lord, you are proved to love God more than yourself, and your neighbor as yourself.[540] Then, therefore, the guardian, i.e., reason, can rest securely because no rival of your soul is able to climb over the top of the walls.

22. By the house walls, in truth, I mean four delights of the heavenly

court, which a human being ought to long for interiorly with attentive meditation.[541] 23. The first is a fervent longing in the heart to see God himself in his eternal glory and those unfailing riches that are never taken away from one who has acquired them. 24. The second is an incessant wish to hear those sweet-sounding voices of the angels in which, without tiring and without end, they praise God and unceasingly adore him. 25. The third is a whole-hearted and fervently longing desire eternally to praise God even as the very angels do. The fourth is a longing to possess the everlasting consolations[542] of the angels and of the holy souls in heaven. 26. Hence it is to be noted that, just as one who is inside a house is always surrounded by walls wherever one turns, so it is with everyone who, day and night, with supreme longing, desires those four things—namely, to see God in his glory, to hear the angels praising God, to praise God together with them, and to possess their consolations. 27. Truly, wherever such a one turns or whatever work he is intent upon, he is then always preserved unharmed inside firm walls so that, as a result, by dwelling among the very angels in this life, he may be said to enjoy the company[543] of God.

28. Oh how much, my Lord, your enemy longs to dig through walls of this sort and to take such inner delights away from the heart and to introduce and entangle into your desire others contrary to them, which could gravely harm your soul. 29. On which account, the guardian, i.e., reason, must have diligent precaution about the two ways by which the enemy usually comes. The first way is the hearing; the second, sight. 30. He comes indeed through the hearing when he introduces into the heart the delights of secular songs and of various sweet-sounding instruments, of useless tales and of narrations of the praises of one's own person.[544] 31. The more these things raise one up through pride in oneself, the more distantly one is separated from the humble Christ. Therefore the guardian, i.e., reason, must resist such delight and say this: 32. "Just as the devil has hatred for all the humility that the Holy Spirit breathes into the hearts of human beings, so I, by the working of God's help, will have hatred for all the pomp[545] and worldly pride that the evil spirit, with his pestilent inflammation, pours into hearts; and it shall be to me as hateful as the stench of rotten corpses, which immediately suffocates those who catch it in their nostrils." 33. Through sight also the enemy is accustomed to come, as if by a second way, to dig through the aforementioned house walls; and he brings with him many tools: namely, all sorts of metals wrought into various objects and forms, precious stones, prestigious clothing, lordly palaces, castles, es-

tates, ponds, forests, vineyards, and all other sorts of costly and lucrative things. 34. For if all these things are fervently desired, they are a proven means of dissipating the aforementioned house walls, i.e., the heavenly delights. Therefore the guardian, i.e., reason, must run out quickly, before such things come into the heart's delight and love, and must say: 35. "If I shall have in my power any of the possessions of this sort, I will lay it away in that chest where thieves or moth are not feared;[546] and with divine grace helping me, I will not offend my God through coveting others' possessions;[547] nor, through ambition for the things of others, will I separate myself in any way from the company[548] of those who serve Christ."

36. By the gates of the said house I mean, in fact, all the body's needs, which indeed the body cannot decline:[549] namely, eating, drinking, sleep, wakefulness, and even occasional distresses and joys. 37. Therefore the guardian, i.e., reason, must stand by these gates, i.e., the body's needs, with concern and, with divine fear, must resist enemies wisely and persistently lest they enter toward the soul. 38. Therefore, just as in taking food and drink one must beware lest the enemy enter through overindulgence, which makes the soul slothful in serving God, so too one must beware lest the foe gain entrance through excessive abstinence, which makes the body weak in doing all things.[550] 39. Let the guardian, i.e., reason, also take note lest, either when you are alone with your household or when guests arrive, for the sake of worldly honor and the favorable opinion of human beings, there be an uninterrupted succession of too many courses; but, out of divine charity, treat each one well while excluding a multiplicity of foods and also extravagant delicacies. 40. Next, the guardian, i.e., reason, must with vigilance and attention consider the fact that, just as food and drink must be moderated, so too must sleep be moderated with fear in such a way that the body may be nimble and in better order for accomplishing all the honor of God so that every waking moment may be usefully spent on the divine offices and on honest labors, with all the heaviness of sleep far removed. 41. Moreover, at the approach of any distress or rancor, the guardian, i.e., reason, accompanied by his companion, namely, fear of God, must swiftly run forth lest, through anger or impatience, it happen that you forfeit divine grace and gravely provoke God against yourself. 42. What is more, when some consolation or joy fills your heart, let the guardian, i.e., reason, imprint the heart more deeply with the fear of God which, with the help of the grace of Jesus Christ, will moderate that consolation or joy in a way that will be of more use to you.

Addition

43. When Lady Birgitta was in Naples, there were revealed to her the innermost secrets of the heart of Elzear—later, a cardinal—and certain wonderful things that were going to happen to him. When he heard these things, he was stunned; and he changed for the better.

In the year of our Lord, 1371, in the month of May, on the day[551] of blessed Urban, pope and martyr, when Lady Birgitta had been living in Rome for many years, after she had returned from pilgrimages in the kingdom of Naples, while she was at prayer on the day and in the month given above, Christ appeared to her and said that she should prepare herself to make a pilgrimage to Jerusalem in order to visit the Holy Sepulchre. Chapter 6.

While Lady Birgitta was living continuously in Rome, she was one day at prayer and her mind was lifted up. Christ then appeared to her and spoke to her, saying this: 2. "Prepare yourselves[552] now to make a pilgrimage to Jerusalem to visit my sepulchre and the other holy places that are to be found there. You will leave Rome when I tell you."

In Rome before Lady Birgitta went overseas,[553] a certain devout Friar Minor consulted the said lady concerning some doubts in his conscience. As this lady prayed, the Virgin Mary appeared to her and gave her complete answers to those doubts and, moreover, said that no matter how sinful the pope or the priests might be—provided that they are not heretics—the pope has the keys of the Church and the true power of binding and loosing and that at the altar the priests fully confect[554] and handle the Blessed Sacrament of the Body of Christ even though they are unworthy of heavenly glory. Chapter 7.[555]

Honor and thanks be given to almighty God and to the Blessed Virgin Mary, his most worthy Mother! It seemed to me, unworthy person that I am, that while I was absorbed in prayer, the Mother of God spoke to me, a sinner, these following words:

2. "Say to my friend the friar, who through you sent his supplication to me, that it is the true faith and the perfect truth that if a person, at the devil's instigation, had committed every sin against God and then, with true contrition and the purpose of amendment, truly repented these sins and humbly, with burning love, asked God for mercy, 3. there is no

doubt that the kind and merciful God himself would immediately be as ready to receive that person back into his grace with great joy and happiness as would be a loving father who saw returning to him his only, dearly beloved son, now freed from a great scandal and a most shameful death.[556] 4. Yes, much more willingly than any fleshly father, the loving[557] God himself forgives his servants all their sins if they assiduously repent and humbly ask him for mercy and they fear to go on committing sins, and, with all the longing of their hearts, desire God's friendship above all things.

5. "Therefore say to that same friar, on my behalf, that because of his good will and my prayer, God in his goodness has already forgiven him all the sins that he ever committed in all the days of his life. 6. Tell him also that because of my prayer the love that he has for God will always increase in him right up to his death and will in no way diminish. 7. Likewise, say to him that it pleases God my Son that he stay in Rome, preaching, giving good advice to those who ask, hearing confessions, and imposing salutary penances, unless his superior should send him sometimes out of the city for some lawful necessity. 8. For their transgressions, the same friar should charitably reprove his other brothers with good words, with salutary teachings, and, when he might be able to correct them, even with just rebukes, to the end that they may keep the rule and humbly amend their lives. 9. Furthermore, I now make known to him that his Masses and his reading and his prayers are acceptable and pleasing to God. 10. And therefore tell him that, just as he guards himself against any excess in food and drink and sleep, so he must diligently guard himself against too much abstinence, in order that he may not suffer any faintness in performing divine labors and services.[558] 11. Also, he is not to have an overabundance of clothing but only necessary things, according to the Rule of Saint Francis,[559] so that pride and cupidity may not ensue; for the less costly and valuable his clothes have been, the more lavish shall be his reward. 12. And let him humbly obey all of his superior's instructions that are not contrary to God and that the friar's own ability permits him to perform.

13. "Tell him also, on my behalf, what he will answer to those who say that the pope is not the true pope and that it is not the true Body of Jesus Christ my Son that the priests confect[560] on the altar. He should answer those heretics in this way: 14. 'You have turned the backs of your heads to God, and thus you do not see him. Turn therefore to him your faces, and then you will be able to see him.' 15. For it is the true and Catholic faith that a pope who is without heresy[561] is—no matter

how stained he be with other sins—never so wicked as a result of these sins and his other bad deeds that there would not always be in him full authority and complete power to bind and loose souls. 16. He possesses this authority through blessed Peter and has acquired it from God.[562] For before Pope John,[563] there were many supreme pontiffs who are now in hell. Nevertheless, the just and reasonable judgments that they made in the world are standing and approved in God's sight.

17. "For a similar reason, I also say that all those priests who are not heretical[564]—although otherwise full of many other sins—are true priests and truly confect the Body of Christ my Son and that truly they touch God in their hands on the altar and administer the other sacraments even though, because of their sins and evil deeds, they are unworthy of heavenly glory in God's sight."

After the abovesaid friar had received from Lady Birgitta the last revelation above, he asked her to pray to God concerning the matter of Christ's private property,[565] and also concerning the authority of the supreme pontiff and of the celebrating priests. As the lady was praying, the Virgin Mary appeared to her and answered all these points as follows. Chapter 8.[566]

"Say to my friend the friar that it is not licit for you to know whether the soul of Pope John XXII is in hell or in heaven.[567] 2. Nor indeed is it licit for you to know anything about the sins that the same pope took with him when, after his death, he came before God's judgment. 3. But tell the same friar that those decretals[568] that the same Pope John made or established concerning Christ's private property contain no error in the Catholic faith nor any heresy. 4. I, indeed, who gave birth to the true God himself, bear witness to the fact that the same Jesus Christ, my Son, had one personal possession and that he alone possessed it. This was that tunic that I made with my own hands. 5. And the prophet witnesses to this fact, saying in the person of my Son: 'Over my garment, they cast lots.'[569] Behold and be attentive[570] to the fact that he did not say 'our garment' but 'my garment.'[571] 6. Know too that, as often as I dressed him in that tunic for the use of his most holy body, my eyes then filled at once with tears and my whole heart was wrung with trouble and grief and was afflicted with intense bitterness. 7. For I well knew the manner in which that tunic would in future be separated from my Son, namely, at the time of his passion when, naked and innocent, he would be crucified by the Jews.[572] 8. And this tunic was that garment over which his crucifiers cast lots.[573] No one had that same tunic while he lived, but only he alone.

9. "Know too that all those who say that the pope is not the true pope and that the priests are not true priests or rightly ordained and that what is consecrated by the priests in the celebration of Masses is not the true Body of my blessed Son, yes, all those who assert such errors are puffed up with the spirit of the devil in hell. 10. For truly these same heretics have committed such serious acts of malice and frightful sins against God that, because of their very great demerits, they are damnably filled with diabolic wickedness, and, through their heresy, they are cut off and cast out from the number of the whole flock of Christianity in the just judgment of the divine majesty, just as Judas was shut out and cut off from the sacred number of the apostles because of his wicked demerits: for he betrayed Christ my Son. 11. Know that, even so, all those who want to amend their lives will obtain mercy from God."

How Christ, speaking to Lady Birgitta during prayer, instructs her to go now to Jerusalem and promises to her bodily strength and the necessary expenses. Chapter 9.

The Son of God speaks to blessed Birgitta his bride and says: "Go now and depart from Rome for Jerusalem. Why do you plead your age? I am the Creator of nature; I can weaken or strengthen nature as it pleases me. 2. I will be with you. I will direct your way. I will guide you and lead you back[574] to Rome; and I will procure for you everything necessary, more adequately than you have ever had before."[575]

The Virgin Mary, speaking to Lady Birgitta, says that in no way is it God's will that clerics should have wives or be contaminated by carnal vice—prohibiting any pope from allowing this marriage of clerics to take place or be established in God's Church. Chapter 10.

Rejoice eternally, O blessed Body of God, in perpetual honor and in perennial victory and in your everlasting omnipotence together with your Father and the Holy Spirit and also with your blessed and most worthy Mother and with all your glorious heavenly court. 2. To you be praise indeed, O eternal God, and endless thanksgiving for the fact that you deigned to become a human being and that for us in the world you willed to consecrate your venerable Body out of material bread and lovingly bestowed it on us as food for the salvation of our souls!

3. It happened that a person who was absorbed in prayer heard then a voice saying to her: "O you to whom it has been given to hear and see spiritually,[576] hear now the things that I want to reveal to you: 4. namely, concerning that archbishop[577] who said that if he were pope, he would give leave for all clerics and priests to contract marriages in the flesh. He thought and believed that this would be more acceptable to God than that clerics should live dissolutely, as they now do. 5. For he believed that through such marriage the greater carnal sins might be avoided; and even though he did not rightly understand God's will in this matter, nonetheless that same archbishop was still a friend of God.

6. "But now I shall tell you God's will in this matter; for I gave birth to God himself. You will make these things known to my bishop and say to him that circumcision was given to Abraham[578] long before the law was given to Moses and that, in that time of Abraham, all human beings whatsoever were guided according to their own intellect and according to the choice of their own will and that, nevertheless, many of them were then friends of God. 7. But after the law was given to Moses, it then pleased God more that human beings should live under the law and according to the law rather than follow their own human understanding and choice. It was the same with my Son's blessed Body. 8. For after he instituted in the world this new sacrament of the eucharist and ascended into heaven, the ancient law was then still kept: namely, that Christian priests lived in carnal matrimony. 9. And, nonetheless, many of them were still friends of God because they believed with simple purity that this was pleasing to God: namely, that Christian priests should have wives and live in wedlock just as, in the ancient times of the Jews, this had pleased him in the case of Jewish priests. And so, this was the observance of Christian priests for many years. 10. But that observance and ancient custom seemed very abominable and hateful[579] to all the heavenly court and to me, who gave birth to his body: namely, because it was being thus observed by Christian priests who, with their hands, touch and handle this new and immaculate Sacrament of the most holy Body of my Son. 11. For the Jews had, in the ancient law of the Old Testament, a shadow, i.e., a figure, of this Sacrament; but Christians now have the truth itself—namely, him who is true God and man—in that blessed and consecrated bread. 12. After those earlier Christian priests had observed these practices for a time, God himself, through the infusion of his Holy Spirit, put into the heart of the pope then guiding the Church another law more acceptable and pleasing to him in this matter: 13. namely, by pouring this infusion into the heart of

the pope so that he established a statute in the universal Church that Christian priests, who have so holy and so worthy an office, namely, of consecrating this precious Sacrament, should by no means live in the easily contaminated, carnal delight of marriage.[580] 14. And therefore, through God's preordinance and his judgment, it has been justly ordained that priests who do not live in chastity and continence of the flesh are cursed and excommunicated before God and deserve to be deprived of their priestly office.[581] 15. But still, if they truthfully amend their lives with the true purpose of not sinning further, they will obtain mercy from God.

16. "Know this too: that if some pope concedes to priests a license to contract carnal marriage, God will condemn him to a sentence as great, in a spiritual way, as that which the law justly inflicts in a corporeal way on a man who has transgressed so gravely that he must have his eyes gouged out, his tongue and lips, nose and ears cut off, his hands and feet amputated, 17. all his body's blood spilled out to grow completely cold, and finally, his whole bloodless corpse cast out to be devoured by dogs and other wild beasts. 18. Similar things would truly happen in a spiritual way[582] to that pope who were to go against the aforementioned preordinance and will of God and concede to priests such a license to contract marriage. 19. For that same pope would be totally deprived by God of his spiritual sight and hearing, and of his spiritual words and deeds. All his spiritual wisdom would grow completely cold; and finally, after his death, his soul would be cast out to be tortured eternally in hell so that there it might become the food of demons everlastingly and without end. 20. Yes, even if Saint Gregory the Pope[583] had made this statute, in the aforesaid sentence he would never have obtained mercy from God if he had not humbly revoked his statute before his death."[584]

This is the beginning of a revelation that Lady Birgitta had in Naples for the lady queen of the same city. But other things contained therein are not set down here because they are secrets that pertain to the status and person of the said lady queen. Chapter 11.[585]

"I am God, the Creator of all. I gave to angels and to humans free decision so that those who willed to do my will might remain with me forever and so that those who thought things contrary to me might be separated from me. 2. And so, certain of the angels became demons because they did not will to love me or to obey me. Then when man had been created and the devil saw my love for man, the devil not only became my enemy but also promoted war against me by inciting Adam to violate my commandments. 3. The devil prevailed on that occasion by my permission and as a result of my justice;[586] and ever since that time, the devil and I are in discord and strife because I want man to live according to my will while the devil exerts himself to make man follow his own desires.[587] 4. Therefore at that moment when I opened heaven with my heart's blood, the devil was deprived of that justice which he seemed to have;[588] and those souls that were worthy were saved and freed. 5. Then indeed the law was established that it should be in man's decision[589] to follow me, his God, in order to obtain the everlasting crown. But if he follows the devil's desires, he will have everlasting punishment. 6. Thus the devil and I do struggle, in that we both desire souls as bridegrooms desire their brides. For I desire souls in order to give them eternal joy and honor; but the devil desires to give them eternal horror and sorrow. Hear what the queen had done[590] to me. I allowed the raising of her to a kingship, etc."[591]

Addition

7. Christ speaks: "Write to her that she should make a clean confession of all that she had done[592] from her youth and that she should have a firm purpose of amendment according to the advice of her confessor. 8. Second, she should diligently recall the manner and the quality of her life during her marriage and during her rule; for she is going to render an account of everything to me. 9. Third, she must have the intention of paying her debts and of restoring that which she knows was wrongly acquired. For the soul is in peril as long as such things are kept; and it does no good to give lavish gifts if debts go unpaid. 10. Fourth, she is not to burden the community with her new inventions,[593] but instead should lighten the burdens which have grown customary. For God will hear the sigh and the crying of those in misery.[594] 11. Fifth, she must have councilors who are just and not covetous; and she must entrust her judgments to such men as love truth and do not fawn upon factions or seek to grow rich but know how to be content with what is necessary. 12. Sixth, every day, at fixed times, she should remember God's wounds and his passion, for by this means the love of God is renewed in the heart. 13. Seventh, at fixed times she should collect the poor, wash their feet, and refresh them. She should love all her subjects with sincere

charity, bringing all those at strife to accord and consoling those who are unjustly offended. 14. Eighth, she should grant her gifts with discretion and according to her means, not oppressing some while making others rich, but wisely relieving some without burdening anyone. 15. Ninth, she is not to be more attentive to the money of criminals than to justice; but setting aside all greed, she is to weigh the quality of the crimes and show more compassion where she sees greater humility. 16. Tenth, during her lifetime, she is to apply all her diligence to ensure that her kingdom can be in a calm state after her death, for I predict to her that henceforth she will not have offspring from her womb. 17. Eleventh, she should be content with the colors and beauty by which God has adorned her face; for extraneous color is very displeasing to God.[595] 18. Twelfth, she is to acquire greater humility and contrition for her sins because, in my eyes, she is a predator of many souls, a prodigal squanderer of my goods, and a rod of tribulation[596] to my friends. 19. Thirteenth, she must have continual fear in her heart because in all the time she has had, she has led the life of a lascivious woman rather than that of a queen. 20. Fourteenth, let her put aside worldly customs and those women who flatter her. The short time that she has left, she should spend in honoring me, for up to now she has treated me as if I were a human being without recollection of her[597] sins. 21. Let her now fear and live in such a way that she may not feel my judgment. Otherwise, if she does not listen to me, I will judge her not as a queen but as an ungrateful apostate; and I will scourge her from head to heel; and she will be a disgrace before me and my angels and my saints."

22. *Item,*[598] *a revelation.* Christ speaks: "Write those things with fewer and gentler words, just as the Holy Spirit will inflame you, and send them through my bishop[599] to the queen."

23. *Item, concerning a certain queen.* A lady was seen standing in a shift spattered with sperm and mud. And a voice was heard: "This woman is a monkey that sniffs at its own stinking posterior.[600] She has poison in her heart and she is harmful to herself and she hastens into snares that throw her down." 24. And again she was seen wearing a crown of twigs spattered with human excrement and with mud from the streets and sitting naked on a tottering beam.[601] 25. At once there appeared a most beautiful virgin who said: "This is that insolent and audacious woman who is reputed by mankind to be a lady of the world, but in God's eyes, she has been cast off, as you see." 26. And the virgin

added: "O woman, think of your entrance and be attentive to your end;[602] and open the eyes of your heart and see that your councilors[603] are those who hate your soul!"

27. *Item, concerning a certain queen.* A woman was seen sitting on a golden seat; and two Ethiopians[604] stood before her—one, as it were, on the right and the other on the left. 28. The one standing on the right called out and said: "O lionlike woman, I bring blood. Take and pour out! For it is a mark of the lioness to thirst after blood." 29. The one on the left said: "O woman, I bring to you fire in a vessel. Take—for you are of a fiery nature—and pour out into the waters in order that your memory may last in the waters as well as on the land."[605] 30. Then a virgin of wondrous beauty appeared, and the Ethiopians fled from her sight. She said: "This woman is in a perilous state. If she prospers in accordance with her will, the result will be tribulation for many. 31. But if she suffers tribulation, the result will be more useful to her for obtaining eternal life. She herself does not wish to give up her own will or to suffer tribulation in compliance with God. Therefore, if she is left to her own will, she will not be the cause of consolation[606] for herself or for others."

32. *Item, a revelation.* The Son appeared and said: "This woman had done[607] some things that did please me. Therefore, because of the prayers of my friends, I am willing to point out to her how she may escape the scorn of mankind and the squandering of her own soul if, indeed, she obeys well; if not, she would not escape the justice of the Judge; for she did not will to hear the Father's voice."

33. *Concerning Lord Gomez.*[608] The Mother of God speaks: "Advise him to do justice wherever he can. If he knows that he has goods that were wrongly acquired, he must not delay in making restitution. 34. He must also be careful not to impose unusual burdens on his subjects, and he must be content with the things that he has because they are sufficient for him if he manages them discreetly and with moderation. 35. Women other than his own wife, he must avoid like poison; and he must not lead out the army against anyone nor take part in the action himself unless he fully knows that justice is on his side and that the war is just. 36. He must also be zealous in making frequent use of confession and in receiving the Body of Christ more frequently and in occupying himself, at fixed times in the day, with the remembrance of Christ's passion and his wounds."

37. *Concerning Anthony of Carleto.*[609] Christ speaks: "Tell the queen to let him stay in his position. If he rises up to greater things, it will be at

the cost of his soul; and neither he himself nor his friends will have any joy out of his promotion." And so it all turned out.

This revelation was given by God to Lady Birgitta in Naples at the request of Lord Bernard, the Neapolitan archbishop.[610] *He asked her to pray to God concerning some doubts he had in his conscience. When she was at prayer, Christ appeared to her, answered all the archbishop's doubts, and gave him instruction and the measures he should maintain in governing his own house and in governing his subjects in his diocese. Chapter 12.*

Christ speaks to his bride and says: "Tell him that if he wishes to be called a bishop in the justice of the divine judgment, he must not imitate the manners and customs of many who are now rulers of the Church. 2. I took on a human body from a virgin in order that by words and deeds I might fulfill the law which, from eternity, had been ordained in the Godhead. I opened the gate of heaven with my heart's blood, and I so illumined the way by my words and deeds that all might use my example in order to merit eternal life. 3. But truly, the words that I said and the deeds that I did in the world are now almost completely forgotten and neglected.[611] 4. For this, no one is as much a cause as the prelates of the churches. They are full of pride, greed, and the rottenness of bodily pleasure. All of these things are contrary to my commandments and to Holy Church's honorable statutes, which my friends established out of great devotion after my ascension and after I had accomplished my will in the world. 5. For those wicked prelates of the churches, who are filled with the malignity of an evil spirit, have left to mankind examples that are exceedingly harmful to souls; and therefore it is necessary for me to exact full justice from them by doing judgment on them, abolishing them from the book of life in heaven and placing them beside my enemy Lucifer in hell, in hellish sees that shall be the seat of their perpetual excruciation.[612] 6. Nevertheless, you ought to know that if anyone is willing to amend himself before death by loving me with all his heart and if he abstains from sins, then I will be prompt in showing my mercy. Tell him also, as if on your own part, these words that follow:[613]

7. "My Lord, it sometimes happens that, from a black furnace, there goes forth a beautiful flame that is useful and quite necessary for fashioning works of beauty. 8. But that does not mean that the furnace must then be praised for its black color. The praise and honor and thanks are

owed to the artist and master of those works. 9. It is a similar situation with me, unworthy woman that I am, if you find[614] something useful in my advice; for then you ought continually to show infinite thanks and willing service, not to me, but to God himself, who made and makes all things and who has a perfect will to do good. 10. My Lord, I begin by first speaking to you of those things that touch the salvation of many souls. I advise you that, if you would have God's friendship, neither you, nor any other bishop acting on your behalf, should be willing to promote anyone to sacred orders 11. unless he has first been diligently examined by good clerics and has been found to be so suitable in his life and character that, by the testimony of wise and truthful men, he is declared worthy to receive such an office. With diligent attention, see to it that all the bishops under you and all the suffragans of your archbishopric do the same. 12. For no one could believe how great God's indignation is against those bishops who do not take care to know and diligently to examine the quality of those whom they promote to orders of such dignity in their bishoprics. 13. Whether they do this at the supplication of others or out of negligence and laziness or because of fear,[615] they shall indeed render a most strict account of this at God's judgment. 14. I also advise you to inquire about the number and the identities of those holders of benefices in your diocese who have the care of souls. Summon them to your presence at least once a year to discuss then with them their own welfare and that of the souls of those under them. 15. And if, by chance, they could not all come together on the same day, then definite dates are to be set on which they may come to you individually during the year so that none of them may be able to excuse himself in any way from consulting you for a whole year. 16. And you are to preach to them about the kind of life to be led by those who have an office of such great dignity. 17. Know too that priests who have concubines and celebrate Mass are as acceptable and pleasing to God as were the inhabitants of Sodom whom God submersed in hell.[616] 18. And even though the Mass, in itself, always is the same and has the same power and efficacy, nevertheless, the kiss of peace that such fornicating priests give in the Mass is as pleasing to God as the kiss by which Judas handed over the Savior of all.[617] 19. Therefore constantly try as much as possible, with words and deeds, by enticing or rebuking or threatening, to work together with them so that they may endeavor to lead a chaste life, especially since they must touch so very holy a Sacrament and, with their hands, administer it to other faithful Christians. 20. Furthermore, for their salvation you should advise all the clergy, both the higher ranks made up of prelates or canons and also the minor clerics—all, that is, who are subject to your rule and have ecclesiastical incomes—that they should correct their lives in every respect. 21. And let no one believe that, for the sake of avoiding sodomy, fornication is at all permissible for clerics; nor, for that reason, is it to be endured that they should defile themselves with women.[618] For every Christian who has the use of intellect and who does not care about eternal life while he is living, will undoubtedly endure after death the most severe punishments of hell for eternity.

22. "I also advise you that your household should not be too large out of pride, but that it should be well proportioned to the needs of your office as a ruler and to the requirements of your status. 23. Those clerics, therefore, who are called your companions, you should keep with you wherever you may be, for the good of your reputation rather than for vainglory or for pomp;[619] and they are to be few in number rather than many. 24. But of those clerics whom you maintain for no other reason than to sing the divine office or to pursue studies or to teach others or to do writing, you may have as many as you please. And nevertheless it is to your advantage to take diligent care, as best you can, for their correction and for the salvation of their souls. 25. Be attentive to the rest of your servants so that each has his own task; and if some of them are superfluous, do not keep them out of vainglory lest your heart be elated[620] at having a larger household than your peers. 26. It is also expedient that you always have in mind those truly necessary members of your household whom you keep with you; painstakingly scrutinize their lives like a true householder,[621] correcting their actions, lives, and characters and, with good formation, encouraging and admonishing them in a fatherly way so that they learn to flee from sins and vices and to love God above all things. 27. It is indeed more acceptable to God and more useful to yourself that you keep with you no member of the household who is unwilling to comply with sound advice and humbly amend his transgressions.

28. "Of your clothing, I advise you never to have in your possession more than three pairs[622] at one time; everything beyond this, you should immediately give to God himself. 29. Of bedcovers, towels, and tablecloths, keep for yourself only what is necessary and useful to you; and give the rest to God. 30. Of silver vessels, reserve for yourself just enough for your own person and for the guests who eat at your own table; 31. donate the superfluous pieces to God with a cheerful mind.[623] For the rest of your household and the guests who sit at other tables

certainly can, without any embarrassment, eat and drink using vessels of tin, clay, wood, or glass. 32. For that custom which now prevails in the houses of bishops and lords of having an overly excessive abundance of gold and silver is quite harmful to souls and very repulsive to God himself, who, for our sake, subjected himself to all poverty.[624] 33. Beware, also, of having too many courses and extravagant delicacies.[625] Nor should you have overly large and expensive horses, but rather those that are moderate in size and price. 34. For such large horses are needed by those who expose themselves to the dangers of war for the defense of justice and the protection of life and not for pride. 35. Indeed, I tell you that as often as prelates, out of pride and vainglory, mount big horses, the devil mounts the prelates' necks. 36. For I know a person[626] who, when the prelates and cardinals proudly lifted their feet to ride on the backs of their big horses, saw demons as Ethiopians[627] who then lifted their feet and mounted the necks of the prelates and sat there laughing. 37. As often as the prelates pompously[628] spurred their horses, the Ethiopians lifted their heads in their glee and kicked their heels into the breasts of those horsemen. 38. Again, I advise you to have your vicars promise under oath that, while carrying out your business, they will not presume to do anything contrary to justice. 39. And if they later do the opposite, you are to have them rebuked in accordance with justice. If you do as I have said, you can be confident that your conscience is quite sound.

40. "And now I give advice for the consolation of the souls of your departed, about whom you asked me whether or not they were in purgatory and what almsdeeds ought to be done for them, etc.[629] 41. I answer and say that every day for one year you are to have two Masses celebrated for them and every day you are to feed two paupers, and every week take care to distribute one florin in coins to the poor. 42. Say also to the parish priests that they are to correct their parishioners and to rebuke them for their open sins in cases that pertain to them in order that they may be able to live better lives.[630] Those parishioners who are unwilling to be rebuked should then be rebuked by you. 43. If, however, you know that some are openly sinning against God and justice, and if they are such great tyrants that you cannot pass judgment on them, then tell them in sweet and gentle words to correct themselves. 44. If they do not wish to obey, you may leave them to God's judgment; and God will see that your intention is good.[631] One must not throw the meek lamb into a wolf's ferocious teeth because this will

make the wolf more ravenous. 45. Nevertheless, it is fitting for you to forewarn them charitably about the peril of their souls, as a father does with his children when they oppose him. 46. Nor are you bound to forego rebukes out of fear for your body unless, by chance, some danger to souls could come from them."

This revelation, made to Lady Birgitta, began in Naples immediately after the death of her son Lord Charles, a knight.[632] *The vision continued, with certain breaks, during her Jerusalem voyage until she arrived at Jerusalem; and there it ended in the Church of the Holy Sepulchre of the Lord. It contains in itself allegations made by the Virgin Mary and by an angel on behalf of the said knight's soul at the divine judgment in the presence of Christ the Judge and allegations made on the devil's part against that very soul and Christ the Judge's verdict for its liberation. Chapter 13.*[633]

The Virgin Mary speaks to Lady Birgitta and says: "I want to tell you what I did for the soul of your son Charles when it was being separated from his body. 2. I acted like a woman standing by another woman who is giving birth,[634] in order that she might help the infant, lest it die in the flow of blood or suffocate in that narrow place through which an infant exits and so that, by her watchful care, the infant's enemies, who are in the same house, might not be able to kill it. 3. I acted in the same way. Indeed I stood near your same son Charles, shortly before he sent forth his spirit,[635] in order that he might not have such thoughts of carnal love in his memory[636] that, for the sake of this love, he would think or say anything against God or will to omit anything pleasing to God or will to perform, to his soul's harm, those things that could be in any way contrary to the divine will. 4. I also helped him in that narrow space,[637] i.e., at his soul's exit from his body, so that in dying he would not endure pain so hard as to cause him to become at all inconstant through despair, and so that in dying he might not forget God.[638] 5. I also guarded his soul from its deadly enemies, i.e., the demons, so that none of them could touch it. As soon as it had left his body, I took custody of it and defended it. 6. This action quickly routed and dispersed that whole throng of demons who, in their malice, yearned to swallow it and torture it for eternity. 7. But as to how, after the death of Charles, judgment was passed on his soul, this will be shown to you completely when it pleases me."

Second revelation on the same matter

8. After an interval of some days, the same Virgin Mary herself again appeared to the same Lady Birgitta, who was wide awake and at prayer, and said: 9. "Through God's goodness, it is now permitted for you to see and hear how judgment was passed on the aforesaid soul when it had left the body. 10. That which then happened in one moment before God's incomprehensible majesty will be shown to you in painstaking detail[639] at intervals by means of corporeal likenesses[640] so that your understanding may be able to grasp it."

11. In the same hour, therefore, Lady Birgitta saw herself caught up to a certain large and beautiful palace where, upon the tribunal,[641] the Lord Jesus Christ sat as if crowned as an emperor in the company of an infinite host of attendant angels and saints. She saw standing near him his most worthy Mother, who listened carefully to the judgment. 12. Also in the presence of the Judge, a soul was seen standing in great fear and panic, naked as a newborn infant, and, as it were, entirely blind so that it could see nothing; but in its consciousness, it understood what was being said and done in the palace. 13. An angel stood on the Judge's right side near the soul and a devil on his left. But neither of them touched the soul or handled it.[642]

14. Then, at last, the devil cried out and said: "Hearken, O most almighty Judge! I complain in your sight about a woman who is both my Lady and your Mother and whom you love so much that you have given to her power over heaven and earth and over all of us demons of hell.[643] She has indeed done me an injustice regarding that soul which now stands here. 15. According to justice, as soon as this soul had left the body, I ought to have taken it to myself and presented it in my company before your court of judgment. 16. And behold, O just Judge: that woman, your Mother, seized this soul with her own hands, almost before it exited from the man's mouth;[644] and in her powerful ward she has brought it to your judgment."

17. Then Mary, the Virgin Mother of God, answered thus: "Hearken, you devil, to my reply! When you were created, you understood the justice that was in God from eternity and without beginning. 18. You also had free choice to do what most pleased you. And even though you have chosen to hate God rather than love him, nevertheless you still understand quite well what, according to justice, ought to be done. 19. I tell you, therefore, that it was my business, rather than yours, to present that soul before God, the true judge. 20. For while this soul was in the

body it had a great love for me, and in its heart frequently pondered the fact that God had deigned to make me his mother and that he willed to exalt me on high above all created things. 21. As a result he began to love God with such great charity that in his heart he used to say this: 'I so rejoice because God holds the Virgin Mary his Mother most dear above all things, that there is in the world no creature and no bodily delight that I would take in exchange for that joy. 22. No, I would prefer that joy to all earthly delights. And if it were possible that God could remove her, in the smallest point, from that dignity in which she stands, I would rather choose for myself, in exchange, eternal torture in the depth of hell.[645] 23. Therefore, to God himself be endless thanksgiving and everlasting glory for that blessed grace and that glory immeasurable that he has given to his most worthy Mother!' 24. Therefore, O devil, see now with what sort of will he passed away. Which now seems to you more just: that his soul come to God's judgment defended by me or that it come into your hands to be tortured without pity?"

25. The devil answered: "I have no right to expect that this soul, which loves you more than itself, would come into my hands before judgment be passed. 26. But even though, at the bidding of justice, you did him this favor before the judgment, nevertheless, after the judgment his works will condemn him to be punished at my hands. 27. Now, O Queen, I ask you why you drove all of us demons from the presence of his body at his soul's exit so that none of us could cause any horror there or strike any fear into him."

28. The Virgin Mary answered: "I did this in return for the ardent charity that he had toward my body and in return for the joy that he had from the fact that I am the Mother of God. 29. Therefore I obtained from my Son the favor that, wherever he was and even where he now is, no evil spirit might approach his body."

30. After this, the devil speaks to the Judge and says: "I know that you are justice and power itself. You do not judge less justly for the devil than for an angel. Therefore adjudge that soul to me! 31. Using the wisdom that I had when you created me, I had written all his sins.[646] Indeed, I had kept watch over all his sins with that malice of mine that I had when I fell from heaven. 32. For when that soul first came to the age of reason and really understood that what it was doing was sinful, its own will then drew it to live in worldly pride and carnal pleasure, rather than resist such things."

33. The angel answered: "When his mother first understood that his will was wavering toward sin, she immediately rushed to his aid with

works of mercy and daily prayers that God might deign to have mercy on him lest he withdraw himself from him.[647] 34. Because of those works of his mother, he finally obtained a godly fear so that, as often as he fell into sin, he immediately hurried to make his confession."

35. The devil answered, "I must tell his sins." And at the very moment he intended to begin, he immediately started to exclaim and lament and carefully search himself, including his head and all the limbs that he seemed to have; and he was seen to tremble all over; and with great confusion he cried out: 36. "Woe to me in my misery! How have I wasted my long labor? Not only is the text blotted out and ruined,[648] but even the material on which everything was written has burnt up completely. 37. Moreover, the material indicates the times that he sinned. And I do not recall the times any more than the sins written down in connection with them."

38. The angel answered: "This was done by his mother's tears and long labors and many prayers. God sympathized with her sighs and gave to her son this grace: namely, that for every sin he committed, he obtained contrition,[649] making a humble confession out of love for God. Therefore those sins have been blotted out and are unheeded by your memory."

39. The devil answered, asserting that he still had a sack full of those writings[650] according to which the abovesaid knight had purposed to make amends for his sins but did not take care [to do so and asserting that the writings gave grounds on which][651] to torture him until, through punishment, satisfaction had been made. And indeed that same knight had not yet taken care to amend those sins during his lifetime.

40. The angel answered: "Open the sack and seek a judgment on those sins for which you must chastise him."

41. At those words, the devil cried out like a madman, saying: "I have been plundered in my power. Not only my sack has been taken, but also the sins that filled it! 42. The sack in which I put all the reasons that I had to punish him was his laziness; for, because of his laziness, he omitted many good things."

43. The angel answered: "His mother's tears have plundered you and have burst the sack and have destroyed the writing. So greatly did her tears please God!"

44. The devil answered: "I still have here a few things to bring forth: namely, his venial sins."

45. The angel answered: "He had the intention[652] to make a pilgrimage from his fatherland, leaving his goods and his friends and visiting,

by many labors, the holy places. He complemented these things, furthermore, by so preparing himself that he was worthy to gain an indulgence from Holy Church. 46. Moreover, he desired, by making amends for his sins, to appease God his Creator. As a result, all those charges, which you just said that you had written down, have been pardoned."

47. The devil answered: "Nevertheless, I still must punish him for all those venial sins that he committed; and therefore, through indulgences, they have not been deleted at all. For there are thousands upon thousands of them, and they have all been written on my tongue."

48. The angel answered: "Extend your tongue and show the writing."

49. The devil answered with loud howling and clamor like a maniac; and he said: "Woe is me. I have not one word to say; for my tongue has been cut off at the root together with its strength!"

50. The angel answered: "His mother did this with her continual prayers and her labor; for she loved his soul with her whole heart. 51. Therefore, for the sake of her love, it pleased God to pardon all the venial sins that he committed from his infancy right up to his death; and therefore your tongue is said to have lost its strength."

52. The devil answered: "I still have one thing carefully stored in my heart, and no one can abolish it. This thing is the fact that he acquired some things unjustly and never attended to their restoration."

53. The angel answered: "His mother made satisfaction for such things with her alms, her prayers, and her works of mercy so that the rigor of justice inclined toward the mildness of mercy; 54. and God gave him the perfect intention of making full satisfaction—according to his opportunities and without sparing any of his own goods—to all those from whom he had taken anything unjustly. 55. God accepted that intention in place of its effect[653] because he was not well enough to live any longer. Therefore, his heirs must make satisfaction for such things to the extent that they can."

56. The devil answered: "If I therefore do not have the power to punish him for sins, I must nevertheless chastise him because he did not practice good deeds and virtues according to his ability while he had his full senses and a healthy body. 57. For virtues and good deeds are those treasures that he ought to bring with him to such a kingdom, namely, to the glorious kingdom of God. 58. Permit me therefore, by means of punishment, to supply what he lacks in virtuous deeds."

59. The angel answered: "It is written that, to one who asks, it shall be given and, to one who knocks with perseverance, it shall be

opened.[654] Listen then, you devil! 60. By her charitable prayers and pious works his mother has perseveringly knocked at the gate of mercy[655] on his behalf; and, for more than thirty years, she has shed many thousands of tears that God might deign to pour the Holy Spirit into his heart so that this same son of hers might willingly offer his goods, his body, and his soul to God's service. 61. And God did so. For that knight became so fervent that it pleased him to live for nothing other than to follow God's will. And behold: God, who had been petitioned for so long a time, did pour his blessed Spirit into his heart. 62. And the Virgin Mother of God has given to him, out of her own virtue, whatever he lacks in those spiritual weapons and garments that are proper for knights who must, in the kingdom of heaven, enter the presence of the highest Emperor. 63. Those saints too, who now have a place in the heavenly kingdom and whom this knight loved during his life in the world, added to his consolation[656] out of their merits. For he himself truly did assemble a treasure as those pilgrims do who daily exchange perishable goods for eternal riches.[657] 64. And because he did so, he will therefore obtain everlasting joy and honor, especially for his burning desire to make a pilgrimage to the holy city of Jerusalem, 65. and for the fact that he fervently longed to risk his life willingly in warfare so that if he had been a match for so great a work, the Holy Land might be restored to the dominion of Christians to the end that the glorious sepulchre of God might be held in due reverence. 66. Therefore you, O devil, have no right to supply those things that he did not personally accomplish."

67. The devil answered: "Still, he lacks a crown. For if I could devise anything to spoil its perfection, I would willingly do so."

68. The angel answered: "It is entirely certain that all who win themselves from hell by truly repenting their sins, by voluntarily conforming themselves to the divine will, and by loving God himself with all their heart, will obtain his grace. 69. And it pleases God himself to give them a crown out of the triumphal crown of his blessed human body if they have been purged according to strict justice. Therefore, it is not at all suitable for you, O devil, to devise anything related to his crown."

70. When the devil heard this, he cried out impatiently, roaring,[658] and said: "Woe is me. For all my memory has been taken from me! I do not now recall in what respect that knight followed my will; and—what is more amazing—I have even forgotten what name he was called by while he lived."

186

71. The angel answered: "Know that now, in heaven, he is called 'Son of Tears.' "[659]

72. The devil cried out loudly and answered: "Oh, what a cursed sow his mother, that she-pig, is,[660] who had a belly so expansive that so much water poured into her that her belly's every space was filled with liquid for tears! Cursed be she by me and by all my company!"

73. The angel answered: "Your curse is God's honor and the blessing of all his friends."

74. Then, however, Christ the Judge spoke, saying this: "Depart, O devil, my enemy!" Then he said to the knight: "Come, O my chosen one!" And so, at once, the devil fled.

75. When the bride saw these things, she said: "O Power eternal and incomprehensible, you yourself, God and Lord, Jesus Christ! You pour into hearts all good thoughts and prayers and tears. You conceal your gracious gifts; and for them you confer eternal rewards in glory. 76. Therefore, to you be honor and service and thanks for all that you have created! O my sweetest God, you are most dear to me and truly to me dearer than my body and soul!"

77. The angel also then spoke to that same bride of Christ and said: "You ought to know that this vision has been shown to you by God not only for your own consolation but also in order that God's friends may be able to understand how much he deigns to do in answer to the prayers, tears, and labors of his friends who charitably pray and labor for others with perseverance and good will. 78. You also ought to know that this knight, your son, would not have had such a grace if he had not, since infancy, had the will to love God and his friends and to amend his life willingly after every fall into sin."[661]

Lady Birgitta had this revelation in the holy city of Jerusalem, the first time that she was in the Church of the Holy Sepulchre.[662] In it, Christ declares the pardon and grace that good pilgrims have in the said church when they come there with a right intention and a holy purpose. Chapter 14.

The Son spoke to the bride: "When you people entered my temple, which was dedicated with my blood, you were as cleansed of all your sins as if you had at that moment been lifted from the font of baptism. 2. And because of your labors and devotion, some souls of your relatives that were in purgatory have this day been liberated and have entered into heaven in my glory. 3. For all who come to this place with a perfect will to amend their lives in accord with their better conscience, and who are not willing to fall back into their former sins, will have all their former sins completely forgiven; and they will have an increase of grace to make progress."

This vision Lady Birgitta saw in Jerusalem in the Church of the Holy Sepulchre in the chapel of Mount Calvary, on the Friday after the octave of the Ascension of the Lord,[663] when, caught up in spirit, she saw the whole passion of the Lord in painstaking detail,[664] as it is here contained at greater length. Chapter 15.

While I was at Mount Calvary, most mournfully weeping,[665] I saw[666] that my Lord, who was naked and scourged, had been led by the Jews to his crucifixion.[667] He was being guarded by them diligently. 2. I then saw too that a certain hole had been cut into the mount and that the crucifiers were round about and ready to work their cruelty. 3. The Lord, however, turned toward me and said to me: "Be attentive;[668] for in this hole in the rock the foot of the cross was fixed at the time of my passion."

4. And at once I saw how the Jews[669] were there fixing and fastening his cross firmly in the hole in the rock of the mount with bits of wood strongly hammered in on every side in order that the cross might stand more solidly and not fall. 5. Then, when the cross had been so solidly fastened there, at once wooden planks were fitted around the trunk of the cross to form steps up to the place where his feet were to be crucified, in order that both he and his crucifiers might be able to ascend by those plank steps and stand atop the planks in a way more convenient for crucifying him.[670] 6. After this, they then ascended by those steps, leading him with the greatest of mockery and scolding. 7. He ascended gladly, like a meek lamb led to the slaughter.[671] When he was finally on top of those planks, he at once, willingly and without coercion, extended his arm and opened his right hand and placed it on the cross. Those savage torturers monstrously crucified it, piercing it with a nail through that part where the bone was more solid.[672] 8. And then, with a rope, they pulled violently on his left hand and fastened it to the cross in the same manner. 9. Finally, they extended his body on the cross beyond all measure; and placing one of his shins on top of the other, they fastened to the cross his feet, thus joined, with two nails.[673] And they violently extended those glorious limbs so far on the cross that nearly all of his veins and sinews were bursting. 10. Then the crown of thorns,

which they had removed from his head when he was being crucified, they now put back, fitting it onto his most holy head. 11. It pricked his awesome head with such force that then and there his eyes were filled with flowing blood and his ears were obstructed. And his face and beard were covered as if they had been dipped in that rose-red blood. 12. And at once those crucifiers and soldiers quickly removed all the planks that abutted the cross, and then the cross remained alone and lofty, and my Lord was crucified upon it.

13. And as I, filled with sorrow, gazed at their cruelty, I then saw his most mournful Mother lying on the earth, as if trembling and half-dead.[674] 14. She was being consoled by John and by those others, her sisters,[675] who were then standing not far from the cross on its right side. 15. Then the new sorrow of the compassion of that most holy Mother so transfixed me that I felt, as it were, that a sharp sword of unbearable bitterness was piercing my heart.[676] 16. Then at last his sorrowful Mother arose; and, as it were, in a state of physical exhaustion, she looked at her Son. Thus, supported by her sisters, she stood there all dazed and in suspense, as though dead yet living, transfixed by the sword of sorrow.[677] 17. When her Son saw her and his other friends weeping, with a tearful voice he commended her to John.[678] It was quite discernible in his bearing and voice that out of compassion for his Mother, his own heart was being penetrated by a most sharp arrow[679] of sorrow beyond all measure.

18. Then too, his fine and lovely eyes appeared half dead; his mouth was open and bloody; his face was pale and sunken, all livid and stained with blood; and his whole body was as if black and blue and pale and very weak from the constant downward flow of blood. 19. Indeed, his skin and the virginal flesh of his most holy body were so delicate and tender that, after the infliction of a slight blow, a black and blue mark appeared on the surface. 20. At times, however, he tried to make stretching motions on the cross because of the exceeding bitterness of the intense and most acute pain that he felt. 21. For at times the pain from his pierced limbs and veins ascended to his heart and battered him cruelly with an intense martyrdom; and thus his death was prolonged and delayed amidst grave torment and great bitterness.

22. Then, therefore, in distress from the exceeding anguish of his pain and already near to death, he cried to the Father in a loud and tearful voice, saying: "O Father, why have you forsaken me?"[680] 23. He then had pale lips, a bloody tongue, and a sunken abdomen that adhered to his back as if he had no viscera within. 24. A second time also, he

cried out again in the greatest of pain and anxiety: "O Father, into your hands I commend my spirit."[681] Then his head, raising itself a little, immediately bowed; and thus he sent forth his spirit.[682] 25. When his Mother then saw these things, she trembled at that immense bitterness and would have fallen onto the earth if she had not been supported by the other women.[683] 26. Then, in that hour, his hands retracted slightly from the place of the nail holes because of the exceeding weight of his body; and thus his body was as if supported by the nails with which his feet had been crucified. 27. Moreover, his fingers and hands and arms were now more extended than before; his shoulder blades, in fact, and his back were as if pressed tightly to the cross.[684]

28. Then at last the Jews standing around cried out in mockery against his Mother, saying many things. For some said: "Mary, now your Son is dead"; but others said other mocking words.[685] 29. And while the crowds were thus standing about, one man came running with the greatest of fury and fixed a lance in his right side with such violence and force that the lance would have passed almost through the other side of the body. 30. Thus, when the lance was extracted from the body, at once a stream, as it were, of blood spurted out of that wound in abundance; in fact, the iron blade of the lance and a part of the shaft came out of the body red and stained with the blood.[686] 31. Seeing these things, his Mother so violently trembled with bitter sighing that it was quite discernible in her face and bearing that her soul was then being penetrated by the sharp sword of sorrow.[687]

32. When all these things had been accomplished and when the large crowds were receding, certain of the Lord's friends took him down. Then, with pity,[688] his Mother received him into her most holy arms; and sitting, she laid him on her knee, all torn as he was and wounded and black and blue. 33. With tears, she and John and those others, the weeping women, washed him. 34. And then, with her linen cloth, his most mournful Mother wiped his whole body and its wounds. And she closed his eyes and kissed them; and she wrapped him in a clean cloth of fine linen.[689] 35. And thus they escorted him with lamentation and very great sorrow and placed him in the sepulchre.

Christ complains to the bride about all the earth's princes and prelates because they will not keep in their memory and recall in their heart these his sorrows and his passion and because they will not consider those sacred places of the Holy Land; and he threatens them if they do not amend themselves. Chapter 16.

After this, in that same hour, Christ spoke to his same bride, Lady Birgitta, saying: "To these things that you have now seen and to the other things that I endured, the world's princes are not attentive;[690] nor do they consider the places in which I was born and I suffered. 2. For they are like a man who has a place designated for wild and untamed beasts and where he sets loose his hunting dogs and takes delight in gazing at the dogs and the wild things as they run. 3. It is a similar case with the princes of the earth and the prelates of the churches and all states of the world. They gaze at earthly delights with greater eagerness and pleasure than at my death and my passion and my wounds. 4. Therefore, I shall now send them my words through you; and, if they do not change their hearts and turn them toward me, they will be condemned along with those who divided my clothing and, over my garment, cast lots."[691]

Addition[692]

5. *Here follows a revelation made to blessed Birgitta in Famagusta.*[693] The Son speaks: "This city is Gomorrah,[694] burning with the fire of lust and of superfluity and of ambition. 6. Therefore its structures shall fall, and it shall be desolated and diminished, and its inhabitants shall depart, and they shall groan in sorrow and tribulation, and they shall die out, and their shame shall be mentioned in many lands because I am angered at them."

7. *Concerning the duke,*[695] *who was privy to his brother's death.* Christ speaks: "This man boldly expands his pride. He boasts of his incontinence and is not attentive to the things that he has done to his neighbor. 8. Therefore, if he does not humble himself, I will act in accord with the common proverb: 'No lighter wails he who afterward weeps than he who wailed afore.'[696] For he shall have a death no lighter than his brother's—no, a death more bitter—unless he quickly amends himself."

9. *Concerning the duke's confessor.*[697] Christ speaks: "What did that friar say to you? Did he not say that the duke is good and cannot live in a better way? Did he not excuse the duke's incontinence? 10. Such men are not confessors but deceivers. They go about like simple sheep, but they are more truly foxes and flatterers. Such are those friends who see and propose 'assumptions and dejections'[698] to human beings for the sake of some temporal trifle. 11. Therefore if that friar had sat in his convent,[699] he would have obtained less punishment and a greater

crown. Now, however, he will not escape the hand of One who rebukes and afflicts."

12. *Certain people advised the lady to change clothes and blacken faces*[700] *because of the Saracens.* Christ speaks: "What advice are they giving you? Is it not to disguise your clothes and blacken your faces? 13. Would I, God, who instruct you, truly be like someone who does not know the future or like someone powerless who fears all things? Not in the least! 14. But I am wisdom itself and power itself, and I foreknow all and can do all. Therefore retain your accustomed manner of clothing and faces, and entrust your wills to me. 15. For I, who saved Sarah from the hands of her captors,[701] will also save all of you on land and sea and will provide for you in a way that is to your advantage."

16. *Concerning a bishop.*[702] The Mother[703] speaks: "My friend ought to love you as a mother, as a lady, as a daughter, and as a sister. 17. As a mother, because of your age and because of the advice that he must seek. Second, as a lady, because of the grace given to you by God, who through you has shown the secrets of his wisdom. 18. Third, as a daughter, by teaching and by consoling and by providing you with more useful things. Fourth, as a sister, by reproving—when this would be opportune—and by admonishing and by inciting to more perfect things through words and examples. 19. Also, tell him that he ought to be like one who carries the best of flowers. These flowers are my words, which are sweeter than honey to those who savor them, sharper and more more penetrating than arrows, and more effective in remuneration. 20. It is therefore the duty of the bearer to protect the flowers from the wind, the rain, and the heat: namely, from the wind of worldly talk; from the rain of carnal delights; from the heat of worldly favor. 21. For one who glories in such things causes the flowers to become worthless and shows himself unsuitable to carry them."

22. *Concerning the queen of Cyprus.*[704] The Son speaks: "Advise the queen not to return to her native land,[705] for this is not to her advantage. But let her stay in the place in which she has been set, serving God with all her heart. 23. Second, she is not to marry, taking a second husband, for it is more acceptable to God to weep for the things that have been done and, by penance, to make up for time that has been uselessly spent. 24. Third, she should guide the people of her kingdom toward mutual concord and charity; and she should labor that justice and good morals be laudably maintained and that the community[706] not be weighed down with unusual burdens. 25. Fourth, for God's sake, she should forget the evils that were committed against her husband and not burn for revenge.

For I am the Judge, and I shall judge for her. 26. Fifth, she should nurture her son[707] with divine charity and appoint as his councilors men who are just and not covetous, and as members of his household, men who are modest, composed, and wise, from whom he may learn to fear God, to rule justly, to sympathize with the unfortunate, to flee from flatterers and sycophants like poison, and to seek the advice of just men, even if they are poor, lowly, or despised. 27. Sixth, she is to put down[708] the shameful custom of women involving tight clothing, display of the breasts, unguents, and many other vanities; for these are things entirely hateful to God. 28. Seventh, she should have a confessor who, having left the world, loves souls more than gifts and who neither glosses over sins nor fears to reprove them. And, in those things that pertain to the salvation of the soul, she is to obey him just as she obeys God. 29. Eighth, she should seek out and be attentive to the lives of holy queens and saintly women;[709] and she is to labor for the increase of God's honor. 30. Ninth, she should be reasonable in her gifts, avoiding both debts and the praises of men, for it is more acceptable to God to give little or even nothing than to contract debts and to defraud one's neighbor."

31. *On the crowning of the new king.*[710] The Son speaks: "It is a great burden to be a king, but also a great honor and a very great enjoyment. It is fitting, therefore, that a king be mature, experienced, prudent, just, and a hard worker who loves his neighbors' welfare more than his own will. 32. Therefore, in ancient times, kingdoms were well ruled when such a man was elected as king—one who had the will and the knowledge and the ability to rule with justice. Now kingdoms are not kingdoms but scenes of childishness, folly, and brigandage.[711] 33. For just as the brigand searches for ways and times to lay his ambush in order to acquire lucre without being marked, so kings now search for inventions by which to elevate their offspring, fill their purses with money, and discreetly burden their subjects. 34. And they all the more gladly do justice in order to obtain temporal good, but they do not love justice in order to obtain everlasting reward. 35. Therefore, a wise man wisely said: 'Woe to that kingdom whose king is a child[712] who lives daintily and has dainty flatterers but feels no anguish at all about the advancement of the community.' 36. But because this boy will not bear his father's iniquity,[713] therefore, if he wishes to make progress and to fulfill the dignity of his kingly name, let him obey my words that I have already spoken concerning Cyprus. 37. And let him not imitate the behavior of his predecessors, but let him lay aside childish levity and

lead a kingly life, having assistants of the sort who fear and who do not love his gifts more than his soul and his honor, who hate flatteries, and who are not afraid to speak the truth and to follow it and to assert it. Otherwise, the boy will have no joy in his people, and his people no joy in the one elected."

When Lady Birgitta was in Jerusalem, she was doubtful as to whether it were better for her to lodge in the monastery of the Friars Minor on Mount Zion or in the pilgrims' hostel in Jerusalem; and then the Virgin Mary appeared to her at prayer and told her that she should lodge in the hostel as a good example to others. Chapter 17.

The Mother of God speaks: "In that place on Mount Zion there are two kinds of human beings. Some love God with all their heart. Others want to have God, but the world is sweeter to them than God is. 2. And therefore, so that the good may not be scandalized and so that you may not give an occasion to the lukewarm or an example to the future, it is therefore better to reside in the place appointed for pilgrims. For my Son will provide for you in all things as it pleases him."

In the kingdom of Cyprus, Lady Birgitta was asked by Lady Eleanor, the queen of the said kingdom, to pray to God for her son the king and for that kingdom. Lady Birgitta then crossed over to Jerusalem; and there one day, while she was at prayer, Christ appeared to her and spoke to her these counsels, which she was to write to the said king and to his paternal uncle, the prince of Antioch. And he instructed her to write those things to them as if from herself and not from the part of Christ. Chapter 18.[714]

The bride writes to the king of Cyprus and to the prince of Antioch: "The first counsel is that each of you, in the presence of his confessor, is to make a clean and complete confession of all the things that he has done against the will of God; and thus you are to receive the blessed Body of our Lord Jesus Christ with fear and love of God. 2. The second counsel is that both of you are to be united in true love so that you may be one heart[715] toward God and his honor, ruling the kingdom for the honor of God and the good of your subjects. 3. The third counsel is that both of you are to be united in true charity with your subjects and that, solely out of reverence for the passion and death of Jesus Christ, you are to forgive and spare all who, by advice, deed, or approbation, cooperated in the death of your father King Peter.[716] 4. Include them in your charity with all your heart in order that God may deign to include you in his mercy and also that he may will to strengthen you to rule the kingdom for his honor. 5. The fourth counsel is that, since divine providence has appointed you the governors of the kingdom, you should use all possible diligence in speaking to all the prelates, both of the churches and of the religious orders, effectively but charitably advising them 6. that they and their subjects should all correct themselves in all those matters in which they have in any way deviated spiritually or temporally from the holy state of their predecessors, the holy fathers of earlier times, and that they should quickly return to living purely in the pristine state of their predecessors, 7. so that their state may be totally reformed in order that they and their subjects, having thus truly amended their lives, may obtain God's friendship and be made worthy to pray that God may mercifully deign to renew in holiness of virtues the state of the universal Church. 8. The fifth counsel is that, for the sake of that great charity with which God has loved your souls, you should will to love the souls of your subjects, 9. advising your military people that all who have in any way offended God should quickly and humbly correct themselves, and that all who are under obedience to the Roman Church and who have reached the age of reason should humbly exercise the practice of confession; that they should reconcile themselves to those neighbors they have offended and establish a concord with them; and that, having amended their lives, they should receive the awesome Body of Christ. 10. Thereafter, moreover, they are to lead a Catholic life: namely, living faithfully in marriage or in widowhood or even in the state of praiseworthy virginity; observing all that Holy Church teaches; 11. leading, with loving heart,[717] the members of their household and their domestics and their subjects and all others possible, by their good example and by word and deed, to do the same; and strengthening those in such states by their good admonitions. 12. And know for very certain that all who are not willing to obey in these matters will suffer the cost in body and soul. 13. The sixth counsel is that you should tell all prelates that they must effectively and frequently admonish all their clerics, namely, the rectors of churches, that each of them is to inquire diligently in his parish as to whether there be any of his parishioners who persist in living wickedly in public sins, causing offense to God and contempt for Holy Mother Church. 14. Any such people whom they find living impudently in their public sins, they are to forewarn with effective admonishments concerning the peril of their souls; and they are to teach them such measures and spiritual remedies by means of which they can and must humbly amend their lives. 15. If, however, some of those who live in public sins will not humbly obey, then the same rectors must not delay in reporting to their superiors and the bishops in order that the prelates may juridically correct the forwardness of such obstinate persons by means of an ecclesiastical censure. 16. If, in fact, because of the sinners' stubbornness and pride or because of their temporal power, the aforesaid bishops and prelates are unable to correct or punish them, 17. then you, my lords, are advised to be, with your powerful hands, co-workers with the lord prelates so that by your help the said sinners may be brought to correct themselves and that having amended their lives they may attain God's mercy."

A revelation made to Lady Birgitta in the holy city of Jerusalem concerning the kingdom of Cyprus and its reformation, which she herself transmitted to the lord king[718] and to the prince of Antioch[719] that they might publish it to the whole kingdom. And because the aforesaid prince did not put complete faith in that revelation, therefore the said lady, on her return trip from Jerusalem, published it in the city of Famagusta on the eighth day of October,[720] in the presence of the said lord king and the queen and the said prince and all the royal council. Chapter 19.[721]

It happened to a person who was wide awake[722] and absorbed in prayer[723] that while she was suspended in an ecstasy of contemplation, she saw herself caught up in spirit to a palace that was of incomprehensible size and indescribable beauty. 2. And it seemed to her that Jesus Christ was sitting among his saints on the imperial seat of majesty. He opened his blessed mouth[724] and uttered these words that are noted down below:

3. "I truly am supreme charity itself; for all things that I have done from eternity, I have done out of charity; and, in the same way, all things that I do and shall do in the future proceed entirely from my charity. 4. For charity is as incomprehensible and intense in me now as it was at the time of my passion when, through my death and out of exceeding charity, I freed from hell[725] all the elect who were worthy of this redemption and liberation. 5. For if it were still possible that I might die as many times as there are souls in hell so that for each of them I might again endure such a death as I then endured for all, my body would still be ready to undergo all these things with a glad will and most perfect

charity.[726] 6. But, in fact, it is now impossible that my body could once more die or suffer any pain or tribulation. 7. And it is also just as impossible that any soul that after my death has been or will be condemned to hell[727] would ever again be freed from there, 8. or would enjoy the heavenly gladness that my saints and chosen ones enjoy at the glorious sight of my body. No, the damned will feel the pains of hell in an everlasting death because they did not will to enjoy the benefit of my death and passion and did not will to follow my will while they lived in the world. 9. However, because no one is judge over the offenses done to me except myself, and, for this reason, my charity that I have ever shown to human beings makes its complaint[728] in the presence of my justice, it therefore pertains to justice to render judgment on this in accord with my will.

10. "Now I make my complaint about the inhabitants of the kingdom of Cyprus as if about one human being. 11. But I do not complain about my friends who dwell there and who love me with all their heart and follow my will in all things; but I speak in complaint, as if to one person, to all those who scorn me and always resist my will and so very greatly oppose me. And therefore I now begin to speak to them all as if to one.

12. "O people of Cyprus, my adversary,[729] listen and be diligently attentive to what I say to you![730] I have loved you as a father loves his only son, whom he has willed to exalt to all honor. 13. I conferred[731] on you a land in which you could have in abundance all things necessary for the sustenance of your body. 14. I sent to you the warmth and light of the Holy Spirit that you might understand the right Christian faith to which you faithfully bound yourself, humbly subjugating yourself to the sacred statutes and to the obedience of Holy Church. 15. Indeed, I placed you in a place that would be quite fitting for a faithful servant, namely, among my enemies, so that in return for your earthly labors and for the physical struggle of battles you would obtain in my heavenly kingdom an even more precious crown. 16. I also carried you for a long time in my heart, i.e., in the charity of my Godhead, and kept you as the apple of my eye[732] in all your adversities and tribulations. 17. And as long as you observed my precepts and faithfully kept obedience and the statutes of Holy Church, then, of a certainty, did an almost infinite number of souls come from the kingdom of Cyprus to my heavenly kingdom to enjoy eternal glory with me for ever. 18. But because you now do your own will and all those things that delight your heart, without fearing me who am your Judge and without loving me who am your Creator and who also redeemed you through my very hard death;

and because you spat me out of your mouth like some foul and unsavory thing;[733] 19. and, indeed, because you have enclosed the devil together with your soul in the chamber of your heart; and because you have driven me thence as if I were a thief and a robber; and because you were no more ashamed to sin in my sight than irrational animals are in their mating,[734] 20. it is therefore a fitting justice and a just judgment that you should be driven out from all my friends in heaven and be placed forever in hell amidst my enemies. 21. And know this without a doubt: that my Father—who is in me, and I am in him,[735] and the Holy Spirit is in us both[736]—is himself my witness[737] that nothing but truth has ever gone forth from my mouth.[738] 22. Wherefore know for a truth that if anyone has been so disposed as you now are and if he will not amend his life, his soul will go the same way along which went Lucifer[739] because of his pride, and Judas, who sold me because of his greed,[740] and Zimri, whom Phinehas killed because of his lust. 23. For Zimri sinned with a woman against my precept; and therefore, after his death, his soul was condemned to hell.[741]

24. "Wherefore, O people of Cyprus, I now announce to you that if you will not correct yourself[742] and amend your life, then I shall so destroy your generation and progeny in the kingdom of Cyprus that I shall spare neither the poor person nor the rich. 25. Indeed, I shall so destroy this same generation of yours that in a short time, your memory will thus slip away from the hearts of human beings as if you had never been born in this world. 26. Afterward, however, it is my pleasure to plant new plants in this kingdom of Cyprus that will carry out my precepts and will love me with all their heart. 27. But, nevertheless, know for a certainty that if any one of you wills to correct himself, amend his life, and humbly turn back to me, then like a loving shepherd, I shall joyfully run out to meet him, lifting him onto my shoulders and personally carrying him back to my sheep.[743] 28. For by my shoulders I mean that if anyone amends his life, he will share in the benefit of my passion and death, which I endured in my body and shoulders; and he will receive with me eternal consolation[744] in the kingdom of heaven.

29. "You should also know for very certain that you, my enemies who dwell in this said kingdom, were not worthy that such a vision or divine revelation of mine should be sent to you. 30. But some friends of mine who live in the same kingdom and faithfully serve me and love me with their whole heart have, by their labors and tearful prayers, inclined me to make you understand, by means of this my revelation, the grave peril of your souls. 31. For, to some of my said friends there, it has been

divinely shown by me how many countless souls from this said kingdom of Cyprus are being excluded from heavenly glory and are being eternally doomed to the death of Gehenna.

32. "However, the above words I speak to those Latin Christians subject to the obedience of the Roman Church, and who, at baptism, vowed to me right Roman Catholic faith, and who, through works contrary to me, have totally withdrawn from me. 33. Greeks,[745] however, who know[746] that all Christians must hold only one Catholic Christian faith and be under only one Church, namely, the Roman, and have, as spiritual pastor over them, only my sole vicar general in the world, namely, the supreme Roman pontiff, 34. and who, nevertheless, will not spiritually subject and humbly subjugate themselves to that same Roman Church and to my vicar because of their stubborn pride or because of greed or because of the wantonness of the flesh or because of some other thing that pertains to the world, are unworthy to obtain pardon and mercy from me after death.[747] 35. But the other Greeks, who would desirously wish to know the Roman Catholic faith, but cannot, and who nevertheless, if they knew it and had the ability, would willingly and devoutly receive it and would humbly subjugate themselves[748] to the Roman Church and who, nonetheless, following their conscience in their state and faith in which they are, do abstain from sin and live piously—to such as these, after their death, I must show my mercy in the matter of punishment when they are called to my judgment. 36. Let the Greeks also know that their empire and kingdoms or domains will never stand secure and tranquil in peace, but that they themselves will always be subject to their enemies from whom they will always sustain the gravest of losses and daily miseries until, with true humility and charity, they devoutly subject themselves to the Church and faith of Rome, totally conforming themselves to the sacred constitutions and rites of that same Church."[749]

37. When, however, these things had thus been seen and heard in spirit as reported above, the said vision disappeared; and the said person remained at prayer, suspended in no little fear and wonder.

In the kingdom of Cyprus, a certain Friar Minor[750] *asked the said lady to advise him as to what he ought to do about some doubts in his conscience, especially concerning the observance of the Rule of his order. When indeed the lady was praying for the abovesaid friar one day*[751] *in the holy city of Jerusalem, Christ appeared to her and spoke to her, saying many things about the Order of Friars Minor. And at the end he threatens all property-owning religious with everlasting death. Chapter 20.*[752]

Infinite thanksgiving and humble service, praise, and honor be to God in his power and everlasting majesty—to him who is one God in three persons! 2. It pleased his immense goodness that his most worthy humanity should speak to a person at prayer, saying this:

3. "Hear, O you to whom it has been given to hear and see spiritual things; and diligently hold in your memory these my words. 4. There was a man named Francis.[753] When he turned away from worldly pride and covetousness and from the flawed delight of the flesh[754] and turned toward a spiritual life of penance and perfection, he then obtained true contrition for all his sins and a perfect intention of amendment, saying: 5. 'There is nothing in this world that I am not willing to give up gladly for the sake of the love and honor of my Lord Jesus Christ. 6. There is also nothing so hard in this life that I am not willing to endure it with gladness because of his love, doing all that I can for the sake of his honor, according to my strength in body and soul. 7. And I want to lead and strengthen all others that I can to love God above all with the whole of their heart.' 8. The Rule of this Francis, which he himself began, was not dictated and composed by his human understanding and prudence, but by me in accord with my will. 9. For every word that is written in it was breathed into him by my Spirit;[755] and afterwards, he brought that Rule forth and held it out to others.[756] 10. So too, all other Rules that my friends began and themselves personally kept and observed and effectively taught and held out to others were not dictated and composed by their own understanding and human wisdom, but by the breathing[757] of that same Holy Spirit. 11. For a number of years, the brothers of this Francis—who are called Friars Minor—held and kept that Rule of his well and very spiritually and devoutly, in whole accordance with my will.

12. "As a result, the devil, the ancient fiend,[758] felt great envy and unrest because he had not the strength to conquer the said friars by his temptations and deceits. 13. Therefore, the devil sought diligently that he might find a man whose human will he could mix together with his own malign spirit. At last he found a cleric who inwardly thought thus: 14. 'I would like to be in a state where I could have worldly honor and my bodily pleasure and where I could amass so much money that I would lack nothing at all that pertains to my needs and pleasures. Therefore, I wish to enter the Order of Francis; and I will pretend to be

very humble and obedient.' 15. And so, with that intention and will, the aforementioned cleric entered the said order; and at once the devil entered into his heart.[759] And thus the said cleric became a friar in the said order. 16. Inwardly, however, the devil considered in this manner: 'Just as Francis with his humble obedience wishes to draw many from the world to receive great rewards in heaven, 17. so this my friar—who will be named "Adversary"[760] because he will be the adversary of the Rule of Francis—will draw many in the Order of Francis from humility to pride, from rational[761] poverty to covetousness, from true obedience to the doing of one's own will and to the pursuit of bodily pleasure.' 18. And when the aforesaid Brother Adversary entered the Order of Francis, at once, at the devil's instigation, he began to think inwardly thus: 19. 'I will show myself so humble and obedient that all will reckon me a saint. When the others are fasting[762] and keeping silence, then I, with special companions, shall do the contrary: namely, by eating and drinking and talking so secretly that none of the others will know or understand this. 20. Also, according to the said Rule, I cannot lawfully touch money or possess gold or silver;[763] therefore I will have some special friend to keep my money and gold secretly with him on my behalf so that I may use that money as I will. 21. I also want to learn the liberal arts and science,[764] so that from them I may be able to have some honor and dignity in the order, having horses and silver vessels and handsome clothes and costly ornaments. 22. And if anyone reproves me for these things, I shall answer that I do it for the honor of my order. 23. If, besides, I could work further and do so much that I would be made a bishop, then I would truly be happy and blessed in such a life as I then could lead, for then I would enjoy my personal freedom and I would have all my bodily pleasure.'

24. "Now hear what the devil had done in the aforesaid Order of Francis. For it is truly so that in the world the friars who, either in action or in will and desire, hold the aforesaid Rule that the devil taught to Brother Adversary, are more numerous than those who keep the Rule that I myself taught to Brother Francis. 25. You should nevertheless know that however much those friars—namely, those of Francis and those of Brother Adversary—are mixed together as long as they live in the world, I will nevertheless separate them after death,[765] for I am their Judge. And I shall judge that those friars of the Rule of Francis are to remain with me, together with Francis, in everlasting joy. 26. But those who belong to Brother Adversary's Rule will be doomed to eternal punishments in the depth of hell if before death they would not will to

correct themselves and humbly amend their lives. 27. Nor is this to be wondered at, for those who ought to give examples of humility and sanctity to worldly human beings actually furnish them with vile and ribald examples[766] through their pride and covetousness. 28. And therefore both the said friars themselves and all other religious who are prohibited by rule from having private property and yet have some property against their Rule, and who wish to appease me by conferring upon me a part of it, should know for very certain that their gifts are abominable to me and hateful and unworthy of any good gift in return. 29. For it is more agreeable and pleasing to me that they diligently observe the blessed poverty that they professed according to their Rules, than that they might present to me all the gold and silver and even all the metals[767] that there are in the world.

30. "You, O woman who hear my words, should also know that it would not have been permitted for you to know this aforespoken vision if it had not been for a good servant of mine who sincerely petitioned me with all his heart on behalf of that Friar Minor, 31. and who, out of divine charity, desired to give to that same friar some advice useful to his soul."

When, however, these things had been seen and heard, this vision disappeared.

A vision that Lady Birgitta had in Bethlehem,[768] where the Virgin Mary showed to her the whole manner of her childbearing and how she gave birth to her glorious Son just as the Virgin herself had promised the same Lady Birgitta in Rome fifteen years before she went to Bethlehem, as can be seen in the first chapter of this the last book.[769] Chapter 21.[770]

When I was at the manger of the Lord in Bethlehem, I saw[771] a Virgin, pregnant and most very beautiful, clothed in a white mantle and a finely woven tunic through which from without I could clearly discern her virginal flesh. 2. Her womb was full and much swollen, for she was now ready to give birth. With her there was a very dignified old man;[772] and with them they had both an ox and an ass.[773] 3. When they had entered the cave,[774] and after the ox and the ass had been tied to the manger, the old man went outside and brought to the Virgin a lighted candle[775] and fixed it in the wall and went outside in order not to be personally present at the birth. 4. And so the Virgin then took the shoes from her feet,[776] put off the white mantle that covered her, removed the veil from her head, and laid these things beside her, remaining in only her tunic, with her most beautiful hair—as if of gold—spread out upon her shoulder blades.[777] 5. She then drew out two small cloths of linen and two of wool, very clean and finely woven, which she carried with her to wrap the infant that was to be born, and two other small linens to cover and bind his head;[778] and she laid these cloths beside her that she might use them in due time.

6. And when all these things had thus been prepared, then the Virgin knelt[779] with great reverence, putting herself at prayer; and she kept her back toward the manger and her face lifted to heaven toward the east. 7. And so, with raised hands[780] and with her eyes intent on heaven, she was as if suspended in an ecstasy of contemplation, inebriated with divine sweetness. 8. And while she was thus in prayer, I saw the One lying in her womb then move; and then and there, in a moment and the twinkling of an eye, she gave birth to a Son,[781] from whom there went out such great and ineffable light and splendor that the sun could not be compared to it. 9. Nor did that candle that the old man had put in place give light at all because that divine splendor totally annihilated the material splendor of the candle.[782] 10. And so sudden and momentary was that manner of giving birth that I was unable to notice or discern how or in what member she was giving birth.[783] 11. But yet, at once, I saw that glorious infant lying on the earth, naked and glowing in the greatest of neatness. His flesh was most clean of all filth and uncleanness.[784] 12. I saw also the afterbirth, lying wrapped[785] very neatly beside him. And then I heard the wonderfully sweet and most dulcet songs of the angels. 13. And the Virgin's womb, which before the birth had been very swollen, at once retracted; and her body then looked wonderfully beautiful and delicate.

14. When therefore the Virgin felt that she had now given birth, at once, having bowed her head and joined her hands, with great dignity[786] and reverence she adored the boy and said to him: "Welcome, my God, my Lord, and my Son!"[787] 15. And then the boy, crying and, as it were, trembling from the cold and the hardness of the pavement[788] where he lay, rolled a little and extended his limbs, seeking to find refreshment and his Mother's favor. 16. Then his Mother took him in her hands and pressed him to her breast, and with cheek and breast she warmed him with great joy and tender maternal compassion.[789] 17. Then, sitting on the earth, she put her Son in her lap and deftly caught his umbilical cord with her fingers. At once it was cut off, and from it no liquid or blood

went out.[790] 18. And at once she began to wrap him carefully, first in the linen cloths and then in the woolen, binding his little body, legs, and arms with a ribbon that had been sewn into four parts of the outer wollen cloth.[791] 19. And afterward she wrapped and tied on the boy's head those two small linen cloths that she had prepared for this purpose.[792] 20. When these things therefore were accomplished, the old man entered; and prostrating on the earth, he adored him on bended knee and wept for joy.[793] 21. Not even at the birth was that Virgin changed in color or by infirmity. Nor was there in her any such failure of bodily strength as usually happens in other women giving birth, except that her swollen womb retracted to the prior state in which it had been before she conceived the boy.[794] 22. Then, however, she arose, holding the boy in her arms; and together both of them, namely, she and Joseph, put him in the manger,[795] and on bended knee they continued to adore him with gladness and immense joy.

A revelation in Bethlehem at the manger of the Lord, on the same matter as above. Chapter 22.[796]

Afterwards again in the same place,[797] the Virgin Mary appeared to me and said: "My daughter, it is a long time ago that I promised you in Rome that I would show to you here in Bethlehem the manner of my childbearing.[798] 2. And even though I showed to you in Naples[799] something about this—namely, what state I was in when I gave birth to my Son—nevertheless, know for very certain that I was in such a state and gave birth in such a manner as you have now seen: on bended knee, praying alone in the stable. 3. For I gave birth to him with such great exultation and joy of soul that I felt no discomfort when he went out of my body, and no pain. But at once I wrapped him in the small clean cloths that I had prepared long before. 4. When Joseph saw these things, he marveled with great gladness and joy from the fact that I had thus, without help,[800] given birth. 5. But because the great multitude of people in Bethlehem were busy about the census,[801] they were therefore so attentive[802] to it that the wonders of God could not be published among them. 6. And therefore know for a truth that however much human beings, following their human perception, try to assert that my Son was born in the common manner,[803] it is nevertheless more true and beyond any doubt that he was born just as I elsewhere told you and just as you now have seen."[804]

It was at the manger of the Lord that this revelation was made to the same lady in Bethlehem: how the shepherds came to the manger to adore the newborn Christ. Chapter 23.[805]

I saw also in the same place,[806] while the Virgin Mary and Joseph were adoring the boy in the manger, that shepherds and guardians of the flock then came to see and adore the infant.[807] When they had seen it, they first wished to inquire whether it were male or female because the angels announced to them that the Savior of the world had been born and had not said "savioress."[808] 3. Therefore the Virgin Mother then showed to them the infant's natural parts and male sex;[809] and at once they adored him with great reverence and joy; and afterward they returned praising and glorifying God for all these things that they had heard and seen.[810]

This revelation she had in Bethlehem, in the chapel where Christ was born. In it, Mary tells her how the three magi kings adored Christ, her Son. Chapter 24.[811]

The same Mother of the Lord also said to me: "My daughter, know that when the three magi kings[812] came into the stable[813] to adore my Son, I had foreknown their coming well in advance. 2. And when they entered and adored him, then my Son exulted, and for joy he had then a more cheerful face. 3. I too rejoiced exceedingly; and I was gladdened by the wonderful joy of exultation in my mind, while being attentive to their words and actions, keeping those things and reflecting on them in my heart."[814]

The Mother of God, speaking to Lady Birgitta, tells her some things about her own humility and that of her Son; and she says that just as she and her Son were humble while they were in the world, so too are they humble now although they are in heaven. Chapter 25.[815]

The Mother speaks: "There is the same humility in my Son now in the power of his Godhead as there was then, when he was laid in the manger. 2. Although he knew all things in accordance with his Godhead, nevertheless, while lying between two animals,[816] he spoke nothing at all, in accordance with his humanity.[817] 3. So too now, sitting at the right hand of the Father, he hears all who speak to him with love;

and he answers through infusions of the Holy Spirit. To some he speaks with words and thoughts, to others as if from mouth to mouth,[818] just as it pleases him.

4. Similarly, I, who am his Mother, am, in my body which has been raised on high above all things created, now as humble as I then was when I was betrothed to Joseph. 5. Moreover, you ought to know for very certain that before Joseph betrothed me, he understood, in the Holy Spirit, that I had vowed my virginity to God and that I was immaculate in thought, word, and deed. 6. He betrothed me with the intention that he might serve me, treating me as his lady, not as his wife. I too in the Holy Spirit knew for very certain that my virginity would remain forever unharmed even though, as a result of God's hidden plan,[819] I was being betrothed to a husband. 7. But after I gave my consent to the messenger of God, Joseph, seeing my womb swell by virtue of the Holy Spirit, feared very greatly. Not suspecting me of anything sinister, but mindful of the sayings of the prophets who had foretold that the Son of God would be born of a virgin,[820] he reckoned himself unworthy to serve such a mother until the angel instructed him in his sleep not to be afraid but to serve me with charity.[821] 8. But of our riches, Joseph and I reserved nothing for ourselves except the necessities of life, for the honor of God. The rest we let go, for the love of God. 9. When my Son's hour of birth was at hand—an hour that I very well knew beforehand—I came, in accord with God's foreknowledge, to Bethlehem, bringing with me, for my Son, clean clothing and cloths that no one had ever used before.[822] In them I wrapped, for the first time, him who was born from me in all purity.

10. "And even though from eternity it was foreseen that I would sit in honor on a most sublime seat above all creatures and above all human beings, yet nonetheless, in my humility, I did not disdain to prepare and serve the things that were necessary for Joseph and myself. 11. Similarly also, my Son was subject to Joseph and to me.[823] Therefore, just as I was humble in the world—known to God alone and to Joseph—so too am I humble now as I sit on a most sublime throne, ready to present to God the rational[824] prayers of all. 12. But some I answer by means of divine outpourings.[825] To others, however, I speak more secretly as is well pleasing to God."

When Lady Birgitta now wished to return from Jerusalem to Rome, she went on the birthday of the Virgin Mary[826] to visit her sepulchre and the other shrines that are there near the city of Jerusalem. As she prayed at the said sepulchre, that same Virgin appeared to her, assuring her about the time of her death and assumption and testifying that this was literally[827] *her sepulchre. Chapter 26.*

When I was in the Valley of Jehoshaphat,[828] praying at the sepulchre of the glorious Virgin, that same Virgin appeared to me, shining with exceeding splendor, and said:

2. "Be attentive, daughter!"[829] After my Son ascended to heaven, I lived in the world for fifteen years and as much time more as there is from the feast of the ascension of that same Son of mine until my death.[830] 3. And then I lay dead in this sepulchre for fifteen days.[831] Thereupon I was assumed into heaven with infinite honor and joy.[832] 4. However, my garments with which I was buried then remained in this sepulchre;[833] and I was then clothed in such garments as those that clothe my Son and my Lord, Jesus Christ. 5. Know also that there is no human body in heaven except the glorious body of my Son and my own body.[834]

6. "Therefore go now, all of you,[835] back to the lands of Christians; ever amend your lives for the better;[836] and in future, live with the greatest of care and attention[837] now that you have visited these holy places, where my Son and I lived in the body and died and were buried."

When Lady Birgitta, in returning from Jerusalem, passed through the city of Naples, at the request of the lady queen and of the archbishop of the said city she prayed to God for that same city's inhabitants. And Christ, speaking to her, reproved the aforesaid inhabitants for their too many sins, showing to them the means by which sinners might reconcile themselves to him, promising them mercy if they would be reconciled and would amend their lives. He also threatens them with the severity of justice if they will not correct themselves but rather persevere in sin. Lady Birgitta published this revelation herself in the presence of the said Lord Bernard the archbishop and three masters of theology and two doctors of canon and civil law and some knights and citizens of the said city. Chapter 27.[838]

To a person who was wide awake at prayer and absorbed in contemplation—and while she was in a rapture of mental elevation—Jesus Christ appeared; and he said to her this:

2. "Hear, O you to whom it has been given to hear and see spiritual things; and be diligently attentive; and in your mind beware in regard to

those things that you now will hear and that in my behalf you will announce to the nations, lest you speak them to acquire for yourself honor or human praise. 3. Nor indeed are you to be silent about these things from any fear of human reproach and contempt; for these things that you are now going to hear are being shown to you not only for your own sake, but also because of the prayers of my friends. 4. For some of my chosen friends in the Neapolitan citizenry have for many years asked me with their whole heart—in their prayers and in their labors on behalf of my enemies living in the same city—to show them some grace through which they could be withdrawn and savingly recalled from their sins and abuses. 5. Swayed by their prayers, I give to you now these words of mine; and therefore diligently hear the things that I speak.

6. "I am the Creator of all and Lord over the devils as well as over all the angels, and no one will escape my judgment. The devil, in fact, sinned in a threefold manner against me: namely, through pride; through envy; and through arrogance, i.e., through love of his own will. 7. He was so proud indeed that he wished to be lord over me and that I should be subject to him. He also envied me so much that if it were possible, he would gladly have killed me in order to be lord himself and sit on my throne. 8. Indeed, his own will was so dear to him that he cared nothing at all about my will so long as he could perform his own will. Because of this, he fell from heaven;[839] and, no longer an angel, he became a devil in the depth of hell. 9. Afterward, however, I, seeing his malice and the great envy that he had toward humankind, showed my will and gave my commandments to human beings that by doing them they could please me and displease the devil. 10. Finally, because of the charity that I have toward human beings, I came into the world and took flesh of a virgin. Indeed, I personally taught them the true way of salvation by work and by word; and to show them perfect charity and love, I opened heaven for them by my own blood.

11. "But what are those human beings who are my enemies doing to me now? In truth, they have contempt for my precepts; they cast me out of their hearts like a loathsome poison; indeed, they spit me out of their mouths like something rotten; and they abhor the sight of me as if I were a leper with the worst of stenches. 12. But the devil and his works they embrace in their every affection and deed. For they bring him into their hearts, doing his will with delight and gladness and following his evil suggestions. 13. Therefore, by my just judgment they shall have their reward in hell with the devil eternally without end. For in place of

the pride that they practice, they will have confusion and eternal shame to such a degree that angels and demons will say of them: 'They are filled with confusion to the very utmost!' 14. And for their insatiable greed, each devil in hell will so fill them with his deadly venom that in their souls there will remain no place that is not filled with diabolic venom. 15. And for the lust with which they burn like senseless animals, they will never be admitted to the sight of my face but will be separated from me and deprived of their inordinate will.

16. "Moreover, know that just as all mortal sins are very serious, so too a venial sin is made mortal if a human being delights in it with the intention of persevering.[840] 17. Wherefore, know that two sins, which I now name to you, are being practiced and that they draw after them other sins that all seem as if venial. But because the people delight in them with the intention of persevering, they are therefore made mortal. And the people in the city of Naples commit many other abominable sins that I do not wish to name to you.

18. "The first of the two sins is that the faces of rational[841] human creatures are being painted with the various colors with which insensible images and statues of idols are colored so that to others, these faces may seem more beautiful than I made them. 19. The second sin is that the bodies of men and women are being deformed from their natural state by the unseemly forms of clothing that the people are using. And the people are doing this because of pride and so that in their bodies they may seem more beautiful and more lascivious than I, God, created them. And indeed they do this so that those who thus see them may be more quickly provoked and inflamed toward carnal desire. 20. Therefore, know for very certain that as often as they daub their faces with antimony and other extraneous coloring,[842] some of the infusion of the Holy Spirit is diminished in them and the devil draws nearer to them. 21. In fact, as often as they adorn themselves in disorderly and indecent clothing and so deform their bodies, the adornment of their souls is diminished and the devil's power is increased.

22. "O my enemies, who do such things and with effrontery commit other sins contrary to my will, why have you neglected my passion; and why do you not attend[843] in your hearts to how I stood naked at the pillar, bound and cruelly scourged with hard whips, and to how I stood[844] naked on the cross and cried out, full of wounds and clothed in blood? 23. And when you paint and anoint your faces, why do you not look at my face and see how it was full of blood? You are not even attentive to my eyes and how they grew dark and were covered with

blood and tears, and how my eyelids turned blue. 24. Why too do you not look at my mouth or gaze at my ears and my beard and see how they were aggrieved[845] and were stained with blood? You do not look at the rest of my limbs, monstrously wounded by various punishments, and see how I hung black and blue on the cross and dead for your sake. 25. And there, derided and rejected, I was despised by all in order that, by recalling these things and attentively remembering them, you might love me, your God,[846] and thus escape the devil's snares, in which you have been horribly bound. 26. However, in your eyes and hearts, all these things have been forgotten and neglected. And so you behave like prostitutes, who love the pleasure and delight of the flesh, but not its offspring. 27. For when they feel a living infant in their womb, at once they procure an abortion by means of herbs and other things so that without losing their fleshly pleasure and further wicked delight, they may thus be always absorbed in their lust and their foul carnal intercourse.[847] 28. This is how you behave. For I, God, your Creator and Redeemer, visit all with my grace, knocking,[848] namely, at your hearts, because I love all. 29. But when you feel, in your hearts, any knock of an inpouring—namely of my Spirit—or any compunction;[849] or when, through hearing my words, you conceive any good intention, at once you procure spiritually, as it were, an abortion, namely, by excusing your sins and by delighting in them and even by damnably willing to persevere in them. 30. For that reason, you do the devil's will, enclosing him in your hearts and expelling me in this contemptible way. Therefore, you are without me, and I am not with you. And you are not in me but in the devil, for it is his will and his suggestions that you obey.

31. "And so, because I have just spoken my judgment, I shall also now speak my mercy. My mercy, however, is this: namely, that none of my very enemies is so thorough or so great a sinner[850] that my mercy would be denied him if he were to ask for it humbly and wholeheartedly.[851] 32. Wherefore, my enemies must do three things if they wish to reconcile themselves to my grace and friendship. 33. The first is that with all their heart they repent and have contrition because they have offended me, their Creator and Redeemer. The second thing is confession—clean, frequent, and humble—which they must make before their confessor. 34. And thus let them amend all their sins by doing penance and making satisfaction in accord with that same confessor's counsel and discretion. For then I shall draw close to them,[852] and the devil will be kept far away from them. 35. The third thing is that after they have thus performed these things with devotion and perfect charity, they are

to go to communion and receive and consume my Body with the intention of never falling back into former sins but of persevering in good even to the end.

36. "If anyone, therefore, amends his life in this manner, at once I will run out to meet him as a loving father runs to meet his wayward son;[853] and I will receive him into my grace more gladly than he himself could have asked or thought. 37. And then I will be in him, and he in me; and he shall live with me and rejoice forever.[854] But upon him who perseveres in his sins and malice my justice shall indubitably come. 38. For when the fisherman[855] sees the fish in the water playing in their delight and merriment, even then he drops his hook into the sea and draws it out, catching the fish in turn and then putting them to death—not all at once, but a few at a time—until he has taken them all. This is indeed what I shall do to my enemies who persevere in sin. 39. For I shall bring them a few at a time to the consummation of the worldly life of this age[856] in which they take temporal and carnal delight. 40. And at an hour that they do not believe and are living in even greater delight, I shall then snatch them away from earthly life and put them to eternal death in a place where they will nevermore see my face because they loved to do and accomplish their inordinate and corrupted will rather than perform my will and my commandments."

41. However, after these things had thus been seen and heard, this vision disappeared.

A revelation of the Virgin Mary which Lady Birgitta had in the city of Naples. And she directs it to Lord Bernard, the Neapolitan archbishop. The revelation reproaches those who do not instruct their servants or infidel slaves, newly converted to the faith, in that same Catholic faith and Christian law. The Virgin Mary also reproves those masters who maltreat these said servants of theirs and exasperate them beyond measure. She also threatens with great punishment fortune-tellers and enchanters and diviners and also those who support them and put faith in them. Chapter 28.

The bride of Christ writes to Lord Bernard, archbishop of Naples, saying: "Reverend Father and Lord! When that person, whom you know well, was praying suspended in a rapture of contemplation, the Virgin Mary appeared to her and said to her this:

2. "I, who speak to you, am the Queen of heaven. I am, as it were, a gardener of this world.[857] 3. For when a gardener sees the rise of a

strong wind harmful to the little plants and the trees of his garden, at once he runs to them quickly and binds them fast with sturdy stakes as well as he can. And thus he comes to their aid, in various ways according to his ability, lest they be broken by the rushing wind or wretchedly uprooted. I, the Mother of mercy,[858] do the same in the garden of this world. 4. For when I see blowing on the hearts of human beings the dangerous winds of the devil's temptations and wicked suggestions, at once I have recourse to my Lord and my God, my Son Jesus Christ, helping them with my prayers and obtaining from him 5. his outpouring of some holy infusions of the Holy Spirit into their hearts to prop them up and savingly confirm them that they may be kept spiritually uninjured by the diabolic wind of temptations lest the devil prevail against human beings, breaking their souls and plucking them up by the stem in accord with his wicked desire. 6. And thus when, with humility of heart and active compliance,[859] human beings receive these said stakes of mine and my assistance, at once they are defended against the diabolic onslaught of temptations; and remaining firm in the state of grace, they bear for God and for me the fruit of sweetness in due season.[860] 7. But as for those who scorn the aforesaid spiritual stakes of my Son and me and are swayed by the wind of temptations through consent to the devil and through action, they are uprooted from the state of grace and, through illicit desires and deeds, are led by the devil even to the profound and eternal pains and darkness of hell. 8. Now, however, know that in the Neapolitan citizenry many different horrible and secret sins are being committed which I am not relating to you. But instead I am speaking to you now about two kinds of open sins that greatly displease my Son and me and all the heavenly court.

9. "The first sin is the fact that in this said city many buy pagans and infidels to be their slaves[861] and that some masters of those slaves do not bother to baptize them and do not want to convert them to the Christian faith. 10. And even if some of them are baptized, their masters bother no more, after the slaves' baptism, to have them instructed and trained in the Christian faith or to train them in the reception of the Church's sacraments than they did before the slaves' baptism and conversion. 11. And so it results that the said convert slaves, after accepting the faith, commit many sins and do not know how to return to the sacraments of penance and communion or how to be restored in the state of salvation and of reconciliation with God and of grace. 12. Moreover, some keep their female servants and slaves[862] in extreme abjection and ignominy, as if they were dogs—selling them and, what is worse, frequently expos-

ing them in a brothel to earn money that is a disgrace and an abomination. 13. Others, in fact, keep them in their own houses as prostitutes both for themselves and for others; and this is extremely abominable and hateful to God and to me and also to the whole heavenly court. 14. Some other masters so grieve and exasperate these said servants of theirs with abusive words and blows that some of the said servants come to a state of despair and want to kill themselves.[863] 15. Indeed these sins and acts of negligence much displease God and all the heavenly court. For God himself loves them because he created them; and to save all, he came into the world, taking flesh from me, and endured suffering and death on the cross. 16. Know too that if anyone buys such pagans and infidels with the intention of making them Christians and wants to instruct and train them in the Christian faith and virtues and intends, during his life or at his death, to set these slaves at liberty so that the said slaves may not pass to his heirs, such a master of slaves merits much by this and is acceptable in the sight of God. 17. But know for very certain that those who do the contrary will be heavily punished by God.[864]

18. "The second kind of sin is that many men and women,[865] with various inordinate marks of respect, keep about them and consult wicked fortune-tellers and diviners and the most evil of enchantresses.[866] 19. For sometimes they ask them to perform witchcraft and incantations in order that they may be able to conceive and beget children. 20. Others require them to perform incantations and to make fetishes[867] that will cause certain men and women, or even their temporal lords, to be enamored of them to the point of distraction and to love them with all their heart. 21. Others, in fact, beg foreknowledge of the future from these same accursed witches. Many others ask them to give them health in their infirmities through their art of enchantment and witchcraft. 22. All indeed who keep these same warlock diviners or enchantresses in their households and at their own expense and all who seek from such people such wicked advice and diabolic remedies, and, indeed, all those same warlock diviners and enchantresses who promise the things mentioned above—all are cursed and hateful in the sight of God. 23. As long as they persevere in such a state and purpose, no infusion or grace of the Holy Spirit will ever descend or enter into their hearts. 24. But nevertheless, if they repent and humbly amend their lives with the true purpose of not falling back again, they will obtain grace and mercy from my Son."

However, when these things had thus been heard, this vision disappeared.

A certain bishop, who was the ruler of the March of Ancona on behalf of the holy Roman Church, asked Lady Birgitta about the fact that he was pricked in conscience on the grounds that he was absent and too remote from his diocese because of his aforesaid office in the marquisate where he resided, and thus could not attend to the sheep entrusted to him in his diocese. And he wondered, therefore, whether it would be more pleasing to God that he reside in his office in the marquisate or that he return to rule the sheep entrusted to him in his diocese. And when at this request the abovesaid lady prayed for the aforementioned bishop, then Christ appeared to her and said to her the words that are contained below. Chapter 29.

Blessed be God forever for all his bounties! Amen. My Lord, most reverend Father, first of all I humbly recommend myself to you.[868] You have written to me with humility that I, a woman unknown to you, should humbly pray to God for you.[869] 2. To this I reply and tell you truthfully, according to my conscience, that I am inadequate for such a task: being a sinner, alas, and unworthy. 3. You have also written to me that I should write to you some spiritual advice for the salvation of your soul. And therefore God, attending to your faith and humility, willed with devoted fatherly love to satisfy your desires and faith and was attentive, not to my sins, but to the heartfelt affection of his humble petitioner.[870] 4. For when I, a sinner unworthy of doing so, was praying for you on the preceding day to my Lord Jesus Christ, he then appeared to me in spirit and spoke with me, using a similitude and saying this:

5. "O you, to whom it has been given to hear spiritually and to see, be attentive now and know for very certain that all bishops and abbots and also all the other ecclesiastical prelates and benefice-holders who have the care of souls and who leave their churches and my sheep, which have been entrusted to them, and who receive and hold other offices and positions of rulership with the intention and purpose that in these offices they may be more honored by human beings and may be exalted and raised to a higher status in the world, 6. then, even though in those offices these rulers neither steal nor plunder anything nor commit any other injustice, nevertheless, because they glory and delight in those offices and honors and, for this reason, leave my sheep and their churches, they are, in doing such things, to my eyes like pigs dressed in pontifical or sacerdotal ornaments.[871] 7. This situation might be expressed by means of the following similitude: There was a great lord

who had invited his friends to supper.[872] And at the hour of the supper, those pigs—dressed as above—entered into the palace in the sight of that lord and in the sight of the banqueters who sat at the table. 8. The lord, however, wished to give to them some of those precious foods on his table; but then the aforesaid pigs cried out with a loud sound, grunting their opposition with their pig voices[873] and refusing to eat those precious foods, although they were avidly eager to eat, in their usual way, the cheap husks meant for pigs.[874] 9. Then, however, when that lord saw and understood this, he loathed their vileness and filth; and at once he said to his servants with great wrath and indignation: 10. 'Expel them from my palace and cast them forth to be refreshed and sordidly sated with the pigs' husks of which they are worthy! For they are neither willing nor worthy to eat of my foods, which have been prepared for my friends.'"

11. By these things, my most reverend Father and Lord, I then understood in spirit that this is what you must do: namely, that you must decide in your own conscience whether or not those sheep of Christ, namely, those entrusted to you in your bishopric, are being well and spiritually ruled in your absence. 12. If in your absence they are being well ruled in accord with what is spiritually appropriate to their souls' advantage and benefit, and if furthermore you see that by ruling the March you can do God greater honor and be more useful to souls than in your own bishopric, 13. then indeed I say that you can quite lawfully stay in your office as ruler of the March in accord with the will of God, provided that it is neither desire for honor nor empty glorying in that office that seduces you into staying there. 14. If, in fact, your conscience dictates to you the contrary, then I advise you to leave that office of the marquisate and go back to reside personally in your own church and in the bishopric entrusted to you: namely, in order to rule those sheep of yours, or rather, of Christ, specially entrusted to you and to feed them by word, example, and work, not negligently and faultily like a wicked hireling, but carefully and virtuously like a true and good shepherd.[875]

15. Be forbearing with me, my Lord, in that I, although an ignorant woman and an unworthy sinner, write such things to you. I ask of him, our true and good Shepherd, who deigned to die for his sheep, that he may bestow on you the Holy Spirit's grace, by which you may worthily rule his sheep and always do his glorious and most holy will, even till death.

The Judge complains[876] to the bride about the universal number of sinners of all states[877] and conditions, narrating the good deeds that he did for them and their ingratitude. He also threatens them with the terrible sentence of his wrath. Nevertheless, he admonishes them to be converted to him; and he will receive them with mercy, like a father. Chapter 30.

I saw a grand palace like the serene sky.[878] In it was the host of the heavenly army, innumerable as the atoms of the sun[879] and having a gleam as of the sun's rays. 2. But in the palace, on a wonderful throne there sat, as it were, the person of a human being, a Lord of incomprehensible beauty and immense power; his clothes were wonderful and of inexpressible brightness. 3. And before him who sat on the throne[880] there stood a Virgin who was more radiant than the sun.[881] All those of the heavenly host, who stood nearby, reverently honored her as the queen of heaven. But then he who sat on the throne opened his mouth and said:[882]

4. "Hearken, all you my enemies who live in the world; for to my friends who follow my will, I am not speaking. Hearken, all you clerics: archbishops and bishops and all of lower rank in the Church! Hearken, all you religious, of whatever order you are! 5. Hearken, you kings and princes and judges of the earth[883] and all you who serve! Hearken, you women: princesses and all ladies and maidservants! All you inhabitants of the world, of whatever condition or rank you are, whether great or small, hearken to these words that I myself, who created you, now speak to you! 6. I complain[884] because you have withdrawn from me and have put faith in the devil, my enemy. You have abandoned my commandments and you follow the will of the devil and you obey his suggestions. 7. You do not attend[885] to the fact that I, the unchanging and eternal God, your Creator, came down from heaven to a Virgin and took flesh from her and lived with you.[886] Through my own self, I opened the way for you and showed the counsels by which you might go to heaven. 8. I was stripped and scourged and crowned with thorns and so forcefully extended on the cross that, as it were, all the sinews and joints of my body were being undone. I heard all insults and endured a most contemptible death and most bitter heartache for the sake of your salvation. 9. To all these things, O my enemies, you are not attentive because you have been deceived. Therefore you bear the yoke and burden of the devil with false sweetness[887] and neither know nor feel them before the approach of sorrow over the interminable burden. 10. Nor is this

enough for you; for your pride is so great that if you could ascend above me, you would gladly do it. And the pleasure of the flesh is so important to you that you would more gladly forfeit me than give up your inordinate delight. 11. Moreover, your greed is as insatiable as a sack with a hole in it; for there is nothing that can satisfy your greed. 12. Therefore, I swear by my Godhead that if you are to die in the state in which you now are, you shall never see my face;[888] but for your pride you shall sink so deeply into hell that all the devils will be above you, afflicting you beyond all consolation. 13. Indeed, for your lust you shall be filled with horrible diabolic venom; and for your greed you shall be filled with sorrow and anguish; and you shall be partakers of all the evil that there is in hell. 14. O my enemies—abominable and ungrateful and degenerate —I seem to you, as it were, a worm dead in winter.[889] Therefore, you do whatever things you will, and you prosper.[890] Therefore, I will arise in summer and then you shall be silent,[891] and you shall not escape my hand. 15. But nevertheless, O my enemies, because I have redeemed you with my blood and because I am in quest of naught but your souls, therefore return to me even now with humility and I will gladly receive you as my children. 16. Shake off from you the devil's heavy yoke and recall my charity and you shall see in your conscience that I am sweet and meek."[892]

In Rome Christ speaks to his bride, blessed Birgitta, foretelling to her the day and manner of her death and ordering what should be done with the books of revelations. He also says that when he so pleases, there will be many in the world who will receive them with devotion and who will obtain his grace. The Lord also makes arrangements concerning the body of his bride and where it ought to be buried. Chapter 31.[893]

It happened five days before the day of the passing[894] of Lady Birgitta, the often-mentioned bride of Christ, that our Lord Jesus Christ appeared to her in front of the altar that stood in her chamber.[895] He showed himself with a joyful face and said to her: 2. "I have done to you what a bridegroom usually does, concealing himself from his bride so that he may be more ardently desired by her. Thus I have not visited you with consolations during this time; for it was the time of your testing. 3. Therefore, now that you have already been tested, go forward and prepare yourself; for now is the time for the fulfillment of that which I promised you: namely, that before my altar you shall be clothed and consecrated as a nun. And henceforth you shall be counted, not only as my bride, but also as a nun and a mother in Vadstena.[896] 4. Nevertheless, know that you will lay down[897] your body here in Rome until it comes to the place prepared for it. For it pleases me to spare you from your labors and to accept your will in place of the completed action."[898]

And having turned toward Rome, he said as if making a complaint:[899] "O my Rome, O my Rome, the pope scorns you and does not attend to my words but accepts the doubtful in place of the certain. Therefore he shall hear my pipe[900] no more; for he makes the time of my mercy dependent on his own choice."[901]

6. Then he said to the bride: "As for you, however: tell the prior[902] to hand over all these words of mine, in all the revelations, to the brothers and to my bishop,[903] to whom I shall give the fervor of my Spirit and whom I shall fill with my grace. 7. And know that when it so pleases me, those human beings will come who, with sweetness and joy, will receive those words of the heavenly revelations that up until now have been made to you; and all the things that have been said to you will be accomplished. 8. And although my grace has been withdrawn from many because of their ingratitude, nevertheless others will come who will arise in lieu of them and who will obtain my grace. 9. But among the very last words of the revelations made to you, put that common and universal revelation that I gave to you in Naples.[904] For my judgment shall be carried out on all the nations who do not humbly return to me, as it has there been shown to you."[905]

10. However, after these and many other things not written here[906] had been said, the bride of Christ made mention of and arrangements for some persons living with her and whom, before death, she said she had seen in God's presence.[907]

11. After those things had been heard, the Lord added these words: "On the morning of the fifth day, after you have received the sacraments, call together one by one the persons who are present and living with you and whom I have just now named to you and tell them the things that they must do. 12. And thus, amidst these words and their hands, you will come to your monastery, i.e., into my joy; and your body will be placed in Vadstena."[908] 13. Then, as the fifth day approached,[909] at the moment of dawn, Christ appeared to her again and consoled her. But when Mass had been said and after she had received the sacraments with very great devotion and reverence, in the hands of the aforesaid persons[910] she sent forth her spirit.[911]

Four Prayers

1. *Proem to the prayers written below, which were divinely revealed to the blessed Birgitta of the kingdom of Sweden.*[912]

2. Since blessed Birgitta always petitioned and asked God to pour into her some acceptable manner of praying, it happened one day, while she was praying, that in a wonderful manner she was lifted up in spirit by an elevation of mind. 3. And then were poured into her from God certain most beautiful prayers concerning the life and passion and praise of Christ and concerning the life, compassion, and praise of the most Blessed Virgin Mary. 4. Afterward she so kept them in memory that every day she would read[913] them devoutly. Wherefore the Blessed Virgin Mary, on a later occasion appearing to her at prayer, said: 5. "I merited for you those prayers. Therefore, when you read them devoutly, you shall be visited with the consolation[914] of my Son."

6. *In this prayer revealed by God to blessed Birgitta, the glorious Virgin Mary is devoutly and beautifully praised for her holy conception and infancy, for all her virtuous acts and labors, for the great sorrows of her whole life, for her most holy death and assumption, etc. The first prayer.*

7. Blessed and revered may you be, my Lady, O Virgin Mary, most holy Mother of God. You are, in truth, his best creation; and no one has ever loved him so intimately as you, O glorious Lady.

8. Glory be to you, my Lady, O Virgin Mary, Mother of God. That same angel[915] by whom Christ was announced to you announced you yourself to your own father and mother;[916] and of their honest wedlock[917] you were conceived and begotten.

9. Blessed may you be, my Lady, O Virgin Mary. In your most holy infancy, immediately after your weaning, you were borne by your parents to the temple of God and were, with other virgins, entrusted to the keeping of the devout high priest.[918]

10. Praise be to you, my Lady, O Virgin Mary. When you reached that age at which you understood that God was your Creator, you forthwith began to love him intimately above all things. Then too you most discreetly ordered your time, both day and night, by means of various offices and exercises in honor of God. Your sleep, too, and the

food for your glorious body were so temperately regulated by you that you were always fit for God's service.

11. Infinite glory be to you, my Lady,[919] O Virgin Mary, who humbly vowed your virginity to God himself[920] and therefore had no concern about who would betroth you, for you knew that he to whom you had first given your faith was more mighty and more good than all others combined.

12. Blessed may you be, my Lady, O Virgin Mary. You were alone and ablaze with ardent love for God and—all your mind and all the strength of your powers being lifted up—you were, with ardor and diligence, contemplating the most high God to whom you had offered your virginity, when the angel was sent to you from God and, in greeting you, announced to you God's will. To him you replied most humbly, professing yourself God's handmaid;[921] and then and there the Holy Spirit wonderfully filled you with all power and virtue.[922] To you, God the Father sent his coeternal and coequal Son, who came into you then and, of your flesh and blood, took for himself a human body. Thus, at that blessed hour, the Son of God became, in you, your son, alive in his every limb and without loss of his divine majesty.

13. Blessed may you be, my Lady, O Virgin Mary. Of your own blessed body, the body of Christ had now been created; and in your womb, you felt his body ever growing and moving even to the time of his glorious nativity. Before anyone else, you yourself touched him with your holy hands; you wrapped him in cloths; and, in accord with the prophet's oracle, you laid him in a manger.[923] With exultant joy, in motherly fashion, you used the most sacred milk of your breasts to nurture him.

14. Glory be to you, O my Lady, O Virgin Mary. While still dwelling in a contemptible house, i.e., the stable,[924] you saw mighty kings[925] coming to your Son from afar and humbly offering to him, with the greatest reverence, their royal guest-gifts.[926] Afterward, with your own precious hands, you presented him in the temple; and, in your blessed heart, you diligently preserved[927] all that you heard from him or saw during his infancy.

15. Blessed may you be, my Lady, O Virgin Mary. With your most holy offspring, you fled into Egypt; and afterward, in joy, you bore him back to Nazareth. During his physical growth, you saw him, your Son, humble and obedient to yourself and to Joseph.

16. Blessed may you be, O Lady Virgin Mary. You saw your Son

preaching, doing miracles, and choosing the apostles, who, being enlightened by his examples, his miracles, and his teachings, became witnesses of truth that your Jesus is also truly the Son of God: publishing to
all nations that it was he who, through himself, had fulfilled the writings
of the prophets[928] when on behalf of the human race he had patiently
endured a most hard death.

17. Blessed may you be, my Lady, O Virgin Mary, who knew beforehand that your Son must be made captive. Later your blessed eyes
with sorrow saw him bound and scourged and crowned with thorns and
fixed naked to the cross with nails. You saw many despising him and
calling him a traitor.

18. Honor be to you, my Lady, O Virgin Mary. In sorrow, you gazed
at your Son as he spoke to you from the cross;[929] and with your blessed
ears, you dolefully heard him, in the agony of death, crying to the Father
and commending his own soul into his hands.[930]

19. Praise be to you, my Lady, O Virgin Mary. With bitter sorrow,
you saw your Son hanging on the cross: from the top of his head to the
soles of his feet,[931] all black and blue and marked with the red of his own
blood, and so cruelly dead. You also gazed at the bitter sight of the
holes—in his feet, in his hands, and even in his glorious side. You gazed
at his skin, all lacerated without any mercy.

20. Blessed may you be, my Lady, O Virgin Mary. With tears in
your eyes, you saw your Son taken down, wrapped in cloths, buried in a
monument, and there guarded by soldiers.

21. Blessed may you be, my Lady, O Virgin Mary. To the grave
intensification of your heart's deep sorrow, you parted from the sepulchre of your Son and, all full of grief, were brought by his friends to
the house of John.[932] But there, at once, you felt a relief of your
great sorrow because you most surely foreknew that your Son would
quickly rise.

22. Rejoice, my most worthy Lady, O Virgin Mary, for in the same
instant that your Son arose from death he willed to make this same fact
known to you, his most Blessed Mother. Then and there he appeared to
you by himself,[933] and later he showed to other persons that he was the
one who had been raised[934] from death after having endured death in his
own living body.

23. Rejoice therefore, my most worthy Lady, O Virgin Mary.
When death had been conquered and death's instigator had been over-
thrown,[935] and heaven's entry had been opened wide through your

Son,[936] you saw him rising and triumphant with the crown of victory. And on the fortieth day after his resurrection, you saw him, in the sight of many, ascend with honor to his kingdom in heaven as himself a king accompanied by angels.

24. Exult, my most worthy Lady, O Virgin Mary. You merited to see how, after his ascension, your Son suddenly transmitted to his apostles and disciples the Holy Spirit with which he had previously filled you to the full. By increasing the fervor of their charity and the rightness of their Catholic belief, he wonderfully enlightened their hearts.

25. Rejoice still more, my Lady, O Virgin Mary; and at your joy, let all the world rejoice. For many years after his ascension your Son permitted you to remain in this world for the consolation[937] of his friends and for the strengthening of the faith, for the relief of the poor and for the sound counseling of the apostles. Then, through your prudent words, your seemly behavior, and your virtuous deeds, your Son converted countless Jews and infidel pagans to the Catholic faith; and by wondrously illuminating them, he enlightened them to confess that you are a virgin-mother and that he, your Son, is God with a true human nature.

26. Blessed may you be, my Lady, O Virgin Mary. In your ardent charity and maternal love, you unceasingly desired at every moment to come to your so well-loved Son now sitting in heaven. While dwelling in this world and sighing after the things of heaven,[938] you humbly conformed to the will of God; wherefore, by the dictates of divine justice, you ineffably increased your eternal glory.

27. To you, O my Lady, O Virgin Mary, be eternal honor and glory. When it pleased God to rescue you from the exile of this world[939] and to honor your soul in his kingdom forever, he then deigned to announce this to you through his angel;[940] and he willed that your venerable body, when dead, be entombed by his apostles in a sepulchre with all reverence.[941]

28. Be glad, my Lady, O Virgin Mary. For in that most light death of yours,[942] your soul was embraced by the power of God;[943] and he, as a watchful father, protected it from all adversity. Then it was that God the Father subjected to your power all things created.[944] With honor, God the Son placed you, his most worthy Mother, beside himself on a most lofty seat. And the Holy Spirit, in bringing you to his glorious kingdom as a virgin betrothed to himself, did wonderfully exalt you.

29. Rejoice eternally, my Lady, O Virgin Mary. For some days after

your death, your body lay entombed in its sepulchre until, with honor and through the power of God, it stood linked anew to your soul.[945]

30. Exult to the full, O Mother of God, O glorious Lady, O Virgin Mary. You merited to see your body revived after your death and assumed with your soul into heaven amidst honor from the angels.[946] You acknowledged that your glorious Son was God with a human nature;[947] and with exultant joy, you saw that he is the most just judge of all and the rewarder of good works.

31. Rejoice again, my Lady, O Virgin Mary. For your body's most holy flesh knows[948] that it now exists in heaven as both virgin and mother. It sees itself in no way stained by any mortal or venial crime. No, it knows that it did all the works of virtue with such charity that God, in justice, had to revere it with highest honor.[949] Your flesh then understood that the more ardently that anyone loves God in this world, the nearer to himself will God place that person in heaven. For it was manifestly clear to the whole court of heaven that no angel and no human loved God with such charity as you did; and therefore it was right and just[950] that with honor God himself placed you, body and soul, on the highest seat of glory.

32. Blessed may you be, O my Lady, O Virgin Mary. Every faithful creature praises the Holy Trinity for you because you are the Trinity's most worthy creature. For wretched souls you obtain prompt pardon, and for all sinners you stand forth as a most faithful advocate and proxy.[951] Praised therefore be God, the most high Emperor and Lord, who created[952] you for such great honor that you yourself became both Empress and Lady everlastingly in the kingdom of heaven, forever to reign with him unto ages of ages. Amen.

33. *This prayer was revealed by God to blessed Birgitta. In it, by means of a painstakingly detailed narrative,*[953] *Christ is beautifully and devoutly praised for his glorious incarnation; for all the actions, labors, and sorrows of his life and of his holy death; for his ascension into heaven; for the sending of the Holy Spirit upon the disciples; etc. The second prayer.*

34. Blessed may you be, my Lord, my God, and my Love most beloved of my soul:[954] O you who are one God in three Persons.

35. Glory and praise be to you, my Lord Jesus Christ. You were sent by the Father into the body of a virgin; and yet you ever remain with the Father in heaven, while the Father, in his divinity, inseparably remained with you in your human nature in this world.[955]

36. Honor and glory be to you, my Lord Jesus Christ. After having been conceived by the power of the Holy Spirit, you physically grew in the Virgin's womb; and in it you humbly dwelt until the time of your birth. After your delightful nativity,[956] you deigned to be touched by the most clean hands of your Mother, to be wrapped in cloths, and to be laid in a manger.[957]

37. Blessed may you be, my Lord Jesus Christ. You willed that your immaculate flesh be circumcised and that you be called Jesus. You willed to be offered by your Mother in the temple.[958]

38. Blessed may you be, my Lord Jesus Christ. You had yourself baptized in the Jordan by your servant John.

39. Blessed may you be, my Lord Jesus Christ. With your blessed mouth, you preached to human beings the words of life; and in their sight, through yourself, within your actual presence,[959] you worked many miracles.

40. Blessed may you be, my Lord Jesus Christ. By fulfilling the writings of the prophets, you manifested to the world in a rational way[960] that you are the true God.

41. Blessing and glory be to you, my Lord Jesus Christ. For forty days, you wonderfully fasted in the desert. You permitted yourself to be tempted by your enemy, the devil, whom—when it so pleased you—you drove from yourself with a single word.[961]

42. Blessed may you be, my Lord Jesus Christ. You foretold your death ahead of time. At the last supper, of material bread you wonderfully consecrated your precious Body and charitably bestowed it on your apostles in memory of your most worthy passion. By washing their feet with your own precious and holy hands, you humbly showed your very great humility.

43. Honor be to you, my Lord Jesus Christ. In fear of suffering and death, you gave forth from your innocent body blood in place of sweat.[962] Nonetheless, you accomplished for us the redemption that you had willed to perform; and thus you manifestly showed the charity that you had toward the human race.

44. Glory be to you, my Lord Jesus Christ. Sold by your disciple and bought by the Jews, you were made a captive for our sake. Solely by your word, you cast your enemies to the earth;[963] and then of your own will you gave yourself over as a captive to their unclean and grasping hands.

45. Blessed may you be, my Lord Jesus Christ. You were led to

Caiaphas, and you, who are the Judge of all, humbly permitted yourself to be given over to the judgment of Pilate.

46. Blessed may you be, my Lord Jesus Christ. From Pilate the judge, you were sent to Herod; and you permitted yourself to be mocked and scorned by him; and you consented again to be remitted to that same Pilate as judge.

47. Glory be to you, my Lord Jesus Christ, for the derision that you endured while you stood invested with purple and crowned with the sharpest thorns. With great patience you endured the spitting on your glorious face, the veiling of your eyes, and, on your cheek and neck, the grave and cutting blows of the deadly hands of the wicked.

48. Praise be to you, my Lord Jesus Christ. Like an innocent lamb,[964] you most patiently permitted yourself to be tied to the column and monstrously scourged; to be led, all bloody, to Pilate's judgment and there be gazed at.

49. Blessed may you be, my Lord Jesus Christ. Most patiently, in Pilate's presence, with your own blessed ears you willed to hear abuse and lies hurled at you and the voices of the people asking that the guilty robber be acquitted and that you, the innocent, be condemned.

50. Honor be to you, my Lord Jesus Christ. With your glorious body covered in gore, the judgment on you was the death of the cross. The cross you bore in pain on your sacred shoulders; and, amidst frenzy, you were led to the place of your passion. Despoiled of your garments, thus you willed to be fixed to the wood of the cross.

51. Glory unmeasured be to you, my Lord Jesus Christ. For us you humbly endured that the Jews[965] stretched out your venerable hands and feet with rope, that they cruelly fixed them with iron nails to the wood of the cross, that they called you a traitor, that in manifold ways they derided you with unspeakable words while above you was inscribed that title of confusion.[966]

52. Eternal praise and thanksgiving be to you, my Lord Jesus Christ. With what great meekness you suffered for us such cruel sorrows! On the cross your blessed body was emptied of all its strength; your kindly eyes grew dark; as your blood decreased, a pallor covered all your comely face; your blessed tongue grew swollen, hot, and dry; your mouth dripped from the bitter drink;[967] your hair and beard were filled with blood from the wounds of your most holy head; the bones of your hands, of your feet, and of all your precious body were dislocated from their sockets to your great and intense grief; the veins and nerves of all

your blessed body were cruelly broken; you were so monstrously scourged and so injured with painful wounds that your most innocent flesh and skin were all intolerably lacerated. Thus afflicted and aggrieved, you, O my most sweet Lord, stood[968] on the cross, and, with patience and humility, awaited in extreme pain the hour of your death.

53. Perpetual honor be to you, Lord Jesus Christ. Placed in this your anguish, with your kind and charitable eyes you humbly looked upon your most worthy Mother, who never sinned nor ever gave to the slightest sin any consent.[969] While consoling her who was your own, you committed her to the faithful keeping of your disciple.[970]

54. Eternal blessing be to you, my Lord Jesus Christ. In the agony of death, you gave to all sinners the hope of forgiveness when, to the robber who had turned to you, you mercifully promised the glory of paradise.[971]

55. Eternal praise be to you, my Lord Jesus Christ, for each and every hour that you endured such great bitterness and anguish on the cross for us sinners. For the most acute pains proceeding from your wounds direly penetrated your happy soul and cruelly passed through your most sacred heart until your heart cracked[972] and you happily sent forth your spirit,[973] and, with bowed head,[974] humbly commended it into the hands of God your Father. Then, having died in the body, you remained there all cold.[975]

56. Blessed may you be, my Lord Jesus Christ. By your precious blood[976] and by your most sacred death, you redeemed souls and mercifully led them back from exile to eternal life.

57. Blessed may you be, my Lord Jesus Christ. You hung dead on the wood of the cross, and straightway you mightily[977] liberated your friends from the prison of hell.[978]

58. Blessed may you be, my Lord Jesus Christ. For our salvation, you permitted your side and your heart to be perforated with a lance, and from that same side you sent forth, in a rich flow, water and your precious blood in order to redeem us.[979] Before the judge's[980] leave had been given, you willed that your most sacred body not be taken down from the cross.

59. Glory be to you, my Lord Jesus Christ. You willed that your blessed body be taken down from the cross by your friends and that it be laid in the hands of your most unhappy Mother. You permitted that it be wrapped in cloths[981] by her and be buried in a monument and that it be guarded there by soldiers.

60. Sempiternal honor be to you, my Lord Jesus Christ. On the third

day, you rose from the dead, and you showed yourself alive to such others as it so pleased you. After forty days, while many watched, you ascended to the heavens; and there, in honor, you placed your friends whom you had delivered from Tartarus.[982]

61. Jubilation and praise eternal be to you, Lord Jesus Christ. You sent the Holy Spirit to the hearts of your disciples; and in their spirits, you immeasurably increased divine love.

62. Blessed may you be, and praiseworthy and glorious unto the ages, my Lord Jesus. You sit upon the throne in your kingdom of heaven, in the glory of your divinity, corporeally alive, with all your most holy limbs that you took from the flesh of the Virgin. Even thus shall you come on the day of judgment to judge the souls of all the living and the dead: you, who live and reign with the Father and the Holy Spirit unto ages of ages. Amen.

63. *In this prayer, revealed by God to blessed Birgitta, praise is given in a beautiful way to all the members of the most holy body of our Lord Jesus Christ and to his body's most virtuous actions. The third prayer.*

64. My Lord Jesus Christ, although I know well that your blessed body is unceasingly praised and glorified by the harmonious jubilee of the citizens of heaven above, and yet, because I am bound by a debt to render to you infinite thanksgiving, therefore I, although a person unwise and unworthy, desire nevertheless with all my heart and with all my mouth to offer to all the members of your precious body such thanks as I can and praise and honor.

65. My Lord Jesus Christ, you are truly the High Priest and Pontiff[983] who first and before all others wondrously consecrated of material bread your true and blessed Body that you might satisfy us with the bread of angels.[984] Therefore, may your glorious priestly seat at the right hand of God your Father, in your divinity, be happy and blessed unto eternity.[985] Amen.

66. My Lord Jesus Christ, you truly are the head of all men and angels, the worthy King of kings and Lord of lords;[986] and you do all your works out of true and ineffable charity. You humbly permitted your blessed head to be crowned with a crown of thorns. Blessed, therefore, be your head and hair; and may they be gloriously adorned with an imperial diadem. May heaven and earth and sea and all things created be subject and obedient to your empire and your power unto eternity. Amen.

67. My Lord Jesus Christ, your splendid forehead never turned away from right justice and truth. Blessed, therefore, be that same forehead of

yours, and, with royal and triumphant glory, may it be perpetually praised by all creatures together. Amen.

68. My Lord Jesus Christ, with your bright eyes of pity you look kindly upon all who with true charity ask of you grace and mercy. Blessed, therefore, be your eyes, your eyelids, and your glorious eyebrows; and may all your fair and lovely sight be unceasingly glorified by the whole heavenly army of citizens on high. Amen.

69. My Lord Jesus Christ, with your kindly ears you gladly hear and hearken to all who humbly address you. Blessed, therefore, be those ears of yours; and may they be eternally filled with all honor. Amen.

70. My Lord Jesus Christ, your most sweet and blessed nostrils did not shrink from the stench of the putrid cadaver of the dead Lazarus or even from the horrid smell that spiritually proceeded from the traitor Judas when he kissed you. Blessed, therefore, be your precious nostrils; and may all expend on them the odor of sweetness and praise forever. Amen.[987]

71. My Lord Jesus Christ, for our bodily and spiritual health and salvation and for our instruction in faith, you, with your own blessed mouth and lips, very often preached the words of life and of doctrine. Blessed, therefore, be your venerable mouth and your lips for every word that proceeded from them.[988] Amen.

72. My Lord Jesus Christ, with your most clean teeth, you most moderately chewed physical food for the sustenance of your blessed body. Blessed, therefore, and honored be your teeth by all your creatures. Amen.

73. My Lord Jesus Christ, your tongue never moved to speak and never kept silence, except with justice and utility and to the extent that such action had been foreordained in your divinity. Blessed, therefore, be that same tongue of yours. Amen.

74. My Lord Jesus Christ, in accordance with your age, you fittingly wore a fine beard on your handsome face. May your venerable beard, therefore, be everlastingly revered and adored.[989] Amen.

75. My Lord Jesus Christ, blessed be your throat, your stomach, and your viscera; and may all your sacred inwards be perpetually honored for the fact that they decently nourished your precious body in due order and perfectly sustained your bodily life for the redemption of souls and to the joy of the angels. Amen.

76. My Lord Jesus Christ, you are worthily called a leader by all because you bore on your holy shoulders and neck the burdensome bulk[990] of the cross before you mightily shattered[991] the gates of hell[992]

and led the souls of the elect back to heaven. Therefore, to your blessed neck and shoulders that so endured, be honor and glory eternally without end. Amen.

77. My Lord Jesus Christ, your blessed, royal, and magnificent heart could never, by torments or terrors or blandishments, be swayed from the defense of your kingdom of truth and justice. You did not spare your most worthy blood in any way; but rather, with your magnificent heart, you faithfully strove for justice and the law and intrepidly preached to your friends and to your enemies the law's precepts and the counsels of perfection.[993] By dying in battle to defend these things, you—and your holy followers with you—have obtained the victory. Therefore, it is right that your unconquered heart be ever magnified in heaven and on earth and be unceasingly praised with triumphal honor by all creatures and soldiers. Amen.[994]

78. My Lord Jesus Christ, the strenuous[995] soldiers and faithful servants of this world gladly expose their own lives to death in war in order that their lords may enjoy safety of life; but you, O my good Lord, quickly hastened to the death of the cross in order that your servants might not miserably perish. Wherefore it is just that your glorious and intrepid breast be eternally adored by all your servants, whom you have thus delivered, and by all others and that it be humbly praised even by the angelic choirs. Amen.[996]

79. My Lord Jesus Christ, with your venerable hands and arms you surpassed the strength of Samson[997] in a wonderful way as you patiently endured that they be fixed to the wood of the cross and thus, with violence, snatched your friends from hell. Therefore to these same limbs of yours, from all whom you have redeemed, may there be shown unceasing reverence, eternal praise, and everlasting glory. Amen.

80. My Lord Jesus Christ, may your precious ribs and your back be blessed and honored unto eternity by all human beings who sweat over labors spiritual and earthly.[998] For from your infancy even to your death, you labored unceasingly for our redemption; and with great pain and burdensomeness, you bore our sins on your back. Amen.

81. My Lord Jesus Christ, supreme purity and true cleanness, may your most innocent loins be blessed and praised above all the angels' cleanness which is in heaven and above the purity of all who have preserved their chastity and virginity in the world; for the chastity and virginity of them all cannot be compared to your cleanness and your purity. Amen.

82. My Lord Jesus Christ, may your knees, with their hams and your

shins, be revered[999] and humbly honored by all creatures in heaven and on earth above all who show reverence and honor by kneeling in the presence of their lords and masters; for you, the Lord of all, in all humility knelt[1000] before your own disciples. Amen.

83. My Lord Jesus Christ, good Teacher,[1001] may your most blessed feet be blessed and perennially adored; for, in this world, to your great sorrow, you walked with unshod feet along the harsher way that you taught to others,[1002] and at the end,[1003] for our sake, you permitted them to be fixed with hard nails to the cross—you who live and reign with God the Father in the unity of the Holy Spirit through all ages of ages. Amen.[1004]

84. *In this prayer, which was divinely revealed to blessed Birgitta, most devout and beautiful praise is given to all the members of the glorious body of the Virgin Mary and to all her body's virtuous actions. The fourth prayer.*

85. O my Lady, my life, O Queen of heaven, O Mother of God, although I am certain that your glorious body is unceasingly praised in heaven with melodious jubilee by all the heavenly court, still I, although an unworthy person, desire with all my heart to render here on earth such praise and thanks as I can to all your precious limbs.

86. Therefore, O my Lady, O Virgin Mary, praised be your hair with all its strands, now decorated with a diadem of glory; for your hair is brighter than the radiance of the sun. Just as the hairs of the head cannot be computed,[1005] even so are your virtues innumerable.

87. O my Lady, O Virgin Mary, may your forehead and your most honest face be together praised above the whiteness of the moon, for none of the faithful in this dark world ever looked to you without feeling some spiritual consolation poured into himself at the sight of you.[1006]

88. Blessed may you be, my Lady, O Virgin Mary. Your eyebrows and your eyelids exceed in the brightness of their splendor the rays of the sun.

89. Blessed be your most chaste eyes, O my Lady, O Virgin Mary. They coveted none of the transitory things that they saw in this world. As often as you lifted up your eyes, their appearance excelled the splendor of the stars in the sight of the whole heavenly court.

90. O my Lady, O Virgin Mary, may both your most blessed cheeks be praised above the beauty of the dawn, which so beautifully rises with its colors white and red. Even thus, while you were in the world, did your lovely cheeks shine with bright splendor in the sight of God and

the angels because you never displayed them for worldly pomp[1007] or vanity.

91. O my Lady, O Virgin Mary, revered and honored be your most honest ears above all the forces of the sea and above the motion of all the waters; for your ears ever manfully militated[1008] against all the unclean flux of worldly hearing.

92. O Virgin Mary, my Mistress, may your most sweet nose glory![1009] By the power of the Holy Spirit, it never drew or sent forth a breath[1010] without all your thought being ever in the presence of the most High. Although at times you slept, you never turned your will from him.[1011] Therefore, to that same nose of yours and to your most blessed nostrils be ever given an odor of sweetness,[1012] praise, and honor above the mingled odor of all the spices and all the herbs that habitually send forth[1013] a delightful fragrance.

93. O my Lady, O Virgin Mary, praised be your tongue—so pleasing to God and to the angels—above all fruitful trees. Every word that your tongue uttered never harmed any person but always came forth to someone's advantage. Your tongue was very prudent, and all found it sweeter to hear than the sweetest fruit is sweet to taste.

94. O my Queen and my Lady, O Virgin Mary, may your blessed mouth and your lips be praised above the loveliness of roses and all other flowers and especially for that your blessed and most humble word[1014] in which, with this same precious mouth of yours, you responded to God's angel when through you God willed to fulfill in the world his will, which he had foretold through the prophets. By virtue of that word, you diminished the power of the demons in hell and honorably restored the choirs of angels in heaven.[1015]

95. O Virgin Mary, my Lady and my consolation, may your neck, your shoulders, and your back be perpetually honored above the charm[1016] of all lilies, for you never bent these members of yours and never straightened them again, except for some useful purpose or for the honor of God. Just as the lily moves and bends at the blowing of the winds, so all your members moved at the infusion of the Holy Spirit.[1017]

96. O my Lady, my strength and my sweetness, may your most holy arms, your hands, and your fingers be blessed and eternally honored above all precious gems, which are comparable to your virtuous works. Just as your virtuous works allured the Son of God to you,[1018] even so did your arms and hands sweetly bind him in a maternal embrace of love.

97. O my Lady and my enlightenment, blessed be your most sacred

breasts[1019] above all the sweetest springs of healing waters.[1020] Just as their welling water supplies solace and refreshment for the thirsty, your sacred breasts, in giving milk to the Son of God, supplied us in our need with medicine and consolation.[1021]

98. O my Lady, O Virgin Mary, blessed be your most precious bosom[1022] above the purest gold. When you stood all sorrowful beneath the cross of your Son, then—at the sound of the hammers—you felt your glorious bosom most sharply constricted as if in a hard press. Although you heartily loved your Son, you nevertheless preferred him to endure that most bitter punishment in order that he might die for the redemption of souls, rather than that he avoid this death to their loss. Thus too did you stand most firm in the virtue of constancy when in every adversity you totally conformed yourself to the divine will.

99. O my Lady, O joy of my heart, O Virgin Mary, may your most venerable heart be glorified and revered. It was so afire for the honor of God—more so than all other creatures of heaven and earth—that the flame of its charity ascended the heights of heaven to God the Father, and, because of this, God's Son descended from the Father into your glorious womb with the fervor of the Holy Spirit. Nevertheless, the Son was not separated from the Father even though, in accordance with the Father's foreordainment, he was most honestly made human in your virginal womb.[1023]

100. O my Lady, most fertile and most virginal Virgin Mary, blessed be your most blessed womb above all fruitfully sprouting fields. Just as the seed that has fallen upon good ground brings forth for its owner fruit a hundredfold,[1024] even so your womb, a virgin-womb and yet most fertile, brought forth for God the Father blessed fruit, more than a thousandfold. Just as the lord of a field glories in its fertile abundance of fruit and just as the little birds and the animals feed in it with delight, even so did the blessed and fertile fruit of the little field of your womb cause high honor for God in heaven, rejoicing for the angels, and, for humans on earth, a lavish flow of sustenance and life.[1025]

101. O my Lady, Virgin most prudent,[1026] may your most sacred feet be eternally praised above all roots that unceasingly bear fruit. May your feet be thus blessed because they carried the glorious Son of God enclosed in your body as its sweetest fruit[1027] while your body itself was inviolate and your virginity remained uninjured forever. Oh with what honesty your most sacred feet went their way! Truly, at each of their prints, the King of heaven stood consoled and all the court of heaven rejoiced and was very glad.

102. O my Lady, O Virgin Mary, O Mother of all, may God the Father, together with the Son and the Holy Spirit, be eternally praised in his incomprehensible majesty for that most sacred cell of your whole body in which God's Son so sweetly rested—he whom the whole army of angels praises in heaven and whom the whole Church reverently adores on earth.

103. And you, my Lord, my King, and my God, to you be perpetual honor, perennial praise, blessing, and glory, and infinite thanksgiving. For you created this Virgin so worthy and so honest; and you chose her for yourself as your Mother for the sake of all who in any way have been consoled in heaven and on earth and for the sake of those in purgatory who have had, through her, assistance and solace. You live and reign with God the Father in the unity of the Holy Spirit, one God, through all ages of ages. Amen.

NOTES

1. The earliest life of Birgitta was apparently prepared soon after her death (23/VII/1373) by her two Swedish confessors: Peter, Cistercian prior of Alvastra (d. 1390), and Peter, a secular priest and master of theology from Skänninge (d. 1378). In Sweden until 1349 and in Italy until Birgitta's death, these men were prominent members of her household, acting as her confessors and as her secretaries (cf. Undhagen, *Book I* 11). Each of the two Peters had a father named Olaf, and thus they confusingly share the same Scandinavian patronymic "Olofsson" or "Olavi." Therefore most documents carefully specify which Peter they mean: the "prior" or the "master." As was the case with other members of the Birgittine circle, both Peters later received a certain local veneration as saints (Lundén, *Svenska helgon* 170–76). The *Life*, however, that the two Peters prepared was, like all the other Birgittine writings, quickly submitted for polishing to Birgitta's learned Spanish confessor, Alphonsus Pecha (cf. note 111), who had been absent on a mission to the papal court in Avignon when she died. Finally, on 17 December 1373, a suitable copy of the *Life* was submitted to the papal curia. Alphonsus, however, seems to have continued to polish and expand the text, which has accordingly come down to us in three main versions, distinguished chiefly by the extent of stylistic improvement and by the number of added passages. An "official" version of the text—neither the shortest of the three, nor the longest—was included in the collection of canonization documents known to us as *Acta et processus canonizacionis beate Birgitte* (ed. Isak Collijn, 73–101). It is this "Process" version of the *Life* that has been translated here, from the edition of Collijn and with the addition of a "chapter" number for each of Collijn's unnumbered paragraphs. For a detailed discussion of the intricate relationships among the various recensions of the *Life*, see Sara Ekwall, *Vår äldsta Birgittavita* (with résumé in French). Ekwall's research has led her to the plausible conjecture that in this "Process" *Life*, the following chapters are the work of Alphonsus and not of the two Peters alone: in chapter 26, the words describing the first two calls from God that frighten Birgitta ("Woman, hear me." She . . . said: "Woman, hear me."); chapters 30 (from the first mention of Gerekin) through 43;

chapters 53 through 57; chapter 69; chapter 72; chapters 76 through 78. I have chosen not to bracket these sections in the present translation in order to avoid giving the false impression that these additions alone mark the only real difference between the "Process" *Life* and the shorter recension of the text. In fact, in the passages common to both recensions, there are numerous small but significant differences of wording and content. Detailed documentation of the textual history of the selections in the present volume lies outside the scope of this book. However, I am grateful to Professor Nyberg for his suggestion that I supply at least this brief summary of the problems connected with the *Life*.

2. *uel eius canale*. The positive use of *canale*, "channel," in Birgittine literature stands in noteworthy contrast to the words of St. Bernard in *Sermones super Cantica Canticorum* 18.3 (Leclercq ed., *Sancti Bernardi Opera* 1: 104): *Quamobrem, si sapis, concham te exhibebis, et non canalem.* "Wherefore, if you are wise, you will show yourself to be a shell and not a channel." Bernard explains that a shell is a better image of the proper balance to be maintained in true Christian service to others. For the shell first fills to its own capacity and then overflows for others. A channel, on the other hand, merely transmits whatever flows into it and retains nothing long enough to transform itself. However, the Birgittine circle—without slighting Birgitta's interior fullness through the gift of contemplation—was equally concerned to stress her role as God's prophet and his mouthpiece; and for stressing this role, the image of the channel is quite effective. For a comparable use of *fistula*, "pipe," see *Rev.* 7.31.5.

3. *principissa Nericie*. In fact, Birgitta's husband Ulf had the Swedish title *Lagman*, "lawman," of Närke. In all of the Latin writings of the Birgittine circle, there is a tendency to use stately Latin equivalents for the rather more straightforward titles used at the Swedish court. The confessors are trying to present Scandinavian realities in terms that will be familiar to the rest of Europe. Throughout this translation I have followed their Latin terminology.

4. Birgitta's royal descent from the ancient Goths is an important detail: when she speaks to popes and kings, she speaks as their social equal. See also Undhagen, *Book I* 6.

5. *loca sanctorum scilicet Jacobi et aliorum*. This use of *loca* to mean the "burial-places" or "relic-shrines" of saints is common in Birgittine Latin and is a noteworthy survival from terminology of the early Church (cf. Brown 10–11).

6. This sentence is potentially misleading. In fact, almost from the first days of Scandinavian Christianity, there were prominent and wealthy pilgrims to Rome and to the Holy Land. *Graenlendiga Saga* 9 (Magnusson 71) tells of Gudrid—mother of Snorri, the first European child born in Vinland—who visited Rome and returned to Iceland to become a nun. The Swedish martyr St. Helen of Skövde died at the hands of her relatives in 1160 after returning from a pilgrimage to Rome and the Holy Land (Lundén, *Svenska* 46–51; Thurston 3: 228). Birgitta's relative, Bd. Ingrid Elovsdotter, O.P. (d. 1282), had made a similar pilgrimage (Klockars, *Svenska* 27; Lundén, *Svenska* 110–16; Sibilia). Klockars (*Svenska* 15) suggests that the frequency of "Israel" and "James" as baptismal names among Birgitta's relatives results from the family's tradition of visiting Jerusalem and Compostella.

7. The MSS mistakenly read "Sigrid," the name of Birgitta's maternal grandmother. Sigrid is, in fact, the unnamed "wife of . . . Benedict" in the anecdote that immediately follows in *Life* 4.

8. Traditionally identified as the Cistercian monastery at Sko (cf. Jørgensen 1: 22–23).

9. The MSS mistakenly read *Henricus,* "Henry." Duke Eric's son Magnus was eventually elected king of Sweden and was the recipient of much criticism from Birgitta before her permanent removal to Italy in 1349. Cf. notes 29, 124, 135, and 449.

10. Apparently, in 1303 (Klockars, *Svenska* 33).

11. *quasi elinguis.*

12. Cf. Luke 2:52.

13. *vidit semel vigilans.* Such a phrase often precedes accounts of Birgitta's visions in order to distinguish them clearly from revelatory dreams received in the course of normal sleep.

14. Katharine Bengtsdotter. She was still alive in the 1350's (Klockars, *Svenska* 20).

15. *solebat obseruare.*

16. *aliquas fallaces oraciones. Fallaces,* "fallacious," here seems to be a euphemism for "superstitious." Propertius (*Carmina* 1.1.19) uses the noun *fallacia* in connection with witchcraft, and perhaps that is exactly what the aunt fears she has discovered.

17. *dominus Wlfo de Wlfason, princeps Nericie.* Cf. note 3.

18. *coniugium honestissimum.* The "honesty" or "honorableness" of marriage is an important theme; cf. *Rev.* 5, Int. 12.18.

19. For the traditional role of tears in the spiritual life see Hausherr,

Penthos. Such prayer with tears is taken for granted in the Rule of St. Benedict (4.57; 20.3; 52.4), and it was important in the teaching of St. Gregory the Great (Leclercq, *Love* 25–34, 58–59), an author known to Birgitta (Collijn, *Acta* 535; Klockars, *Böckerna* 209, 214–16). This aspect of Birgitta's devotion was much exaggerated in the notorious "roarings" of her imitator Margery Kempe (cf. Butler-Bowdon, Collis, and Meech).

20. *a multis genuflexibus et crudelibus disciplinis.* This is not the modern "genuflection" of the Roman Rite but a prostration, or half-prostration, with the forehead touching the floor. Now rarely seen in the Western Church except on Good Friday, these repeated prostrations are still performed by the whole congregation in the Byzantine Rite during Lent and during the octave of the Holy Cross in September. "Disciplining" is a common monastic euphemism for "scourging" (cf. Blaise, *Lexicon* 310).

21. Although the *Life* speaks of only one prayer, this was in fact the moment at which Birgitta received the *Four Prayers* translated in this volume. Cf. note 913.

22. *consolacionem.* "Consolation"—the New Testament's *paraklēsis* —has an important place in Birgitta's vocabulary.

23. Master Matthias (d. ca. 1350), a canon of Linköping, was a noted biblical scholar. He was Birgitta's chief adviser in the years before she left Sweden, and he played a major part in the first collection of her early revelations. Matthias's own works deserve more attention than they have received (cf. Strömberg). For Matthias's local veneration as a saint in the Dominican church in Stockholm, see Lundén, *Svenska* 168–69. The "gloss" mentioned is a commentary in the form of notes on obscure, obsolete, or unusual words in the text.

24. At first Birgitta read only Old Swedish; her serious Latin studies began after the death of her husband. Her role in financing Old Swedish biblical translations deserves further investigation. On them, see Haugen 250.

25. It should be noted that Birgitta and Ulf were persons of considerable wealth, owning farms, mines, and other valuable properties throughout Sweden (Jørgensen 1: 69; Klockars, *Svenska* 54, 61).

26. It is not clear if this incident is the birth of Birgitta's son Charles; if so, there may be a further allusion to it in *Rev.* 7.13.2. In all, Birgitta had eight children: Benedict, Birger, Cecilia, Charles, Gudmar, Ingeborg, St. Katharine, and Martha.

27. The most famous of their teachers is Blessed Nicholas Hermansson, a notable Latin poet, who died as bishop of Linköping in 1391 (Thurston 3: 178–79; Lundén, *Svenska* 182–93).

28. Presumably June 23, Midsummer's Eve.

29. There is a hint here at the highly sensitive political situation in which Birgitta's family was involved. King Magnus was suspicious of their possible designs on the throne, to which they had a certain distant claim by blood. The unsatisfactory Magnus was finally deposed in 1365 (Hallendorf 55–70).

30. *horas.* Also known as the Little Office of the Blessed Virgin Mary, these "hours" were a simplified parallel to the full daily Liturgy of the Hours (or Divine Office) of the Roman Rite. Appearing first in the tenth century, by Birgitta's time the Book of Hours had virtually supplanted the full psalter as the most popular prayerbook among the literate laity. See: Janet Backhouse, *Books of Hours* (London: British Library, 1985); Robert G. Calkins, *Illuminated Books of the Middle Ages* (Ithaca: Cornell University Press, 1983), 207–82; and John Harthan, *The Book of Hours* (New York: Park Lane, 1982).

31. St. Denis, the bishop of Paris, was martyred ca. 258. In Birgitta's day he was still confused with the mystical writer, Denis the Pseudo-Areopagite, who wrote under a pen name taken from the Athenian St. Denis the Areopagite of Acts 17:34. (See Thurston 4: 66–68; Ryan 616–22.) The composite "St. Denis" was naturally venerated as the patron of mystics and contemplatives. The apparition of this saint is therefore highly significant. Note, however, that here the saint himself alludes only to his identity as the apostle of Paris. For the writings of the Pseudo-Areopagite, see *Pseudo-Dionysius: The Complete Works,* trans. Colm Luibheid (New York: Paulist Press, 1987). See also note 726 below. On the whole, an explicitly Dionysian terminology is not characteristic of the Birgittine writings, although they are aware of and concerned with the balance between apophatic and cataphatic approaches to God. See notes 159, 180, 263, 359, 442, 454, and 499.

32. There are some disputed issues in the chronology of Birgitta's life. As a result of certain suggestions made (31/III/87) by Prof. Nyberg, one or two salient points should be clarified here. A number of key dates in Birgittine chronology rest on the solid fact of the saint's death in 1373. We are told (*Life* 73) that the period of her life specially marked by having the Spirit of God was 28 years. This would seem to indicate 1345 as the year of her "vocation vision" (*Life* 26). But in classically correct Latin computations, the year *of* an event is itself

counted as the first year "before" or "after." Thus Latin texts—if they are following strict classical tradition—add one number more than we would use today. Thus these "28 years" should perhaps be taken as 27 in modern reckoning, with a resulting date of 1346 for the "vocation vision." This vision, however, took place *post aliquos dies*, "some days later" (*Life* 26), after her husband's death (February 12). But in what year? I have followed Collijn in putting 1344 (*Life* 25) for Ulf's death, a date supported by his late fourteenth century tombstone at Alvastra. Collijn, however, notes (*Acta* 80) that at least two MSS end this sentence without giving any date at all. It has been argued by Ekwall ("Årscylken" and "Den Heliga") that, like certain other dates, this 1344 is an error (being perhaps the year Ulf entered the monastery), and that the true date of his death is 12 February, 1346. Although Collijn prints 1345 (*Life* 27), and notes one MS giving 1346 (*Acta* 81), Ekwall observes that most MSS give, in fact, 1346. Her redating has been contested by Liedgren ("Två") and by Klockars (*Svenska* 85–92), but her arguments do give a plausible solution to an apparent difficulty. Professor Nyberg himself accepts 1346 as the correct date for both events. He also feels that the reader should be assured that such expressions as "seventh year," "tenth year," or "twelfth year" (*Life* 9, 10, and 11) have the same meaning in Latin as in modern English: i.e., the years that *end* on the seventh, tenth, or twelfth birthdays. There is a similar nuance to "fourth year" and "third year" in *Life* 28 and 29. Professor Nyberg warns that failure to observe the exact meaning of such expressions has resulted in many inaccuracies and useless controversies with regard to Birgittine chronology.

33. *qui expertus est duorum spirituum secundum discrecionem.* "Discernment of spirits" is a technical phrase used to describe the gift of being able to determine whether an inspiration comes from God or from the devil. See 1 Corinthians 12:10. Concerning the "bright cloud," see Matthew 17:5.

34. Cf. note 2.

35. "Etc." here and in the following sentence represents the *etcetera* of the original. The authors of the *Life* assume that the reader has access to a complete text of Birgitta's *Revelations* and they occasionally allude to passages in this shorthand way. For the purposes of the present volume, it has not always proved worthwhile to reproduce these other passages fully in the notes. For the particular revelation cited here (apparently *Prologus magistri Mathie* 33–40), see Undhagen, *Book I* 10.

36. Cf. note 35.

37. Cf. note 32.

38. In this section, the confessors are applying to Birgitta's experiences the three traditional Augustinian categories of visions; 1) corporeal, in which there is a perceptible manifestation external to the seer; 2) spiritual or imaginary, in which the seer internally perceives sense-images; and 3) intellectual, in which the seer's understanding receives the divine manifestation without dependence on sense-imagery. The classical statement of this teaching on visions occurs in St. Augustine's *De Genesi ad litteram* 12.7.16 (J.-P. Migne, *Patrologia Latina* 34: 459, hereafter abbreviated as PL).

39. St. Botvid, a layman, was murdered by a Finnish slave whom he had baptized and freed. He is venerated as a martyr and as one of the early apostles of Sweden. See Thurston 3: 204; Lundén, *Svenska* 41–45.

40. Cf. Luke 2:12.

41. Birgitta's pilgrimage to the Holy Land took place in 1372, the year before her death. Incidents concerning the journey form the major part of the Seventh Book of her *Revelations*. The Seventh Book is translated in full in the present volume.

42. Cf. 1 Samuel 21:1–6; Matthew 12:3–4; Mark 2:25–26; Luke 6:3–4.

43. Cf. Luke 2:12.

44. Cf. Klockars, *Biskop Hemming;* Lundén, *Svenska* 177–81.

45. Cf. 2 Corinthians 5:20; Ephesians 6:20.

46. Cf. note 35. See also Colledge, *Epistola solitarii.*

47. Vårfruberga, "Our Lady's Mount," on Lake Mälaren.

48. Genesis 1:1. Apocalypse 1:8; 21:6; 22:13. Cf. *Rev.* 5, Int. 16.36–37. Birgitta strictly follows the tradition of the Greek and Latin texts and writes "O" rather than "Omega."

49. Cf. 2 Timothy 4:7–8.

50. Cf. Luke 2:12.

51. Cf. *Life* 71.

52. This whole passage provides important testimony about the intertwined process of composition and translation that lies behind the Latin text of the *Revelations*. The confessors take pains to stress that Birgitta understood and approved their Latin version. They are unfortunately not quite so forthcoming about the inevitable question of their own contribution to the verbalization of her insights and to the theological refinement of her thought. But it should be noted that they never attempted to hide the fact that the final text was not the work of Birgitta

alone. Cf. Pourrat 2: 96–98; Undhagen, *Book I* 5–14; and my discussion of the Birgittine Problem in the Translator's Foreword to this volume.

53. Nicholas Orsini, count of Nola, rector of the Patrimony of St. Peter, d. 1399 (cf. note 865); Gomez Garcias de Albornoz, rector of Spoleto, d. 1377 (cf. note 608); Onorato Caetani, count of Fondi, excommunicated in 1399 for supporting the antipope Clement VII, d. 1400. On these men, see Collijn, *Acta* 659, 673.

54. In contrast to this statement, note *Rev.* 7.8.1–2, where Birgitta, who had asked about the possible damnation of Pope John XXII, is politely told to mind her own business.

55. This *Book of Questions* is the Fifth Book of the complete *Revelations* and is translated in full in this volume.

56. Cf. note 38.

57. *diuinitus coruscantibus.*

58. The confessors again lay great stress on Birgitta as a prophet in the full biblical sense: speaking out for God, reminding the people of the examples of the past, evaluating the present, and urging all to think of reward or punishment in the future.

59. Birgitta's early interest in reading the Bible (*Life* 18) developed into a lifelong study. As she became more proficient in Latin, she began to ask questions about the details of the text and certain difficulties that it contains; and throughout the books of her *Revelations* there are many traces of her solutions to these questions.

60. Revelations concerning the life of Christ are chiefly, but not exclusively, found in the Seventh Book. It might be objected that Birgitta's interest favors the passion at the expense of the resurrection; but it should be noted that throughout the *Revelations*, Birgitta is in constant dialogue with the risen Lord. For her, the resurrection is not simply a past event to be devoutly recalled but a present and continuing reality in which she daily participates through her experience of Christ, in himself and in his Church. One cannot too strongly emphasize the fact that within the Birgittine corpus, the visions of Christ's life are very few in number. Birgitta's visions were not really for the purpose of supplying curious new details. Their true purpose was to reawaken in the Church an awareness and an appreciation of the things that have been revealed from the first.

61. *posita sum quasi in spisso vitro valens audire.* In the context, one would expect "see" rather than "hear"; but sight is reserved for those in heaven. In purgatory, the holy souls can only be said to "hear" heaven's

NOTES

distant and joyful sounds. This image may ultimately be derived from a mystical interpretation of Luke 15:25.

62. *quod memoria mei fiat per annum*. Note the eucharistic flavor of these words, based as they are on the traditional terminology of the ancient eucharistic prayers of the universal Church. *Per annum* could also be rendered as "for a year." But this soul seems to be asking for the customary Month's Mind Masses that can be celebrated throughout the year and also for daily remembrance at Mass.

63. *Benedictus tu, Deus meus, qui me creasti et liberasti, te confiteor teque benedico*. The opening phrase of this little prayer and the use of *confiteor*, "I confess," and *benedico*, "I bless," as synonyms for "I praise" ultimately derive—through the Latin Bible—from the Jewish tradition of *berakoth* or "blessings." Cf. Bouyer, *Introduction* 31, 95–96, 99–101; *History* 23–26; *Eucharist: Theology and Spirituality of the Eucharistic Prayer*, trans. Charles U. Quinn (Notre Dame: University of Notre Dame Press, 1968), 29–90.

64. *vidi Christum quasi stantem in cruce*. Birgitta almost always speaks of Christ "standing" on the cross, and she seems to intend it literally of his posture rather than metaphorically of his "state."

65. Cf. Luke 2:12.

66. *in societatem magnorum es ventura*. Cf. Rev. 5, Rev. 9.1: *in societatem magnorum venisti*, "you came into the society of the great."

67. Cf. Psalm 80(81):11. (Birgittine references to the Psalms will normally be found in Jerome's version "according to the Septuagint" —the historic psalter of the Roman Rite.) See also Exodus 4:10–16; Jeremiah 1:6; Matthew 10:19–20; and Luke 12:11–12. In what sense are we to understand this "answer": as a separate visionary experience or as a special illumination received while listening to the verse of the psalm?

68. Professor Nyberg suggests that this bishop could be Sigge Jonsson of Skara (elected 1340, d. 1351/52), one of the executors of King Magnus's will of 1 May 1346, in which Vadstena was given to Birgitta (cf. notes 124 & 135). See *Skara I: Före 1700* (Skara: 1985), 433.

69. Perhaps Birgitta is thinking of King Codrus, who sacrificed his life to save the city of Athens. His story is told in *Speculum humanae salvationis* 24 (Wilson 37, 189) as an allegory of the death of Christ.

70. *subtilitates*.

71. Perhaps there is an allusion here to the struggle between the old paganism of Scandinavia and the relatively new religion of Christ, first introduced by St. Ansgar (d. 865) and reintroduced by St. Sigfrid (d.

1045) after the first mission collapsed. Otherwise, the contrast would be between God as revealed in the OT and God as revealed in the NT. That the demon would worship the Creator God rather than the "new God" is curiously reminiscent of the second-century heresy of Marcion.

72. Cf. note 1. Although this passage of the *Life* is now attributed to Alphonsus, Prior Peter himself must be the source for this description of his own initial reluctance to become involved in Birgitta's literary career. While the anecdote conveys the note of personal experience, it also reflects the medieval author's traditional protestation of modest unwillingness to write (cf. Curtius 83–85).

73. *Osgocia.* In modern Swedish: *Östergötland.*

74. The allusion is to King David; cf. 2 Samuel 12:16–23; 23:2; Matthew 22:43.

75. The allusion is to Hosea 1:2 and 3:1.

76. It was a fairly widespread medieval custom to begin sermons with the recitation of the Hail Mary or some other prayer to our Lady.

77. Cf. note 35. The bishop is presumably Hemming of Åbo, mentioned in *Life* 32.

78. Benedict (d. 1346), Birgitta's youngest child.

79. Cf. *Rev.* 7.13.72, where the son in question is Charles.

80. *filius lacrimarum.* Cf. *Rev.* 7.13.71. The phrase is from St. Augustine's *Confessions* (3.12): "It cannot happen that the son of those tears would perish." The story of St. Monica's tears is perhaps one of the most frequently told sermon stories in the history of the Western Church. See Klockars, *Böckerna* 212–13.

81. A similar occurrence of birdsong between the bed and the wall is recorded in the last hours of St. Elizabeth of Hungary (d. 1231); cf. Thurston 4: 390; Jørgensen 1: 219.

82. *attencius.* The word *attendere,* "to attend," and its derivatives are very important in the vocabulary of Birgitta's spirituality. Their occurrences should be noted with care. In a sense, Birgitta's chief mission from God is to renew the Church's attention to the sacred mysteries of the Christian faith. When, through overfamiliarity or boredom, these life-giving mysteries are no longer the object of frequent and loving attention, then the spiritual life of the Church is in mortal danger. This insistence on the need for attention is particularly notable in the Seventh Book of the *Revelations.*

83. *castrimargia.* The normal Latin name for this deadly sin is *gula.* The word used here is a corruption of the Greek *gastrimargia* and

introduces into the text a reminiscence of the vocabulary of St. John Climacus and the Desert Fathers. In fact, the whole following incident has an "Egyptian" flavor. On the survival of Greek terminology in Latin spiritual writers, see Leclercq, *Love* 99–105.

84. *in spiritu visus fuit ei Ethiops unus.* The usual term for black people in both Greek and Latin is *Aethiopes*, "Ethiopians." The reporting of visions of demons in the guise of "Ethiopians" unfortunately has a long tradition in the spiritual writings of both East and West. There is an early and undoubtedly influential instance in St. Athanasius's *Life of Saint Anthony* 6 (trans. Robert C. Gregg [New York: Paulist Press, 1980], 34–35). Birgitta was very probably familiar with St. Benedict's vision of the "black boy" recorded in St. Gregory's *Dialogues* 2.4. Regrettable as this tradition undoubtedly is, its racist implications cannot simply be credited without reservation to a woman living in fourteenth-century Sweden. In her reading of the *Lives* of the Desert Fathers, Birgitta should have encountered the noble figure of St. Moses the Black, priest and martyr, among whose anecdotes certain incidents of racial bigotry are bluntly recorded (Thurston 3: 435–36). Toward the end of her life, her revulsion at the mistreatment of slaves—of unspecified color—is recorded in *Rev.* 7.28.9–17. Finally, there is a tradition among the Birgittine nuns that the saint was sent a black girl "from India" as a gift from Queen Joanna of Naples, and that after Birgitta's death this girl was raised by her household under the name of Katharine. Katharine went with Birgitta's relics to Sweden and died there as a nun, at Vadstena, in the odor of sanctity (Tjader, *Mother Elizabeth* 185). Note that by the words *in spiritu*, "in spirit," the confessors are classifying this vision as spiritual or imaginary (cf. note 38). For Ethiopian translations of Birgitta, see James, *Apocryphal* 150.

85. *custodiam.* This "youth" is Birgitta's *angelus custos*, her guardian angel.

86. *saccum terrenum.* Birgitta often refers to the body as *saccus*, which can be rendered "sack" or "sackcloth" according to the context. Cf. *Rev.* 5, Int. 10.1 & 16, where "sackcloth" is called for by the contextual reference to the divine condescension of Christ's incarnation.

87. Cf. *Life* 52 and note 71.

88. *Obmutesce negociator; inuide, quia ista est assignata michi.* This bartering devil may display all the envy he likes; through Mary's patronage, Birgitta's position is secure.

89. *gule.* Here at the end, the Latin term is used; cf. note 83.

90. *ideo tu conare et ora.*

91. The Ave Maria or Hail Mary.

92. *suaue.* Cf. Psalm 33(34):9, a verse traditionally applied to the reception of the eucharist.

93. *dimittere consuetam lecturam et addiscere gramaticam.* Cf. *Life* 18 and note 24. Birgitta was now in her forties, and there is evidence that she did not find this plunge into Latin studies very attractive or easy. In *Rev.* 4.46, we read:

> The Mother [of God] responded: "What are you doing right now and every day?" And I responded: "I learn grammar, I pray, and I write." And then the Mother said: "It is not fitting to give up such labor for the sake of physical labor."

In *Rev.* 4.105, Birgitta is disturbed because she lacks the time to visit the shrines in Rome; and the Mother of God replies:

> Daughter, for the sake of these things, do not give up your school lessons in grammar nor holy obedience to your spiritual Father.

Birgitta persevered in her study of Latin because of its practical importance in her day and because, for her, it was the key to biblical study. She saw that a knowledge of Latin is the necessary and permanent precondition for discovering the spiritual treasures of the Western Church.

94. There is a touch of humor in the information that Birgitta had help with her Latin from a native speaker, the martyred Roman whom the *Golden Legend* describes as a schoolgirl (Ryan 110).

95. Cf. note 1.

96. *sciuit pro parte legere, intelligere et proferre sermonem latinum.* These words need careful consideration. *Proferre,* "utter," may mean as much as "speak" and as little as "pronounce." Certainly there is evidence that Birgitta eventually spoke Latin (Jørgensen 2: 43–44); but, concerning her initial proficiency, the confessors are perhaps being diplomatic. Cf. Undhagen, *Book I* 7–8.

97. The kingdom of Sicily, embracing much of the southern mainland of Italy.

98. Cf. *Rev.* 7.4.1–22.

99. *vobis.* Christ uses the plural to include Birgitta's household.

100. *Rev.* 5, Rev. 12, and Rev. 13.

101. Cf. Tobit 5:15 and 20; 12:3 (according to the numbering of the verses in the Vulgate and in Challoner).

102. Cf. *Rev.* 7.1.1–6.

103. *Rev.* 7.21.1–22.
104. Cf. note 99.
105. Cf. notes 41 and 60.
106. Cf. *Life* 36.
107. Cf. *Rev.* 7.16.9–11.
108. Cf. Lokrantz.
109. *de statu Vrbis et de reparacione omnium statuum.* Since *status* means both social "standing" and the political "state," it seems best to preserve this ambiguity in the translation. Naturally the reform of all social classes would result in a renewal of the country.
110. Urban V was pope from 1362 to 1370. His temporary return of the papacy to Italy took place in 1367–1370. Against Birgitta's wishes, he went back to Avignon, where he died within three months. He was beatified in 1870. Cardinal Beaufort succeeded him as Gregory XI, and after much urging from St. Catherine of Siena, he returned the papacy to Rome in 1377, four years after the death of Birgitta. It was for Gregory that the confessors wrote the present *Life*. Gregory XI died in Rome on 27 March 1378. According to the French theologian John Gerson (1363–1429), Pope Gregory's dying words were a warning against further trust in the guidance of visionaries (Pourrat 2: 98). After his death, the Church experienced the horrors of the Great Schism and the unedifying spectacle of three rival popes. The French party naturally had no interest in canonizing Birgitta, who had always denounced the idea of a Church centered on Avignon. The Roman pope, however, canonized her on 7 October 1391. The Pisan antipope did the same in 1415. At the end of the schism, in 1419, Pope Martin V reconfirmed her canonization. The French party made a last effort to discredit her by attacking her writings at the Council of Basel (1433–1436). Their list of 123 alleged heresies was successfully refuted by Cardinal John Torquemada (cf. Michel), the saintly uncle of the notorious inquisitor (Mansi 30: 750–814). Birgitta's involvement in the question of the Avignon papacy is a major theme in the totality of her writings and should be kept in mind in spite of the fact that the Avignon question is not often mentioned in the particular selections that have been translated in this volume.
111. Alphonsus Pecha (ca. 1330–19 August 1389), former bishop of the Spanish diocese of Jaen, retired to Italy for unknown reasons in 1368 to live the life of a "hermit." By 1370 he had met Birgitta, and, from then until her death three years later he was almost constantly with her, even accompanying her on the pilgrimage to Jerusalem. In 1373,

Birgitta sent him to the pope in Avignon; and he was still absent in Avignon when Birgitta died in July of that year. His principal duty in the Birgittine circle was to oversee the final redaction of the Latin text, ensuring the clarity and correctness of its Latinity and the doctrinal orthodoxy of its statements. Up till then the two Peters had been in charge of translating and preserving the individual revelations. It was Alphonsus' task to turn these disparate materials into a publishable book, as this section of the *Life* makes clear. It is therefore chiefly to Alphonsus that we owe the present form of the *Heavenly Book of Revelations*—apart from Prior Peter's later "additions" (cf. note 522). See Colledge, *Epistola;* Undhagen, *Book I* 11–13.

112. Luke 11:28, which however has "word" of God. The confessors' reading is unattested in either Greek or Latin. Doubtlessly, like many of the Fathers, they are quoting from memory.

113. *genuflexiones, inclinaciones, et venias.* Cf. note 20. *Venia,* "pardon," came to have, in monastic usage, the meaning of a full prostration on the ground. In Greek, a comparable meaning developed for *metanoia,* "repentance." On the use of *metania* or *metanoea* as Latin words and for Peter the Venerable's evidence that they were translated as *venia,* see Leclercq, *Love* 100 and 110, notes 52 and 53. Cf. Blaise, *Lexicon* 949.

114. *inmissis vnguibus suis ita in eis arauit.* Cf. *Ilias Latina* 1017: infelix Hecube saevisque arat unguibus ora. With regard to this section of the *Life,* I can only repeat the traditional and prudent observation that in the *Lives* of the saints certain imprudent actions are recorded to arouse us to amazement, but not to imitation.

115. *libenter.* Usually this word means "willingly." But from the context it is clear that the confessors mean to say that as an act of penance, Birgitta refused herself the pleasure of initiating conversations. Cf. the similar use of *libenter* in *Life* 85.

116. *in corda illa, que ad dicendum pater noster in pectore suo pendebat.* One early form of the rosary involved the repetition of the Our Father alone, and the beads themselves were sometimes simply called "a paternoster." Attaching medals and other pious reminders to one's rosary remains to this day an instinctive Catholic custom.

117. Cf. note 115.

118. *statim in eadem murenula, que ad collum pendebat, signatum reseruabat.* Cf. note 116. *Murenula* is the diminutive of *murena*—in Greek, *myraina*—meaning "moray eel." In St. Jerome's *Letters* (24.3), we read that *murenula* was a popular nickname for a type of necklace;

and, in the Vulgate, there are instances of *murenula* as "necklace": Songs 1:10; Isaiah 3:20.

119. Over the centuries, plant names can undergo drastic alterations in popular usage; and it has therefore seemed to me more prudent, in the present instance, not to attempt to identify the modern name of this *genciana*.

120. *nam quandoque deuastata calciamenta sua occultabat, dum aliis nova donari rogabat.* An unforgettable picture, expertly punctuated by both rhyme and *cursus*.

121. *detestacionem peccatorum.* cf. Daniel 9:11

122. *Rev.* 7.19.1–37.

123. *Rev.* 7.27.1–41.

124. *et amodo reputaberis non solum sponsa mea, sed eciam monacha et mater in Wastenis.* These famous words are often inscribed on pictures of the saint. Vadstena was a royal property given to Birgitta by King Magnus (cf. notes 9 and 135) as the future site of the first of the double monasteries of the Order of the Most Holy Savior (O.Ss.S.). Three years after receiving the gift, Birgitta left Sweden forever; and it was only after her death that her daughter St. Katharine of Sweden finally established the monastery and completed the construction of the great church and the other buildings that Birgitta had described in her revelations. These buildings still stand. There, in the famous Blue Church, the relics of St. Birgitta and St. Katharine are still preserved and venerated. The history of the Birgittine Order, its Rule and liturgy, and its twentieth-century revival are topics that lie outside the scope of this volume. Documenting the history of the order has been the major contribution of Professor Nyberg, and his important works should be consulted. The interested reader should also note in the bibliography: *Biographie;* Blunt; Eklund, *Regula* & *Sermo;* Ennis; Fletcher; Grad; Graf; Johnston; Koenig-Bricker; Laubenberger; Lundén, *Officium;* Odenius, *Bridgit;* Stein; *Syon House;* Tjader; Undhagen, *Birger;* Wallin; Waugh.

125. *depones,* "lay down," can also have the sense of "deposit." This word is rich in liturgical and patristic echoes.

126. *voluntatem tuam recipere pro effectu.* The contrast and interaction between "willing" and "doing" is very important in Birgittine thought. See, for example, *Rev.* 7.13.55.

127. *Hijs dictis et multis alijs mencionem fecit et ordinacionem aliquarum personarum secum existencium, quas ante mortem coram Deo vidisse se dicebat astare.* The Latin has been given for this whole section because the words are extremely ambiguous and unclear. Apparently the

confessors felt obliged to respect the privacy not only of the messages but also of the people who received them.

128. *conuoca singillatim omnes, quos superius nominaui, et eis dicas facienda et sic inter verba et manus eorum venies ad monasterium tuum, jd est in gaudium meum, et corpus tuum locabitur in Wastenis.* Again, the preservation of the secrets of Birgitta's last moments has led the confessors to write with obscurity. The point of the wording *inter verba et manus eorum* is hard to grasp. The final words of Christ, however, are very beautiful. He is consoling Birgitta for the fact that she will never see her monastery in this life by offering her entry into the heavenly monastery of his everlasting joy. The idea is ultimately based on the Greek text of John 14:2: *en tēi oikiāi tou patros mou monai pollai eisin.* In monastic usage, *monai* can mean "monasteries." Therefore, to a reader of Greek, the verse can be given a mystical meaning: "In my Father's house there are many monasteries." Once the idea started, it was easy for it to spread. Finally, note the overtones of *locabitur,* "will be placed," in light of note 5. Vadstena will be Birgitta's *locus,* her "shrine."

129. 23 July 1372, the memorial of St. Apollinaris of Ravenna, bishop and martyr.

130. *inter manus predictarum personarum.* Cf. note 128.

131. *emisit spiritum.* Matthew 27:50. In the moment of death Birgitta is totally conformed to the crucified Lord. The confessors may also intend to suggest the double meaning that has traditionally been seen in the verbs that the Gospels use for the death of Christ: not simply "expired" but "sent forth his Spirit." Finally, note that these sections (*Life* 95, 96, 97) are repeated almost verbatim in *Rev.* 7.31.1–13. Great care has been taken to reproduce the repetitions in the English.

132. This heading has been supplied by Birger Bergh in his *Sancta Birgitta, Revelaciones, Book V: Liber Questionum* (Uppsala: Almqvist, 1971), 93. A full account of the textual history of the Birgittine corpus would be out of place in this volume, and interested readers are referred to the thorough discussions provided in the editions of Bergh and others.

133. This admirably clear and simple prologue gives all the information needed to understand the setting of the one long visionary experience that unfolds in the Fifth Book. The prologue is not found in all MSS of the *Revelations.* It is presumably by Alphonsus Pecha, the final editor of the text (cf. note 111 & Undhagen *Book I* 17).

134. Cf. *Life* 40.

135. King Magnus donated the Vadstena property on 1 May 1346; Birgitta left Sweden forever at the end of 1349. The most that can be said about the incident that follows is that it occurred between those two known dates. See note 421.

136. Cf. *Life* 52.

137. Cf. note 124.

138. *scalam*. Cf. Genesis 28:12. The image of the ladder to heaven was immortalized by St. John Climacus (d. ca. 649) in his *Klimax* or *Ladder of Divine Ascent* (trans. Colm Luibheid and Norman Russell [New York: Paulist Press, 1982]). The theme of the ladder was also portrayed by artists; see Adolf Katzenellenbogen, *Allegories of the Virtues and Vices in Medieval Art: From Early Christian Times to the Thirteenth Century* (New York: Norton, 1964), 22–26. There is a detailed depiction of the heavenly ladder in Straub 196–97.

139. *religiosum quendam sibi notum adhuc corpore tunc viuentem*. As a result of the extreme discretion of the Birgittine circle, this man's identity remains a secret to this day. He is most commonly referred to as *religiosus*, "a religious"—a term that covers all members of any religious order: monks, canons regular, friars, etc. The Old Swedish narrows this to "monk"—which could simply be a careless use of an easier word rather than an authentic piece of additional information. Alphonsus and the confessors always stress that the religious was "at that time still alive in the body." By this insistence they mean to distinguish this particular vision from the many others that Birgitta had of the judgment or punishment of people after their death. But Jørgensen (1: 239) has clearly misinterpreted Prior Peter's use of *adhuc*, "still" (Collijn, *Acta* 522), when Jørgensen asserts that the religious was still alive in 1379.

140. *seriosius*. For this interpretation, see Bergh, *Book V* 178. However, the word *seriosus* gives trouble in several passages, and I cannot help but wonder if the Birgittine Latinists did not make some false connection between *seriosus*, "serious," and *series*, "series." In some of these places, the meaning "step-by-step" would be quite in context. See Blaise, *Lexicon* 841.

141. A precious bit of testimony: Birgitta sometimes wrote out her revelations in Old Swedish. Some texts in the saint's handwriting are extant (cf. Haugen 233–34; Högman; Undhagen, *Book I* 7). The idea that the extant Old Swedish version (ed. Klemming) may partly consist of other pre-Latin texts has been perhaps too quickly rejected by some.

NOTES

See Eklund, "Re-assessment"; and my summary in the Translator's Note to this volume. See also *Life* 37.

142. *in lingua litterali*—i.e., Latin.

143. Cf. 1 Kings 22:19; 2 Chronicles 18:18; Apocalypse 4:2.

144. Cf. note 139.

145. *gradu*. Not only a "rung," but also a "step" or "grade."

146. *Item*. From here on, most of the questions and responses begin with this word—literally meaning "again"—that traditionally marks each new "item" in a list. The repetition of *item* gives to the *Book of Questions* the flavor of a formal scholastic debate. For a comic use of the device see Shakespeare, *Two Gentlemen of Verona* III.1.305–69.

147. The awkward repetition of *quia*, "because," in this section 7 is a fairly simple instance of one of the less attractive aspects of the Birgittine style. It is possible that in rambling sentences like this we have come very close to Birgitta's oral formulation of her thoughts. At times this impression of oral composition can be very strong.

148. *similitudinem*. Birgittine Latin almost always uses this very general term for a literary "comparison," rather than specify one of the subtypes such as "parable," "fable," etc.

149. For examples of how the limbs can signify virtues, see *Rev.* 5, *Rev.* 4.1–22 and the third and fourth of the *Four Prayers*.

150. *Item cur dedisti hominibus et mulieribus semen commixtionis et naturam, si non secundum appetitum carnis effundatur?* Note that Birgittine Latin often uses *homo*, "human being," to mean "male"—thus making any attempt to conform the *Revelations* to our modern ideas of gender-free language almost impossible. *Natura* and its derivatives as "sex" or "genitals" is typically Birgittine. Cf. *Rev.* 7.23.3.

151. This is the first in a series of thirteen revelations unevenly interwoven with the interrogations and culminating in the great riddle with which the *Book of Questions* ends. The Old Swedish arranges the interrogations and revelations in two separate blocks, but Bergh's study of the textual tradition has led him to prefer the interwoven arrangement of the Latin MSS.

152. The best MSS do not begin this question with *item*.

153. Cf. note 19.

154. Cf. *Rev.* 7.28.9–17.

155. *similitudine*, cf. note 148.

156. Cf. note 147. There is something about the topic of animals that inevitably leads Birgitta into thickets of verbiage where one can scarcely

NOTES

follow. Klockars (*Böckerna* 220) has linked this passage to the *Elucidarium* of Honorius of Autun (PL 172: 1117).

157. Genesis 1:31.

158. *inquisicio tua.* There is a certain humor in the thought of God being questioned by the inquisition.

159. *Ideo per similitudinem quandam verborum respondeo tibi.* Throughout Birgitta's *Revelations* we encounter this awareness that her written words and material imagery only dimly approximate the full realities of God. Nevertheless, both words and imagery come from God in some way, and do not falsify him, provided that their innate limitations are understood. This is a theme that becomes increasingly important in the unfolding of the *Book of Questions.*

160. This is one of a number of beautiful Birgittine similitudes based on a vivid perception of the image of sunlight (cf. Klockars *Böckerna* 299). It is used here with great refinement and theological sophistication to refer to the problem that arises from John 3:5—namely, whether entry into heaven is strictly limited to those who have actually been baptized in this life. Birgitta is alluding to one popular solution: a "fringe" place where there is neither sight of God nor punishment. The text however avoids the traditional expression *limbus puerorum*, "fringe for children." Perhaps this reflects the fact that, while Catholic theology strictly holds the teaching of John 3:5, it remains open to other possible solutions to the fate of unbaptized babies (cf. Ott 113–14). Birgitta's teaching here was vindicated by Cardinal Torquemada in his sixtieth article. (Cf. note 110. N.B.: A number of the 123 objections answered by Torquemada involve faulty readings or other trivialities, as the cardinal never fails to point out. These notes will only refer to those of his articles that involve points of serious interest.)

161. *contraria*, a favorite Birgittine expression.

162. Cf. Exodus 22:1–4 (Vulgate numbering).

163. This theme of the just God's respect for the free will of his creatures is very important to Birgitta.

164. *commoda.*

165. *necessarium est ire magis post mundi vilitatem quam post eius pulchritudinem.*

166. Cf. Genesis 1:31.

167. *occasionem dampni.*

168. *Tu quidem habuisti de patre vilissimam putredinem et immundiciam.* Please note that Birgitta is trying to awaken our humility by reminding us that we all come from semen, which 1) does not command

a high price, 2) quickly spoils, and 3) makes a mess. These are simple facts of life, quite familiar to this happily married wife, the mother of eight children. Birgitta's blunt references to sex should not automatically be interpreted as a neurotic hatred of the flesh. Among moral writers there is a tendency to teach through startling exaggeration (cf. Leclercq, *Love* 131–33). The Talmud (*Pirke Aboth* 3.1) gives almost exactly the same humiliating description of semen. One should also recall that Birgitta, a born aristocrat (cf. note 4), is here recording the much-needed reprimand of a man whose aristocracy has gone to his head.

169. Cf. Luke 12:48.

170. *Nam omnia temporalia bona communia esse debent et ex caritate indigentibus equalia.* The statement needs to be seen in the larger context of Birgitta's thought. She does not condemn private property *per se.* It was the retention of her own private property that made possible her maintenance of her household and the production of the *Heavenly Book.* On the question of Christ's ownership of private property, see *Rev.* 7.8.1–8. Birgitta, however, sees a legitimate distinction between ownership and superfluous consumption. Cf. Acts 2:44; 4:32.

171. *congregando.*

172. A unique instance of one response to two questions.

173. Cf. Mark 10:18.

174. Cf. James 1:17.

175. Birgitta may be thinking of Sts. Cosmas and Damian, Arabian martyrs daily commemorated in the Roman Mass. Their legend (Ryan 575–78) describes them as brothers and physicians who practiced medicine solely for the love of Christ and who absolutely refused all remuneration for their cures. In the Byzantine liturgical books they are always called *hoi anargyroi,* the "silverless" or "free" physicians.

176. The thought and vocabulary of this response are reminiscent of the Roman priest's prayer while purifying the chalice after communion: *de munere temporali fiat nobis remedium sempiternum,* "of the temporal gift let there be made for us a remedy everlasting."

177. Cf. note 163. This statement was the subject of Torquemada's article 62. In defending *facerem vtique eis iniuriam,* "I would indeed do them an injustice," the cardinal cites Matthew 20:13.

178. Cf. Romans 1:20–25.

179. The allusion is either to Sinai (Exodus 19:16) or to the mountain of Christ's transfiguration (Matthew 17:1–9; Mark 9:1–7; Luke 9:28–36).

180. This is perhaps the most important statement of this whole eighth interrogation, which centers around the favorite Birgittine themes of God's respect for the free will of his creatures and the relation between the apophatic and cataphatic approaches to the encounter with God. Cf. note 159.

181. *homo, qui recipit secum peccatores.*

182. *Deus exiget mortem.*

183. *magistralis medicus.*

184. Again one thinks of Sts. Cosmas and Damian, the free physicians (cf. note 175).

185. *excedant.*

186. *iuxta vulgare proverbium. Proverbium* in the rare sense of "similitude" is peculiar to John 10:6; 16:25, 29. The source of this proverb has not been identified. Whenever Birgitta pursues the topic of animals in this book, there are problems.

187. As a result of the usual discretion of the Birgittine circle, the actual situation referred to in the latter part of this revelation remains unknown.

188. *vas terrenum.* Cf. *Life* 61 and note 86.

189. This statement was defended by Torquemada in article 63. He simply observes that anyone should understand that this *speciale insigne virtutum* was wrought in Mary by God himself and that she cooperated with his grace.

190. *dignum et iustum est.* These words from the preface dialogue of the Roman Rite Mass seem to have been a favorite expression with Birgitta. Prior Peter tells of a knight, Canute Folkesson, who resented Birgitta's moral influence over King Magnus and who, one day in Stockholm, drenched her with water as she walked through the narrow street beneath his window. Her immediate response was *dignum et iustum est:* "It is right and just that I endure such things! But may God spare him and not repay this to him in the age to come!" Later in that same day, through her brother Israel Birgersson, Birgitta sent the knight a visionary warning from Christ to beware of dying "from blood." Canute said: "To dreams I do not attend! God is merciful and damns no one!" Not long afterward, Canute Folkesson died of a nasal hemorrhage. Everyone in Stockholm could bear witness to the truth of this story (cf. Collijn, *Acta* 492–93).

191. This old idea ultimately rests on Deuteronomy 32:8 (LXX): ". . . he established the limits of the nations in accord with the number of the angels of God." Cf. Pelikan 3: 140.

192. *flebilis ingressus et egressus.* Cf. 1 Kings 3:7. Through the Latin Bible Birgitta has learned the Jewish description of moral behavior as *halakah,* "walking."

193. Torquemada (article 64) sees nothing objectionable in this simple observation.

194. Cf. Genesis 1:28; Psalm 8:7–9.

195. *rote posteriores subsequuntur priores.* There is something unclear about this *exemplum.* Could Birgitta have originally been thinking of the turning of each wheel, with the "back" of the wheel following the "front"?

196. *estas et frigus.* Literally, "summer and cold." Some MSS give *estus et frigus,* "heat and cold."

197. Cf. *Rev.* 5, Int. 8.14–20 and note 180.

198. Cf. Isaiah 60:19–20; Apocalypse 22:5.

199. Cf. *Rev.* 5, Int. 2.9 and *Four Prayers* 63–103.

200. *corona.* Birgitta is referring to its circular shape.

201. Cf. the important point of Catholic understanding about Mary given in note 189. Birgitta has a particular fondness for this idea that our Lady's holiness drew the Son of God down to his incarnation in her womb.

202. Cf. Songs 5:11.

203. *continencia omnium illicitorum motuum.* For this sense of *continentia,* see Lewis & Short, s.v. *abstinentia.* For the doctrinal considerations, see Ott 202–03. Birgitta was a firm proponent of the doctrine of the Immaculate Conception as later defined by the Church.

204. Cf. Songs 5:10.

205. *morum.*

206. Cf. Luke 1:38.

207. Cf. Psalm 18(19):11.

208. *locus ex virtuosis lapidibus.* On *locus* in Birgittine Latin, see notes 5 and 128. For *virtuosus* as "exquisite," see Bergh *Book V* 179.

209. The parallel between Mary's faith, which first accepted God, and her womb, which then conceived him, is hinted at in St. Justin's *Dialogus cum Tryphone* 100 (J.-P. Migne, *Patrologia Graeca* 6: 709, hereafter abbreviated PG), and is elaborated by St. Augustine, *Sermones* 25.7–8 (PL 46: 937–38). Cf. Edward Schillebeeckx, O.P., *Mary, Mother of the Redemption* (New York: Sheed and Ward, 1964), 69–72. See also Luke 1:45.

210. Prudence, justice, temperance, and fortitude are the four cardinal virtues and are crowned by the three theological virtues: faith, hope,

and charity. All seven virtues are interwoven into sections 19–20, accompanied by the important virtue of perseverance. Cf. Klockars, *Böckerna* 122.

211. *non abhorrui.* Cf. the hymn *Te Deum: non horruisti Virginis uterum,* "you felt no horror of the Virgin's womb."

212. Birgitta is continuing the theme of the divine condescension involved in Christ's incarnation. For God to clothe himself in flesh is a voluntary humiliation comparable to putting on penitential sackcloth. Cf. note 86. Such vocabulary is traditional and should not simply be equated with an unnatural loathing of the flesh. Cf. note 168.

213. *secundum patrem.*

214. *absque contactu hominis.* It is important for understanding the development of this *exemplum* to recall that in Birgittine Latin *homo* can mean "male." Cf. note 150.

215. Cf. Luke 1:38.

216. Psalm 44(45):3.

217. Psalm 18(19):7. The Stuttgart Vulgate gives Birgitta's *a summo celo* as a variant reading.

218. Psalm 22(23):5; 64(65):10.

219. *conuersari.* Cf. Baruch 3:38.

220. Cf. 1 John 4:8.

221. Cf. Wisdom 11:25 (Vulgate numbering).

222. *in precium et premium.*

223. Cf. John 4:24.

224. Cf. Psalm 32(33):9.

225. Cf. Acts 17:25.

226. Cf. Exodus 3:14.

227. Cf. John 3:8.

228. *merito incomprehensibilis est omnia comprehendens.* This "comprehension" or "grasping" should be understood in the fullest sense: both "understanding" and "containing." The paradox is not simply that "comprehension" can happen *despite* "incomprehensibility," but that the two take place simultaneously. Birgitta's frequent and skillful use of this sort of theological paradox is a trait that brings her close to the Byzantine liturgy.

229. *conditor.*

230. Cf. Habakkuk 3:2, in the Septuagint: *en mesōi dyo zōiōn,* "in the midst of two living things." Birgitta would have known this Greek reading through the Old Latin version as sung, until recently, after the first reading of the Mass of the Presanctified on Good Friday: *in medio*

duorum animalium innotesceris, "in the midst of two animals you shall be known." (Like *zōiōn, animalium* means either "animals" or "living things," and thus can be applied either to the ox and ass of Bethlehem or to the two thieves on Calvary.) Cf. Isaiah 1:3 and notes 773 & 816.

231. Cf. Psalm 71(72):10–11.

232. Cf. Malachi 3:1.

233. *persequendum ab inimicis.* This could also be "pursued by enemies." The context of the nativity would seem to narrow the allusion to the flight into Egypt or the killing of the Holy Innocents. Matthew 2:13–21 cites two prophecies: Hosea 11:1 and Jeremiah 31:15. For this whole section 27, Bergh (*Book V* 127) cites the fifth responsory for Christmas in the *Breviarium lincopense* (ed. K. Peters [Lund: 1950–1958]), 214–15.

234. *per interualla temporum.*

235. *ex origine Abrahe secundum patrem.*

236. *secundum matrem, licet sine peccato.*

237. *antiquo populo.* Cf. Isaiah 44:7. Birgitta calls the Jews by that crucial biblical title—*populus,* "people"—which tends to lose some of its force in English.

238. Cf. Matthew 3:13–17; Mark 1:9–11; Luke 3:21–22; John 1:29–34.

239. *et ego Dei filius ostensus sum in homine vero.* Although I have not traced the exact source of this phrase, there is a Greek feeling to this use of *ostensus sum,* "I was shown." The Greek equivalent *edeikhthēn* in such a context would be quite normal in the Byzantine liturgy.

240. Birgitta follows many of the Fathers in interpreting the baptism of the sinless Christ as primarily a prophetic act comparable to the frequent acts of prophetic behavior recorded in the Jewish scriptures. Christ underwent the experience of baptism not because he needed cleansing but so that the action itself might be shown to the world: a prophetic "opening" of heaven, a prophetic descent of the Holy Spirit, and a prophetic sanctification of all water through contact with the human body of the Son of God. All of these prophecies found fulfillment in the paschal mystery of the crucified and risen Lord.

241. Exact and accurate statements of orthodox trinitarian doctrine play an important part in Birgittine spirituality. This apparition of the Trinity at the Jordan is the greatest of the mysteries shown to the world in the baptism of our Lord. For this reason, the Byzantine liturgy prefers for this feast the title Theophany, "apparition of God."

242. Cf. John 14:6.

243. *confracta est testa legis et apparuit nucleus.* Cf. Matthew 5:17; Romans 3:31. For the image, cf. Pelikan 3: 248.

244. *confirmatus est in me ipso baptismus.* There is a punning allusion to the close link between the sacraments of baptism and confirmation.

245. Ephesians 2:3.

246. *annichilacionis.* Cf. Bergh, *Book V* 176.

247. Cf. note 82.

248. The Desert Father Evagrius (d. 399) popularized a method of countering temptations through *antirrhēsis*, "talking-back" in words mostly drawn from Scripture. Despite his condemnation for certain points of heresy, some elements of his spiritual teaching have had a lasting influence.

249. *dampnum rerum concessarum.* These *res concessae* seem to have puzzled the Old Swedish translator, who simply omits them.

250. Cf. Job 1:21.

251. *tribue.* Birgitta is playing with the words *tribulatio*, "trouble," *tribulo*, "I trouble," and *tribuo*, "I allot."

252. Cf. Mark 10:18.

253. *et obliuiscitur Deus.* According to the normal rule for deponent verbs, this would mean "and God forgets"—a rather harsh shift in the thought of the sentence. In a private letter (10/XII/86), Professor Bergh has indicated to me his preference for the less usual passive meaning here, citing *Rev.* 1.55.4; 2.17, 24, 34; 3.25; 4.63. However, although the transition is harsh, Birgitta could be thinking of the idea that the ultimate outcome and punishment for sin is to be forgotten by God forever in hell. The words "memory" and "remember" are central terms in all the traditional liturgies for the departed (cf. note 62). Cf. Sirach 35:9 in the Vulgate numbering.

254. Cf. John 19:28 and 30.

255. Cf. John 5:24.

256. Cf. Romans 8:28.

257. Cf. note 159.

258. Torquemada (article 66) defends this statement, saying that it is true if it is understood correctly, "as the words of saints ought to be understood." The word "inseparable" must not be taken to mean any coercive limitation of God.

259. Cf. Psalm 67(68):3.

260. Cf. Exodus 33:20.

261. Cf. Exodus 20:18–19.

262. *corporalis non sim nec corporaliter effigiatus.* Cf. *Rev.* 5, Int. 16.6.

263. This whole response presents a very clear statement of Birgitta's view of the relation between apophatic and cataphatic approaches to mysticism. Birgitta's spiritual writing is predominantly cataphatic (or "affirmative") in emphasis, using words and images as a path toward God. But she was aware of the apophatic (or "negative") way associated with the name of Denis the Pseudo-Areopagite (cf. note 31), and she several times repeats the traditional apophatic warning about the need to remember that there is always something of God that goes beyond both our comprehension and our imagery.

264. The famous image of "chewing" or "ruminating" is central to the tradition of meditative reading called *lectio divina*. See Bouyer, *Introduction* 45–55, 81–82; Charlier 242–80; Cousins 5–20; Fry 95–96, 446–47, 467–77; Hall 7–56; Kezel 85–92; Leclercq *Love* 15–17, 72–77; Squire 117–27; Tugwell 3–15.

265. Cf. Hebrews 4:15.

266. John 19:30.

267. *vsque ad vltimum punctum.* Like the English "point," *punctum* is ambiguous, meaning either "moment" or "detail."

268. Cf. Psalm 67(68):34; 117(118):16–17; 138(139):18; Luke 24:44–47; Acts 2:30–31.

269. Cf. Matthew 27:40.

270. *ego innocens steti stabiliter in cruce. Et per stabilitatem meam omnia instabilia stabiliui et infirma confirmaui.* Birgitta's usual reference to "standing" on the cross (cf. note 64) here gives rise to a fine example of Birgittine wordplay.

271. *viriliter.* Cf. Judith 15:11 and see note 150 on the problem of gender-free language.

272. Cf. Genesis 29:20. Rachel is a traditional symbol of the contemplative life.

273. By the substitution of Leah for Rachel on the wedding night (cf. Genesis 29:23–24). Leah symbolizes the active life.

274. Cf. Genesis 29:26. As Birgitta immediately explains: first take Leah (action) and then receive Rachel (contemplation).

275. Cf. 1 Peter 5:8.

276. *licet frigidus factus et tepidus.* This mixed metaphor would seem to be based on Apocalypse 3:15–16.

277. *natura hominis.* Here *natura* seems at first to mean "nature"; but as the argument proceeds, the meanings "sex" and "genitals" become important (cf. note 150).

278. *in illo membro, quod ad maiorem fructum institutum fuit.*

279. Torquemada (article 67) defends Birgitta against a misquotation of her text which would cause her to imply that sexual intercourse would never have existed without the fall of Adam and Eve. The Cardinal quotes the text correctly and shows that Birgitta says that sexuality, which had existed before the fall and could have been ruined by the fall, was rescued from ruin and turned in a good direction by the specific command of God.

280. The *semita*, "path," of virginity, and the *via*, "road," of marriage apparently mean that fewer people are chosen to walk along the former way. Cf. note 192.

281. There are too many themes interacting here to permit a full analysis in this note. The key is the traditional practice of interpreting many instances of *terra*, "earth," in the OT as mystical references to the Mother of God. Mary was a virgin-mother; and so too the earth, the mother of Adam, was a virgin, as yet unstained by Cain's murder of Abel or by any other bloodshed.

282. The sun's penetration of the unbroken glass is a traditional image for the inviolate virginity of the Mother of God (cf. Ott 206). For "attend," see note 82.

283. Cf. note 18. Torquemada (article 68) defended the following image.

284. Cf. note 228. The paradox of Mary containing the uncontainable God is very popular in the Marian hymns of both East and West.

285. *misterium pietatis mee*. Birgitta is here proposing a pious adaptation of the Vulgate's bafflingly literal rendering (*pietatis sacramentum*) of a very difficult phrase in 1 Timothy 3:16, *to tēs eusebeias mystērion*, "the mystery of piety." There is no exact agreement among the commentators concerning the details of the meaning; but as Birgitta has seen, the phrase as a whole refers to the incarnation, which is described in the words that follow in the text of the epistle. Elsewhere, Birgitta often refers to the *pietas* that Christ manifested by coming to redeem the world. See also note 59. On *sacramentum*, see Pelikan 3: 206–07.

286. Cf. 2 Thessalonians 2:3. Birgitta is again quoting from another difficult passage. For a detailed study, see Charles H. Giblin, S.J., *The Threat to Faith: An Exegetical and Theological Re-examination of 2 Thessalonians 2*, Analecta biblica 31 (Rome: Pontifical Biblical Institute, 1967).

287. Cf. Matthew 2:14.

288. One of the oldest themes of Christian theology (cf. the *Didache* 1.1).

289. *iustum et dignum fuit.* Cf. note 190.

290. Cf. Isaiah 42:8; 48:11.

291. Hosea 11:1; cf. Matthew 2:15.

292. Cf. Matthew 2:16.

293. *misterium vocandorum et caritatis diuine.*

294. The words for "infant" in both Greek (*nēpios*) and Latin (*infans*) literally mean "speechless one," i.e., too young to speak. The Christmas liturgies and the sermons of the Fathers often play with this double meaning. To make the present passage clear, the word "speechless" has been added to "infants" and "infancy."

295. Cf. Psalm 8:3.

296. *ibi sanguis effusus accumulabat perfectissimum bonum.*

297. Cf. 2 Samuel 16:5–13. Birgitta does not mention that in 1 Kings 2:8–9, the dying David urged Solomon to kill this man.

298. The Latin suddenly shifts to the plural for this sentence.

299. There is a variant version of this revelation in *Rev.* 6.19, which ends with a *declaratio* (cf. note 522) that identifies the man in this revelation as a dissolute monk "of the monastery of St. Lawrence," who was murdered by his enemies.

300. Cf. Psalm 139(140):2. The inner logic of this revelation only becomes apparent when one realizes that these are the opening words, slightly condensed, of the responsory after the second reading at the Mass of the Presanctified on Good Friday according to the medieval books of the Roman Rite. It was immediately followed by the singing of the Passion according to John. See the *Liber antiphonarius* (PL 78: 676). This chant, however, is not part of the oldest arrangement for Good Friday; and it has been omitted from the latest edition of the *Graduale sacrosanctae romanae Ecclesiae: De tempore & de sanctis* (Solesmes: Abbaye Saint-Pierre de Solesmes, 1974). It is, however, found in the pre-Vatican II *Liber usualis* (Paris: Desclée, 1960), 725–27. On the late date of its composition, see Willi Apel, *Gregorian Chant* (Bloomington: Indiana University Press, 1958), 494, 511. This revelation is therefore dramatically rooted in the liturgy for Good Friday; and, through the striking picture of the bad man singing the chant before the Passion, the reader is powerfully confronted with a key Birgittine theme—already foreshadowed at *Rev.* 5, Int. 11.31–35—namely, the sufferings of Christ.

NOTES

301. Cf. the words of Canute Folkesson in note 190.

302. Birgitta, who was intensely devoted to the Scriptures, is recording a remarkable example of hypocrisy and skepticism on the part of this man who had such thoughts even while publicly chanting the psalms in church during the liturgy. This cantor is even ungrateful for the very mystery of Christ's suffering, in honor of which he is supposed to be singing.

303. Cf. notes 64 and 82. Here however the "standing" and the "state" are both part of the picture.

304. Cf. Sirach 22:24, in the Vulgate numbering.

305. Torquemada (article 69) could see nothing objectionable in this expression of filial affection.

306. *ideo sicut abortiuum et pannus menstruate proicieris.* Cf. Numbers 12:12 and Isaiah 64:6. This passage is an example of the rhetorical scheme called "zeugma," in which a single verb *proicieris* is working with two separate nouns *abortiuum* and *pannus* in two different senses: "cast forth" and "cast away." Birgitta is quite familiar with the facts of a woman's life. In a miscarriage, the fetus is "cast forth" from the woman's body, as Numbers 12:12 says. In the case of menstruation, the soiled napkin is naturally thrown away. The fact that the fetus has been "cast forth" does not entail any rejection by God; this is simply a tragic event, evoking pity and a sense of loss—a dramatic warning about the untimely loss of one's soul. The fact that the dirty cloth is "cast away" implies that the woman herself is thereby rendered clean—a strong warning to anyone who fails to undergo spiritual cleansing. Of the two instances, only the second carries the warning of divine rejection. Especially note that the word "abominably," which occurs in the heading, does not actually appear in this part of Birgitta's own text. See also St. Paul's description of himself as an "abortion" in 1 Corinthians 15:8. Here at the end of this dramatic revelation, the wicked cantor has received two warnings. The first is gentle: "You will be cast forth." The second is blunt: "You will be cast away."

307. Birgitta often uses this idea that God will reward—even if only in some temporal way—every slightest trace of goodness that he finds in his creatures. Cf. note 163.

308. 1 Samuel 13:11–14—Saul's sacrifice.

309. 2 Samuel 11 & 12—David and Bathsheba.

310. 1 Samuel 28:7–20. Birgitta uses the word *phitonissam*, "pythoness," which she found in the Vulgate. The original "pythoness" was the pagan Greek priestess who gave prophecies at the Pythian oracle of

Apollo at Delphi. The original Python was the guardian serpent of the shrine, slain by Apollo. In time, *pytho* came to mean almost any "divining spirit" that gave oracles through a human medium (cf. Acts 16:16). The Old Swedish (Klemming 2: 305) gives a very apt rendering, *trolkononne*, "troll-woman." In Medieval Scandinavian literature, the "troll" is sometimes pictured as a reanimated corpse, e.g., *The Saga of Grettir the Strong* 32–35 (trans. George A. Hight [London: Everyman-Dent, 1913]; 86–100).

311. 1 Kings 11:4.

312. Cf. note 82.

313. *creans malum.* Isaiah 45:7. These startling words provide another instance of Birgitta's interest in exegetical questions (cf. notes 59, 285, and 286). The Hebrew and the Vulgate agree in using the same word-root here for "creating" as they use for "created" in Genesis 1:1. (The LXX uses synonyms.) How can the Bible say that God creates evil? The heretic Marcion used such OT verses to support his theory of two Gods: an evil Jewish God and a good Christian one (cf. note 71 and Jean Daniélou, S.J., *Origen*, trans. W. Mitchell [New York: Sheed and Ward, 1955], 142–43). Birgitta's solution to the difficulty is that the word *creans* is being used in a tropical or "non-literal" sense through the device of synecdoche, in which the whole stands for the part: God's act of creating includes his act of permitting created beings to act in accord with their natures (cf. note 163). Therefore, any ensuing evil—either moral or ontological—comes from the Creator only by permission and not by volition. Note that this problem phrase is followed by the famous passage *rorate caeli desuper*, "Drop dew, O heavens, from above." Birgitta may have first noticed this exegetical problem while praying the Roman liturgical offices of Advent.

314. Cf. 1 Corinthians 11:31–32.

315. Cf. John 5:24.

316. *supportantur.* Cf. Bergh, *Book V* 178.

317. *non compunctos.* On the importance of *compunctio* in traditional spiritual vocabulary, see Leclercq, *Love* 29–32. *Compunctio* is that moment of "puncturing," when God pierces through and awakens our *attentio* (cf. note 82). The virtue of "compunction" is the habitual retention of that original sharpness of realization that characterized the moment when God "pierced through." These ideas lie at the heart of Birgitta's spiritual message.

318. *defluit in vanitates.*

319. *Nam Petrus apostolus in iuuentute obliuiosus erat, Iohannes*

ydiota. In what way Peter was "forgetful" is not made clear; but, in Acts 4:13, both Peter and John are called *sine litteris et idiotae.* I suspect that Birgitta's exegetical curiosity has been whetted by the Greek word *idiōtai,* "private individuals," or "non-experts." (Cf. note 59.) Here only John is called *ydiota;* but we find *Petrus ydiota* in *Extravagantes* 23.4. And it is also to another book of the *Revelations* (4.5) that we must look for a solution to the nature of Peter's forgetfulness. There Peter appears to Birgitta; and, among other things, he says:

> As to the fact that you ask me to give you the gift of memory, I answer you: Have you not heard how forgetful I was? I was indeed fully instructed as to the way of God; and, by an oath, I bound myself to take a stand and die with God. But when I was questioned, at the word of one woman I denied the truth. And why? Because God left me to myself, and I did not know myself. But what did I then do? Then indeed I considered myself: that I was nothing of myself. And I rose, and I ran to the truth: to God, who impressed upon my heart such a memory of his name that not before tyrants, nor amidst scourges, nor even in death, could I forget him. Do this therefore yourself. Rise through humility to the Master of memory, and seek memory from him!

320. Cf. Proverbs 9:10.

321. This is apparently the only reference to Aristotle in the writings of Birgitta. Klockars (*Böckerna* 308) also cites *Rev.* 5, Int. 15.6, which does not apply to any form of the text that I have seen.

322. Cf. Numbers 22:21–31; 2 Peter 2:15–16. The Latin Bible always refers to Balaam's *asina* in the feminine, reflecting the gender of the Hebrew. One can easily suppose that Birgitta used this particular *exemplum* with a certain ironic relish.

323. Cf. Daniel 13:44–64.

324. Cf. Exodus 7:2–4.

325. *pinguedinem.* Literally, "fatness," this word is here used to mean "fertilizer." Birgitta tends to use *pinguedo* in symbolic passages which must be translated in a way that conveys the idea of "fatness," "oiliness," or "richness."

326. *zizanie.* Cf. Matthew 13:24–30, 36–43.

327. Cf. Exodus 7:8–11:10.

328. *amplectatur.* In Latin poetry, the noun *amplexus,* "embrace," is often used as a sexual euphemism; and the verb here carries some of those overtones. The combination *amplectatur abstinenciam,* "embrace

refrainment," is a discreet, but clever, example of oxymoron or "apparent contradiction." For the alert, there are many subtle charms to be savored in the Birgittine texts.

329. Cf. 2 Samuel 14:14; Ezekiel 18:23, 32; 33:11; 1 Timothy 2:4.

330. Cf. notes 163, 189, 201, and 313.

331. Cf. Matthew 25:14–30.

332. *afficit.* Cf. Bergh, *Book V* 176.

333. Cf. Isaiah 66:10–13.

334. This is not true of Birgitta in the literal sense (cf. *Life* 2–4 and note 25).

335. Cf. *Life* 47.

336. *obliuio Dei.* No doubt the primary meaning here is "forgetfulness toward God"; but see note 253.

337. Torquemada (article 70) defended this statement as "very true, not only of St. Birgitta, but also of anyone in the state of grace. . . ." He cites Songs 2:4.

338. Here the words in John 10:38; 14:10–11, 20; 17:21, 23—concerning the interrelation of the Father, the Son, and the faithful—are applied to the interrelation of the Son, the Holy Spirit, and the individual soul. Birgitta is alluding to the doctrine of perichoresis or "reciprocal indwelling" of the Three Divine Persons in one another. Cf. note 241 and Ott 71.

339. *inquisicio tua.* Cf. note 158.

340. *ad aliorum caritatem.*

341. *qui maiori vtitur racione.*

342. *Nam aut erit eis ad celeriorem vite finem aut ad minorem miserie laborem et nature fortis consumpcionem aut propter mutacionem temporum aut ex incuria hominis labore proueniente.* This is one of the most unclear passages in the *Book of Questions.* Even the subject of the sentence is not certain. Is it "suffering" or "great justice"? The following list of "causes" is an incoherent collection: "for a swifter end . . . for less labor . . . and consumption . . . or because of the change . . . or out of the carelessness . . ." The final two words, an ablative absolute, seem to mean that men are careless about the animals' sufferings so long as they can get work out of the animals. But *labore* could possibly refer to "labor pains"—although that meaning would make the passage even more obscure. It seems best to give a very literal, but tentative, translation together with the full Latin wording.

343. Cf. Exodus 19:8–11.

344. *Et quia inordinacio cepit in homine et per hominem, iusticia mea*

est, vt eciam aliis creaturis, que sunt propter hominem, aliqua amaritudo sit propter temperamentum delectamenti sui et fomentum nutrimenti sui. In this, the last of the difficult animal passages, the problem lies in the final eight words. First, *propter*, "for," or "because of," can indicate both efficient and final cause. Which is it here? "Tempering of delight" is no problem; but *sui* is. In Medieval Latin, the rules for determining the word to which *suus* refers are often ignored; and in a passage like this, the classical rules cannot be relied upon. *Sui* here means either "his" (i.e., man's) or "their" (i.e., the animals'). Finally, *fomentum nutrimenti*, "foment of nutriment," has several sharply contradictory possibilities. *Fomentum* can be positive (foster) or negative (alleviate)—based on its use as the name of any warm medicinal application that is used to heat a cold patient or to alleviate swelling or pain in the body. *Nutrimentum* is even more ambiguous, meaning "nutriment," "the act of nourishment," or even "nursling." To compound our confusion, in Deferrari 407–08 we read that *fomentum* is a synonym of *nutrimentum* in the sense "nutriment." Here again, I have chosen to put a very literal rendering that does give some sense—together with the Latin wording in this note.

345. Cf. Ezekiel 18:20. See also *Rev.* 7.16.36.

346. Cf. Exodus 20:5.

347. Cf. Wisdom 11:17.

348. Cf. Romans 11:34.

349. *qui omnium operor salutem.* God works our salvation in a way that respects our freedom (cf. note 163). We will not receive his salvation unless, through the help of his grace, we cooperate with his work (cf. Philippians 2:13). These are major themes of this *Book of Questions* and of all of Birgitta's thought. And it is to Mary, the Mother of God, that Birgitta looks for a perfect model of divine salvation and human cooperation (cf. notes 189 and 201).

350. A favorite Birgittine theme; cf. note 307.

351. *pro quibus in presenti flagellandi sunt aut expectandi.* The phrase is elliptical to the point of unintelligibility on a first reading. Presumably, *flagellari*, "to be scourged," or *flagellatum iri*, "to be about to be scourged," must be understood at the end of the sentence.

352. Cf. note 192.

353. This is a reflection on the ancient maxim: "Call no man happy before his death." The thought is attributed to Solon in Herodotus (1.32). Birgitta, however, rephrases it so that the circumstances of the death are not the final standard of judgment as in the pagan sense.

354. Cf. note 163.

355. *et decepcionem, sicut in illis libris, qui Apocrifi intitulantur, in-uenitur, vt post mortem quasi iusti laudentur.* Despite the clue in the text and a diligent search, I have not been able to trace this reference.

356. *euolarent.*

357. *perismata.* A mistranscription of the Greek *peripsēmata* (cf. Bergh, *Book V* 178) found in 1 Corinthians 4:13, but only attested in the singular *peripsēma* (Vulgate: *peripsima*). Although Birgitta uses the word in a context different from St. Paul's, she correctly understands its meaning, "offscourings." Here again we have evidence of her interest in biblical language and in the exegesis of those Greek words that the Vulgate simply transliterates (cf. notes 59, 285, 286, 313, and 319).

358. Cf. 1 Kings 13:20–30. Klockars (*Böckerna* 216) notes that the same story is told in St. Gregory's *Dialogues* 4.25 (cf. notes 19 and 84).

359. Cf. note 263.

360. Bergh (*Book V* 155) gives references to *Rev.* 4.102 and its "Addition," and to *Rev.* 6.9.

361. *insinuaretur.*

362. The usual mystical interpretation of these names derived from St. Augustine, *Enarrationes in psalmos* 50.22: *Interpretatur Sion speculatio, et Jerusalem visio pacis.* "Zion means 'watching,' and Jerusalem 'vision of peace.'" Therefore Zion was often interpreted as the Church on earth, and Jerusalem as heaven.

363. Cf. Isaiah 43:8; Matthew 13:13. The cruel mistreatment that has befallen the Jews as a result of an indefensible use of biblical verses wrenched out of historical context is now so widely demonstrated that such comments as this of Birgitta's are disturbing in their possible results. In the saint's defense, one might point out that despite the adjectives "blind" and "deaf," her main statement is that the Jews are the Lord's people. Cf. note 237.

364. There is a striking resemblance between this image and Plato's cave (*Republic* 7.1–3). The intermediate source seems to be St. Gregory's *Dialogues* 4.1 (cf. Klockars, *Böckerna* 215–16). Klockars (*Böckerna* 232) also cites Henry Suso's *Little Book of Eternal Wisdom* as a possible source. Finally, there is a study that I have been able to consult only in abstract: Adalbert de Voguë, O.S.B., "Un avatar du mythe de la caverne dans les Dialogues de Grégoire le Grand," *Homenaje a Fray Justo Perez de Urbel, O.S.B.*, Studia Silensia 4 (Burgos: Abadía de Silos, 1977), 19–24. For the final words, cf. John 20:29.

365. Bergh (*Book V* 157) refers to a Medieval Swedish proverb: Man ma swa vaenias vidh ilt at onth aer fulgoth.

366. *alia ad municiones et misteria consilii sui.* The transition from "fortifications" to "secret council chamber" seems rough. Could the Birgittine Latinists have confused *munitiones,* "fortifications," with *munimenta,* "archives"?

367. On Easter night, in the *Exsultet,* the Roman liturgy similarly praises the bee for its making of wax. See also Sirach 11:3.

368. Cf. *Rev.* 5, Int. 8.14–20.

369. Cf. 2 Corinthians 12:7–9.

370. *ne excedat in malicia.* For this sense of *excedat,* see Bergh, *Book V* 177.

371. Cf. note 307.

372. *Omnis, quicumque bonus est, michi soli Deo cognitus est et quid meretur.* The first half might also be rendered: "Only I, God, know *who* each good person is. . . ."

373. Cf. Job 23:10; Proverbs 17:3; Sirach 2:5; Zechariah 13:9; Malachi 3:3; 1 Peter 1:7; Apocalypse 3:18.

374. Cf. Job 1:12–2:10.

375. *qui eum preueni benediccionibus meis.* Cf. Psalm 20(21):4. The verb *praevenire,* "come before," is difficult to translate into modern English; the cognate, "prevent," is very rarely appropriate. Where Birgitta uses it in a "preventive" sense, I have generally put "forestall." Where, as here, Birgitta is alluding to the doctrine of "antecedent" or "prevenient" grace (Ott 226–27), I have used the somewhat unsatisfactory "anticipate."

376. Cf. John 3:8.

377. Cf. Wisdom 1:4. Note that Birgitta transfers these words from God's Wisdom to his Spirit. She has also put *vase,* "vessel," where Wisdom 1:4 has *corpore,* "body." This may be another instance of Birgitta's interest in "hard words" in the Bible. *Vas* is often encountered there in the senses of "instrument," "body," or even "wife." See *skeuos* in Walter Bauer, et al. *A Greek-English Lexicon of the New Testament and Other Early Christian Literature,* 2nd ed. (Chicago: University of Chicago Press, 1979), 754. In 1 Thessalonians 4:4, the word *vas* has some unclear sexual connotation; and the Birgittine use of *vase* here may reflect the view that Wisdom 1:4 is referring primarily to sexual sins. It should also be noted that Birgitta very often refers to the Mother of God as *vas,* or "vessel." Cf. *Rev.* 5, Int. 10.7–11. This Marian meaning of *vas* is based on a mystical interpretation of the vessel of manna mentioned in Exodus 16:33, and this tradition is still familiar today from its use in the Litany of Loreto: *vas spirituale, vas honorabile, vas*

insigne devotionis—"spiritual vessel, vessel of honor, singular vessel of devotion."

378. Cf. 1 John 4:8 and 16.

379. Cf. 2 Corinthians 3:17.

380. Cf. note 163.

381. Cf. 1 Samuel 16:14; 18:12; 28:15–16.

382. Cf. Numbers 22:5–24:25. See also note 322.

383. Birgitta uses this Latin word that originally denoted the Roman official who attended magistrates in public and who often also carried out legal sentences involving scourging or decapitation. The lictor's sign of office was the *fasces*—a bundle of rods from which an ax protruded.

384. This statement is so concise that it is slightly unclear. Birgitta apparently means that the pagan infants go to limbo while the Christian infants go to heaven. Note, however, that the word *limbus* is not in the text. Cf. note 160.

385. Cf. *Rev. 5*, Int. 14.10–12 and note 342.

386. *exigentibus meritis.*

387. *saluber.* In Latin, the word *salus* and its derivatives can mean either "health" or "salvation"; and it is on this double meaning that much of the following imagery depends.

388. *de frigido ferro et duro lapide.* In Latin, *ferrum*, "iron," is a common metonymy for "sword."

389. *calibs.* Usually *chalybs* is taken to mean "steel" in contrast to *ferrum*, "iron." However, Latin usage is not entirely consistent on this point, and perhaps we should not look for any significance in the text's shift to this second term.

390. *montem sulphureum.* The problem here is that *mons*, which normally means "mountain," can also mean "mound" or "large rock." The following allegory is not absolutely clear in its details, but a "sulphurous mound" or a "sulphurous rock" could be envisioned as burning more conveniently than a "sulphurous mountain." However, this is an allegorical composition; and not all of the details should be criticized according to the principle of verisimilitude.

391. *oliua.* In this revelation, the feminine *oliva* means both "olive tree" and "olive oil"—the latter is usually put in the neuter form *olivum.*

392. *pinguedine.* Cf. Judges 9:8–9; Romans 11:17; and note 325.

393. *ille maritus tuus, quem pre ceteris carnaliter dilexisti.* This is an important testimony to the happiness of Birgitta's marriage and to her

true and very human love for her husband Ulf. It should be remembered that the events recorded in the *Book of Questions* took place in the early years of Birgitta's widowhood.

394. The allegory is here given support by wordplay involving *mundana,* "mundane," and *monti,* "mountain."

395. *conuersacio.* In Christian Latin, this word normally means "way of life"—translating the New Testament's *politeia* or *politeuma.* While the primary stress of *conversatio* is "living together" or "familiarity with," the notion of "talking to" is hardly excluded. Certainly here, as a parallel to the "words of the gospels," some word for "talking" seems necessary. The reference is to Birgitta's love of books and reading, which permitted her to hear the discourses of the fathers of the Church. It should also be remembered that the tradition of *lectio divina* stressed reading with the ears as well as with the eyes (cf. Leclercq, *Love* 72–73 and note 264).

396. *revelacionum in spiritu.* Cf. note 38.

397. Cf. Zechariah 14:4; Apocalypse 14:1. The text does not clearly say that this mountain is the aforementioned sulphurous mountain.

398. Cf. note 396.

399. Cf. Matthew 25:33.

400. Cf. Matthew 24:36; Mark 13:32.

401. *vbique et semper.* This reversal of the phrase used in the Preface of the Roman Rite Mass is repeated several times in the Judge's reply.

402. Cf. *Rev.* 5, Int. 11.6.

403. Cf. *Rev.* 5, Int. 11.19.

404. Cf. note 159. Here Birgitta is criticizing those who attribute absurdities to the Bible through their failure to respect its literary devices, such as allegorical language in the parables. The theme of the correct method of exegesis is a major concern of this final Interrogation and forms part of the climax of the *Book of Questions.* Birgitta was attacked for saying that "right" and "left" in these gospel passages are similitudes and are not to be taken literally. Cardinal Torquemada defended her teaching (article 71), saying that it is *verus et conformis verbis sanctorum,* "true and conformed to the words of the saints."

405. *vt habeat paruulus, quod sugat, et perfecti, ut perfecciores fiant.* Cf. Hebrews 5:12–14; 1 Peter 2:2. There seem to be echoes of Isaiah 66:11 and Luke 2:19, 51; 11:27–28.

406. Cf. Luke 2:34–35.

407. Cf. note 400.

408. Cf. Luke 2:52.

409. Birgitta is building on the thought in John 5:19. Cf. note 338.

410. *vna substancia, vna deitas et voluntas.* Cf. note 241 and Ott 44.

411. The question of Christ's human knowledge is always difficult to phrase correctly (cf. Ott 162–68). Birgitta was attacked for her teaching in this passage. Cardinal Torquemada defended her (article 72) and said: *si respiciatur oculo pio, eo modo, quo dicta sanctorum sunt consideranda, videtur continere veritatem et consonare dictis sanctorum*—"if it be looked at with a pious eye—in the way that the saints' sayings must be considered—it is seen to contain truth and to be consonant with the sayings of the saints." This is the last of Torquemada's articles that relates to the *Book of Questions.*

412. *dissonancia.*

413. Cf. 1 Corinthians 12:7–11.

414. Cf. Apocalypse 6:6.

415. *ipsum momentum statere.* Cf. Wisdom 11:23; Isaiah 40:15; and 4 Ezra 3:34. Here again we have an example of Birgitta's interest in exegetical problems (cf. note 377). In the first two biblical passages, this unclear Latin expression means "a particle sufficient to turn the scales" (cf. Lewis & Short, s.v. *momentum*). But the context here seems to imply that like the apocryphal 4 Ezra 3:34 (Stuttgart Vulgate), Birgitta took the phrase as a reference to the movement itself, rather than to the particle that causes the motion. In a private letter (10/XII/86), Professor Bergh has indicated to me his conclusion that Birgitta means the "moving parts" of the scales, i.e., the needle, etc. Since, in English the word "movement" has the same ambiguity as the Latin *momentum*, i.e., "motion" or "moving parts," it seems best to me to leave the ambiguity for the reader to appreciate.

416. *alii ad inueniendam occasionem.*

417. Birgitta is apparently referring to those occasions such as Matthew 13:10–23 and 36–43, on which Christ privately interpreted his parables for the disciples.

418. Cf. Luke 1:1.

419. 24. *Ideo non mirum, si hii, qui narracionem euangeliorum ordinauerunt, quod posuerunt diuersa sed tamen vera, quia quidam eorum posuerunt verbum ad verbum, quidam sensum verborum, non verba.* 25. *Quidam scripserunt audita, non visa, alii priora posterius, alii plura de deitate mea et vnusquisque, prout Spiritus Sanctus dabat loqui illis.* I have given the full Latin text of this remarkable passage because it is an important and little-known testimony to the continuity of Catholic teaching on this subject. Birgitta's approach, which seems so modern,

can also be found in Chaucer's *Canterbury Tales*, in the prologue to the "Tale of Melibee" (VII.943–52; Benson 216). Bergh (*Book V* 166) points out Medieval Latin parallels for the redundant use of *quod* after *si* in section 24; in the English the redundant *quod* is not represented. For the final words of section 25, cf. Acts 2:4.

420. Since the second century, the acceptance of no more and no fewer than the four canonical gospels—with all their differences and their apparent discrepancies—has been a distinguishing mark of Catholic Christianity. Birgitta is here emphasizing that the other ancient texts called "apocryphal gospels" have never been accepted by the Church and have no valid claim to such acceptance.

421. Cf. John 2:19; but the text as cited in this revelation is abbreviated and John's *excitabo*, "I shall raise up," has been altered to *reedificabo*, "I shall rebuild," inspired by *reaedificat* "he rebuilds," in Matthew 27:40. See also Matthew 26:61 and Mark 14:58; 15:29, in all of which the verb is a form of *aedificare*, "to build." Although the text is shortened and conflated, the context makes it clear that Birgitta is referring to a reading from John, presumably at Mass on the day that this series of visions took place. One clue to the date may be the fact that in the Tridentine lectionary, John 2:13–25 was read on the Monday of the fourth week of Lent. This is a point that awaits further study based on the lectionaries used in medieval Sweden.

422. Cf. Matthew 26:60–61.

423. Cf. John 2:21.

424. Cf. John 6:54, 61, 67. Birgitta's chronology is confused.

425. Cf. John 6:64.

426. *idest spiritualem habent intellectum et virtutem.*

427. Here, after the climactic discussion of the gospels, the pattern of answers is about to be abruptly broken; and we see the anonymous religious apparently beginning to show signs of understandable fatigue.

428. Birgitta, of course, is still riding her horse in ecstasy on the road to Vadstena.

429. Master Matthias; cf. note 23.

430. Cf. sections 18 and 31 of this Interrogation.

431. Cf. *Life* 34 and note 48.

432. Cf. Romans 5:20. Christ alludes to himself as a physician in Matthew 9:12; Luke 4:23 and 5:31.

433. *appropinquabant.* This could also be rendered as "were approaching." But Birgittine Latin is not always concerned about the distinction between imperfect and perfect tenses.

434. Cf. note 401.

435. This is the first time that the Spirit speaks in the *Book of Questions;* up till now, only the Mother of God and then Christ himself have spoken to Birgitta in the various "revelations." For a joint mention of the Spirit and the bride, see Apocalypse 22:17.

436. *non ad diem vnum mansurus est viuus.* The words *ad diem unum* are ambiguous: "one day" or "one more day." I have tried to preserve the ambiguity. See note 139.

437. Cf. *Rev. 5*, Int. 11.6–9; Int. 14.6.

438. *Sed ecce iam cum affeccionibus et cogitacionibus finietur spes et vita eius.* Again the text is very discreet about this man and his fate. The use of *iam* can be ambiguous; it is rarely so strong as *nunc* in meaning "now." *Iam* usually means "at this time" or "at that time" in relation to the time of the main verb, which is here future. Cf. notes 139 and 436.

439. *impinguatur.* Cf. notes 325 and 392.

440. The identity of this man is buried under the usual Birgittine discretion. In the context of what follows, he would hardly seem to be the same man whom we have been shown on the ladder. And yet perhaps we are dealing with two layers of revelation: one grim and threatening just punishment, addressed to the man himself; the other patient and full of mercy, meant chiefly for the instruction of the visionary. In that case, this could be the man on the ladder. In the end, we are left with a very interesting literary puzzle—one that we are apparently not meant to solve. Bergh (*Book V* 170) notes that the first three sections of this revelation are repeated in *Rev.* 8.21. There they have a few final lines added in which the king is warned not to interfere in this man's case.

441. *colores.* Cf. Bergh, *Book V* 176.

442. *et tunc rei, cui apponentur, magis conuenient et virtutem meam conuenienter colorabunt.* There is an allusion here to the ancient use of *colores*, "colors," as a general term for the ornaments of rhetoric that give "color" to a writer's words. The term became very popular in the Middle Ages (Leclercq, *Love* 128, 173). Birgitta is using the idea of "color" here in the context of her teaching about the relation of apophatic and cataphatic elements in religious language (cf. notes 159, 180, 263, and 359). She is saying that the reality of God—here, his "virtue" —is "applied" to mankind through the medium of words; but that the application involves "fitting" the words to the reality they represent and to the capacity of the receiver. With patience, the right moment will arrive; and then the words will fittingly display to the hearer the

NOTES

fair color of God's virtue. For a similar expression, see François Martine, ed., *Vie des pères du Jura,* Sources chrétiennes 142 (Paris: Cerf, 1968), 240; 3: *non decoloret uirtutum amplitudinem sermonis angustia,* "the narrow scope of the style would not discolor the grandeur of the virtues."

443. *pinguedine.* Cf. note 325. Birgitta is thinking of the tallow-burning lamps of northern Europe, much like the "betty lamps" of colonial America. For an illustration, see La Fay 87.

444. *lichinus.* Cf. Bergh, *Book V* 177. I think that it is clear from the context that Birgitta means a burning wick.

445. Cf. note 147.

446. *aruinam.*

447. *recipitur.* Cf. Bergh, *Book V* 84–87, 178. Literally, it seems as if the text says: "by which it is received." Bergh (84) points out: "the sense must be considered utterly strange: the soul receives grace and words by which it is received." Some manuscripts read *reficitur,* "it is refreshed." But there are other meanings of *recipere:* "entertain at a meal" (cf., in English, a "reception," meaning a party with food served for those who want it); "feed"; "support"; "pardon." In *Rev.* 5, Rev. 3 (cf. note 181), *recipere* means "take responsibility for." It is possible that *recipere* is also taking on some of the meanings of *suscipere,* which translates *antilambanesthai,* "take the side of" or "come to the aid of," in Luke 1:54 and Acts 20:35. The attempted wordplay with *recipere* has not been entirely successful; and the passage remains difficult. To some extent, the development of the image is governed by: "When fat is put into it, the wick soon draws near. . . ." in section 5. The "fat" of God's words attracts and "receives" the burning "wick" of the soul. In the translation, I have followed Bergh (87) and have put "sustained" as the best way to respect the ambiguities of the passage.

448. *protraccione.*

449. The kingdom is Sweden. The exact sin is discreetly left unspecified. But Birgitta's outspoken objection to the public injustices and private immoralities associated with the court of King Magnus and Queen Blanche is well documented.

450. The Latin text's shift in the sequence of tenses has been retained in the translation. The difficulties of this revelation are worth noting.

451. Presumably, Rome.

452. *aperiatur.*

453. This is the first time that God the Father speaks in the *Book of*

276

Questions. His appearance, following that of the Holy Spirit in Int. 16.50, turns the end of this book into a theophany of the Trinity (cf. note 241).

454. These words introduce the magnificent conclusion of the *Book of Questions:* the statement and solution of a great riddle. The literary *genre* of the riddle was extremely popular in the early literature of all the Germanic-speaking countries: England, Scandinavia, Germany, etc. Here Birgitta takes this popular form and exalts it into a final example of her teaching about religious language. Each of the five parts of the riddle consists of a series of *kataphaseis*, "affirmations," immediately balanced by *apophaseis*, "negations." For Birgitta, there is no question of rejecting words and imagery; rather, she uses them and passes through them to the God who is above and beyond comprehension. In private conversation, Professor Bergh has pointed out to me that this great riddle is a fine example of the medieval tradition of *coincidentia oppositorum*, "the coincidence of opposites." For a study of this device in the century before Birgitta, see Ewert H. Cousins, *Bonaventure and the Coincidence of Opposites* (Chicago: Franciscan Herald Press, 1978).

455. *loca.* Cf. note 5.

456. *qui agnoscebatur et incognitus fuit.* Unlike the other phrases in the riddle, this one has not been constructed with an exact repetition of the key word. Here and elsewhere the slight variations in the parallelism have been reproduced in the translation.

457. *Vas.* Cf. note 377.

458. Mary's parents are not mentioned in the Bible; but since the second century, they have been given the names Joachim and Ann (cf. Thurston 3: 189–190; 336). Birgitta is here adding to our Lady's name the traditional Scandinavian patronymic: *Maria Joakimsdotter.*

459. *mater humanitatis Christi.* There is no trace of Nestorianism in this expression. Throughout the *Revelations*, Birgitta refers to Mary as Mother of God, i.e., *Theotokos.* Here Birgitta is stressing one true part of the full doctrine of Mary's divine maternity (cf. Ott 196–97).

460. Cf. Psalm 17(18):5—"torrents" as an image of evil.

461. Cf. Psalm 35(36):9—"torrent" as an image of good.

462. *mater filii mei.* Here Birgitta gives the correct balance to her statement in section 9 (cf. note 459).

463. *paruum et modicum in humilitatis sue contemptu.* The phrase is ambiguous. Here the principal meaning seems to be: "her outwardly contemptible position of lowliness." On Mary's "humility" or "lowliness," see Luke 1:48.

464. *vacuum ab omni voluptate et peccato.* The words at the end form a hendiadys and could be rendered "sinful pleasure."

465. Cf. notes 201 and 209.

466. Cf. Songs 4:7.

467. Birgitta's words "not clean" may seem strange to modern Catholics, who accept the doctrine of Mary's own Immaculate Conception in the womb of her mother as defined at Rome in 1854. Birgitta herself accepted that doctrine, and she states it correctly here. Through the foreseen merits of Christ, Mary was preserved from all stain of original sin in the first moment of her conception. At the same time, Mary was a true daughter of Adam; she was conceived in the normal way, and she was a redeemed member of our unclean race even though the uncleanness of our race never actually touched her. Therefore, the only thing that one might term "not clean" about Mary is the fact that she is related to us. Cf. Ott 199–202.

468. Traditionally, Jerusalem.

469. This first part of the riddle is solved in great detail to demonstrate the correct method of solution. The following parts will be solved more briefly, leaving much to the reader's own ingenuity.

470. Cf. Genesis 49:9; Numbers 24:9; Apocalypse 5:5.

471. Cf. Isaiah 53:7; Jeremiah 11:19; John 1:29, 36; Acts 8:32; 1 Peter 1:19; Apocalypse 5:12.

472. *ponebatur.* Cf. note 125 on *depones.*

473. Cf. Numbers 21:6–9; John 3:14.

474. Cf. Acts 1:9–12.

475. Cf. Jeremiah 48:40. See also Psalm 17(18):11; 103(104):3.

476. *innouabatur.* Cf. Psalm 102(103):5; Isaiah 40:31.

477. *habebit.*

478. Cf. Psalm 33(34):9. See note 92.

479. With these prophetic words, the *Book of Questions* comes to an end. In 1349, Birgitta left Sweden on a pilgrimage to Rome for the Holy Year of 1350. She settled there permanently and never saw Sweden again. In 1372, she finally reached the Holy Land; and there she visited the "places" that had been foretold to her in this riddle. In Jerusalem and in Bethlehem, she was indeed "shown more" (cf. *Rev.* 7:prologue 3; chapters 14–15; 21–26; *Life* 64–70).

480. This is the heading as given in Birger Bergh, ed., *Den Heliga Birgittas Revelaciones: Bok VII* (Uppsala: Almqvist, 1967), 111. This is the critical edition followed in the present translation, and readers

interested in the textual history of the Seventh Book should consult Bergh.

481. Again we find an introductory prologue. Like the prologue to the *Book of Questions* (cf. note 133), this prologue too is not found in all the MSS but chiefly in those of the Prague redaction (Undhagen, *Book I* 32); and it too is perhaps by Alphonsus Pecha (cf. note 111), although Undhagen (*Book I* 17) suggests that this is unlikely. The description of this as the "last book" would only be true in the seven-book edition of the *Revelations* that Alphonsus prepared for the canonization process. Later he himself added an eighth book; and still later others added the remaining sections of the *Revelations* as it has come down to us (Undhagen, *Book I* 14–22). However, in the Prague redaction, Alphonsus's Eighth Book and the other supplements are inserted after the Second and Fourth Books so that the Seventh can continue to stand as the "last book."

482. The prologue is here alluding to the fact that the Seventh Book divides into two parts at chapter 9. Before that chapter, there are revelations related to the theme of pilgrimage and setting the scene for the journey to the Holy Land in 1372. From chapter 9 on, the arrangement is presumably a chronological one, involving incidents directly related to the 1372 pilgrimage. It is this remarkable adherence to some sort of chronological sequence that makes the Seventh Book unique in the Birgittine corpus. For the shrine of St. Michael on Monte Gargano, see Ryan 579 and Thurston 2: 249–50.

483. *vltra mare.*

484. Cf. *Rev.* 7.9.1–2.

485. Cf. *Rev.* 5, Rev. 13.1–23.

486. *in Vrbe.* Birgitta died in Rome on 23 July 1373.

487. *lacius.* For further information on the material in Book Seven, see Andersson, *Holy Land;* Jørgensen 2: 232–309. Concerning the origins and meaning of such pilgrimage, see Brown and Sumption; for a documented account of such a pilgrimage shortly after Birgitta's time, see the works of Prescott in the bibliography. For maps, see Aviel and Nebenzahl.

488. *habuit.*

489. A.D. 1350. This was the second officially proclaimed Holy Year; and it was the occasion, and perhaps the royal excuse, for Birgitta's permanent removal to Italy.

490. *oracioni vacaret.* Literally "was empty for prayer." Cf. Tobit

6:17–18 (Vulgate); 1 Corinthians 7:5. *Vacare* has never found a really adequate English rendering that conveys the image of being *vacuus*, "empty," for the purpose of being filled by something, in this case, by prayer. In Book Seven, *vacare orationi*, "to be empty for prayer," acquires a special importance from its association with the major Birgittine theme of *attentio*, "attention" (cf. notes 82, 312, and 317). See Leclercq, *Otia* 42–49.

491. *de partu virginis.* That is to say, the birth of Christ from the ever-virgin Mary (Cf. Ott 203–07).

492. *preelegit.* Cf. *Rev.* 7.4.12.

493. *Et sic amoris dulcedine inebriata stabat supra se alienata a sensibus in quodam extasi mentalis contemplacionis suspensa.* In various combinations the words of this description recur formulaically in the *Revelations*.

494. *Attende.* The first clear statement of the great theme of the Seventh Book: "attention." (Cf. note 490.)

495. *ibique ostendam tibi in loco proprio totum modum, qualiter ego peperi eundem filium meum Ihesum Christum.* This deceptively simple promise is the prelude to a startling disappointment for Birgitta (*Rev.* 7.21.10), who apparently misunderstands Mary's words (cf. *Rev.* 5, Rev. 10.1–8 on the ways in which a revelation may be misunderstood).

496. According to the rubric for *Rev.* 7.21, Birgitta received this promise in 1357 (or 1358, cf. note 32), fifteen years before her visit to Bethlehem in August 1372. There is further information on sections 5–6 in Collijn, *Acta* 96 (= *Life* 69), 516, 633.

497. *Sancte Marie Maioris.* Founded near the site of the earlier Liberian Basilica, this church was consecrated by Pope Sixtus III (435–440). It is traditionally regarded as the oldest church dedicated to our Lady in the West; and its anniversary day (August 5) is still kept in the Roman liturgical calendar. St. Mary Major has a special significance here at the start of Book Seven: it contains the *Praesepe Domini*—a chapel built in imitation of the cave of Bethlehem, containing a nativity scene and enshrining the reputed relics of the original manger brought from the Holy Land.

498. February 2; also called Candlemas from the blessing of candles on that day. The original Roman title was Hypapante (meaning "Encounter"); since 1969, the title is "Presentation of the Lord." The feast commemorates, on the fortieth day after Christmas, the presentation of Christ in the temple and his encounter with Simeon (cf. Luke 2:22–38).

499. *rapta fuit dicta domina in spiritualem visionem.* These words are

also formulaic. On "spiritual vision" and on the relevant apophatic warning, see notes 38 and 263.

500. *quasi.* Birgitta's use of this qualifying expression should always be carefully noted. It is an important element in her balancing of the cataphatic-apophatic tension mentioned in the preceding note. Birgitta herself insists on the importance of noting the literary genre as a part of correct exegesis of the Scriptures (cf. *Rev.* 5, Int. 16:6–10, 15–31). For St. Gregory on *quasi,* see Evans 88.

501. Cf. Luke 2:24.

502. Cf. Luke 2:35. Birgitta, with her perennial interest in exegetical difficulties (cf. note 377), is proposing one traditional explanation of the "sword" mentioned by Simeon. In doing so, she is preparing us for the great revelation of the crucifixion in chapter 15.

503. *rependitur.* The theme of divine recompense remains important in this book (cf. note 307).

504. October 4.

505. San Francesco a Ripa.

506. *se et suos.*

507. *Bene veneris!* Birgitta commonly uses this very literal idiom for "welcome!" But the term will have its true moment of glory in the unforgettable words of *Rev.* 7.21.14.

508. *domus.* The meaning "house" should not be overstressed here. Birgitta is following the early Christian distinction between God's People meeting in their "assembly" (*Ecclesia,* "the Church") and the "building" in which they assembled (*domus Ecclesiae,* "the house of the Church.") Unfortunately, in most languages, this distinction has disappeared; and both the people and the building are called "church."

509. *preceptore.* Latin words derived from *praecipio* have the same ambiguity as the English "instruct": "command" or "teach."

510. Bergh here cites *Opuscula sancti patris Francisci assisiensis,* Bibliotheca franciscana ascetica medii aevi I (Quaracchi: 1904), 80, and *Speculum perfectionis* 46.

511. Cf. John 4:34.

512. Another interpretation of St. Francis' "food" and "drink" is given in *Extravagantes* 90.1:

> When blessed Birgitta was in the church of the friars in Assisi, she heard and saw Christ saying: "My friend Francis descended from the mountain of delights into a cave, where his bread was divine charity, his drink was continual tears, and his bed was meditation of my works and commandments."

513. This revelation introduces an important Franciscan element into the Seventh Book. Birgitta's links to the Franciscan Order are by no means as simple as Franciscan tradition maintains. Certainly, in this late period, the relationship is very obvious. But for the earlier part of Birgitta's life in Sweden, her choice of confessors seems significant: secular priests and a Cistercian. No doubt there were also Dominican influences: note her family ties to Bl. Ingrid Elofsdotter (cf. Klockars, *Svenska* 27; Lundén, *Svenska* 110–16; Sibilia; and note 6). Here, however, at the beginning of the Seventh Book, the figure of St. Francis, who became Christlike to the point of receiving the stigmata, is a perfect model for Birgitta as she prepares spiritually for her journey to the Holy Land.

514. *Vni persone vigilanti in oracione.* This phrase too is a common formula introducing Birgitta's visions. For the force of *vigilanti*, "awake," see *Life* 9 and note 13.

515. John 3:8.

516. Cf. Hebrews 1:1.

517. Cf. Matthew 6:21; Luke 12:34.

518. *loca.* Cf. note 5.

519. The relics of St. Thomas are chiefly associated with Edessa; and the date (July 3) of their translation to Edessa is now the feast of St. Thomas in the Roman liturgy (cf. Thurston 4: 591).

520. Psalm 113(115):13(5)–15(7).

521. *quem elegi et preelegi.* Birgitta is curiously applying to the apostle words from the responsory *Elegit eam Dominus, et praeelegit eam,* "the Lord chose her and forechose her," traditionally associated with the offices of the Blessed Virgin and of saintly virgins (cf. *Liber responsalis sive antiphonarius,* PL 78: 848).

522. Throughout the printed editions of Birgitta's *Revelations,* there are numerous chapters with addenda entitled "addition" or "declaration." These addenda consist of authentic materials that were either withheld (cf. note 591) from the edition of Alphonsus (cf. note 111) or were inaccessible to him, having been left behind in Sweden. After Prior Peter Olofsson (cf. note 1) returned to Sweden with Birgitta's relics in 1374, he began to deal with these unpublished items. Those that related to existing chapters in Alphonsus's edition were inserted there as "additions" or "declarations." Everything else was collected into a separate appendix, which has come down to us as *Reuelaciones extrauagantes,* "stray revelations." Incorporating Prior Peter's additions into the existing manuscript tradition outside Vadstena involved

many problems, and a final arrangement was only achieved in Ghotan's first printed edition of 1492. See Undhagen, *Book I* 1–4, 26–33.

523. Cf. 2 Samuel 12.

524. Cf. Genesis 12:15.

525. Cf. section 7 of the present chapter.

526. Cf. Matthew 5:14.

527. Cf. John 3:19.

528. This revelation concerning St. Thomas the Apostle further prepares Birgitta for her pilgrimage to Jerusalem. In Assisi, she had seen St. Francis, who is the model of conformity to the pattern of Christ: in his own body he received the wounds of Christ. At Ortona, Birgitta sees St. Thomas, who doubted the resurrection and was invited to touch the wounds of the risen Christ (John 20:24–29). In Jerusalem and Bethlehem, Birgitta will personally see and hear the birth and death scenes of Christ at the original locations. It is worth stressing here that these particular visions are very different from the other revelations about the life of Christ in various books of the *Revelations*—in which Birgitta simply *hears* narrations of these scenes from Christ or his Mother. The Holy Land experiences will be for Birgitta comparable to St. Thomas's palpable experience of the risen Lord. Finally, note that for this whole fourth chapter, there is eyewitness corroboration from Prior Peter in Collijn, *Acta* 495.

529. *Elziarius.* This name has puzzled some past translators. Its most famous bearer was an earlier count of Ariano, St. Elzear de Sabran (d. 1323), one of the notable lay saints of the Middle Ages. St. Elzear's wife, Bl. Delphine de Glandèves, survived him until 1360. St. Elzear was canonized by his own godson, Bl. Urban V (cf. note 110) in 1369 (cf. Thurston 3: 661–62). The Elzear mentioned in this chapter was a later member of the same family. He became a cardinal and was a witness in Birgitta's canonization process (cf. Collijn, *Acta* 245–55).

530. *viriliter.* Cf. note 271.

531. There are references to this revelation in Collijn, *Acta* 251–53, 322–23, and 520.

532. The opening of this allegory is similar to *Gesta Romanorum* 1 and to the legend of St. Barbara (cf. Thurston 4: 487–89).

533. *murorum.*

534. *parietes domus.*

535. *parabola.* Almost always Birgittine Latin prefers the term *similitudo* (cf. note 148).

536. Cf. 1 Chronicles 28:9; Wisdom 1:6.

537. *machinamentis.*

538. *gloriaberis.* Cf. Bergh, *Bok VII* 218.

539. *familie tibi vere necessarie et non propter vanam gloriam super-flue.* Book Seven contains several examples of the "mirror of kings" or "mirror of prelates" genre. Among the detailed and practical advice in these chapters there is always great insistence on the need to avoid superfluity.

540. Cf. Matthew 22:37–39.

541. *attenta meditacione.* Birgitta here combines her themes of "attention" (cf. note 82) and *lectio divina* (cf. note 264). To them she is adding now a specific recommendation of the traditional monastic "devotion to heaven" (cf. Leclercq, *Love* 53–70). Birgitta's devotion is solidly based on the biblical and liturgical traditions that characterize patristic and monastic spirituality. Pourrat (2: 92–98) was quite justified in classifying Birgitta as the last medieval flower of Benedictine spirituality. See also note 938.

542. Cf. note 22.

543. *conuersacionem.* Cf. note 395. The idea of leading the angelic life on this earth is one of the oldest themes in monastic literature (cf. Leclercq, *Love* 57–58).

544. *fabularum inutilium atque proprie persone laudes narrancium.* Does *narrantium* modify *fabularum,* "tales narrating," or is it a substantive, "those narrating"? "Narrations" preserves the ambiguity.

545. *pompam.* The word *pompa,* "procession" or "pomp," quickly acquired diabolic overtones in Early Christian Latin. This connotation has lasted to modern times as a result of the prominence of the words *pompis* or *pompēi* in the renunciation of Satan just before the administration of baptism in both the Roman Rite and the Byzantine.

546. Cf. Matthew 6:20–21; Luke 12:33.

547. Cf. Exodus 20:17; Deuteronomy 5:21.

548. *societate.*

549. *excusare.* Cf. Bergh, *Bok VII* 217.

550. The topic of "discretion" and balance in the ordering of one's life—particularly with regard to penances—is a frequent theme in the Seventh Book.

551. May 25. Cf. Collijn. *Acta* 636.

552. *vos.* Cf. note 99.

553. *vltra mare.* The reference is to her Jerusalem journey.

554. *plene conficiunt.* The word *conficere,* "to confect," is a technical

term of Catholic theology meaning the complete and valid performance of a sacramental rite.

555. There are references to this chapter in Collijn, *Acta* 382; Klockars, *Böckerna* 206. The friar was Peter of Trastevere (Bergh, *Bok VII* 221). Birgitta received this revelation in the church of "St. Mary the Round," i.e., the ancient Pantheon.

556. Cf. Luke 15:20.

557. *pius.* Cf. note 285.

558. Cf. note 550.

559. Cf. *Regula Sancti Francisci* 2.

560. Cf. note 554.

561. In the context of the doctrine of papal infallibility, which protects the official teaching of the pope *ex cathedra*, Catholic theology traditionally has debated the possibility of a pope who, as a private person, publicly falls into personal heresy. If such a theoretical fall occurred, that pope would—in the opinion of some—*ipso facto* lose his papal office and authority. For a detailed modern discussion of this theological issue, see Cardinal Charles Journet, *The Church of the Word Incarnate: An Essay in Speculative Theology,* trans. A. H. C. Downes, 2 vols. (London: Sheed and Ward, 1955) 1: 482–84. Birgitta's remark on this subject was defended by Cardinal Torquemada in the first of his articles (108) relating to the Seventh Book.

562. Cf. Matthew 16:18–19; John 21:15–17.

563. Pope John XXII (1316–1334) is perhaps mentioned in this context because of his controversial opinion about the delayed fate of the dead before the resurrection of the body (cf. Ott 475–76). The point had never been previously defined, and Pope John stubbornly held out against his critics, making a retraction only on 3 December 1334, the eve of his death at the age of ninety. For Peter of Trastevere's personal interest in this pope, see the chapter that immediately follows.

564. "Heretical" in this case would apparently be relevant only if the priests were heretical in their concept of the eucharist in a way that would adversely affect their intention of truly consecrating the Body and Blood of Christ. See Ott 342–44.

565. *super materia de proprio Christi.* It is these words that explain Peter of Trastevere's concern with John XXII and the question of heretic popes and heretic priests. The reference is to the debate over the absolute poverty of Christ and the apostles which raged in the time of John XXII, who eventually condemned the position of those Fran-

ciscans who claimed that absolute poverty was the way in which Christ had lived. The controversy dragged on for many years, much of it full of bitter and intemperate abuse of Pope John. Here, some fifty years later, Birgitta is still addressing these issues. Given the usual discretion of the Birgittine circle, it is not entirely clear whether Friar Peter's questions arise from personal leanings in the direction of the condemned Franciscan Spirituals or from distress at inability to effectively refute their propaganda. On the quarrel, see Bernard McGinn, *Apocalyptic Spirituality* (New York: Paulist Press, 1979), 149–81.

566. This revelation and the preceding one derive from the same visionary experience in the Pantheon (cf. note 555). For additional information, see Collijn, *Acta* 382; Ekwall, *Birgittavita* 134–35; Klockars, *Böckerna* 205–06.

567. Cf. note 54. The *Revelations* are several times very open about the fact that Birgitta's questions sometimes went too far and that her expectations were rebuffed. See note 495.

568. Bergh cites Aemilius Friedberg, ed., *Corpus iuris canonici* (Leipzig, 1879–81) 2: 1229–30.

569. Cf. Psalm 21(22):19.

570. *attende.* Cf. note 82.

571. For another example of Birgittine exegesis (cf. note 59) based on the exact grammatical form of the words, see *Rev.* 7.23.2. Birgitta is also perhaps alluding to the monastic custom of using "our" about items that a secular would instinctively describe as "my."

572. Birgitta here refers to "the Jews" as actual participants in the act of executing Christ. Her words are impossible to reconcile with the wording of Matthew 27:27–37 and Mark 15:16–24, where it is clear that the *stratiōtai*, "soldiers," are the executioners. The verbs in Luke 23:26 and John 19:16–17 are less clear and would seem, from the context, to have "crowd" or "high priests" as their subject. No gospel says "the Jews" did the execution.

573. Cf. Matthew 27:35; Mark 15:24; Luke 23:34; John 19:24.

574. Cf. note 101.

575. For another form of this revelation, see Collijn, *Acta* 95–96 (= *Life* 68) and 633.

576. Cf. note 38.

577. His identity is veiled under the usual Birgittine discretion. Bergh (*Bok VII* 221) suggests "Bernardus de Bosqueto?" and cites S. Baluzius and G. Mollat, *Vitae paparum Avenionensium* (Paris, 1916–1928) 2: 543. This archbishop is not to be confused with "my

bishop" (mentioned in section 6), a frequent Birgittine epithet for Alphonsus of Jaen (cf. Bergh, *Bok VII* 221).

578. Cf. Genesis 16:10–14; 17:24–27.

579. *videbatur multum abhominabilis et exosa.* The words may seem unnecessarily strong to us, but the requirement of abstention from sexual intercourse before any physical contact with the eucharist is a very old idea and certainly not peculiar to Birgitta. The first rubric of the Byzantine Eucharistic Liturgy states that the priest (ordinarily a married man and not always a daily celebrant) ought to abstain (*egkrateuesthai*) from the evening before, and this abstinence is traditionally interpreted as sexual. See the 1950 Roman edition of the *Hieratikon* (89). The more recent Roman editions (1961, 1967) of the Chrysostom Liturgy omit this rubric. See also Casimir Kucharek, *The Byzantine-Slav Liturgy of St. John Chrysostom: Its Origin and Evolution* (Allendale: Alleluia Press, 1971), 214–17. In the West, it was the devout laity who practiced this custom for many centuries (cf. St. Francis de Sales, *Introduction to the Devout Life* 2.20).

580. *nullo modo viuerent in matrimoniali contaminosa delectacione carnali.* The exact force of the rare word *contaminosus* is not clear. Cf. Bergh (*Bok VII* 217), who notes that it is not exactly "contaminated" (which would be open to theological objection), but more like the Italian *contaminoso,* "easily contaminated," or "prone to contamination." Note also the obsolete English "contaminous," meaning "infectious."

581. *sunt maledicti et excommunicati apud Deum et digni carere sacerdotali officio.* It is not clear in what sense Birgitta means "excommunicated." In Latin, *excommunicatio,* "exclusion from the community," can be used in senses far less drastic than "excommunication from the Church" (cf. Deferrari 369); and this milder sense is frequently used in the *Rule of St. Benedict* (cf. Fry 415–36, 514). For *carentia* and *careo* in the sense of "deprivation" or "forfeiture," see Deferrari 132–33. Note the doctrinal precision of Birgitta's words: priests can never be deprived of their sacramental priesthood but only of the "office" or exercise of it (cf. Ott 457).

582. *spiritualiter.* The importance of this qualifying adverb should not be overlooked (cf. note 500). In Birgittine vocabulary, "spiritual" especially refers to the attempt to convey the ineffable by means of imagery, an attempt which can only be partially successful (cf. note 38).

583. St. Gregory the Great seems to have been a favorite writer with Birgitta; see notes 19, 84, 358, and 364.

584. Birgitta's teaching here seems unnecessarily harsh in its support of a disciplinary tradition of the Western Church. Even Cardinal Torquemada's defense (article 109) betrays a certain uneasiness, and he wants it clearly understood that no matter what Birgitta may seem to say, the pope does have power to make changes in this area. Torquemada does agree with Birgitta's opinion about the inadvisability of such a change in the Church of his own times. He felt that such a step would only add to the clerical corruption that was already a flagrant scandal and that if any pope issued such a measure in support of such corruption, he would indeed displease almighty God.

585. The tragic role of Queen Joanna of Naples (1326–1382) in Birgitta's final years is greatly obscured by the scrupulous discretion of the Birgittine circle, owing in part to the fact that Joanna was herself one of the witnesses to Birgitta's sanctity and wrote twice to Pope Urban VI on behalf of Birgitta's canonization (cf. Collijn, *Acta* 54–55). Because of her stormy reign, her marital problems, her adulteries, and her support of the Avignon papacy, Queen Joanna was the recipient of stern criticism from the saint. But her worst offense was her questionable relationship with Birgitta's dying son Charles in the winter of 1371–1372, when Birgitta and her household were waiting in Naples for their spring sea voyage to the Holy Land. Charles died on 12 March 1372, before the pilgrimage had been able to continue, and the thought of his eternal fate preoccupied Birgitta on the outward voyage (cf. *Rev.* 7.13.1–78). In spite of this tragedy, Birgitta stayed with Joanna for several days on her return journey from Jerusalem. After Birgitta's death, Queen Joanna came to grief through her support of the Avignon antipope. She was excommunicated by Urban VI in 1381, and her throne passed to Charles of Durazzo. On 12 May 1382, by order of the new king, she was strangled in her prison bed. See Jørgensen 2: 119–24, 186–90, 234–38, 286–87. Specifically in connection with the present revelation, Bergh cites Collijn, *Acta* 325, 373, 382–83.

586. *permissione mea ex iusticia mea*. Birgitta is referring to her frequent theme of God's respect for the free will of his creatures; see notes 163, 307, 313, 330, and 380.

587. *dyabolus vero nititur, vt homo sequatur desideria sua*. The word *sua*, "his own," is hopelessly ambiguous. Given the confused state of medieval Latin usage of *suus* (cf. note 344), it can be taken to refer here either to "devil" or to "man." Fortunately, in the present sentence, either interpretation makes perfectly good sense.

NOTES

588. *dyabolus priuatus est iusticia, quam videbatur habere.* With these words Birgitta introduces a cautiously worded allusion to another, and far less theologically satisfactory, concept of the devil's claim to "justice" in the sense that he somehow owned the sinful race of Adam and that God had to buy us back by paying the devil with the blood of Christ. Such an idea can be found in not a few of the early fathers as a result of their attempt to explain the biblical concept of "redemption" or "buying-back." This concept of paying the devil was vigorously rejected by such different theologians as St. Gregory Nazianzen, St. Anselm, and St. Thomas Aquinas. See Ott 186 and William A. Jurgens, *The Faith of the Early Fathers,* 3 vols. (Collegeville, Liturgical Press, 1970–1979), passages 508, 928, 1016, 1257, 1675, 2311 and the notes appended to them.

589. *arbitrio.*

590. *fecerat.* Medieval Latin is sometimes idiosyncratic in its use of the pluperfect.

591. *Ego permisi eam exaltare in regnum etc.* Here, as the revelation begins to apply personally to Joanna, the text breaks off with a discreet "etc." Note that the subject of *exaltare,* "to exalt," is not expressed before the fragment ends, and some MSS and the *editio princeps* therefore put *exaltari,* "to be exalted," thus obviating the difficulty. I have used a similar solution to the problem in the English. However, as the reader can immediately see, the revelation does continue with a series of additions (cf. note 522) which presumably contain at least some of the material that had originally been suppressed. For a discussion of the additions here, see Bergh, *Bok VII* 78 and 88.

592. *egerat.* Cf. note 590.

593. *non oneret communitatem suis nouis adinuencionibus.* In Birgittine Latin, *communitas* can mean either the whole "community" or the "common people" (cf. Bergh, *Bok VII* 216, Hollmann, *Extravagantes* 237, Undhagen, *Book I* 446–47). The more restricted meaning is not clearly required here, and, in view of the fact that the whole community is subject to the addressee, I have put "community." *Adinventiones,* "inventions," may be listed among Birgitta's exegetical "hard words." Various forms of the word occur in the Vulgate, very often in the sense of the "schemes" or "connivings" of the wicked, e.g., Deuteronomy 28:20; Psalms 27(28):4; 80(81):13; 105(106):29; etc.

594. Oppression of the poor is traditionally reckoned as one of the sins that "cry to heaven for vengeance"; see Exodus 2:23–24.

595. Cf. *Rev.* 7.27.18–21. For a similar view on tight dresses and daring décolletage, see *Rev.* 7.16.27. For a command against blackening the face in order to travel incognito, see *Rev.* 7.16.12–15.

596. *virga et tribulacio.* Cf. Proverbs 29:15—*virga atque correptio,* "rod and rebuke"—a hendiadys.

597. *sua.* As mentioned in notes 344 and 587, medieval usage of this word is not entirely consistent. But in this context, "her" seems more relevant than "his."

598. Cf. note 146. The first of several brief "items" about "a certain queen" who is, of course, Joanna of Naples.

599. Presumably, Alphonsus of Jaen. See notes 111 and 577 and Bergh, *Bok VII* 221.

600. *Videbatur domina stare in camisia respersa spermate et luto et audita est vox: "Hec est symia odorans fetencia posteriora."* For the proverbially foul bottoms of monkeys, see T.H. White, *The Bestiary: A Book of Beasts* (New York: Capricorn-Putnam's, 1960), 34–35. See also Curtius 538–40.

601. *Item videbatur habere coronam de viminibus respersis stercore humano et luto platearum et sedere nuda in trabe casura.* An extraordinary image expressed in a remarkable display of Birgittine word-music! Cf. Esther 14:2 (= C:13 in NAB).

602. *cogita ingressum tuum et attende finem.* The Jewish image of *halakah,* "walking," to mean "moral behavior." See note 192. Cf. 1 Kings 3:7.

603. *consiliarii.* This could also be "counselors"; but, in light of the use of the same word in section 11 of this revelation, the reference there and here would seem to be to members of the queen's council.

604. *Ethiopes.* Cf. note 84.

605. For sections 28–29, Bergh refers to chapters 16 and 17 of the Apocalypse; he also cites I. Andersson, *Källstudier till Sveriges historia 1230–1436* (Lund: 1928), 139.

606. *in consolacionem.* Cf. note 22.

607. *fecerat.* Cf. notes 590 and 592. This use of the pluperfect seems to be a particular characteristic of the present revelation.

608. *De domino Gomecio.* Gomez Garcias de Albornoz, nephew of Cardinal Giles de Albornoz, held various important posts in the administration of the Papal States and knew Birgitta well during her years in Italy. He died as a senator in Rome in 1377. Cf. note 53. Concerning this revelation, see Collijn, *Acta* 381–82.

609. Anthony of Carleto, a merchant in Naples, entered the service of Queen Joanna and was a good friend of Birgitta. See Collijn, *Acta* 335, 390–91, 544, 652.

610. Bernard de Rodez, Archbishop of Naples from 1368 until his death in 1379. See Collijn, *Acta* 325, 382–83, 653.

611. Such statements play an important part in the negative formulations of Birgitta's theme of "attention": the words and deeds of Christ (cf. Acts 1:1) are being neglected and forgotten. See note 82.

612. *in sedibus infernalibus perpetuo cruciandos.* The Latin uses *sedes,* "seat," in several interrelated senses: "place," "chair," "episcopal see." These damned prelates include bishops who have exchanged their earthly "thrones" or "sees" for new and unspeakable ones in hell. For *sedis infernae,* "of the infernal region," see Valerius Maximus, *Facta et dicta memorabilia* 2.6.8.

613. From here to the end of this revelation, Christ speaks as if he were Birgitta. She is to relay these dictated words to Bernard without saying that they have a source outside herself.

614. *inveneritis.* In speaking to the archbishop, Birgitta always uses the formal plural of Medieval Latin.

615. *Quod siue hoc fecerint propter [negligenciam siue propter] aliorum supplicacionem siue propter negligenciam et desidiam seu propter timorem.* Birgitta's lists of "causes" often get her into trouble (cf. notes 342 and 344). Here there is a textual problem. Some MSS—but not Ghotan's *editio princeps*—insert the bracketed words *negligenciam siue propter* and then repeat *propter negligenciam* a few words later. Bergh prints the addition in brackets as being doubtful. It has seemed better to omit the repetition in this translation. For further discussion, see Bergh, *Bok VII* 101.

616. Cf. Genesis 19:1–29.

617. Cf. Matthew 26:48–49; Mark 14:44–45; Luke 22:47–48. The warning example of Judas is traditionally associated with the kiss of peace before communion in the Roman Mass. The Byzantine Liturgy explicitly recalls his false kiss by the regular use of the troparion *Tou deipnou sou,* "Of your supper," before or during communion.

618. Cf. Apocalypse 14:4.

619. *pompa.* Cf. note 545.

620. Cf. Deuteronomy 8:12–14, which contains a very succinct summary of Birgitta's theme of "attention" (cf. notes 82 and 611).

621. *paterfamilias.* Birgitta uses the formal term of Roman law—lit-

erally "father of a household"—which occurs in the Vulgate at Matthew 20:1; 21:33; Luke 12:39; 14:21.

622. *tria paria.*

623. *hylari mente.* Cf. Sirach 35:11; Romans 12:8; 2 Corinthians 8:7. See also Proverbs 22:8 in the Septuagint.

624. The theme of Christ's poverty has already been prominently mentioned in *Rev.* 7.8.3–8.

625. Cf. *Rev.* 7.5.39.

626. *scio personam.* Cf. 2 Corinthians 12:2.

627. *demones quasi Ethiopes.* Cf. note 500 and notes 84 and 604.

628. *ex pompa.* Cf. notes 545 and 619.

629. This "etc." is given by the best MSS but is omitted in the Ghotan *editio princeps.*

630. *corrigant parrochianos suos et pro manifestis peccatis eos corripiant in casibus ad eos pertinentibus, vt melius possint viuere.* Medieval Latin is not always careful about the distinction between *eos* "them" and *se* "themselves" (cf. notes 344, 587, and 597). This sentence is unclear in its use of *eos*, "them," which seems to mean the parishioners with *corripiant*, "rebuke," and then the priests with *pertinentibus*, "pertaining." The subject of *possint*, "be able," could arguably be either the priests or the parishioners, but the latter group would seem to be the more likely.

631. *vestram beniuolam respiciet voluntatem.* Cf. note 126.

632. The wayward Charles (cf. note 585) died repentant on 12 March 1372. The exact date of his birth is not known, but both he and Queen Joanna would have been in their later forties. Charles had already been coughing up blood when he arrived in Rome to join Birgitta's pilgrimage. Therefore, his death was not entirely without forewarning; but at the deathbed, the wake, and the funeral, Birgitta's extreme self-control caused not a little comment. See Collijn, *Acta* 249, 370–71, 436.

633. Specifically concerning this revelation, see Collijn, *Acta* 329, 386, 533.

634. Although Mary is here explicitly speaking of the death of Charles under the imagery of childbirth, there is perhaps in Birgitta's mind some connection with the incident related in *Life* 20–21. Cf. note 26.

635. Cf. note 131.

636. *vt carnalem amorem non sic in memoria haberet.* No doubt

Charles' carnal love for Joanna is uppermost in Birgitta's mind, but the situation is being treated with true Birgittine discretion.

637. *in illo arto spacio.* Mary is still describing the death under the image of human childbirth. Cf. note 634.

638. *et ne Deum in morte obliuisceretur.* An important aspect of Birgitta's theme of *attentio,* in which we must persevere until the end. Cf. notes 82, 312, and 611. On "forgetting," see note 253.

639. *seriose.* Cf. Bergh, *Bok VII* 219. See also note 140.

640. *similitudine corporali.*

641. *pro tribunali.* A common Roman legal idiom indicating presence on the *tribunal* (dais) in an official capacity. Cf. John 19:13 and Acts 25:6 and 17.

642. The whole description in 12 and 13 reflects the common medieval portrayal of the disembodied soul as a small human figure. Here the soul is an infant (cf. note 294) and cannot speak in its own defense; it is blind because it has not yet been judged worthy of the sight of God (cf. note 61). The final words, however, reject the common, but crude, depiction of angels and demons engaged in a tug-of-war over the helpless soul.

643. The theme of Mary's power over the devil is recounted in many medieval legends, most memorably that of Theophilus, the cleric who had sold his soul (Ryan 528–29; Thurston 1: 247–48). Barely a century after Birgitta's death, this theme received a most startling expression from François Villon ("Ballade pour prier Notre-Dame" 2): *Emperière des infernaux palus,* "Empress of the swamps of hell."

644. In the ancient world, such reverence was felt for a dying person's last breath that the next-of-kin would often attempt to catch it into their own mouths rather than see it lost in the open air. Such a sentiment was common to both pagans (cf. Vergil, *Aeneid* 4.684–85; Ovid, *Metamorphoses* 12.424–25) and Christians (cf. St. Ambrose, *De excessu fratris sui Satyri* 1.19). In the ancient languages, the words for "wind," "breath," "soul," and "spirit" tend to overlap. Thus this image of the last breath easily became a "corporeal likeness" of the immaterial soul's departure from the body. Cf. Blindheim, plate 20; Broby-Johansen 95, 173, and 202.

645. In 20 and 21, two points deserve notice. First, that contemplation of Mary properly leads to great love for God. And, second, that this soul states his love of Mary in the exaggerated tradition of courtly love, which leads him to the expression of a theological impossibility:

namely, that God could ever "trade off" (*in permutacionem*, "in exchange") Mary's glory against her lover's voluntary self-damnation. Cf. Birgitta's own prayer in *Rev.* 7.1.2–3.

646. In article 110, Cardinal Torquemada replied to criticism of this passage by pointing out that Birgitta means "wisdom" in the sense of *cognitio naturalis*, "natural knowledge," and that "written" here is simply a metaphor for "retained in the mind" comparable to the image in Jeremiah 31:33.

647. *vt ei Deus misereri dignaretur, ne ab ipso se elongaret.* The original is not absolutely clear, but the meaning seems to be that God might have mercy on the man in order that the man might not distance himself from God. However, in light of the confusing usage of *se*, the sentence could conceivably be read to mean that God might have mercy and that God himself might not withdraw.

648. In spite of the very different wording, there seems to be an echo here of Colossians 2:14. On the motif of the devil's loss of his "writings," see Klockars, *Böckerna* 175, which cites a miracle of St. Augustine in the Old Swedish *Golden Legend* (Jansson 650; Ryan 499) and *Rev.* 6.39. See also Broby-Johansen 189.

649. *contricionem optinuit.*

650. *scripturis.* These "writings" are apparently the "penances" that are "prescribed" before absolution by one's confessor as part of the sacrament of reconciliation. It was the "prescription" of such penances that seems to have given rise to our older terminology for confession: "shrift," "shrive," etc. The devil mentions these writings, or penances, here precisely because he claims that the soul is guilty of neglecting to perform them.

651. There is a serious textual problem here in the form of an anacoluthon, a grammatical breakdown. The text, as transmitted in most MSS reads: ". . . but did not take care to torture him. . . ." Several MSS and the first edition have tried to emend the text by additions or omissions, but the problem remains. The words here placed in square brackets are my own suggestion of a way to make sense of the text. For further discussion, see Bergh, *Bok VII* 102–05. Note that this is the only reply of the devil that is given in the accusative-with-infinitive construction—a factor that might figure in the cause of the problem.

652. *optinuit voluntatem.* It was, in fact, while attempting to carry out this intended pilgrimage, that Charles died in Naples.

653. *Istam enim voluntatem accepit Deus pro effectu.* Cf. notes 126 and 631.

654. Cf. Matthew 7:8; Luke 11:10.

655. Cf. Psalm 117(118):19.

656. Cf. notes 22, 542, and 606.

657. *caduca bona commutant in eternales diuicias.*

658. *rugiens.* Cf. 1 Peter 5:8, a traditional reading at compline in the Roman Rite.

659. *filius lacrimarum.* Cf. note 80.

660. *O, quam maledicta est illa scrofa seu porca mater eius.*

661. This long chapter, with its setting outside earthly space and time, has provided the Seventh Book with an effective transition from the sad scene at the court of Naples to the wonderful visions in the Holy Land. On the way to Jerusalem, Birgitta's chief thought has been for the eternal salvation of her recently deceased son. At this point the *Revelations* make no reference to the earthly incidents of her journey, not even to the disastrous shipwreck just before her landing at Jaffa. (Cf. Collijn, *Acta* 205 and 371–72.)

662. Birgitta arrived in Jerusalem on Thursday, 11 May 1372, the octave of Ascension Day. (Cf. Andersson, *Holy Land* 30.) On the problems of exactly dating the events in chapters 14 and 15, see Ekwall, *Birgittavita* 79, note 6.

663. Cf. note 662. The *editio princeps* omitted the word "octave." See also Collijn, *Acta* 385.

664. *seriose.* Cf. notes 140 and 639.

665. Cf. note 19. Note that the precise cause of Birgitta's tears is not explicitly stated. They are simply juxtaposed with the vision of Christ's passion. On the propriety of weeping over the passion, tradition provides both cautions and examples (Hausherr, *Penthos* 6, 50). Birgitta's approach to the passion is not entirely unaffected by the late medieval tendency, in the West, to let feelings of sympathy and grief predominate over the equally legitimate reactions of wonder, praise, and thanksgiving. In the words of Jean Guitton (*The Virgin Mary*, trans. A. Gordon Smith [New York: Kenedy, 1952], 45):

> Fundamentally, it must be remembered, Christ's Passion consisted less in the agonies he endured than in his submitting to them in a spirit of perfect obedience to his Father. This helps us to understand how mother and Son were united at that *Hour.*

666. On the rarity of such "seeing," cf. notes 60 and 528.

667. *ductum per Iudeos ad crucifigendum.* Cf. note 572. See also Raymond E. Brown, S.S., *A Crucified Christ in Holy Week: Essays on the Four Gospel Passion Narratives* (Collegeville: Liturgical Press, 1986),

NOTES

13–16, 28–29, 38–39, 53–54, 62–63. On Birgitta's references to the Jews, see also notes 237 and 363.

668. *Attende tu.* At this climactic moment, we again encounter the great theme of "attention" (cf. notes 82, 611, and 617). The *foramine petre*, "hole in the rock," mentioned was an actual hole venerated in the shrine on Calvary (cf. Andersson, *Holy Land* 43).

669. *a Iudeis.* Cf. note 667.

670. Although unusual in modern times, the depiction of Christ being crucified in a standing position has been known in Byzantine art since the ninth century. It often occurs in Italian works of the thirteenth and fourteenth centuries. (Cf. Schiller, *Iconography* 2: 86–88; Kontoglou 1:216.) In the two earlier crucifixion revelations—in which Birgitta merely *hears* Mary's narration of the passion—the standing posture is clearly described in *Rev.* 4.70 and is probably, but less clearly, presupposed in *Rev.* 1.10.22–23. See Anker 2: plate 156.

671. Cf. Isaiah 53:7 and Jeremiah 11:19.

672. *per illam partem, qua os solidius erat.* This detail is usually associated, in modern times, with knowledge of the famous relic of Christ's reputed shroud with its mysteriously imprinted images of a crucified man. This relic is now preserved in Turin, Italy; but, in Birgitta's time, it was in France. There is no mention of this relic in Birgitta's writings; and there is no reason to suppose that she had heard of its relatively recent emergence in France. This detail about the place of the nails could simply be the result of commonsense reflection on the anatomical structure of the human hand. Birgitta, rather than the shroud, is more likely to be the source, in the early seventeenth century, for this unusual placement of the nails in the work of various Counter-Reformation artists, especially in the paintings of Rubens and his school and in the ivory crucifixes of Georg Petel (cf. Schiller, *Iconography* 2: 149, 229–30; illus. 494, 814).

673. *posita fuit vna tibia eius super aliam et sic iunctos pedes affixerunt in cruce duobus clauis.* Birgitta's description of the nailing of Christ's feet has caused much confusion. In *Rev.* 1.10.23, she simply says *dexterum pedem crucifixerunt et super hunc sinistrum duobus clauis,* "the right foot they crucified and, over it, the left with two nails." In *Rev.* 4.70, the wording is more difficult: *Et pedes similiter ad foramina sua distenduntur, cancellatique et quasi infra a tybijs distincti, duobus clauis ad Crucis stipitem per solidum os, sicut et manus erant, configuntur,* "and the feet, likewise, are stretched to their holes and having been arranged like latticework and, as it were, distinguished below from the shins,

they are affixed with two nails to the upright of the cross through the solid bone, just as the hands were." The difficulty of visualizing these words has given rise to a rare and rather desperate solution in what might be hesitatingly termed "Birgittine" crucifixes. In them, it is the shins (and not the feet) that are "arranged like latticework" in such a way that the ankles are crossed like an *x* and the two feet are nailed separately on the wrong side of each other. Examples of this extraordinary iconography can be found as early as the fifteenth century (Andersson, *Holy Land* 124, illus. 33B; 126), and as recently as the turn of this century (e.g., the Neo-Gothic window of the crucifixion in the Dominican Church in New Haven, Connecticut). In fact, it seems to me that Birgitta was not thinking of anything quite so different from the traditional idea of the crucifix. I believe that she simply wanted to make two points: 1) that one foot was on top of the other and 2) that two nails were used.

674. Birgitta is here reflecting the highly controversial late medieval devotion toward our Lady's alleged *spasmus* or "swoon." Such devotion went into abrupt decline after 1503, when Cardinal Cajetan published a negative analysis of this unscriptural motif, in consequence of which Pope Julius II refused to issue indulgences for the devotion. Later theologians openly termed the idea of the "swoon" as "akin to error" (Maldonatus) and "rash, scandalous, and dangerous" (Medina). There is no doubt that it accords poorly with the testimony of John 19:25–26. See Gabriel M. Roschini, O.S.M., *Mariologia*, 2nd ed. (Rome: Belardetti, 1948) II.2: 208–13; Charles Journet, "The Swoon," *The Mary Book*, ed. Frank J. Sheed (New York: Sheed and Ward, 1951), 179–80. It is interesting to note that no objections were raised on this point in Torquemada's time. Iconographically, the motif is much older than Birgitta (cf. Schiller 2:11, 152–53). One example can be dated to 1272 in Armenia (cf. Bezalel Narkiss, et al., *Armenian Art Treasures of Jerusalem* [New Rochelle: Caratzas, 1979], 63). Orthodox iconography still accepts it in a restrained form: the holy women support Mary lest she fall (Kontoglou 1:176). It is precisely in such a restrained Byzantine form that Birgitta returns to this motif in sections 16 and 25 of this revelation.

675. *Iohannes et alie sorores eius.* Birgitta is offering an interpretation of the exegetical difficulty of the number of women listed and the meaning of "sister" in John 19:25. See Raymond E. Brown, S.S., *The Gospel according to John (XIII–XXI)*, The Anchor Bible 29A (Garden City: Doubleday, 1970), 904–06.

676. Cf. Luke 2:35 and note 502.

677. Cf. notes 674, 675, and 676.

678. Cf. John 19:26–27.

679. Cf. Psalm 37(38):3; 44(45):6; Lamentations 3:12–13.

680. Cf. Psalm 21(22):2; Matthew 27:46; Mark 15:34.

681. Cf. Psalm 30(31):6; Luke 23:46.

682. Cf. Matthew 27:50. See notes 131 and 635. The design of Book Seven revolves around the central placement of chapters 13 and 15; and we are meant to reflect upon the juxtaposition of the death of the repentant son of Birgitta and the death of the innocent Son of Mary. We will encounter Matthew 27:50 again—with overtones of Psalm 103(104):30—in the moment of the Christ-like death of Birgitta herself (*Rev.* 7.31.13).

683. Cf. note 674.

684. As in the case of the nailing of the feet (cf. note 673), Birgitta's words in sections 26 and 27 are hard to visualize. The chief confusion seems to come from *retraxerunt*, "retracted." In the context of what follows, it seems at first as if she means that Christ's arms "pulled down" upon the nails after his death. But she does say "his *hands* retracted," that is to say, they were no longer visibly pulling the body upward because they had relaxed in death and "were now more extended than before." The chief support of the body now appeared to be its lowest point: the nailed feet.

685. The Synoptics record that various groups—but not "the Jews" —mock the crucified Christ *before* his death. (John says nothing about this.) But in all four gospels, the death of Christ becomes a moment of signs and wonders, of faith and repentance. Luke 23:48 even says: "And all the multitude of them that were come together to that sight, and saw the things that were done, returned striking their breasts." In the gospels, no mockery is spoken of the dead Christ or of his Mother. Here Birgitta's own vivid imagination and the corrupting legacy of medieval anti-Semitism have, perhaps unintentionally, combined with very regrettable results. See note 667 and the references given there.

686. Cf. John 19:31–37. Here too, in her effort to heighten our appreciation of Christ's mistreatment at the hands of cruel sinners, Birgitta departs from the literal sense of John. There the opening of Christ's side is presented simply as a *coup de grâce*, followed by the wonderful flow of blood and water and the testimony of the eyewitness. Here Birgitta has contaminated the incident with the figure of the man who ran and filled a sponge with vinegar and held it up on a reed that

Christ might drink (cf. Matthew 27:48; Mark 15:36). She says that the piercing was done, not as a *coup de grâce*, but *cum furia maxima ... vehementer et valide*, "with great fury . . . with . . . violence and force." She speaks of its aftermath in purely human and pathetic terms, never mentioning the flow of water or the testimony of the eyewitness.

687. Cf. Luke 2:35. See also notes 502 and 676. For the exegetical background and other possibilities, see Raymond E. Brown, S.S., *The Birth of the Messiah: A Commentary on the Infancy Narratives in Matthew and Luke* (Garden City: Image-Doubleday, 1979), 441, 460–66; and Raymond E. Brown, S.S., et al., *Mary in the New Testament: A Collaborative Assessment by Protestant and Roman Catholic Scholars* (Philadelphia: Fortress Press; New York: Paulist Press, 1978), 154–57. See also Blindheim, plate 13.

688. *pie.* The familiar representation of this scene of Mary holding the dead Christ is traditionally called in English "Our Lady of Pity." See Andersson, *Holy Land,* 127–34.

689. In sections 32–34, the words *reclinauit eum ... inuoluit eum,* "she laid him . . . she wrapped him," repeat, in reverse order, the words of Luke 2:7, describing Mary's actions at the birth of her Son. See *Rev.* 7.21.17–22.

690. Here, at the center of Book Seven, we find one more forceful reiteration of Birgitta's great theme of "attention." The fact that kings are cited as the worst offenders in this regard explains the following transition to a series of revelations concerned with the kingdom of Cyprus, which Birgitta had visited on her way to Jerusalem.

691. Cf. Psalm 21(22):19; Matthew 27:35; Mark 15:24; Luke 23:34; John 19:23–24.

692. Cf. note 522. In this 16th chapter, we have reached May of 1372, the time of Birgitta's arrival in Jerusalem. Now these "additions" suddenly carry us back to the preceding April when Birgitta's pilgrim ship made a stop at the island of Cyprus. The original chronological pattern of Book Seven will resume with chapter 17. The chief reason for the preoccupation with Cyprus at this point in Book Seven is that while on the island, Birgitta was asked for advice on a number of pressing issues. From chapter 18 on, we will be reading the series of answers in the order that they were revealed to Birgitta in the Holy Land. As we learn from the rubric to chapter 19, Birgitta returned to Cyprus in the late summer and early fall of 1372 and delivered her messages.

693. This rubric apparently applies to the whole "addition" from

section 5 to section 37. Birgitta landed in Famagusta on 14 April 1372 (Andersson, *Holy Land* 25). For further comments on the various parts of this 16th chapter, see Bergh, *Bok VII* 79.

694. Cf. Genesis 18:20–19:29.

695. Duke John of Antioch allegedly conspired in the death of his brother King Peter I of Cyprus in 1369. They were members of the Lusignan family, to whom the island had been granted by King Richard the Lion-Hearted. (See Bergh, *Bok VII* 221; Jørgensen 2: 239–40.) It was to an unidentified member of this family that St. Thomas Aquinas addressed his unfinished *De regno, ad regem Cypri*. The death of Peter I was sufficiently famous to be included, with some inaccuracy, in Chaucer's *Canterbury Tales* ("The Monk's Tale" VII.2391–98; Benson 247, 933.)

696. *Non leuius plorat, qui post flet, quam qui plorabat ante.* The source of this proverb is not identified. It can be understood in more than one relevant way: either "grief delayed is not grief eliminated," or "grief in this world is not as serious as grief in the next."

697. Simon, a Dominican friar (Bergh, *Bok VII* 221). In his testimony for Birgitta's canonization process (Collijn, *Acta* 429–31), Charles Malocello of Genoa testified that there was:

> . . . a certain Brother Simon of the Order of Friars Preachers, who said—among other things—about the said Lady Birgitta: "The woman's mind is affected; for never has it been heard from of old that, since Christ appeared and spoke to Moses face to face, he visibly appeared to any living person and said such things as Christ said to her. Do not believe those things in any way, for it is an act of foolishness to believe such things."

This confrontation with Simon took place on Birgitta's return journey. In the canonization process, Magnus Petersson (274–75), St. Katharine (334–35), Alphonsus Pecha (390), and Prior Peter (544) testified that in dealing with this deceitful Simon, Birgitta perceived the sulphurous stench described in *Life* 71–72. Alphonsus (390) notes that Simon was "a great theologian and astronomer, knowing the planets and the stars but not himself."

698. *assumpciones et deiecciones.* Cf. Lamentations 2:14, *viderunt autem tibi adsumptiones falsas et eiectiones,* "they, however, have seen for you assumptions false and ejections." Birgitta may have first noticed this exegetical curiosity in the second lesson of the medieval office of Tenebrae on Good Friday. In fact, Birgitta is quoting only certain

words of the biblical text; and it is difficult to say whether *deiecciones*—the unanimous reading of the Birgitta MSS—is a deliberate alteration or an inadvertent misspelling. Birgitta apparently knew that these words were a stock phrase for the positive and negative utterance of false prophecy. The traditional rendering by Challoner is: "revelations and banishments."

699. *si iste frater sedisset in conuentu.* "Sitting" is a technical term of monastic contemplation, based on a mystical interpretation of Lamentations 3:28 and Luke 10:39 (cf. Leclercq, *Otia* 135–36). "Convent," although usually restricted in Modern English to houses of religious women, is traditionally also applied to the houses of men, especially friars, in this case, the Dominicans.

700. The plural is used to include Birgitta's companions. So too, in sections 14 and 15, the imperatives are plural.

701. Cf. Genesis 12:10–20; 20:1–18.

702. Alphonsus Pecha (cf. Bergh, *Bok VII* 221). See note 111.

703. The Mother of God.

704. Queen Eleanor, the widow of the murdered Peter I (cf. note 695) and the regent for her young son, King Peter II. (Cf. Bergh, *Bok VII* 221.)

705. Aragon, in Spain (cf. Jørgensen 2: 240).

706. *communitas.* See note 593.

707. Cf. note 695.

708. *sexto, quod deponat.* Birgitta phrases this point with diplomatic ambiguity, and thus it is not clear whether the queen is being told to "lay aside" something that she herself is doing or to "put an end to" things being done by others. For the latter, post-classical sense of *deponere*, see the Vulgate: Exodus 15:7.

709. Reading the lives of the saints was a favorite activity with Birgitta (cf. *Life* 18). Here she recommends it to the queen as a way to develop that attention to divine things that is an essential part of all prayer.

710. Peter II of Cyprus (cf. note 704).

711. Birgitta's contemporary, Giovanni Boccaccio, used Cypriote misgovernment and brigandage as the premise for *Decameron* 1.9. On this passage, Bergh (*Bok VII* 172) cites I. Andersson, *Källstudier till Sveriges historia 1230–1436* (Lund: 1928), 132.

712. Cf. Ecclesiastes 10:16. In both the Hebrew and the Latin, the word here translated "child" (*puer*) can also mean "servant."

713. Cf. Ezekiel 18:20.

714. Concerning this revelation, see Collijn, *Acta* 266 and 326.

715. *ita quod sitis cor vnum.* Cf. Acts 4:32. (Note the variant reading of the Clementine Vulgate.)

716. Birgitta is perhaps thinking of the Florentine saint, John Gualbert, who encountered the murderer of his only brother and pardoned him for the sake of the passion of Christ (cf. Thurston 3: 81–82).

717. *caritatis visceribus.* Cf. Philippians 2:1.

718. Peter II. Cf. note 704.

719. Cf. note 695.

720. A.D. 1372. By a curious coincidence, Birgitta was canonized on 7 October 1391; and for many centuries her memorial was celebrated on October 8. In the Roman calendar, since 1969, her memorial has been restored to the correct and original date, July 23, the day of her death in 1373.

721. Concerning this revelation see Collijn, *Acta* 100, 266, 326, 372–73, 383, 430, 636.

722. Cf. notes 13 and 514.

723. Cf. note 490.

724. Cf. Matthew 5:2.

725. *inferno.* Literally, "the underworld." The term "hell" traditionally includes the "limbo of the fathers," where the souls of the just awaited the coming of Christ and his reopening of paradise. After Christ's death, the saved no longer experience any temporary stay in this "hell," as *Rev.* 7.19.7 mentions. Of course, Christ's death has also enabled all of the saved to escape "hell" in the strict sense. Cf. Ott 191–92, 476.

726. Birgitta is here paraphrasing a famous passage from Denis the Pseudo-Areopagite (cf. note 31; Luibheid 280) on the passion of Christ and found in his *Letter* 8.6 (P.G. 3: 1100), in which Jesus appears to a man named Carpus and says: ". . . I am ready to suffer even again for the sake of humans being saved anew. . . ."

727. *infernum.* Here "hell" is used in the strict sense of the place of eternal punishment for those who die unrepentant in personal serious sin (cf. Ott 479–82).

728. *conqueritur.* The legal overtones of a complaint are obvious, but one should also note the importance of "complaint" as a part of the vocabulary of Latin love poetry from at least the time of Catullus and on throughout the Middle Ages. The amatory nature of Christ's "complaint" is emphasized in two ways. First, the complaint is made by *caritas*, "charity," the *agapē* of the Greek New Testament. The more

usual medieval procedure was to describe a debate between "justice" and "mercy." Second, the complaint is addressed to the people of Cyprus collectively, with substantives and verbs in the singular, *quasi ad vnam personam*, "as if to one person." These singular forms will be apparent in the English in only a few places.

729. *michi aduersarie.* On the significance of the singular, see note 728.

730. *ausculta et attende diligenter.* Once again the theme of "attention" is given great prominence.

731. *disposui.* Cf. Luke 22:29–30.

732. *sicut pupillam oculi.* Cf. Deuteronomy 32:10; Psalm 16(17):8. The psalm-verse was traditionally associated with the night office of compline.

733. For the thought, see Apocalypse 3:16.

734. *quam irracionabilia animalia in commixtione sua.*

735. Cf. John 14:10.

736. Cf. notes 241 and 338.

737. Cf. John 5:37; 8:18.

738. For the thought, see Isaiah 53:9; 1 Peter 2:22.

739. The Latin *lucifer*, "light-bringer," is an epithet for the morning star. Its application to Satan derives from a mystical interpretation of Isaiah 14:12. Cf. Luke 10:18; Apocalypse 8:10; 9:1; 12:7–9. In Latin, *lucifer* is not necessarily satanic; on Easter night, in the *Exsultet*, the Roman liturgy applies the title to Christ. Cf. 2 Peter 1:19.

740. Cf. Matthew 26:15.

741. Cf. Numbers 25:6–15; 1 Maccabees 2:26. Note that these texts say nothing explicit about Zimri's eternal fate.

742. *te.* Cf. note 729.

743. Cf. Luke 15:4–6.

744. Cf. note 22.

745. Birgitta now begins to give vent to her very strong feelings on the subject of the historical alienation of the Western and Eastern Rites of the Church.

746. *qui sciunt.* Although stated in the indicative rather than the subjunctive, this verb does significantly qualify the strong words that follow.

747. Harsh though they sound, Birgitta so qualifies her words that they are technically defensible: those who know that a thing is God's will, and, for inadequate reasons, do not obey him are indeed unworthy of pardon and mercy. But Birgitta immediately goes on to state that in

her opinion there are Greeks who do *not* know such things and who do *not* act out of such inadequate motives. They are "following their conscience" and "live piously."

748. *se humiliter subiugarent.* Birgitta's insistence on the verb *subiugare*, "subjugate," hardly makes union with Rome seem very attractive.

749. *donec ipsi cum vera humilitate et caritate ecclesie et fidei Romane se deuote subiecerint, eiusdem ecclesie sacris constitucionibus et ritibus se totaliter conformando.* If, in fact, Birgitta is calling for the abandonment of the Eastern Rites, such a position is entirely out of harmony with the mind of the Roman Church in modern times (cf. the decree *Orientalium Ecclesiarum;* Abbott 373–86). However, in early fifteenth-century documents related to proposals for reunion with Constantinople, *ritus* usually means "faith," and only rarely "rites" in the narrower sense. Cf. Joseph Gill, S.J., *Eugenius IV: Pope of Christian Union* (Westminster, MD: Newman Press, 1961) 182–84. On the "Greek" section of this revelation, see also Collijn, *Acta 525.*

750. Martin of Aragon (cf. Bergh, *Bok VII 222).*

751. Once again Birgitta's editors are publishing their material in the order in which her revelations were *received,* rather than following the chronological sequence in which her petitioners presented their problems.

752. With this revelation we return to the Franciscan atmosphere of the earlier part of Book Seven, especially chapters 3, 7, and 8. See Collijn, *Acta* 269, 383–84, and 525, where we learn that Martin was Queen Eleanor's secretary and that after hearing this revelation he sold his books and other personal property and eventually became the guardian of Bethlehem. See also Klockars, *Böckerna* 204–05.

753. St. Francis of Assisi (cf. *Rev.* 7.3.1–7).

754. *carnis viciosa delectacione.*

755. *a Spiritu meo fuit sibi aspiratum.*

756. Bergh (*Bok VII* 183) cites *Speculum perfectionis* 1.8.

757. *aspiracione.*

758. *hostis antiquus.* Cf. Matthew 13:39; Apocalypse 12:9; 20:2.

759. Cf. Luke 22:3; John 13:2, 27.

760. *Aduersarius.* It is the detail of this symbolic name that leads me to suppose that this friar is an allegorical figure, rather than some historical individual such as the notorious Brother Elias. See Klockars, *Böckerna* 205.

761. *racionabili.* This is the traditional Latin translation of the Greek New Testament's *logikos,* "rational," "spiritual," etc. (Cf. Romans 12:1

and 1 Peter 2:2, and also the epiclesis *Quam oblationem* of the Roman Canon.) The word refers especially to the enrichment and sanctification of an action by means of the rational doer's accompanying conscious intention and spiritual state of mind.

762. Bergh (*Bok VII* 185) cites *Regula II Fratrum Minorum* 3.

763. Bergh (*Bok VII* 185) cites *Regula II Fratrum Minorum* 4.

764. *artes liberales et scienciam.* Cf. *Rev.* 7.5.10.

765. Cf. Matthew 13:24–30, 37–43, 47–50.

766. *exempla vilia et ribaldica.* As a technical literary term, *exemplum* means "an exemplary story"—especially the type of moral tale so often found in the popular sermons of the medieval friars. One cannot help but wonder if Birgitta is not specifically thinking of the "vile and ribald" tales about the friars told by her contemporary, Giovanni Boccaccio, for whom alone she spares but five short lines at the bottom of her page (fol. 232r) in Hartmann Schedel's *Nuremberg Chronicle.*

767. *metalla.* This word can also mean "mines."

768. In mid-August of 1372 (cf. Andersson, *Holy Land* 79).

769. Cf. *Rev.* 7.1.6. On "last," see note 481.

770. This is undoubtedly the most famous chapter that Birgitta ever wrote and the most important for its lasting influence on the iconography of Christ's nativity. See Collijn, *Acta* 96, 270, 328, 385, 619, 633, 636. Klockars (*Böckerna* 227) detects in it the influence of the anonymous *Meditationes vitae Christi.* Of the numerous iconographic commentaries on this chapter, note: Andersson, *Holy Land* 79–81, 110–17; Broby-Johansen 80; Butkovitch 28–34, 71–73; Cornell 1–45; Jørgensen 2: 332; Kontoglou 1: 156–58; Kup, *Bene veneris* 5–11; Kup, *Christmas* 39; Schiller 1: 78–80.

771. Again it must be emphasized how very rarely Birgitta actually claims to have "seen" events from the life of Christ. Many representations of Birgitta's vision of the nativity include her own figure kneeling off to one side.

772. *senex quidam honestissimus.* Apparently out of a peculiar notion of propriety, St. Joseph has often been portrayed as a very old man, without any scriptural warrant for this detail. Bergh (*Bok VII*) here cites the apocryphal *Historia Iosephi* 4.

773. *et secum habebant ambo vnum bouem et asinum.* Note the unclassical syntax of *ambo*, "both." On the origins of the unscriptural ox and ass, see note 230 and Schiller 1: 58–61.

774. *speluncam.* The place of the nativity has been spoken of as a cave since the second century (cf. Justin, *Dialogus cum Tryphone* 78.5).

775. This lighted candle—often shown still in Joseph's own hand—is perhaps the most distinctive and enduring "Birgittine" detail in later nativity scenes.

776. Cf. Exodus 3:5 and Joshua 5:16.

777. *spatulas*. A number of MSS have the classical synonym *scapulas*. In Medieval Latin, the colorful *spatula* often weakens into "shoulder" (cf. Arsène Darmesteter, *La vie des mots: Étudiée dans leurs significations* [Paris: Delagrave, n.d.], 164). The detail of Mary's uncovered hair will remain very popular; but her simple clothing, and especially its white color, will often be ignored by later artists.

778. Cf. John 20:7. This is the first of a number of details about the swaddling of Christ that seem to be deliberate echoes of the scenes of his burial and resurrection (cf. note 689). Such echoes had already appeared in art (cf. Schiller 1: 75).

779. *tunc virgo genuflexa est*. This kneeling is the most revolutionary and indispensable detail of the "Birgittine" nativity scene. In both the East and the West, from the sixth century to the fourteenth, the Mother of God was portrayed reclining beside the figure of her Son lying in his manger. As Cornell (1–7) has made clear, in the school of Giotto we begin to find departures from this "patristic" model, culminating in the portrayal of Mary kneeling beside the manger. But these pictures must be classified as "Adorations at the Manger"; they are clearly not meant to show the actual moment of the birth. Birgitta is the first to say that the birth itself took place while Mary was kneeling, and in a true "Birgittine" nativity the Child lies naked on the ground before the kneeling Mother. Such a portrayal first appeared in Naples shortly before 1380; and as Birgitta's vision became more widely known, the "Birgittine" nativity firmly established itself throughout the Western Church.

780. Despite the novelty of our Lady's kneeling posture, Birgitta sees her carefully praying according to the earliest traditions of the Church: with lifted hands and facing the east.

781. Cf. Matthew 1:25; Luke 2:7.

782. The radiance in the cave is an ancient apocryphal detail and not peculiarly Birgittine; but Birgitta throws it into prominence with her reference to the candle. By artists who are clearly using other Birgittine motifs, the radiance is rarely omitted.

783. *Et tam subitus et momentaneus erat ille modus pariendi, quod ego non poteram aduertere nec discernere, quomodo vel in quo membro parie-bat*. Curiosity about this anatomical detail seems to have awakened in

Birgitta as a result of misunderstanding the word *modum,* "manner," in *Rev.* 7.1.6, and now she suddenly realizes that her exaggerated expectations are being rebuffed. On Mary's virginity *in partu,* see Ott 205–06.

784. The traditional "patristic" nativity scene (cf. note 779) had usually included a secondary motif: one or more midwives bathing the Child Jesus. Perhaps Birgitta intends these words as a rejection of that tradition. Cf. *Rev.* 7.22.4.

785. *inuolutam.* Cf. John 20:7. In the midst of these homeliest of details, we hear echoes of the paschal mystery. See note 778.

786. *honestate.*

787. *Bene veneris, Deus meus, Dominus meus et filius meus.* Cf. John 20:28. This echo of the confession of St. Thomas further heightens the paschal atmosphere of this Christmas vision, and we are reminded of Birgitta's visions at Ortona that prepared her for her pilgrimage (cf. *Rev.* 7.4.1–22). These simple and unforgettable words of our Lady are often found inscribed in Latin on early depictions of the "Birgittine" nativity scene. For *bene veneris,* "welcome," see also note 507.

788. *pauimenti.* Note, however, that in Romanian *pavimentum* has become simply "earth." Cf. Psalm 118(119):25 and Blaise, *Dictionnaire* 601.

789. *compassione.* This word powerfully evokes the thought of Good Friday and the traditional image of Our Lady of Pity (cf. note 688).

790. *nec inde aliquis liquor aut sanguis exiuit.* Again we find traces of the paschal mystery: cf. John 19:34. *Liquor,* "liquid," is a frequent poetic equivalent for *aqua,* "water." Note, however, that Birgitta had not seen the flow of water in her vision on Calvary (cf. note 686).

791. *cum fascia, que suta erat in quatuor partes superioris panniculi lanei.* This detail is not entirely clear.

792. Cf. note 778.

793. *prosternens se ad terram genibus flexis adorando eum plorabat pre gaudio.* Birgitta is stressing the fact that *adorare* can mean the physical act of "prostration" as well as the interior act of "adoration," and that this act can be a sign of joy. On tears of joy as the crown of *penthos,* see Hausherr 137–156.

794. On the tradition of our Lady's painless childbearing, see Ott 205–06.

795. Cf. Luke 2:7, where Mary alone performs this act.

796. This chapter marks a brief interlude in what seems, in fact, to be a single incident of "seeing" that will resume with the account of the shepherds' visit in chapter 23.

NOTES

797. *in eodem loco,* i.e., "at the Lord's manger in Bethlehem" (cf. *Rev.* 7.21.1). The repetition of this phrase at *Rev.* 7.23.1 establishes a unifying link between these three chapters; and, in spite of the words "afterwards" and "again" in this sentence, I believe that the three chapters represent the stages of a single incident, rather than three separate revelations on three different occasions.

798. Cf. *Rev.* 7.1.6 and the rubric to *Rev.* 7.21. See also note 783.

799. Cf. *Life* 79. I have been unable to find any detailed account of this nativity revelation in Naples.

800. *sine adiutorio.* Cf. note 784. However, even the apocryphal traditions generally describe Joseph as arriving with the midwives only after Mary has already given birth "without help."

801. Cf. Luke 2:1.

802. *attendebant.* Cf. note 82.

803. *per modum communem.* Cf. note 783.

804. As a recapitulation of the preceding vision and as an indictment of human inattention, compare this chapter to *Rev.* 7.16.1–4.

805. Cf. Collijn, *Acta* 386. In this chapter, I believe that we are returning to the incident of "seeing" that was interrupted by the words recorded in chapter 22. In fact, chapters 21 and 23 can be read in sequence—omitting chapter 22—without any alteration in the opening words of 23. Cf. note 796.

806. Cf. note 797.

807. Cf. Luke 2:8 and 16.

808. *saluator ... et non "saluatrix" dixerant.* Cf. Luke 2: 11 and 17.

809. *Tunc igitur virgo mater eis ostendit naturam et sexum masculinum infantis.* In this surprising addition to the gospel details, Birgitta is expressing her complete faith in the full reality of Christ's incarnation.

810. Cf. Luke 2:20.

811. Cf. Collijn, *Acta* 386. There Alphonsus includes both the shepherds and the magi under the single verb *vidit,* "she saw." Here, however, the text makes it clear that the extraordinary revelation through "seeing" ended with the shepherds' departure from the cave. Birgitta learns about the magi through her more normal experience of "hearing" a narration spoken by the Mother of God.

812. *tres reges magi.* Matthew 2:1–16 speaks only of "magi." Birgitta's addition of "kings" ultimately derives from a very early mystical interpretation of Psalm 71(72):10–11 and Isaiah 60:6.

813. *venerunt in stabulum.* Birgitta is attempting to solve the famous

exegetical problem of reconciling the *phatnēi,* "manger," of Luke 2:7, 12, and 16 with the *oikian,* "house," of Matthew 2:11. Because both *oikia* and its Latin translation *domus* can also mean "building" in a more general sense, Birgitta interprets "house" as *stabulum,* "stable," i.e., the "building" in which stood the "manger." Thus Birgitta can locate the visits of the shepherds and of the magi in one and the same place—the cave-shrine of the Basilica of the Nativity in Bethlehem. Cf. note 508 and *Rev.* 7.22.2.

814. Cf. Luke 2:19, 51; 11:28. Mary is offered to us as the model of perfect "attention" (cf. note 802).

815. For the influence of the apocryphal gospels in this and the following chapter, Klockars (*Böckerna* 167) believes Birgitta's source to be the Old Swedish equivalent of the *Golden Legend,* edited under the title *Fornsvenska legendariet* by Stephens and, more recently, by Jansson. For evidence that Birgitta had such an Old Swedish *Lives of the Saints,* see the testimony of Christina Bosdotter (Collijn, *Acta* 66).

816. *inter duo animalia.* Cf. notes 230 and 773.

817. Birgitta is indirectly alluding to the patristic paradox of the *Infans Verbum,* "the speechless Infant Word" (cf. note 294).

818. Cf. Numbers 12:8.

819. *dispensacione.* The traditional Latin rendering of the *oikonomia,* "economy," of the New Testament and of the Greek fathers.

820. Cf. the Septuagint version of Isaiah 7:14, cited in Matthew 1:22–23.

821. Cf. Matthew 1:20.

822. Cf. *Rev.* 7.21.18. See also the gospel descriptions of the Palm Sunday ass (Mark 11:2; Luke 19:30) and of the Holy Sepulchre (Luke 23:53; John 19:41). Once again we find that Birgitta's view of Christmas contains a foretaste of the paschal mystery.

823. Cf. Luke 2:51.

824. *racionabiles.* Cf. note 761.

825. *per infusiones diuinas.*

826. 8 September 1372.

827. *proprie.*

828. The Valley of Jehoshaphat is the location of Mary's empty sepulchre according to the statements of the apocryphal gospels and was accepted as such by most later writers and liturgical texts, and the shrine of her sepulchre is still venerated there. The name "Jehoshaphat" means "Yahweh judges" and occurs in Joel 3(4):2, 12 as the ultimate place of divine judgment. In later tradition we commonly find it being

identified with the Kidron Valley outside Jerusalem, near Gethsemane. See note 815.

829. *Attende, filia!* Again, at the beginning of the last revelation received by Birgitta in the Holy Land, we find the heavenly summons to attention. Cf. note 814.

830. That is to say, after the actual day of Christ's ascension, Mary lived until the fifteenth anniversary of the ascension and then for as many more days as there were until the day of her own death in that year. Birgitta is presumably locating Mary's death on August 15, the day eventually settled on in the liturgical calendars for the celebration of Mary's "dormition," or "assumption."

831. There are two points to be noted: first, that Birgitta accepts the tradition that Mary actually died before her body and soul were assumed into heaven. On this point, she is aligning herself with a very ancient and widely held opinion. Cf. Walter J. Burghardt, S.J., *The Testimony of the Patristic Age concerning Mary's Death*, Woodstock Papers 2 (Westminster: Newman Press, 1961). However, when the belief in Mary's bodily assumption was dogmatically defined in Rome (1 November 1950), the exact manner in which she "completed the course of earthly life" was left undecided (Ott 208–11). The second noteworthy point is the "fifteen days." Klockars (*Böckerna* 168) cites evidence that the Old Swedish *Legendariet* (cf. note 815) had originally read 40 (XL) and that this number was altered, in at least one MS, to 15 (XV), the number that Birgitta accepted as correct.

832. Birgitta's affirmation of Mary's burial and bodily assumption and her statement (5) that only Christ and his Mother have human bodies in heaven figure among the points criticized at the Council of Basel. Torquemada (article 111) defended Birgitta's position as being without cause for suspicion.

833. Through the centuries, these garments have provided many alleged relics of the Blessed Virgin. The Byzantine Rite still celebrates the enshrinement in Constantinople of our Lady's robe (July 2) and her belt (August 31).

834. There is a remarkable parallel to this passage in a sermon of St. Gregory Palamas (*In Dormitionem Deiparae;* PG 151: 464–68; trans. in Robert Payne, *The Holy Fire: The Story of the Fathers of the Eastern Church* [New York: Harper, 1957], 276).

835. *Vos.* Mary begins to use plural forms, thus imparting to the whole group of Birgittine pilgrims a dismissal and a moral charge.

836. *vitas vestras semper in melius emendate.* Cf. the responsory *Emendemus in melius,* "Let us amend for the better," still sung during the distribution of ashes on the first day of Lent.

837. Cf. note 829.

838. For corroborating testimony concerning Birgitta's great address to the city of Naples, see Collijn, *Acta* 100 (= *Life* 93), 265, 325, 373–74, 562–63. See also *Epistola solitarii* 6 B, Alphonsus Pecha's introduction to his compilation of an eighth book of Birgitta's revelations. See also notes 585 and 610.

839. Cf. *Rev.* 7.19.22.

840. *Ceterum scias, quod, sicut omnia peccata mortalia grauissima sunt, ita eciam peccatum veniale, si homo delectatur in eo cum voluntate perseuerandi, efficitur mortale.* Birgitta's laconic presentation of this delicate issue is not entirely felicitous, and it is understandable that this would be one of the points criticized at the Council of Basel. Cardinal Torquemada (article 112) explained the truth in Birgitta's words with great care, relying chiefly on the treatment of this question by St. Thomas (*Summa theologiae* 1a–2ae: 88.4). There are two *false* interpretations that might be drawn from what Birgitta said: 1) that one and the same sin can be venial at the moment it is committed and then reclassified as mortal; and 2) that repeated venial sins add up to the guilt of a mortal sin. There are, however, two truths in Birgitta's words: 1) Although the matter of a given sin may be intrinsically venial, if one so fixes one's delight in that sinful act as a final end in itself, to the despite of God our true end, then it is entirely possible that the soul's choice of this intrinsically venial act may be seriously sinful. 2) Persistent repetition of venial sins has a tendency to create a disposition favorable to the committing of mortal sin.

841. *racionabilis.* Cf. note 761.

842. *colore stibio et extraneo.* Cf. 2 Kings 9:30 and Jeremiah 4:30.

843. Cf. note 690.

844. Cf. notes 64 & 270.

845. *dolorata.* As Bergh (*Bok VII* 200) notes, a small number of MSS read, perhaps correctly, *decolorata,* "discolored."

846. *vt ex tali recordacione et attenta memoria me, Deum vestrum, diligeretis.* These few words contain the true core of Birgitta's spiritual message. Cf. note 837.

847. *Ideo facitis sicut meretrices, diligentes voluptatem et delectacionem carnis, non autem prolem. 27. Cum enim senciunt infantem viuum in*

vtero suo, statim procurant abortiuum herbis et aliis rebus, ne careant carnis voluptate et continua delectacione pessima, vt sic semper vacent luxurie et fetide commixtioni carnali.

848. Cf. Songs 5:2; Apocalypse 3:20.

849. Cf. note 317.

850. *tantus et tam magnus peccator.*

851. *humili et perfecto corde.* For *perfectum cor* as "whole heart," see 1 Kings 11:4.

852. *appropinquabo me eis.* Cf. Bergh's apparatus (*Bok VII* 201).

853. Cf. Luke 15:20.

854. Cf. John 6:57–58.

855. The theme of the divine fisherman occurs in patristic literature, chiefly in connection with the problematic view of the redemption as an entrapment or deception of the devil, the bait being Christ's flesh and the hook his cross (cf. note 588). The image was popular enough to be included in the Greek *kontakia* of St. Roman the Melode (*Hymnes*, ed. José Grosdidier de Matons, 5 vols. Sources chrétiennes 99, 110, 114, 128, 283 [Paris: Les Éditions du Cerf, 1964–1981]; 4: 150, 558–59; 5: 206–07). The theme was also illustrated; see Straub 52–53, 86–87. Birgitta here interprets this old idea of the divine fisherman in the light of Ecclesiastes 9:12 in such a way that the act of fishing represents the destruction of sinners. In the gospels, however, fishing usually contains some allusion to the rescue of the elect (cf. Matthew 4:19, 13:47–48; Mark 1:17; Luke 5:10; John 21:11).

856. *Nam paulatim consumabo eos de hac vita mundana huius seculi.* The future form *consumabo* could represent an irregular variant of *consumam*, "I shall take" (reflecting *consumpserit* "he has taken" in the preceding sentence); but I prefer to follow Bergh (*Bok VII* 217) in equating it with *consummabo*, "I shall bring to an end." Pelikan (3: 156) cites a similar play on "consumption" and "consummation" in St. Bernard, *De diligendo Deo* 7.19 (Leclercq 3: 135).

857. *ortulanus huius mundi.* It is unusual for Mary to be called "gardener of the world." The Vulgate uses *hortulanus* of Christ (John 20:15); and other, similar words are used in the Scriptures for God: e.g., *agricola*, "farmer" (John 15:1). In 1 Corinthians 3:9, St. Paul says *Dei agricultura estis*, "you are God's husbandry." This image of God, who planted and farms this world, is still very much alive in the Byzantine liturgy: e.g., in the *kontakion* for the Sunday of All Saints. But Birgitta's transference of the image to Mary is surprising. Note that even in applying the word *hortulanus* to herself, Mary uses it with the masculine

ending. On the boldness of Catholic devotional language about Mary and on the usefulness of such language in depicting—through the sublime example of Mary—the possibility of human participation in the life of God through cooperation with grace, see note 201.

858. *mater misericordie.* The title has a double meaning: "merciful mother" and "mother of God, who is true mercy itself." This title, and the title "queen of heaven" in 2 above, figure prominently in the Marian antiphons *Regina caeli* and *Salve regina* sung at the end of compline in the Roman Rite.

859. *execucione operis.*

860. *in tempore oportuno.* Cf. Psalm 31(32):6; 144(145):15.

861. *ad seruitutem suam.*

862. *suas seruas vel sclauas.* Here, and once in the rubric to this revelation, Birgitta uses the word *sclavus* "slave," which ultimately derives from "Slav." By Birgitta's time *sclavus* had become a generic term; and its use is unlikely to contain any clue to the ethnic identity of these slave women. Elsewhere in this revelation, Birgitta uses for "slave" the classical word *servus*, which can also mean "servant."

863. There is a curiously close parallel to this sentence in Robert Burton, *The Anatomy of Melancholy*, 3 vols. (London: Everyman-Dent, 1968) 1: 334; I.2.4.2:

> Many masters are hard-hearted, and bitter to their servants, and by that means do so deject, with terrible speeches and hard usage so crucify them, that they become desperate, and can never be recalled.

No source is cited; but in his long preface, "Democritus Junior to the Reader," Burton mentions "St. Bridget" (1: 118).

864. Birgitta's own father, Birger Persson, had been a principal author of Sweden's Uppland lawcode, promulgated by King Birger Magnusson on 2 January 1295. In the Uppland laws, slavery was abolished out of reverence for the memory of Christ who was sold by Judas and thus redeemed the world (cf. Jørgensen 1: 14–16; 2: 282, 335). See also note 84.

865. *homines et femine.* Cf. note 150.

866. As an example of witchcraft in the Naples area, Bergh (*Bok VII* 206) cites Collijn, *Acta* 234–35. There we read a vivid account of one Picziolella, an elderly and unattractive woman from Nola, who was raped every night by a violent unclean spirit in human form. At first, she had the neighbor women sit up with her at night, and then her daughter and son-in-law; but the spirit continued to come and rape her after

extinguishing the lights and paralyzing the helpless bystanders. Reception of the sacraments brought her no relief and she turned to witchcraft. After Raymond, the priest of Lauro, gave her a magic charm to wear in her hair, the attacks came less frequently. The old woman then turned to Nicholas Orsini, the count of Nola (cf. note 53); and he referred her case to Alphonsus Pecha, who was in Nola at the time. Alphonsus took the woman to Naples to see Birgitta. After Birgitta showed miraculous knowledge of the charm in the woman's hair, the woman finally admitted her involvement with witchcraft and threw the charm away. At Birgitta's command, she fasted and prayed, heard Mass, and received communion. Thereafter she was quite free of her vexation. The canonization process received a written document containing the count of Nola's personal testimony to the truth of this incident.

867. *facturas.*

868. *Domine mi, reuerendissime pater, humili recommendacione premissa.* Literally: "My Lord, most reverend Father, humble recommendation having been fore-sent," the final words of this highly elliptical utterance were commonly used in the later Middle Ages as an introductory formula for letters. For other examples in Birgittine literature, see Bergh, *Bok VII* 99.

869. *vobis.* Birgitta addresses the bishop in the formal plural of Medieval Latin. Bergh (*Bok VII* 222) identifies him as John of Oleggio.

870. *non attendens ad peccata mea sed ad cordialem affectum humiliter postulantis.* For the construction, compare the Roman priest's prayer at Mass before the kiss of peace: *Domine Iesu Christe, qui dixisti . . . , ne respicias peccata mea, sed fidem Ecclesiae tuae,* "Lord Jesus Christ, who said . . . , look not upon my sins but upon the faith of your Church." Note that even if man is neglectful in attending to God, Birgitta has no doubt that God pays attention to man.

871. *similes sunt coram me porcis indutis pontificalibus seu sacerdotalibus ornamentis.* The following satirical similitude of the piggy prelates is one of the most enduringly famous passages in the writings of Birgitta.

872. Cf. Matthew 22:1–10; Luke 14:15–24.

873. *voce porcina et refutatoria grunientes.*

874. *viles siliquas porcinas.* Cf. Luke 15:16.

875. Cf. John 10:11–14.

876. Cf. note 728.

877. Cf. note 109.

NOTES

878. *Vidi palacium grande simile celo sereno.* This may have been intended to mean "I saw a palace as high as the serene sky."

879. *athomi solis.* Birgitta is doubtlessly thinking of the motes that one sees in a sunbeam. This application of the word *atomus* is already suggested in St. Isidore's *Etymologiae* 13.2.1.

880. *ante sedentem in throno.* In the Apocalypse, "the One sitting on the throne" is four times used as a mysterious periphrasis for the divine name (4:9; 5:13; 6:16; 21:5). Twice it is explicitly used to modify "God" (7:10; 19:4). In this last revelation before the description of Birgitta's death, we are confronted with a vision of eschatological glory and judgment.

881. Cf. Apocalypse 12:1.

882. Cf. Matthew 5:2.

883. Cf. Wisdom 6:2.

884. Cf. note 728.

885. Again we encounter the great theme of "attention" (cf. note 846).

886. *conuersatus sum vobiscum.* Birgitta is alluding to the traditional mystical interpretation of Baruch 3:38. Cf. notes 395 and 543.

887. There are verbal echoes here of Matthew 11:30 which reads, according to the Vulgate: "For my yoke is sweet and my burden light."

888. Cf. Apocalypse 22:4. See also Acts 20:25, 38.

889. *videor vobis quasi vermis mortuus in hyeme.* Beneath the surface of this image there is an allusion to the crucified Christ's apparent defeat at the hands of his enemies; cf. Psalm 21(22):7. Moreover, in the Germanic languages (including older English), the word "worm" can be used of snakes. In the great riddle at the end of the *Book of Questions* (*Rev.* 5, Rev. 13.7, 21), we find the dead Christ compared to a "serpent" (cf. note 473).

890. Cf. Jeremiah 12:1.

891. Cf. Psalm 75(76):9–10. These verses—indirectly alluded to here—have a paschal connotation in the Roman Rite from their use in the Offertory chant on Easter Sunday.

892. Cf. Matthew 11:29–30. The ending thus balances the allusion to the same verses in section 9 above (cf. note 887).

893. On the contents of this chapter, see Collijn, *Acta* 20–21, 318–20, 442–43; and *Epistola solitarii* 6 K (cf. note 838).

894. *quinque diebus ante diem obitus.* Birgitta died on 23 July 1373. If the confessors are reckoning in the classical fashion, we should trans-

late: "four days before . . ." (cf. note 32). As an introduction to the scenes of Birgitta's "passing," the phrase is comparable to John 12:1.

895. This chamber can still be seen in the House of St. Birgitta on the Piazza Farnese in Rome. See Laubenberger; and Tjader, *Mother Elizabeth* 5–7, 38–44, 53–77, 133–34, 162–63, 169–176, 228.

896. For section 3, see *Extravagantes* 67.6. Cf. notes 124 and 135.

897. Cf. note 125.

898. Cf. note 126. On sections 1–4 of this chapter, see Collijn, *Acta* 101 (= *Life* 95) and 506. Birgitta's body was first buried at Rome in the Church of St. Lawrence *in Panisperna*, where a major relic of her arm is still venerated today. In December of 1373, the saint's bones began their homeward journey to Sweden by way of Ancona, Trieste, Austria, and Poland (via the shipyards of Gdansk, where a parish church now bears her name), reaching Vadstena on 4 July 1374. For their later history and the survival of their original wooden shrine, see Lindblom, *Birgittas gyllene skrin.*

899. *quasi conquerendo.* Cf. notes 728 and 876.

900. *fistulam.* A "pipe" in the sense of "tube" or a musical instrument. Probably "tube" is meant; and this would seem to be another way of speaking of Birgitta as God's *canale*, "channel" (cf. note 2). But, in the context of this loving "complaint," the choice of a word with musical connotations may have been influenced by Luke 7:32.

901. *quia tempus misericordie mee ponit in arbitrio suo.* An allusion to Birgitta's desire to see an end of the Avignon papacy, a desire with which the pope was in no hurry to comply (cf. note 110). Cf. Judith 8:13. N.B.: Section 5 has no parallel in the *Life.*

902. Peter Olofsson. Cf. notes 1 and 72.

903. Alphonsus Pecha. Cf. note 111.

904. *Rev.* 7.30.1–16.

905. For sections 6–9, see Ekwall, *Birgittavita* 62. These four sections have no parallel at the end of the *Life*, but some of this material is summarized in *Life* 78.

906. Cf. John 20:30.

907. Cf. note 127. Sections 10–13 are closely paralleled by *Life* 96–97. The small differences in wording have been carefully reproduced in the English: e.g., *Life* 96 reads *coram Deo astare*, "standing in God's presence."

908. Cf. note 128. The phrase *inter verba et manus eorum* is open to various interpretations: "among their words and hands," "between their words and hands," etc. The true meaning of *inter . . . manus eorum*

is clarified in the final sentence (13) by *inter manus predictarum person-arum*, "in the hands of the aforesaid persons." The problem of *verba*, "words," remains. I have proposed a translation which supposes that these *verba* are those of Birgitta herself (cf. section 11) rather than those of the bystanders at her deathbed.

909. Cf. notes 129 and 720.

910. Cf. notes 130 and 908. In the house of St. Birgitta in Rome (cf. note 895), pilgrims still venerate the long, planklike top of the table on which an old tradition says she spent her final hours (cf. Lindblom, *Birgittas gyllene skrin* 9–11). The choice of this uncomfortable deathbed may seem strange, but it is not without precedent. Over the centuries, the dying have sometimes been placed "on wood" in their final moments that they might die in closer conformity to Christ, who died upon the wood of the cross.

911. Cf. note 131.

912. Professor Eklund has pointed out to me that none of the Latin MSS offers any prologue to the *Four Prayers*. His own forthcoming critical edition of the text will print the rubric and proem (itself a notable variant of *Life* 15) as given in Ghotan's *editio princeps* of 1492. I have therefore followed his text here rather than the introductory matter and list of rubrics as printed by Durante in 1628. The prayers themselves are, however, translated from Durante's text. In the winter of 1986–87, they were checked by Professor Eklund against his own unpublished critical edition. As a result, certain modifications of Durante's readings have been incorporated into the present English rendering, together with an explanatory note in each instance. The new section-numbering of the Eklund edition has also been followed. For an account of the recent discovery of a fragment of another recension of the text of the *Four Prayers*, see Eklund, "A Re-assessment of the Old Swedish Bridgettine Text Corpus," and the Translator's Foreword included in the present volume.

913. *legebat*. Here and in *Life* 15, the verb *legere* could also be taken in the medieval sense "recite." The words were, however, written down at some point for the purpose of being "read." Note that *Life* 15 speaks of "a prayer" although the text, as we know it, clearly has four distinct sections. Cf. note 21.

914. Cf. notes 22, 542, 606, 656, and 744.

915. Gabriel. Cf. Luke 1:26.

916. Joachim and Ann. Cf. note 458.

917. *coniugio honestissimo*. Cf. notes 18 and 283.

NOTES

918. *devoti Pontificis.* The Vulgate regularly equates the pagan title *pontifex,* "pontiff," with the Greek *arkhiereus,* "high priest." The newly-discovered Oslo fragment here has *deuoti episcopi,* "of the devout bishop," corresponding to the Old Swedish use of *biskoper,* "bishop," in references to the Jewish high priests. Apparently a process of correction has taken place: the Christian *episcopus* has been emended to its non-Christian synonym *pontifex.* See Eklund, "Re-assessment" 14–15. The text is alluding to the second-century tradition that Mary was actually raised in the Jerusalem temple. The feast of her "Presentation" or "Entrance into the Temple" is still celebrated by East and West on November 21. See Thurston 4: 398–99; Ryan 523.

919. From the beginning of section 7 until these words in section 11, the entire text has survived in the recension of the Oslo fragment. The most notable difference between the texts has already been discussed in note 918. Most of the other variations in word order or synonymous vocabulary would hardly repay the effort to reproduce them in an English form. But the absence of the following words might be noted: (7) ... and revered ... has ever ...; (8) ... my Lady ... [the "angel" sentence has been entirely recast] ... their ...; (9) ... In your most holy infancy ... [the rest of the sentence has been rephrased with synonyms]; (10) ... most discreetly ... and exercises ... glorious ... so ... always [= "more" in the Oslo fragment] ...; (11) Infinite. ... Both Latin texts and the Old Swedish rendering are printed in Eklund, "Re-assessment" 22–24.

920. Cf. Luke 1:34. Because Mary herself raises the matter of her virginity, her concern on this point has been taken, at least since the time of St. Gregory of Nyssa (d. ca. 395), as an indication that she had previously made a conscious commitment to virginity as a perpetual state. On the actual doctrine of Mary's perpetual virginity, see Ott 203–07. On the difficulties of interpreting Luke 1:34, see Raymond E. Brown, S.S., *The Birth of the Messiah: A Commentary on the Infancy Narratives in Matthew and Luke* (Garden City: Image-Doubleday, 1979), 303–09.

921. Cf. Luke 1:38.

922. *et illico Spiritus Sanctus omni virtute mirabiliter te impleuit.* This is the Eklund text; Durante 1628 lacks *illico,* "then and there," and has the synonym *repleuit* for Eklund's *impleuit,* "filled." Note that, like the Greek *aretē,* the Latin *virtus* literally means "manliness" and was extended to "strength," "power," "virtue," and "miracle"—the latter two being frequent Christian senses of the word.

NOTES

923. Cf. Luke 2:7. The prophet's *vaticinium*, "oracle," must be Isaiah 1:3.

924. Cf. note 813.

925. Cf. note 812.

926. *Regalia xenia.*

927. Cf. Luke 2:19 and 51; 11:28.

928. ... *apostolos* ..., *qui eius exemplis miraculis et doctrinis illuminati veritatis testes effecti sunt Ihesum tuum et Dei filium veraciter existere diuulgando cunctis gentibus, quod ipse erat, qui prophetarum scripturas per seipsum adimpleuerat.* ... This is the Eklund text. Durante 1628 punctuates rather differently and follows Ghotan in printing *diuulgantes*—which is, I believe, simply a classicizing equivalent for the medieval participial usage of the gerund *diuulgando*, "publishing." Even then the text remains difficult; and some MSS have apparently tried to clarify it by giving *asserentes diuulgando* in the sense "... witnesses of truth *asserting* that your ... *by* publishing to all. ..." The original makes good sense, however, if one recalls that Medieval Latin is sometimes clumsy in its use of the accusative-with-infinitive construction (cf. note 651). The clause "that your Jesus ... Son of God" can be taken as a noun clause in apposition with *veritatis*, "of *the* truth. ..." However, I agree with Professor Eklund that by its placement in the word order, *veritatis* is better taken in an adjectival sense: "witnesses of truth," or "true witnesses." Here, *testes* ("witnesses") seems to have the force of a verb of speech and thus leads into the accusative-with-infinitive construction. Professor Eklund also notes that one might translate thus: "... that Jesus was your and God's Son. ..." He observes that in line with usage elsewhere in the traditional text of the *Four Prayers*, the final *quod*-clause is unlikely to be causal.

929. Cf. John 19:26.

930. *animam suam in eius manibus recommendantem.* Cf. Psalm 30:6; Luke 23:46.

931. *a vertice capitis usque ad plantas pedum.* Birgitta has noticeably altered this famous phrase: cf. Deuteronomy 28:35; 2 Samuel 14:25; Job 2:7; Isaiah 1:6.

932. Birgitta accepts the ancient identification of the Beloved Disciple (John 19:26) with the apostle John, son of Zebedee.

933. The gospels do not mention that the risen Christ appeared to his Mother, but it is a pious belief of considerable antiquity and still widely accepted. The Byzantine Rite explicitly mentions this apparition in its liturgical books: e.g., in the *Octoechus*, see the *apolytikion anasta-*

simon of the second plagal tone, *Aggelikai Dynameis epi to mnēma sou . . . hypēntēsas tēi Parthenōi,* "Angelic Powers at your tomb! . . . You met the Virgin."

934. *resuscitatum.* Cf. Acts 2:32 & 13:33. "*As Man,* indeed God the Father raised him to Life, and so holy Scripture affirms; but *as God,* he raised himself." (John Mannock, OSB, *The Poor Man's Catechism: Or the Christian Doctrine Explained, with Short Admonitions,* 3d ed. [London: Coghlan, 1770], 77). See Ott 192–93. Ott's reference to the *Catechism of the Council of Trent* should read: *Cat. Rom.* 1.5.11.

935. *mortis actore supplantato.* The devil, or perhaps, as often in Byzantine art and poetry, Death personified as "Hades." His bound figure is often portrayed in Scandinavian church art: see Anker 2: plates 223, 228; Blindheim, plate 15; Broby-Johansen 217. Cf. Apocalypse 20:13–14.

936. *celique introitu patefacto per filium tuum.* This is Eklund's text. Durante 1628 lacks *per,* "through," and reads thus: ". . . had been opened wide, you saw your Son rising and . . . ."

937. Cf. notes 22, 542, 606, 656, 744, and 914.

938. Our Lady is here depicted as practicing the medieval "devotion to heaven" (cf. note 541). See Evans, *Gregory* 99–101; Leclercq, *Love* 53–70; Stephen A. Hurlbut, *The Picture of the Heavenly Jerusalem: In the Writings of Johannes of Fecamp,* De contemplativa vita, *and in the Elizabethan Hymns* (Washington: St. Alban's Press, 1943). *Speculum humanae salvationis* 44 (Wilson 205) lists Mary's longing for reunion with her risen Son as the seventh of her sorrows.

939. *a saeculi huius exilio eripere.* Cf. the antiphon *Salve Regina* sung at compline: *Ad te clamamus, exsules filii Evae. Ad te suspiramus, gementes et flentes in hac lacrimarum valle,* "To thee do we cry, poor banished children of Eve. To thee do we send up our sighs, mourning and weeping in this valley of tears." Mary can understand the cry of her petitioners because she too has shared in their exile and in their longing for heaven and the sight of her Son: *Iesum, benedictum fructum ventris tui, nobis post hoc exsilium ostende,* "After this our exile, show unto us the blessed fruit of thy womb, Jesus."

940. Birgitta is alluding to the apocryphal gospels and their account of Mary's death and assumption. These stories had come down to her by way of the *Golden Legend* (Ryan 449–65). Concerning the dogma of Mary's assumption and the disputed question of her death, see note 831.

941. Birgitta visited the shrine of Mary's sepulchre near Jerusalem on 8 September 1372; see *Rev.* 7.26.1–6.

942. *in illa leuissima tua morte.* This is Eklund's text; and for *levissima,* "most light," there is the variant *lenissima,* "most lenient." Durante 1628, however, gives the surprising *laeuissima,* "most sinister." In fact, with the medieval use of *e* for the classical *ae,* Durante's interpretation is possible. (And it is possible that his text is a typographical error.) The idea of Mary's soul being protected "in the midst of most sinister death" does fit Birgitta's view of death as a perilous event. Recall the death of Charles (*Rev.* 7.13.1–7) and how our Lady stood by him to help him *in illo arto spacio,* "in that narrow space." But, in fact, this text is not about death in general; the words *illa . . . tua,* "that . . . of yours," must be taken into account: "in that most sinister death of yours." Neither Professor Eklund nor I see any likelihood that Birgitta would intentionally use so negative an epithet for Mary's own death, which was the model of *bona mors,* "a happy death," suffered in the state of grace and after the example of Christ.

943. The traditional Byzantine icon of the *koimēsis,* "dormition," or "falling-asleep," of Mary shows Christ appearing by the corpse of his Mother and holding in his hands her soul, which is portrayed as a small child (cf. Kontoglou 1:259–61). This motif was well known in the West, and it may have influenced Birgitta's choice of words here.

944. *Et tunc Deus Pater omnia, quae creata sunt, tuae potestati subiecit.* The New Testament speaks of all things being subject to Christ or to his feet: e.g., 1 Corinthians 15:24–28; Ephesians 1:22; Philippians 3:21; Hebrews 2:8. But Christ's saints truly share in this triumph of his, as the seventy-two recognize in Luke 10:17. What can be said of the saints can be said with even greater confidence of Mary: even the demons are subject to her. See notes 189, 201, and 857.

945. Cf. note 940.

946. Cf. note 831.

947. *tuumque Filium gloriosum cum humanitate Deum existere agnouisti.* Although Birgitta's text apparently implies that Mary had not previously acknowledged the incarnation of the Word, it seems more likely that she is trying to say that Mary acknowledged the incarnation in a more perfect way now that she was physically in heaven and could see the full truth of what she had previously believed. Note that throughout this prayer there is a repeated affirmation that Mary's son is the Son of God; see *Four Prayers* 16 and 25. For Mary's confession of Christ's divinity at the moment of his birth, see *Rev.* 7.21.14.

948. The line of Birgitta's thought here becomes clearer. The truths mentioned in this section are indeed things that Mary had previously

known or believed (e.g., her own virginal motherhood); but now, as a result of her physical presence in heaven, her *flesh* knows the reality of these things in a more perfect way.

949. *quod Deum ex iustitia oportuit summo honore venerari.* The virtues of Mary are the fruit of God's grace; and, in revering them, he is revering his own gifts to her. But, by her cooperation with the mystery of grace, Mary's virtues are also, in some way, truly her own; and they call for a just reward. See notes 163, 189, and 307.

950. *dignum et iustum fuit.* Cf. notes 190 and 289.

951. *procuratrix.*

952. *creata.* This reading in Durante 1628 yields no sense. Not having access to the MS readings here, I have tentatively translated as if the form were *creavit.*

953. *cum narratione seriosa.* Cf. notes 140, 639, and 664.

954. *amor . . . dilectissime anime mee.* This is Eklund's text. Durante 1628 has *amator . . . dilectissimae animae meae,* "Lover of my own most beloved soul." The medieval use of *e* for *ae* has led Durante to misinterpret the masculine vocative *dilectissime* as a feminine genitive in *-ae.*

955. Exact and accurate statements of orthodox trinitarian and christological doctrine play an important part in Birgittine spirituality. Cf. note 241.

956. *post iucundam Natiuitatem tuam.* This is probably intended as an allusion to Mary's painless childbearing. See note 794.

957. Cf. Luke 2:7.

958. *a Matre tua in Templo offerri voluisti.* In using *offerri,* "to be offered," of Mary's action, Birgitta notably departs from the wording of Luke 2:22: *sisterent,* "present." However, this use of "offer" does occur several times in Peter Abelard's hymn, *Adorna, Sion, thalamum,* now assigned to Lauds on Candlemas. See also *Rev.* 7.2.3.

959. *praesentialiter.* Cf. Blaise, *Lexicon* 724; Deferrari, *Dictionary* 830–31. Note, however, that the Vulgate (2 Peter 1:16) uses *praesentia* as one way to translate *parousia,* the "advent" or "coming" of Christ. Birgitta is saying that Christ wrought these miracles during his first *parousia,* i.e., his incarnate "presence" in the world.

960. *rationabiliter.* The word is rich in overtones; see note 761.

961. *solo verbo.* In the midst of the other words that Christ says, Matthew 4:10 records only one serenely effortless command of dismissal: *vade,* "go." Birgitta's text may also be translated: "by word alone."

962. Cf. Luke 22:44.

963. Cf. John 18:5–6. Here *unico tuo verbo*, "solely by your word," refers to Christ's declaration, *ego sum*, "I am," which is equivalent to the divine name "Yahweh" of Exodus 3:13–14. Before the majesty of the name, Christ's enemies fall to the ground. Therefore, Birgitta may also mean "by your single word"; cf. note 961.

964. Cf. note 471.

965. Cf. notes 572 and 667.

966. Cf. John 19:19–22.

967. *ex amarissimo poculo.* That the dying Christ was given vinegar to drink is mentioned in Matthew 27:48; Mark 15:36; Luke 23:36; and John 19:29–30. Matthew, Mark, and John mention that the vinegar was held in a "sponge"; and nowhere is there any mention of a *poculum*, "cup," although the use of one is perhaps assumed in Matthew 27:34 and Mark 15:23, where Christ is offered drugged wine before the crucifixion begins. Therefore *poculum* here must be a metonymy for "drink." Note that in *Rev.* 7.15.29–30, Birgitta has conflated details of the proffered sponge of vinegar with the piercing of Christ's side after his death (cf. note 686).

968. Cf. notes 64, 270, and 844.

969. On the lifelong sinlessness of Mary, see Ott 202–03; this is a belief distinct from and complementary to the dogma of her immaculate conception in the womb of her mother (cf. note 467).

970. Cf. John 19:26–27.

971. Cf. Luke 23:39–43.

972. *cor tuum sacratissimum crudeliter pertransibant, donec crepante corde.*

973. Cf. Matthew 27:50. See notes 131, 635, and 636.

974. Cf. John 19:30.

975. Birgitta's wording reflects her concern for doctrinal accuracy (cf. note 955). At death Christ's human soul separated from his body; but, as a result of the hypostatic union, his body remained inseparably united to his divine Person (cf. Ott 150–51). Therefore Birgitta rightly says: " 'you' remained."

976. Cf. 1 Peter 1:19.

977. *potenter.* Professor Eklund has indicated that this is the unanimous reading of the MSS and of the Ghotan edition. Durante 1628 has misprinted *potentes*, producing the strange reading: "you liberated your mighty friends."

978. *de inferni carcere.* Cf. 1 Peter 3:19.

979. Cf. notes 686 and 967.

NOTES

980. Pontius Pilate. Cf. Matthew 27:57–58; Mark 15:42–45; Luke 23:50–52; John 19:38.

981. *reclinari voluisti et ... pannis involui ... permisisti.* See notes 689 and 778.

982. *a tartaris.* Birgitta here applies to the "limbo of the fathers" (Ott 191–92), the ancient pagan name for the place of punishment after death. In 2 Peter 2:4, *tartarum* is "hell" in the strict sense. Cf. note 978.

983. *Summus Sacerdos et Pontifex.* In Christian Latin these words are synonymous. See note 918.

984. Psalm 77(78):25; 104(105):40; Wisdom 16:20; John 6:30–35.

985. *Ideo Gloriosa Sacerdotalis sedes tua sit ad dexteram Dei Patris tui in tua diuinitate Beata, & benedicta in aeternum.* I owe the solution of this puzzling sentence to my brother John. Other less satisfactory renderings might be: "Glorious, therefore, be your priestly seat at God your Father's right hand in your blessed divinity; and blessed may it be unto eternity." Or (a possibility noted by Professor Eklund): "Therefore may your glorious priestly seat be at God your Father's right hand. . . ."

986. Cf. Deuteronomy 10:17; 1 Timothy 6:15; Apocalypse 19:16.

987. After mentioning the raising of Lazarus (John 11:1–44) and the traitorous kiss of Judas, Birgitta adds to both of these references a veiled allusion to Lazarus' sister Mary, who anointed Christ's feet with fragrant nard, an action that Judas criticized as a pointless expense (John 12:1–8). Cf. note 1012.

988. Cf. Deuteronomy 8:3; Matthew 8:4.

989. Through the hypostatic union (cf. note 975), the human nature of Christ is so intimately united to the divine nature and person of the Word that the human nature, in all its parts, quite rightly shares in the one single adoration of the incarnate Word. Thus *latreia*, "adoration," is owed to Christ's face, wounds, blood, heart, etc. Birgitta's statement of adoration for Christ's beard is certainly unusual; but it is theologically orthodox. See Ott 157–60.

990. *sarcinam.* Literally: "bundle," "pack," or "knapsack." The perfect, but archaic, English rendering is "fardel."

991. *confringeres.* This is the Eklund text and the unanimous reading of the MSS. However, Ghotan's *editio princeps* has *constringeres*, "constrained" (= forced?); and this apparent misprint survived in Durante 1628.

992. The mention of "shoulders" and "gates" contains a veiled allusion to Samson, whose carrying off of the gates of Gaza (Judges 16:3) is

324

listed as a type of the resurrection of Christ in *Speculum humanae salvationis* (ch. 32 in Shailor, *Vol. I* 45; ch. 28 in Wilson 196).

993. The counsels of perfection or evangelical counsels are traditionally reckoned to be poverty, chastity, and obedience.

994. This example of the medieval devotion to the Sacred Heart is noteworthy for its emphasis on the heart as an image of Christ's courage in the face of death. Birgitta is here drawing on the description of heroic royal warriors as found in the traditional poetry of the Germanic countries.

995. *extrenui.*

996. In this praise of Christ's breast, Birgitta's thought remains in the world of the early Germanic epics and sagas with their heroic kings and tragic deaths in battle. The image of Christ as a hero hastening to the cross occurs in the Anglo-Saxon *Dream of the Rood* 33–41.

997. Cf. Judges 16:25–30. Samson stretching out his arms to pull down the two columns and destroy the Philistines is listed as a type of the crucifixion in the twelfth-century *Pictor in carmine* 101 (James 162). This type is not used in either *Biblia pauperum* or *Speculum humanae salvationis*. It is even more surprisingly absent from the noteworthy series of Samson-types used in the Klosterneuburg enamels (cf. Floridus Röhrig, *Der Verduner Altar* [Klosterneuburg: Stift Klosterneuburg, 1955]).

998. *a cunctis hominibus spiritualibus, et terrenis laboribus insudantibus.* This is the text and punctuation of Durante 1628. It would seem to mean: "by all humans, who are spiritual and yet who sweat at earthly labors"; or: "by all spiritual men [i.e., the clergy], and by those who sweat at earthly labors [i.e., the laity]." Neither of these renderings seems natural. If the comma is removed, a reading of the text is possible that coincides with that of the Old Swedish version; and, with the concurrence of Professor Eklund, it is the commaless interpretation that I have adopted.

999. *venerentur ... genua tua cum poplitibus, & tibijs tuis.* For *venerentur*, the Eklund text has the synonymous *reuereantur.*

1000. Cf. John 13:4–16. The gospel does not actually say that Christ knelt; and in art he is shown kneeling only in the West after the mid-eleventh century (cf. Schiller 2: 46). The source of this kneeling posture seems to be medieval rubrics for the "maundy" or foot-washing as performed liturgically on Holy Thursday.

1001. *Magister bone.* Cf. Mark 10:17 and Luke 18:18.

1002. *per asperiorem viam, quam alios docuisti.* This is the Eklund text. Durante 1628 lacks *per*, "along." The text might also be rendered "along a harsher way *than* you taught to others" (cf. Eklund, "Re-assessment" 16). Since the beginning, however, Christian theology has stressed *two* ways: one good, the other evil (cf. note 288). The rendering "than" would seem to introduce a *third* way, one peculiar to Christ. Such a rendering would also seem inconsistent with Birgitta's own words in *Rev.* 5, Int. 10.31: "Everyone who wills to establish or begin a new way must himself, as the establisher and beginner of the way, walk on it ahead of others." Clearly the way walked by Christ and by his followers must be one and the same. This way is "harsher" than "the way that leads to perdition" (cf. Matthew 7:13–14). The Oslo fragment gives this passage with a shift in the imagery: *Domine mi Ihesu Christe, benedicentur perhenniter tui pedes super omnes magistros, qui sapienciam adepti sunt, quoniam duriorem viam elegerunt, quam alios incedere docuerunt:* "My Lord Jesus Christ, your feet shall be perennially blessed above all teachers who have acquired wisdom: because they [i.e., Christ's feet] chose the harder way that they taught others to go." Here too *quam* might be rendered "than," but "that" seems preferable. Christ's feet are themselves teachers by their example: their choice was itself an act of teaching. This image of the *feet* as the teachers has been reworked in the traditional text so that *Christ* becomes the teacher and the verbs are changed from the third to the second person.

1003. *in fine.* This is the Eklund text. Durante 1628 has *in finem*, "unto the end."

1004. *Four Prayers* 81–83 survives in the Oslo fragment. The Oslo text is quite different in places and has a concluding paragraph that has not come down in the traditional recension. Therefore I am here appending it in translation; the section numbers are those of Eklund, "Re-assessment" 22. The Oslo fragment reads:

42. My ... Jesus Christ, blessed shall your loins be; and praised be they above all the angels' cleanness in heaven and above the purity of all who have preserved their chastity in this world: because the chastity of them all is in no way able to be compared to your cleanness. 43. My Lord Jesus Christ, glorified be your knees, with their hams and shins, above all who show honor to their masters [as in Durante 1628: *magistris*, "masters" or "teachers"], because, with all humility, they were bent before your own disciples. 44. My Lord Jesus Christ, your feet shall be perennially blessed above all teachers [*magistros*] who have acquired wisdom: because they chose the

326

harder way that they taught others to go. 45. Lord Jesus Christ, honor and joy be to all your most sacred body with all its members from the top of your crown to the bottom of your soles: because [*quod*], in memory of your most worthy passion, you show yourself to human eyes in the appearance of bread; but, in the presence of the angels and all the heavenly court, out of your ineffable charity, you show yourself living with humanity and Godhead.

The Oslo fragment has no final doxology but immediately goes on to the opening words of the text that we now know as *Four Prayers* 7–11. Note that despite Professor Eklund's reservations about *quod*, "because," in the traditional recension (cf. note 928), here parallelism with the earlier sections and the syntax of the clause strongly support "because."

1005. God, however, knows their number: cf. Matthew 10:30; Luke 12:7; Acts 27:34.

1006. Birgitta's image is suggestive of the popular interpretation of the face in the moon as our Lady's, interceding for the world. The idea is perhaps more widespread in Greece and the Romance countries, where the words for "moon" are feminine, but it is certainly not unknown in the United States.

1007. Cf. notes 545, 619, and 628.

1008. *viriliter militabant.* Cf. note 271.

1009. *glorietur nasus tuus suauissimus.* Birgitta has begun her catalogue of body parts, and she can hardly leave our Lady's nose out. If we fail to see a touch of humor and playfulness in such passages, we have rather missed the medieval point. See notes 322 and 809.

1010. *ex virtute Spiritus sancti numquam anhelitum attraxit, vel emisit.* Birgitta is playing with the double meaning of *spiritus*, "breath" and "spirit." For the overtones of *emittere*, "send forth," see Psalm 103(104):30; Matthew 27:50.

1011. For the thought, cf. Songs 5:2.

1012. *odor suauitatis.* Cf. Genesis 8:21; Sirach 24:20 and 23; 39:18; Ezechiel 20:41; Ephesians 5:2. This phrase connotes literal or spiritual sacrifice (cf. Leviticus 1:9 and 17). The verses in Sirach 24 are often found in offices of the Blessed Virgin.

1013. *emittere.* Cf. note 1010.

1014. Cf. Luke 1:38.

1015. Cf. note 191.

1016. *venustatem.* By virtue of its derivation from "Venus," the

Latin word connotes a subtle contrast between Mary, the chaste "lily," and the pagan goddess of love.

1017. Birgitta is again playing on the various meanings of *spiritus*, "breath," "wind," "spirit," etc. Here she also uses *ventorum*, "of the winds," in the literal sense. Cf. notes 644 and 1007.

1018. *sicut virtuosa opera tua Filium Dei ad te alliciebant*. Cf. note 201.

1019. Cf. Luke 11:27.

1020. *omnes dulcissimos fontes aquarum*. In Latin, *aquae*, "waters," is especially used to mean "medicinal springs"; and this meaning has survived in the place names "Aix" and "Aachen." That this is the significance of *aquae* here is clarified by the mention of *medicinam*, "medicine," at the end of this salutation.

1021. For a strikingly similar comparison of "springs" and "breasts" in patristic literature, see Clement of Alexandria, *Paedagogus* 3.7(39).

1022. *pectus*. This praise of Mary's courage and constancy is comparable to *Four Prayers* 78.

1023. These last two sections (98 and 99) concerning Mary's bosom and heart directly echo *Four Prayers* 77 and 78 but in reverse, or "chiastic," order. Here in 99, Mary's heart has the more usual significance of "charity." This permits Birgitta to return to her theme of Mary's total cooperation with grace as a decisive factor in God's decision to descend into her womb. See notes 201 and 1018.

1024. Cf. Matthew 13:8; Luke 8:8.

1025. Birgitta firmly roots this ancient image of fertility in the ground of the Scriptures by introducing references to the parable of the sower and to Mary as the *agellus*, "little field," in which sprang up the Bread of Life. For Mary as a fertile field, in the Eastern tradition, see the *Akathist Hymn* (delta & epsilon stanzas) and its kanon (ode 3: troparion 2). For Western knowledge of the *Akathist Hymn* from the eighth century on, see Bouyer, *History* 2: 253. For "earth" as a type of Mary, see note 281.

1026. Cf. Matthew 25:1–13, the parable of the wise (*prudentes*) and foolish virgins.

1027. Birgitta returns one last time to the image of Mary as "earth" and "field" (cf. note 1025), which ultimately rests on the words of Elizabeth (Luke 1:42), repeated in the Hail Mary: "Blessed art thou amongst women; and blessed is the fruit of thy womb: Jesus!"

SELECT BIBLIOGRAPHY

Birgittine source material, whether primary or secondary, is extensive and somewhat bewildering in its diversity and richness of detail. The present list is limited to a selection of works that are directly about Birgitta or give essential background information, together with a few general reference books and the works that are cited by short title in the notes. Other items, of importance only to a particular note, are cited in the notes with full bibliographical data and are not repeated here. To avoid confusion for English-speaking readers, the Scandinavian å, ä, ö, and ø have been alphabetized as English a and o, rather than in their correct position at the end of the alphabet. Full lists of technical and scholarly items are given in the critical editions of Bergh, Collijn, Eklund, Hollman, Lundén, and Undhagen. For several items that would otherwise have gone unused, I must acknowledge my debt to the kind interest of Bishop Basil Losten of Stamford and to the vigilant eyes of Brother David Amico, O.F.M. Cap.

Abbott, Walter M., S. J., ed. *The Documents of Vatican II.* New York: Guild Press, 1966.

Åmark, Mats. "La chapelle Finsta." *La cathédrale d'Upsal: Petit guide.* Uppsala: Almqvist, 1950. 11–12.

Andersson, Aron, ed. *Den heliga Birgitta och Vadstena: Ett sexhundraårs minne.* Stockholm: Almqvist, 1970.

———. *St. Birgitta and the Holy Land.* Trans. Louise Setterwall. Stockholm: Museum of National Antiquities, 1973.

———. *Saint Bridget of Sweden.* London: Catholic Truth Society, 1980.

———. *S. Katarina av Vadstena.* N.p.: Ljungberg, 1981.

Anker, Peter, and Aron Andersson. *The Art of Scandinavia.* Trans. Vivienne Menkes. 2 vols. London: Hamlyn, 1970

Attwater, Donald. *A Dictionary of Saints: Based on Butler's Lives of the Saints, Complete Edition.* New York: Kenedy, 1958.

Aviel, Yaakov, ed. *Choice of Illustrations from Yaakov Aviel's Collection of Holy Land.* Tel-Aviv: Aviel, 1984.

Baring-Gould, S. *The Lives of the Saints*. Rev. ed. 16 vols. Edinburgh: Grant, 1914.

Baumgarten, N. de. *Olaf Tryggwison roi de Norvège et ses relations avec Saint Vladimir de Russie*. Orientalia christiana 24: 73. Rome: Pontificale Institutum Orientalium Studiorum, 1931.

Benson, Larry D., ed. *The Riverside Chaucer*. 3d. ed. Boston: Houghton, 1987.

Bergh, Birger, ed. *Den Heliga Birgittas Revelaciones, Bok VII*. Samlingar utgivna av svenska fornskriftsällskapet 2, 7: 7. Uppsala: Almqvist, 1967.

———, ed. *Sancta Birgitta, Revelaciones, Book V: Liber Questionum*. Samlingar utgivna av svenska fornskriftsällskapet 2, 7: 5. Uppsala: Almqvist, 1971.

Binder, Georg. *Die Heilige Birgitta von Schweden und ihr Klosterorden*. N.p.: n.p., 1891.

Biographie e preghiere dei santi dell'ordine brigidino. Rome: Casa di S. Brigida, 1979.

Blaise, Albert. *Dictionnaire latin-français des auteurs chrétiens*. 1954. Turnhout: Brepols, 1967.

———. *Lexicon latinitatis medii aevi*. Corpus christianorum: Continuatio mediaevalis. Turnhout: Brepols, 1975.

———. *Manuel du latin chrétien*. Strasbourg: Le latin chrétien, 1955.

Blindheim, Martin. *The Stave Church Paintings: Medieval Art from Norway*. New York: Mentor-Unesco-NAL, 1965.

Blosius, Ludovicus. *Monile spirituale. Manuale vitae spiritualis*. Ed. Charles Newsham. London: Richardson, 1859. 277–367.

Blunt, John Henry, ed. *The Myroure of Oure Ladye: Containing a Devotional Treatise on Divine Service, with a Translation of the Offices Used by the Sisters of the Brigittine Monastery of Sion, at Isleworth, during the Fifteenth and Sixteenth Centuries*. 1530. Early English Text Soc. Extra Ser. 19. London: Trübner, 1873.

Bodenstedt, Sister Mary Immaculate. *The* Vita Christi *of Ludolphus the Carthusian*. Catholic University of America Studies in Medieval and Renaissance Latin Language and Literature 16. Washington: Catholic University of America Press, 1944.

Boland, Paschal, O.S.B. *The Concept of* Discretio Spirituum *in John Gerson's "De Probatione Spirituum" and "De Distinctione Verarum Visionum a Falsis."* Catholic University of America Studies in Sacred Theology (Second Series) 112. Washington: Catholic University of America Press, 1959.

SELECT BIBLIOGRAPHY

Bouyer, Louis, Cong. Orat. *Introduction to Spirituality*. Trans. Mary Perkins Ryan. Collegeville: Liturgical Press, 1961.

Bouyer, Louis, Cong. Orat., et al. *A History of Christian Spirituality*. 3 vols. 1963–1969. New York: Seabury Press, n.d.

"Brigidē." *Thrēskeutikē kai ēthikē egkyklopaideia*. 12 vols. Athens: A. Martinos, 1963. 3: 1043.

Brilioth, Yngve. *Den påfliga beskattningen af Sverige: Intill den stora schismen*. Uppsala: Appelberg, 1915.

Broby-Johansen, R. *Den danske billedbibel: De middelalderlige kalkmalerier i de danske kirker*. Copenhagen: Gyldendal-Nordisk, 1948. 80, 153.

Brown, Peter. *The Cult of the Saints: Its Rise and Function in Latin Christianity*. Chicago: Phoenix-University of Chicago Press, 1982.

Butkovich, Anthony. *Revelations: Saint Birgitta of Sweden*. Los Angeles: Ecumenical Foundation of America, 1972.

Butler, Cuthbert. *Western Mysticism: The Teaching of Augustine, Gregory and Bernard on Contemplation and the Contemplative Life*. 2nd ed. 1926. New York: Torchbooks-Harper, 1966.

Butler-Bowdon, W., ed. *The Book of Margery Kempe 1436: A Modern Version*. New York: Devin, 1944.

Bumpus, T. Francis. *The Cathedrals and Churches of Norway, Sweden, and Denmark*. New York: Pott, n.d.

Cecchetti, Igino, et al. "Brigida di Svezia, santa, fondatrice dell'Ordine del S. Salvatore." *Bibliotheca sanctorum*. 12 vols. Rome: Istituto Giovanni XXIII, 1961–1970. 3: 439–533.

Charlier, Celestin. *The Christian Approach to the Bible*. Trans. Hubert J. Richards and Brendan Peters. Westminster: Newman Press, 1958.

Clarus, Ludwig. *Leben und Offenbarungen der Heiligen Brigitta*. 4 vols. Regensburg: G. Joseph Manz, 1856.

Colledge, Eric. "*Epistola solitarii ad reges:* Alphonse of Pecha as Organizer of Birgittine and Urbanist Propaganda." *Medieval Studies* 18 (1956): 19–49.

Collijn, Isak, ed. *Acta et processus canonizacionis beate Birgitte*. Samlingar utgivna av svenska fornskriftsällskapet 2: 1. Uppsala: Almqvist, 1924–1931.

———, ed. *Birgerus Gregorii, Legenda sancte Birgitte: Efter Cod. Lund. Perg. 21 och Cod. Holm. A 75 A*. Samlingar utgivna av svenska fornskriftsällskapet 2: 4. Uppsala: Almqvist, 1946.

Collis, Louise. *Memoirs of a Medieval Woman: The Life and Times of Margery Kempe*. 1964. New York: Colophon-Harper, 1983.

SELECT BIBLIOGRAPHY

Conlan, Sr. Mary Samuel, O.P. "Bridget of Sweden, St." *New Catholic Encyclopedia*. 15 vols. New York: McGraw, 1967. 2: 799.

Cornell, Henrik. *The Iconography of the Nativity of Christ*. Uppsala Universitets Årsskrift (1924) 3. Uppsala: A.-B. Lundequistska Bokhandeln, 1924.

Cousins, Kathryn, et al. *How to Read a Spiritual Book*. New York: Paulist Press, 1981.

Cumming, William Patterson, ed. *The Revelations of Saint Birgitta: Edited from the Fifteenth-Century MS in the Garrett Collection in the Library of Princeton University*. Early English Text Society: Original Series 178. London: Oxford University Press, 1929.

Curtayne, Alice. *St. Brigid of Ireland*. 1933. New York: Sheed, 1954.

Curtius, Ernst Robert. *European Literature and the Latin Middle Ages*. Trans. Willard R. Trask. 1953. New York: Torchbook-Harper, 1963.

Deferrari, Roy J. *A Latin-English Dictionary of St. Thomas Aquinas*. Boston: St. Paul Editions, 1960.

Durante, Consalvus, ed. *Revelationes S. Brigittae*. Rome: Paulinus, 1606.

———, ed. *Revelationes Sanctae Brigittae*. 2 vols. Rome: Grignanus, 1628.

———. *Tractatus de visionibus, revelationibus, apparitionibus, extasi, & raptu. Revelationes Sanctae Brigittae*. 2 vols. Rome: Grignanus, 1628. 1: 1–210.

Egan, Harvey D., S.J. "Christian Apophatic and Kataphatic Mysticisms." *Theological Studies* (September, 1978): 399–426.

———. *What Are They Saying about Mysticism?* New York: Paulist Press, 1982.

Eklund, Sten. "A Re-assessment of the Old Swedish Bridgettine Text Corpus." *Kungl. Humanistiska Vetenskaps-Samfundet i Uppsala*. 1983–84: 5–23.

———, ed. *Sancta Birgitta, Opera minora I: Regula Salvatoris*. Samlingar utgivna av svenska fornskriftsällskapet 2, 8: 1. Lund: Berlingska, 1975.

———, ed. *Sancta Birgitta, Opera minora II: Sermo angelicus*. Samlingar utgivna av svenska fornskriftsällskapet 2, 8: 2. Uppsala: Almqvist, 1972.

Ekwall, Sara. "Årscylken i Acta et processus canonizacionis b. Brigide." *Personhistorisk tidskrift* 69 (1973): 1–9.

————. "Den Heliga Birgittas makes dödsår än en gång." *Personhistorisk tidskrift* 72 (1976): 32–35.

————. *Vår äldsta Birgittavita och dennas viktigaste varianter.* Kungl. vitterhets historie och antikvitets akademiens handlingar: Historiska serien 12. Stockholm: Almqvist, 1965.

Emery, Richard W. "Birgitta, St., of Sweden." *The Literatures of the World in English Translation: Volume I, The Greek and Latin Literatures.* Eds. George B. Parks and Ruth Z. Temple. New York: Ungar, 1968. 300.

Ennis, Arthur John, O.S.A. "Bridgettines." *New Catholic Encyclopedia.* 15 vols. New York: McGraw, 1967. 2: 800.

Evans, Gillian Rosemary. *The Thought of Gregory the Great.* Cambridge Studies in Medieval Life and Thought: Fourth Series 2. Cambridge: Cambridge University Press, 1986.

Farmer, David Hugh. *The Oxford Dictionary of Saints.* 2nd ed. Oxford: Oxford University Press, 1987.

Ferraige, Maistre Iaques, trans. *Les révélations célestes et divines de Sainte Brigitte de Suède.* 1651. 2 vols. Avignon: Seguin, 1850.

Fry, Timothy, O.S.B., et al. *RB 1980: The Rule of St. Benedict in Latin and English with Notes.* Collegeville: Liturgical Press, 1981.

Fletcher, John Rory. *The Story of the English Bridgettines of Syon Abbey.* South Brent, Devon: Syon Abbey, 1933. [A more detailed version was published serially as *The History of Syon* in issues of Syon Abbey's magazine *The Poor Souls' Friend* 1957–1969.]

Fogelklou, Emilia. *Die Heilige Birgitta von Schweden.* Trans. Maja Loehr. Munich: E. Reinhardt, 1929.

Garrigou-Lagrange, Reginald, O.P. *The Three Ages of the Interior Life: Prelude of Eternal Life.* Trans. Sister M. Timothea Doyle, O.P. 2 vols. St. Louis: Herder, 1949.

Glare, P. G. W., ed. *Oxford Latin Dictionary.* Oxford: Clarendon Press, 1982.

Grad, Toni, ed. *Festschrift Altomünster 1973: Birgitta von Schweden † 1373; Neuweihe der Klosterkirche nach dem Umbau durch J. Michael Fischer 1773.* Aichach: Mayer, 1973.

Graf, Ernest, O.S.B. *Fourth Centenary of Syon Abbey's Martyr: Blessed Richard Reynolds, Bridgettine Monk of Syon, Martyred at Tyburn, 4th May, 1535.* Exeter: Catholic Records Press, 1935.

Gronberger, Sven Magnus. *St. Bridget of Sweden: A Chapter of Mediaeval Church History.* Ed. James J. Walsh. Publications of the Writers

Club of Washington 1.2 (1917). [Reprint from *American Catholic Quarterly Review* 42 (1917): 97–148.]

Guibert, Joseph de, S.J. *The Theology of the Spiritual Life.* Trans. Paul Barrett, O.F.M. Cap. London: Sheed and Ward, 1956.

Hall, Thelma, R.C. *Too Deep for Words: Rediscovering Lectio Divina.* New York: Paulist Press, 1988.

Hallendorff, Carl, and Adolf Schück. *History of Sweden.* Trans. Lajla Yapp. Stockholm: Fritze, 1929.

Haugen, Einar. *The Scandinavian Languages: An Introduction to Their History.* Cambridge: Harvard University Press, 1976. 233–34.

Hausherr, Irénée, S.J. *Penthos: The Doctrine of Compunction in the Christian East.* Trans. Anselm Hufstader, O.S.B. Cistercian Studies Series 53. Kalamazoo: Cistercian Publications, 1982.

Heidenstamm, Verner von. *Heliga Birgittas pilgrimsfärd.* Stockholm: Bonniers, 1915.

Heuser, A., ed. *Revelationes Selectae S. Birgittae.* Cologne: Heberle, 1851.

Högman, Bertil, ed. *Heliga Birgittas originaltexter.* Samlingar utgivna av svenska fornskriftsällskapet 205. Uppsala: Almqvist, 1951.

Hollman, Lennart, ed. *Den heliga Birgittas Revelaciones extravagantes.* Samlingar utgivna av svenska fornskriftsällskapet 2: 5. Uppsala: Almqvist, 1956.

Hörmann, Simon, O.Ss.S., ed. *Revelationes caelestes seraphicae matris S. Birgittae.* Munich: Rauch, 1680.

James, Montague Rhodes, ed. and trans. *The Apocryphal New Testament: Being the Apocryphal Gospels, Acts, Epistles, and Apocalypses with Other Narratives and Fragments.* Oxford: Clarendon Press, 1924.

———. "*Pictor in Carmine.*" *Archaeologia* 94. London: Society of Antiquaries, 1951.

Jansson, Valter, ed. *Fornsvenska legendariet.* Samlingar utgivna av svenska fornskriftsällskapet 181. Uppsala: Almqvist, 1938.

Johnston, F.R. *Syon Abbey: A Short History of the English Bridgettines.* Eccles: Eccles and District History Society in association with Syon Abbey, 1964.

Jørgensen, Johannes. *Saint Bridget of Sweden.* Trans. Ingeborg Lund. 2 vols. London: Longmans, 1954.

Kezel, John Ryle. *Aelfric the Benedictine and His Spells for the Assumption.* Diss. Fordham University, 1983. Ann Arbor: University Microfilms International, 1983. 83-26687.

Kilström, B. I., and C.-G. Frithz, eds. *Bibliographia Birgittina: Skrifter av och om den heliga Birgitta samt om birgittinska kloster och birgittinskt fromhetsliv, i urval.* Strängnäs: Societas Sanctae Birgittae, 1973.

Kirby, Benedict, O.Ss.S. "St. Bridget's Legacy." *Sign* 60 (1981): 2.

Klauser, Theodor. *A Short History of the Western Liturgy: An Account and Some Reflections.* Trans. John Halliburton. 2nd ed. Oxford: Oxford University Press, 1979. 111–12.

Klemming, Gustav Edvard, ed. *Heliga Birgittas uppenbarelser: Efter gamla handskrifter.* 5 vols. Stockholm: Norstedt, 1857–1884.

Klockars, Birgit. *Birgitta och böckerna: En undersökning av den heliga Birgittas källor.* Kungl. vitterhets historie och antikvitets akademiens handlingar: Historiska serien 11. Stockholm: Almqvist, 1966.

———. *Birgittas svenska värld.* Stockholm: Natur och kultur, 1976.

———. *Biskop Hemming av Åbo.* Skrifter utg. av Svenska litteratursällskapet i Finland 379. Helsingfors: Svenska litteratursällskapet i Finland, 1960.

Eine Klosterfrau der ewigen Anbetung in Mainz. *Blüthenlese aus den Schriften der Heiligen Birgitta von Schweden.* Mainz: Franz Kirchheim, 1877.

———. *Leben der Heiligen Birgitta von Schweden.* Mainz: Franz Kirchheim, 1875.

Knowles, David. *The Nature of Mysticism.* Twentieth Century Encyclopedia of Catholicism 38. New York: Hawthorn, 1966.

Koenig-Bricker, Woodeene. "Revival of an Ancient Monastic Order." *Our Sunday Visitor* 15 Mar. 1987.

Kontoglou, Phōtēs. *Ekphrasis tēs orthodoxou eikonographias.* 2 vols. Athens: Astir, 1960.

Kup, Karl. Bene veneris . . . filius meus: *An Early Example of St. Birgitta's Influence on the Iconography of the Nativity.* New York: New York Public Library, 1957. [Reprint from *Bulletin of the New York Public Library.* Dec., 1957.]

———. *The Christmas Story: In Medieval and Renaissance Manuscripts from the Spencer Collection.* New York: New York Public Library, 1969. 39.

Kurth, Willi, ed. *The Complete Woodcuts of Albrecht Dürer.* Trans. Silvia M. Welsh. 1927. New York: Dover, 1963. 22–23; plates 128–42.

La Fay, Howard. *The Vikings.* Washington: National Geographic Society, 1972.

Lapide, Cornelius a, S.J. *Commentaria in sacram scripturam.* 22 vols. Paris: Vivés, 1866.

Laubenberger, M. Hilaria, O.Ss.S. *Saint Birgitta's House in Rome.* Guild of St. Birgitta Booklet 2. [Darien: Vikingsborg,] 1967.

Leclercq, Jean, O.S.B. "Deux témoins du IXe siècle: 1.—Un apôtre: Saint Anschaire . . ." *Témoins de la spiritualité occidentale.* Paris: Cerf, 1965. 39–58.

———. *Études sur le vocabulaire monastique du moyen âge.* Studia anselmiana 48. Rome: Herder, 1961.

———. *The Love of Learning and the Desire for God: A Study of Monastic Culture.* Trans. Catharine Misrahi. 3d ed. New York: Fordham University Press. 1982.

———. *Otia monastica: Études sur le vocabulaire de la contemplation au moyen âge.* Studia anselmiana 51. Rome: Herder, 1963.

Leclercq, Jean, O.S.B., et al., eds. *S. Bernardi opera.* Rome: Editiones cistercienses, 1957–77.

Lewis, Charlton T., and Charles Short. *A Latin Dictionary.* 1879. Oxford: Clarendon Press, 1966.

Liedgren, Jan. "Två Birgittinska data." *Personhistorisk tidskrift* 70 (1974): 51–54.

Lindblom, Andreas. *Birgittas gyllene skrin.* Kungl. vitterhets historie och antikvitets akademiens handlingar: Antikvariska serien 10. Stockholm: Almqvist, 1963.

———. *På Birgittas vägar.* Stockholm: Norstedt, 1962.

Linderoth, Fred, and Sven Norbrink. *Den svenska kyrkan: Kyrkokunskap för kyrka, skola och hem.* 4th ed. Stockholm: Svenska kyrkans diakonistyrelses bokförlag, 1952.

Lokrantz, Margherita Giordano. "Intorno al viaggio italiano di Birgitta di Svezia: Il soggiorno milanese (autunno 1349)." *Vestigia: Studi in onore di Giuseppe Billanovich.* Ed. Rino Avesani. 2 vols. Rome: Edizioni di storia e letteratura, 1984. 387–98.

Lundén, Tryggve, trans. *Den heliga Birgitta: Himmelska uppenbarelser.* 4 vols. Malmö: Allhems, 1957–59.

———, ed. *Den heliga Birgitta och den helige Petrus av Skänninge: Officium parvum beate Marie Virginis.* Studia Historico-Ecclesiastica Upsaliensia 27. Lund: Skånska, 1976.

———. *Svenska helgon.* Stockholm: Verbum, 1972.

[Magni, Olaus, ed. *Revelationes Sanctae Brigittae.*] Rome: In aedibus diuae Brigittae viduae, per Franciscum Mediolanensem de Ferrarijs, 21 Augusti, 1557.

Magnusson, Magnus, and Hermann Pálsson, trans. *The Vinland Sagas: The Norse Discovery of America.* Harmondsworth: Penguin, 1965.

Marin, Antonio Royo, O.P. *Teologia de la perfeccion cristiana.* 3d ed. Biblioteca de autores cristianos 114. Madrid: Editorial catolica, 1958.

Maritain, Jacques, and Raïssa Maritain. *Prayer and Intelligence.* Trans. Algar Thorold. New York: Sheed and Ward, 1943.

Mayr, Vincent. "Birgitta von Schweden." *Lexikon der Christlichen Ikonographie.* Ed. Wolfgang Braunfels. 8 vols. Rome: Herder, 1973. 5: 400–03.

Meech, Sanford Brown, ed. *The Book of Margery Kempe.* Early English Text Soc., Orig. Ser. 212. London: Oxford University Press, 1940.

Memorial: Sixth Centenary of the Death of St. Birgitta of Sweden 1373–1973. Rome: Casa Santa Birgitta, n.d.

Merton, Thomas. *The Ascent to Truth.* New York: Harcourt, 1951.

Michel, A. "Torquemada (Jean de), ou Jean de Turrecremata, dominicain espagnol (1388–1468)." *Dictionnaire de théologie catholique.* Eds. A. Vacant et al. Paris: Letouzey, 1946. 5: 1235–39.

Moberg, Vilhelm. *Min svenska historia: Berättad för folket. Första delen: Från Oden till Engelbrekt.* Stockholm: Norstedt, 1970.

Nebenzahl, Kenneth. *Maps of the Holy Land: Images of* Terra Sancta *through Two Millennia.* New York: Abbeville Press, 1986.

Nordenfalk, Carl. "St. Bridget of Sweden as Represented in Illuminated MSS." *Essays in Honor of E. Panofsky.* Ed. Millard Meiss. 2 vols. De artibus opuscula 40. New York: New York University Press, 1961. 1: 371–93.

Nyberg, Tore. "Analyse der Klosterregel der Hl. Birgitta." *Festschrift Altomünster.* Ed. Toni Grad. Aichach: Mayer, 1973. 21–34.

———. "Birgitta/Birgittenorden." *Theologische Realenzyklopädie.* 16 vols. to date. Berlin: de Gruyter, 1977– . 6: 648–52.

———. *Birgittinische Klostergründungen des Mittelalters.* Bibliotheca historica lundensis 15. Lund: Gleerup, 1965.

———. *Dokumente und Untersuchungen zur inneren Geschichte der drei Birgittenklöster Bayerns, 1420–1570.* 2 vols. Quellen und Erörterungen zur bayerischen Geschichte 26. Munich: Beck, 1972–74.

———. *St. Birgitta and Her Order.* Rev. ed. Guild of St. Birgitta Booklet 1. [Darien: Vikingsborg], 1964.

———. *Sankt Peters efterfølgere i brydningstider: Omkring pavedømmets historie, Rom og Nordeuropa 750–1200.* Odense University Studies in History and Social Sciences 58. Odense: Universitetsforlag, 1979.

———. *Storia dell' ordine di Santa Brigida/The Development of the Order of St. Birgitta.* Rome: Bulzoni, 1974.

———. "Vadstena Then and Now." *St. Ansgar's Bulletin* 69 (1972): 16–18.

Öberg, Jan. *Kring Birgitta.* Kungl. vitterhets historie och antikvitets akademien: Filologiskt archiv 13. Stockholm: Almqvist, 1969.

O'Connell, Patrick. *New Light on the Passion of Our Divine Lord: From a Comparison between the Evidence from the Holy Shroud and the Visions of St. Bridget of Sweden and Other Contemplatives.* 3d. ed. Dublin: Gill, 1961.

O'Connell, Patrick, and Charles Carty. *The Holy Shroud and Four Visions.* St. Paul: Radio Replies Publication Society, n.d.

Odenius, Oloph. "Alvastra, Abbey of." *New Catholic Encyclopedia.* 15 vols. New York: McGraw, 1967. 1: 360.

———. "Bridgit, Abbey of." *New Catholic Encyclopedia.* 15 vols. New York: McGraw, 1967. 2: 801.

Origo, Iris. *The Merchant of Prato: Francesco di Marco Datini, 1335–1410.* New York: Knopf, 1957. 235.

Ott, Ludwig. *Fundamentals of Catholic Dogma.* Trans. Patrick Lynch. 1955. Rockford: TAN, 1974.

Peacey, Edith, O.Ss.S. *St. Birgitta of Sweden.* London: Washbourne & Bogan, 1933.

Pelikan, Jaroslav. *The Christian Tradition: A History of the Development of Doctrine.* 5 vols to date. Chicago: Phoenix-University of Chicago Press, 1971-89.

Plé, A., O.P., et al. *Mystery and Mysticism.* New York: Philosophical Library, 1956.

Pourrat, Pierre. *Christian Spirituality.* Trans. W. H. Mitchell et al. 4 vols. 1927. Westminster: Newman, 1953–55.

Prescott, Hilda Frances Margaret. *Friar Felix at Large: A Fifteenth-Century Pilgrimage to the Holy Land.* New Haven: Yale University Press, 1950.

———. *Once to Sinai: The Further Pilgrimage of Friar Felix Fabri.* New York: Macmillan, 1958.

Rácz, Istvan, and Riitta Pylkkänen. *Art Treasures of Medieval Finland.* Trans. Diana Tullberg and Judy Beesley. New York: Praeger, 1967.

Rambusch, Robert E. "Presentation of St. Birgitta." *Saint Birgitta.* Guild of St. Birgitta Booklet 3. Darien: Vikingsborg: [1977].

Redpath, Helen M. D., O.Ss.S. *God's Ambassadress: St. Bridget of Sweden.* Milwaukee: Bruce, 1947.

Revelations of St. Bridget: On the Life and Passion of Our Lord, and the Life of His Blessed Mother. [Reprint, n.d.] Fresno: Academy, 1957.

Ryan, Granger, and Helmut Ripperger, trans. *The Golden Legend of Jacobus de Voragine.* New York: Longmans, 1941.

Schedel, Hartmann. *Register des buchs der croniken und geschichten mit figuren und pildnissen von anbeginn der welt bis auf dise unnsere zeit.* 1493. New York: Brussel, 1966. fol. 232r. [The *Nuremberg Chronicle.*]

Schiller, Gertrud. *Iconography of Christian Art.* Trans. Janet Seligman. 2 vols. Greenwich: New York Graphic Society, 1971–72.

Schmid, Toni. "Le culte en Suède de Sainte Brigide l'Irlandaise." *Analecta Bollandiana* 61 (1943): 108–15.

Schnerich, Alfred. *Wiens Kirchen und Kapellen.* Wien: Amalthea, 1921. 132, 135.

Shailor, Barbara A. *Catalogue of Medieval and Renaissance Manuscripts in the Beinecke Rare Book and Manuscript Library, Yale University. Volume I: MSS 1-250.* Medieval and Renaissance Texts and Studies 34. Binghamton, NY: Medieval and Renaissance Texts and Studies, 1984. 14–15, 39–40, 51, 182.

————. *Catalogue of Medieval and Renaissance Manuscripts in the Beinecke Rare Book and Manuscript Library, Yale University. Volume II: MSS 251-500.* Medieval and Renaissance Texts and Studies 48. Binghamton, NY: Medieval and Renaissance Texts and Studies, 1987. 399–400.

Sibilia, Anna Lisa. "Ingrid Elofsdotter, santa." *Bibliotheca sanctorum.* 12 vols. Rome: Istituto Giovanni XXIII, 1961–70. 7: 816–17.

Söderwall, K. F. *Ordbok öfver svenska medeltids-språket.* 3 vols. Svenska fornskrift-sällskapet: Samlingar 23. Lund: Berlingska, 1884–1918.

Sperry, Margaret. "Saint Birgitta of Sweden as Pilgrim." *St. Ansgar's Bulletin* 69 (1972): 1–3.

Squire, Aelred, O.P. *Asking the Fathers.* New York: Morehouse-Barlow, 1973.

Starr, Eliza Allen. "Santa Brigida." *Pilgrims and Shrines.* 2nd ed. 2 vols. Chicago: Starr, 1885. 1: 237–40.

Stein, Ruthie. "Monks Who Make Fudge in Camelot." *Catholic Digest* Aug. 1983: 43–46.

Stephens, George, ed. *Ett forn-svenskt Legendarium: Innehållande medeltids kloster-sagor om helgon, påfvar och kejsare ifrån det I:sta till det XIII:de århundradet.* 3 vols. Samlingar utgifna af svenska fornskrift-sällskapet 4. Stockholm: Norstedt, 1847.

Straub, A., and G. Keller. *Herrad of Landsberg: Hortus Deliciarum (Garden of Delights).* Trans. Aristide D. Caratzas. New Rochelle: Caratzas, 1977.

Strömberg, Bengt. *Magister Mathias och fransk mendikantpredikan.*

SELECT BIBLIOGRAPHY

Samlingar och studier till svenska kyrkans historia 9. Stockholm: Svenska kyrkans diakonistyrelses bokförlag, 1944.

Sumption, Jonathan. *Pilgrimage: An Image of Mediaeval Religion.* Totowa, New Jersey: Rowman and Littlefield, 1975.

Sundén, Hjalmar. *Den heliga Birgitta: Ormungens moder som blev Kristi brud.* Stockholm: Wahlström, 1973.

Syon House: The Story of a Great House with a Short Guide for Visitors. London: Syon House Estate, 1950.

Tanquerey, Adolphe, S.S. *The Spiritual Life: A Treatise on Ascetical and Mystical Theology.* Trans. Herman Branderis, S.S. 2nd rev. ed. Tournai: Desclée, 1930.

Thurston, Herbert, and Donald Attwater, eds. *Butler's Lives of the Saints: Complete Edition.* 4 vols. New York: Kenedy, 1956.

Tjader, Marguerite. "Den nya svenska grenen av den heliga Birgittas orden." *Den heliga Birgitta och Vadstena.* Ed. Aron Andersson. Stockholm: Almqvist, 1970. 51–71.

———. *Mother Elisabeth: The Resurgence of the Order of Saint Birgitta.* New York: Herder, 1972.

Torquemada, John Cardinal, O.P. *Defensiones quorundam articulorum rubrorum Revelationum S. Birgittae factae in Concilio Basileensi.* [1435.] *Sacrorum conciliorum nova et amplissima collectio.* Ed. Joannes D. Mansi et al. 31 vols. 1759–1798. Paris: Welter, 1900–1924. 30: 699–814.

Tugwell, Simon, O.P. *Prayer: Living with God.* Springfield: Templegate, 1975.

Undhagen, Carl-Gustaf, ed. *Birger Gregerssons Birgitta-Officium.* Samlingar utgivna av svenska fornskriftsällskapet 2, 6. Uppsala: Almqvist, 1960.

———, ed. *Sancta Birgitta: Revelaciones, Book I: With Magister Mathias' Prologue.* Samlingar utgivna av svenska fornskriftsällskapet 2, 7: 1. Stockholm: Almqvist, 1977.

Undset, Sigrid. *Saga of Saints.* Trans. E. C. Ramsden. New York: Longmans, 1934.

Vernet, F. "Brigitte de Suède." *Dictionnaire de spiritualité: Ascétique et mystique; doctrine et histoire.* Ed. Marcel Viller, S.J., et al. Paris: Beauchesne, 1932– . 1: 1943–58.

Voelkle, William M., et al. *Italian Manuscript Painting 1300–1550.* New York: Pierpont Morgan Library, 1984. 17.

Voguë, Adalbert de, O.S.B. "Un avatar du mythe de la caverne dans les

Dialogues de Grégoire le Grand." *Homenaje a Fray Justo Pérez de Urbel, O.S.B.* Studia silensia 4. Burgos: Abadía de Silos, 1977. 19–24.

Wallin, Sven. *Vadstena (Sweden): Its Abbey, Castle, and Memories.* Motala: Borgströms, 1937.

Waugh, Evelyn. *Edmund Campion.* 1946. Garden City: Image-Doubleday, 1956. 138–46.

Wilson, Adrian, and Joyce Lancaster Wilson. *A Medieval Mirror:* Speculum humanae salvationis *1324–1500.* Berkeley: University of California Press, 1984.

INDEX

INDEX

INDEX

INDEX

INDEX

sinners, 216–217
sword of sorrow, 160
Thomas the Apostle relics,
161–163
translation of, 58
writing of, 159
sexuality, 104
signs, visible, 112–114
Silén, Sven, 10
sin, 139–141, 143, 146
sinners, 216–217
Sixth Book, 33, 34, 35, 36–37
Societas Sanctae Birgittae, 8
Söderblom, Nathan (Archbishop), 8
souls, 143–145, 148–149, 152
spelling, 66–67
spirituality, 13
Steffen, R., 8
Stolpe, Sven, 7
Strindberg, August, 5
Strömberg, Bengt, 17
structure, 56–57
Sundén, Hjalmar, 17, 21, 26, 27
Suso, 6
sword of sorrow, 160

temporal goods, 103
temptation, 91, 127–128
Teresa of Avila, 4
Third Book, 33, 34–35, 36, 37
Thomas the Apostle, relics of,
161–163
translations
and Alphonsus' role in texts, 65
and authenticity, 62
and Bible English, 57
bibliography for, 68
and *Extravagantes*, 65–66
of Fifth Book, 57–58
flavor of, 57
of *Four Prayers*, 58
imagery in, 56
Latin to Old Swedish, 61
of *Life*, 57

meaning in, 55–56
names in, 67
notes on, 59
Oslo version in, 61–62, 63
and priest-translators, 63
recent, 55, 58–59
"revelation" in, 63–65
of *Revelations*, 8
section numbering in, 58
of Seventh Book, 58
spelling in, 66–67
structure in, 56–57
texts chosen for, 57
tribulations, 134, 135

Ulf. *See* Lord Ulf
union, 46
Urban V, Pope, 11, 95

Vadstena Convent's Destiny, The
(Lindblom), 7
vengeance, 103–104, 108–109
Virgin Mary
and birth of Christ, 128–132
childbearing of, 202–204
Immaculate Conception of, 31
limbs of, 118–120
members of, praise of, 232–235
praise of, 221–225
and sword of sorrow, 160
virtues
of five sacred places, 154–156
humility, 123–124
inward and outward, 105–106
self-denial, 123–124
in words of revelations, 147–148
Vita. See Life
Vita C 15, 15
Vita Processus, 15

war, 108–110
wealth, 110–111, 123–124
Westman, Knut B., 5, 21, 36
work, 43–44

350

Other Volumes in this Series

Julian of Norwich • SHOWINGS

Jacob Boehme • THE WAY TO CHRIST

Nahman of Bratslav • THE TALES

Gregory of Nyssa • THE LIFE OF MOSES

Bonaventure • THE SOUL'S JOURNEY INTO GOD, THE TREE OF LIFE, AND THE LIFE OF ST. FRANCIS

William Law • A SERIOUS CALL TO DEVOUT AND HOLY LIFE, AND THE SPIRIT OF LOVE

Abraham Isaac Kook • THE LIGHTS OF PENITENCE, LIGHTS OF HOLINESS, THE MORAL PRINCIPLES, ESSAYS, AND POEMS

Ibn 'Ata' Illah • THE BOOK OF WISDOM and Kwaja Abdullah Ansari • INTIMATE CONVERSATIONS

Johann Arndt • TRUE CHRISTIANITY

Richard of St. Victor • THE TWELVE PATRIARCHS, THE MYSTICAL ARK, AND BOOK THREE OF THE TRINITY

Origen • AN EXHORTATION TO MARTYRDOM, PRAYER AND SELECTED WORKS

Catherine of Genoa • PURGATION AND PURGATORY, THE SPIRITUAL DIALOGUE

Native North American Spirituality of the Eastern Woodlands • SACRED MYTHS, DREAMS, VISIONS, SPEECHES, HEALING FORMULAS, RITUALS AND CEREMONIALS

Teresa of Avila • THE INTERIOR CASTLE

Apocalyptic Spirituality • TREATISES AND LETTERS OF LACTANTIUS, ADSO OF MONTIER-EN-DER, JOACHIM OF FIORE, THE FRANCISCAN SPIRITUALS, SAVONAROLA

Athanasius • THE LIFE OF ANTONY, A LETTER TO MARCELLINUS

Catherine of Siena • THE DIALOGUE

Sharafuddin Maneri • THE HUNDRED LETTERS

Martin Luther • THEOLOGIA GERMANICA

Native Mesoamerican Spirituality • ANCIENT MYTHS, DISCOURSES, STORIES, DOCTRINES, HYMNS, POEMS FROM THE AZTEC, YUCATEC, QUICHE-MAYA AND OTHER SACRED TRADITIONS

Symeon the New Theologian • THE DISCOURSES

Ibn Al'-Aribī • THE BEZELS OF WISDOM

Hadewijch • THE COMPLETE WORKS

Philo of Alexandria • THE CONTEMPLATIVE LIFE, THE GIANTS, AND SELECTIONS

George Herbert • THE COUNTRY PARSON, THE TEMPLE

Unknown • THE CLOUD OF UNKNOWING

John and Charles Wesley • SELECTED WRITINGS AND HYMNS

Meister Eckhart • THE ESSENTIAL SERMONS, COMMENTARIES, TREATISES AND DEFENSE

Francisco de Osuna • THE THIRD SPIRITUAL ALPHABET

Jacopone da Todi • THE LAUDS

Fakhruddin 'Iraqi • DIVINE FLASHES

Menahem Nahum of Chernobyl • THE LIGHT OF THE EYES
Early Dominicans • SELECTED WRITINGS
John Climacus • THE LADDER OF DIVINE ASCENT
Francis and Clare • THE COMPLETE WORKS
Gregory Palamas • THE TRIADS
Pietists • SELECTED WRITINGS
The Shakers • TWO CENTURIES OF SPIRITUAL REFLECTION
Zohar • THE BOOK OF ENLIGHTENMENT
Luis de León • THE NAMES OF CHRIST
Quaker Spirituality • SELECTED WRITINGS
Emanuel Swedenborg • THE UNIVERSAL HUMAN AND SOUL-BODY
INTERACTION
Augustine of Hippo • SELECTED WRITINGS
Safed Spirituality • RULES OF MYSTICAL PIETY, THE BEGINNING OF WISDOM
Maximus Confessor • SELECTED WRITINGS
John Cassian • CONFERENCES
Johannes Tauler • SERMONS
John Ruusbroec • THE SPIRITUAL ESPOUSALS AND OTHER WORKS
Ibn 'Abbād of Ronda • LETTERS ON THE SŪFĪ PATH
Angelus Silesius • THE CHERUBINIC WANDERER
The Early Kabbalah •
Meister Eckhart • TEACHER AND PREACHER
John of the Cross • SELECTED WRITINGS
Pseudo-Dionysius • THE COMPLETE WORKS
Bernard of Clairvaux • SELECTED WORKS
Devotio Moderna • BASIC WRITINGS
The Pursuit of Wisdom • AND OTHER WORKS BY THE AUTHOR OF THE
CLOUD OF UNKNOWING
Richard Rolle • THE ENGLISH WRITINGS
Francis de Sales, Jane de Chantal • LETTERS OF SPIRITUAL DIRECTION
Albert and Thomas • SELECTED WRITINGS
Robert Bellarmine • SPIRITUAL WRITINGS
Nicodemos of the Holy Mountain • A HANDBOOK OF SPIRITUAL COUNSEL
Henry Suso • THE EXEMPLAR, WITH TWO GERMAN SERMONS
Bérulle and the French School • SELECTED WRITINGS
The Talmud • SELECTED WRITINGS
Ephrem the Syrian • HYMNS
Hildegard of Bingen • SCIVIAS